Becoming the Second City

Becoming the Second City

Chicago's Mass News Media, 1833–1898

RICHARD JUNGER

UNIVERSITY OF ILLINOIS PRESS
Urbana, Chicago, and Springfield

Manufactured in the United States of America
1 2 3 4 5 C P 5 4 3 2 1
This book is printed on acid-free paper.

Library of Congress Cataloging-in-Publication Data
Junger, Richard.
Becoming the second city : Chicago's mass news media,
1833–1898 / by Richard Junger.
p. cm.
Includes bibliographical references and index.
ISBN 978-0-252-03589-0 (cloth : alk. paper) —
ISBN 978-0-252-07785-2 (pbk. : alk. paper)
1. Journalism—Illinois—Chicago—History—19th century.
I. Title.
PN4899.C37J86 2010
071.773'1109034 2010012859

Contents

Introduction

The press of Chicago has, in a great degree, made the city. Blot it out of existence and the city is done for. Support it literally, and nothing can make a more handsome return.
—(Chicago) *Daily Democratic Press,* May 10, 1853

Chicago has long been a butt of newspaper and magazine jokes. When a New York paper mocked a report that a wolf had been seen running loose on a Chicago street in 1840, a hometown editor couldn't resist the retort that Chicago "was growing so fast that the wild animals just can't keep out of the way." A popular mid-nineteenth-century newspaper tale told of a St. Louis man who died while visiting Chicago. St. Peter, seated at the Pearly Gates with a "goodly mug of steaming whiskey toddy" at his side supposedly asked the man, "Where did you live down below?" "I lived at St. Louis, but I died at Chicago, Illinois," was the reply. "Chicago?" St. Peter said shaking his head, "There's no such place, sir." When confronted with a map showing Chicago, the good Saint replied, "It's there, sure enough, so walk in, sir, but I'll be blest if you ain't the first man that has ever gone home here from that place." "A Chicago woman died a few days ago while saying her prayers," the *Indianapolis Sentinel* wrote. "The Coroner's jury finds that the cause of death was lonesomeness."[1]

A Chicago man supposedly told his wife, "Tomorrow is the Fourth of July" according to the humor magazine *Puck.* "'Yes,' replied [the wife] musingly, 'the day that this country got its divorce from England.'" "Do you paint?" an artistic Eastern young man asked a fetching Chicago girl according to the *Brooklyn Eagle.* "O, no indeed," was the reply, "but I've long suspected that ma does." The *Minneapolis Journal* wrote that "Chicago, were it not for its inhabitants and its location, would be a nice town," and a joke popular among some elevator operators was to announce "Chicago" whenever an elevator reached the ground floor. When an indignant Chicagoan told a Washington,

D.C. hotel clerk, "I'll leave the house, sir," the clerk asked where he was from. "What's that got to do with it?" the man snapped. "O nothing, only the last Chicago man who was here wanted to take the house with him."

As quoted in the *Chicago Tribune,* a man lectured a group of Chicago school boys on the value of education, telling them that if each of them studied diligently, he had a chance of becoming president. One child, listening attentively, turned to the next and said, "Say, Jim, I will sell you my chance for two bits." "Hootch Hoo" was said to be the name of Chicago's social register during Prohibition, and New York Mayor James "Jimmy" Walker made famous the statement that "I'd rather be a lamppost in New York City than Mayor of Chicago."[2]

My grandfather never put stock in such witticisms. A commonsense, say-it-as-it-was businessman, to him Chicago was simply "the mistake by the lake." Angry that it had situated itself so inconveniently between our hometown of Milwaukee and his summer retreat at Michigan City, Indiana, my grandfather took personal exception to the fact that the first Mayor Richard Daley had manipulated the paths of all of the "free" interstates so that they crossed through Chicago's already congested downtown Loop area, adding hours to our trip. My grandfather also disliked what he considered to be Chicago's poorly behaved professional sports fans, but the worst insult to him was that the *Chicago Tribune* controlled the syndication rights to the Charlie Brown comic strip so that it was unavailable to Milwaukee's two daily newspapers. It saddened him that I grew up thinking that Linus, Peppermint Patty, Lucy, Snoopy, and "good ol'" Charlie Brown were television rather than the newspaper characters they really were, a transgression against the entire city in my grandfather's eyes.[3]

Years after my grandfather died, I became aware of what a fascinating city his traffic bottleneck really was. For instance, I learned that many Chicago sports fans were decent if occasionally misguided people. And I discovered that Chicago's two daily newspapers had positive attributes, not just monopolistic comic strip practices. As I studied the city's history in graduate school and read excellent books such as Bessie Louise Pierce's *A History of Chicago* and Harold M. Mayer and Richard C. Wade's *Chicago: Growth of a Metropolis,* I couldn't help but wonder how great newspapers such as the *Chicago Tribune* were so inconspicuous in their discussions of the city's formative years. Scholars have written about everything Chicago from critical mass to mass consumption. Why not mass communication?[4]

Consider sociologist Robert Park's 1940 statement on the natural connection between cities and mass communication, that "news performs somewhat the same functions for the public that perception does for the individual man." Or sociologists Peter L. Berger and Thomas Luckmann, who found that participants in social systems like cities use mental representations of each other to create their meaning of everyday life. This process, called the social construction of reality, is strongly influenced by the mass news media. British social scientist Colin Cherry wrote about how mass communication technologies reduced the restraints of time and space in the nineteenth century, making communication and commerce possible between cities and their rural hinterlands.

Donald L. Shaw and Maxwell E. McCombs spoke to the levels of prominence selectively attached to public issues by the mass news media and how such decisions influence the public and private sectors, a process known as agenda setting. W. Phillips Davis wrote about how mass media consumers assume that persuasive communication will have more of an effect on others than on themselves, a process known as the third-person effect. Herbert Gans theorized on "enduring values in journalism" including an often misguided faith in capitalism and rural values. And George Gerbner postulated that a mass medium (television—but it could have been nineteenth-century print) can create a different perception of reality in its consumers, a process he called the cultivation theory. Surely, at least some of this social science has some relevance on our understanding of past times, events, people, and places. So how could it be that a pervasive nineteenth-century mass news media did not figure more prominently in nineteenth-century Chicago, at least as it was reconstructed in history books?[5]

Of particular usefulness in my thinking on this conundrum was the work of two American sociologists, David Croteau and William Hoynes. They constructed a model of how the mass news media functions as a well-delineated system of messages, readers, and technology within a social world that includes (but is not limited to) government, economic activities and conditions, and citizenry. Nonmedia institutions such as the public and private sectors influence the news media and are, in turn, influenced. News media companies influence how their employees operate, identifying, changing, and reinventing perceptions, and consumers are influenced by what they read and see in the mass news media. "From a sociological perspective, the media play a crucial role in almost all aspects of daily life," the pair wrote. Although the Croteau and Hoynes model was created to explain a contemporary world, it wasn't hard to envision early Chicago residents acting with and being influenced by their mass news media as well. "In all these cases, media products are connected to the ways we interact with other people on a daily basis," Croteau and Hoynes wrote. "Media products provide a diversion, a source of conflict, or a unifying force."[6]

To test the relevance of their and other mass communication theories on Chicago's past, I considered a variety of events for a possible case or field study. I thought of examining the evolving perceptions of Chicago's newspapermen (there were few newswomen before the twentieth century), or specific, media-oriented events such as the 1855 Lager Beer riot, the 1871 fire, or the 1886 Haymarket Square bombing, or how early Chicago's mayors and city councils interacted with the press. But as I sifted through existing source materials, I was attracted to another, lesser known event in early Chicago history, the path taken that led it to become the nation's "Second City." No person enters a race intending to finish second, but reminiscent of Croteau and Hoynes's model, nineteenth-century Chicagoans of all stripes who could otherwise agree on virtually nothing somehow came together in one mass belief (or delusion) that their city would somehow become the most populous on the North American continent. Not everything that went on in early Chicago was specifically intended to advance that cause, but there seems to have always been at least some undercurrent, some desire, for Chicago to leapfrog past its local and regional rivals (something it did during the 1840s and 1850s), surge past a defiant St. Louis (which it did commercially around 1855 and population-wise by 1880), and out-populate New York (something it did briefly during the mid-1890s before the incorporation of Greater New York City) to become Number One. That, and the story of the race to become the Second City was a good one as well.

At virtually every step along this path, Chicago's mass news media was intimately involved in the process, as Croteau and Hoynes might have predicted, creating a unifying force among Chicago's disparate population and classes. In a chemical sense, Chicago's nineteenth-century newspapers were the accelerants of its urbanization process, the potassium nitrate in its gunpowder or the liquid oxygen portion of its kerosene rocket fuel. Alone and unread, a newspaper is inert, nonreactive, benign, harmless, something in which to wrap fish or used to line a birdcage. But in the complex machinery of a city on the move it is challenging, disturbing, incendiary, even explosive. As Gunther Barth correctly observed in *City People: The Rise of Modern City Culture in Nineteenth-Century America,* the metropolitan press revealed the common humanity and identified the pursuit of money as the common denominator of nineteenth-century American urban life. But there was more. Those newspapers and their creators were the links between public officials, the business community, and residents, the grain of sand in the oyster. As Chicago demonstrated, an American city cannot be born, grow, and prosper without some home news medium.[7]

Primary source materials for nineteenth-century Chicago are sketchy, especially since the 1871 fire did such an expert job of consuming its early written records. I consulted letters, diaries, speeches, drawings, photographs, maps, memoirs, and other primary sources as they were available, but it was painfully obvious to me that the process also needed to be reconstructed through the thousands of articles that appeared in early Chicago's English-language daily newspapers. This presented a different challenge. "To do local history well, one must read broadly," historian Michael G. Kammen wrote, but standard historical epistemology balks at newspapers as primary sources. Instead, newspapers are "sometimes worse than useless when they purport to give the inside history of decisions," Pulitzer Prize–winning historian and presidential advisor Arthur Schlesinger Jr. complained. "Their relation is often considerably less than the shadows in Plato's cave." In *Understanding History,* Louis Gottschalk warned that "the careful historian will not use all the statements of . . . newspaper dispatches with equal confidence." In *The Modern Researcher,* a book I read in graduate school, Jacques Barzun and Henry G. Graff claimed that "the intelligent newspaper reader . . . daily encounters 'incredible' stories and tries automatically to 'verify' them." This, Barzun and Graff instructed, could involve "reading between the lines," temporarily accepting a story's conclusion, or "looking for further reports." "No matter the medium in which it is delivered . . . every news report is in some sense selective therefore 'biased,'" Martha Howell and Walter Prevenier wrote in *From Reliable Sources.*

Alarmingly, Stephane Levesque warned in 2008 of "derivative" primary sources, "evidence left for posterity [that] unveils a public or official character," that include church records, memoirs, business records, and unfortunately, newspapers. Levesque even took one Canadian newspaper editor to task in his *Thinking Historically* for adding to a Reuters news service report when it was published in his paper. "Newspapers are entitled to deliberately modify the wording of a news-agency's story to reflect the ideology of their editors and subscribers, even if the modifications can cause serious political or epistemological imbroglios about the changes themselves," Levesque warned. "Clearly, there is a lot at stake with this type of reasoning, which only amplifies the necessity of critical examination of sources." "The bias of much of the historical profession . . . is reflected in what has become the pattern of selecting for training those who are to be future members of the profession," historian J. H. Hexter wrote. "Once in graduate school the successful applicant is pressed even more firmly into the mold for which he previously opted."[8]

By comparison, the *Indianapolis Journal* observed in 1889 that "making every allowance in the press of both parties for partisan prejudice, mistakes, misinformation, exaggeration, and even a little lying in the heat of controversy, the publicity which the press gives public affairs and the constant check it furnishes on official action far more than counterbalances its defects." Irish Chicago barkeeper Martin Dooley, the fictional creation of *Chicago Evening Post* editorial writer Finley Peter Dunne, told his patrons in the 1890s that "th' newspaper is watchin' most iv us fr'm th' cradle to th' grave, an' befure an' afther. . . . Ye can get anny kind iv information ye want to in ye'er fav'rite newspaper about ye'ersilf or annywan else." To twentieth-century newspaper columnist and critic Walter Lippmann, the "function of news is to signalize an event . . . and make a picture of reality on which men can act." "Behind all [the] salient aspects of newspaper usefulness [to historians]," historian Allan Nevins wrote around 1929, "of course, lies the broader fact that the press forms an unrivaled source for the study of opinion, and for gaining some insight into the spirit of the age."

On a different note, veteran *Chicago Tribune* newspaperman Arthur M. Evans told the first class of Northwestern University journalism students in 1921 that "by far the greatest cause of error in a representative metropolitan newspaper is not 'inaccuracy' on the part of the reporter, but 'ivory' [contemporary slang for spinning or the putting on of a pleasing exterior] on the part of established sources of information." "The first difficult circumstance [about newspapers] is time," former *Washington Post* editor Benjamin C. Bradlee wrote some sixty years later. "The second thing is that people don't tell the truth. I mean it's just as simple as that. Including those people who think they are telling you the truth. One of the really glorious aspects of modern history, for me, is to read the versions of participants in major events and to see how they differ. Each one thinks he's telling the truth, and it comes out different. . . . You're no better than what people tell you."[9]

While historians will continue to disagree on the usefulness or uselessness of newspapers as primary historical sources, there is no doubt that reading old newspaper files "offers an opportunity to engage one's mind in what R. G. Collingwood . . . has defined as the historical enterprise, 'the imaginative recreation of the past,'" as Allan J. Lichtman and Valerie French put it. Doing so can also avoid incorrect characterizations or generalizations of the temper or tone of a particular time, for local newspapers have always exchanged information with out-of-town newspapers, even in the days before wire services, and we always see the forest better when the trees aren't in our way. In the twenty-first century, the use of newspapers may include digitized newspaper collections, which provide what librarians call vertical or longitudinal files, collections of articles on people, places, events, and virtually any other topic from a variety of publications over time periods as long as a newspaper's complete run, in comparison to a single newspaper article or article clusters. The wider scope and time frames possible with newspaper databases provides information reported by a series of reporters without the innate biases of morgue librarians or others who arbitrarily categorize and organize old articles. Newspaper databases allow a thoughtful, careful researcher to search for and make factual and logical connections not possible through traditional newspaper research, to do what Jacques Barzun called the cross-questioning of historical information.

So, what took University of Chicago history professor Bessie Louise Pierce's graduate students two decades to complete for her three- (and unfinished fourth) volume *A History of Chicago*, namely the reading, copying, and categorizing on 3-by-5 index cards of thousands of Chicago newspaper articles, can today be performed systematically, thoroughly, and with less human interference, in seconds. With careful reading and analysis, complications such as incomplete, biased, sensationalized, suppressed, erroneous, and misinterpreted information can be better detected, addressed, and even presented as historical evidence itself. And a researcher can cross-reference articles in other, nondigitized newspaper collections to further minimize factual errors.

Careful database searches of the *Chicago Tribune* and *Chicago Inter Ocean*, along with databases of other African American, early American, and out-of-town American newspapers from the *New York Times* and the *Washington Post* to the *Lake Superior Miner* and numerous other microfilmed newspapers, provided a wealth of information, accounts, and perspectives for my research on nineteenth-century Chicago's bid to be number one. "The use of newspapers as historical sources has grown steadily greater and bolder during the last generation," Allan Nevins told his history students in 1929, and as more newspapers are digitalized, their usefulness will continue to grow, especially through efforts such as the U.S. Newspaper Program, initiated in 2005 and funded by the National Endowment for the Humanities and the Library of Congress. Dare I speculate that a day will be coming when information from digitalized newspaper collections will be a part of all urban histories?[10]

Armed with such findings, the first chapter of this book examines Chicago's earliest public perception when there were no local papers, how technology changed the nature of news for early Chicagoans, the founding of the *Chicago Tribune*, and the impact of the so-called 1855 Lager Beer riot on the city. The second chapter considers the connections and role the mass news media played in promoting and regulating Chicago's growing commodities trade, its first indigenous commercial endeavor, the Civil War–era founding of the *Chicago Times* (the *Tribune*'s leading nineteenth-century competitor), the *Tribune*'s role in the nomination of Abraham Lincoln, and the emergence of the *Times* as a paper of its own merit through the unintentional efforts of the Union Army—all developments that led to Chicago becoming the Midwest's leading information center. Chapter 3 examines the development of a "fast" Chicago, its growing diversity, size, and self-importance, the 1871 fire, and how Chicago was able to remake itself from its ashes with the aid of the mass news media to surpass St. Louis as the most populous midwestern city in 1880. Chapter 4 considers how newspapers influenced the birth and development of Chicago's labor movement, how the newspapers exacerbated and contributed to the 1886 Haymarket Square bombing, trial, and executions, and partially redeemed themselves covering the 1894 Pullman Strike. Chapter 5 details the Battle of the Bigs, the war of words between Chicago and New York that brought the 1893 World's Columbian Exposition, the archetypal world's fair, to Chicago. And chapter 6 considers the confusing and complicated relationship between the mass news media and nineteenth-century Chicago vice, how changing technology affected the perception Chicagoans had of their city council and its so-called Gray Wolves aldermen, and how Chicago became the nation's Second City.

Debts are many for a book such as this, with space to acknowledge them limited. Staff members at the University of Chicago Library, Newberry Library, Chicago Historical Society, William L. Clements Library, University of Illinois–Chicago, and Robert R. McCormick Research Center helped me to mine the miles of books, archival documents, and related materials in their collections. Though they likely will never see this book, I extend my acknowledgment to the many Chicago homeless people who spend their hot summer and cold winter days in the downtown Harold Washington Library Center. In particular, I would like to thank a gentlemen named Michael and another I called "the captain" (for his omnipresent sailor's hat) who photocopied, carried books, and did other research tasks for me.

Without Western Michigan University's Waldo Library staff, especially its resource sharing center, I could not have attempted this book. Faculty colleagues Richard Gershon, Sue Ellen Christian, Arnie Johnston, and the late Herb Scott helped inspire and assist me as did a host of students who quietly listened as I rambled about my Chicago research. My parents, Eugene and Marjorie Junger, encouraged my passion for history and journalism, and I am indebted to you. Greg, Mark, Zack, and Cassie, this is what I was doing when I was away from home or in front of the computer for so many hours. Last and most importantly, thank you, Pennie, for your able assistance, gentle patience, loving support, and for sharing Lake Michigan sunrises and sunsets with me on the road and rail to and from the Second City.

Becoming the Second City

1

From Zero to 29,963 in Just Fifty-five Years

If the intent of the original Congress had prevailed, much of Chicago, its north and western suburbs, and cities such as Galena and Rockford would today be a part of Wisconsin. The original border between what would become Illinois and Wisconsin, set by the Congress of Confederation in the Northwest Ordinance of 1787, was sixty-one miles south of where it presently lies, stretching from the southwesterly bend of Lake Michigan westward to Rock Island on the Mississippi River. Astute early Illinoisans led by territorial delegate-to-Congress Nathan Pope saw the illogic of such a division in 1818 even if none of the other representatives had ever heard of the aggregation center some called Chicago. In petitioning for Illinois statehood that year, he negotiated for the approximately eight thousand square miles that now comprise the fourteen northernmost counties of Illinois, including most of Cook County. Pope was rewarded for his advanced thinking by being named Chicago's first federal district court judge in 1848.[1]

The issue resurfaced in 1840 when representatives of nine Illinois counties gathered in Rockford to give voice to a contention that their northern region had more in common with Wisconsin's Yankee-born population than Southern-flavored downstate Illinois, especially south of Springfield. They lobbied a young Chicago newspaper editor and congressman, nicknamed "Long" John Wentworth, to join their cause. If Wentworth would champion them, the new state of Wisconsin would make him one of its first two U.S. senators. Wentworth was too careful a student of public opinion to fall for such a transparent scheme. "Despite echoes of this sentiment . . . the movement by 1842 was in partial, if not complete, collapse," Bessie Louise Pierce wrote. Gatherings of old cross-border settlers continued for years, and the boundary issue resurfaced a final time in 1846 when Wisconsin petitioned for statehood. But, by that date, the impracticality of dividing the Illinois and Michigan canal between two states ensured that Chicago would remain forever a part of Illinois.[2]

From a wet prairie to a gathering place for native peoples to a Euro-American symbol of personal wealth and success, Chicago gradually entered the American consciousness through the pages of the mass news media during the late eighteenth and early nineteenth centuries. In particular settlers began streaming toward it through the promotional or "booster" efforts of Chicago's earliest newspaper editors. By the time of the arrival of the first telegraph line to the city in 1848 to a claim of "Lightning Flashes! Time and Space Annihilated!" Chicago was an urban wonder of its age, one of the fastest growing and most memorable cities in the world, its progress aided by journalists such as the *Chicago Democrat*'s Wentworth and the *Tribune*'s Joseph Medill along with the help of new newspaper technology. The newspapers were not always responsible for the perceptions of Chicago and its residents that they created within their pages—but it mattered little because new settlers surged daily into the city from points as distant as Ireland and Germany, creating a population officially estimated at 29,963 in 1850. As Chicago approached 1860, it was girding itself for an eventual bid to become the most populous city on the North American continent.[3]

The "Most Vicious, Chilling, Comfortless Place I Ever Visited"

It is likely that a number of Europeans passed through the area that would become Chicago during the early seventeenth century, but absent written records the credit for the first mapping of the area belongs to Frenchmen Louis Joliet and Father Jacques Marquette. The pair visited the site of Chicago—also known as Chicaga, Checagou, Chigagou, Cheagoumeman, Checago, Checagou, Chekagou, Chicagoux, Chigagou, Chicagoua, Chicagoüa, Chicagoux, and other variants—on the final leg of their historic exploration of the upper Mississippi River Valley during the summer of 1673. However it was spelled, the name was usually attributed to an abundance of malodorous plant life (wild garlic, leeks, onions, or worse) growing at the confluence of the river and Lake Michigan. Partisans such as the *Chicago Tribune*'s Col. Robert R. McCormick preferred a connotation to water, but sports journalist Ring Lardner once explained the name as "a Cree Indian word meaning, primarily, 'at the place of the skunk.'" Regardless, a map published in France in 1697 showed a fort located between the river "Des Illinois" and "Lac du Mighiganc ou des Illinois" labeled "Chicagou." A century later, the spelling "Chicago" was suggested in a 1786 *Massachusetts Spy* article. "The Illinois river furnishes a communication with Lake Michigan, by the Chicago river," the paper wrote. However, the federal government preferred the spelling "Chikago" in the 1795 Treaty of Greenville, which gave the United States a six-mile tract of land at the mouth of the Chicago River, and egregious misspellings such as "Eschecagou" and "Eschikagou" persisted into the early nineteenth century before newspapers and common usage settled on the preferred version.[4]

None of the earliest Europeans remained for long; the honor of being Chicago's first non-Native American resident belongs to Jean Baptiste Point de Sable, French for "John the Baptist of the Sand Point," a Canadian-born, free black fur trader. De (not the Anglicized "Du") Sable constructed a farm of nine buildings during the mid-1780s to the north of the "sand point" mouth of the river, just yards from the early twenty-first-century Tribune Tower. De Sable, probably born in Montreal in or around 1745 and the son of free blacks, was an illiterate Frenchman who spoke poor English. He worked in the Great Lakes fur trade until he was captured by the British in 1779 on suspicions of siding with Americans in the Revolutionary War. After the war, De Sable transported his belongings to "Eschikagou" and married a Native American woman named Catherine, his holdings growing to form a plantation with barns, mill, bake house, smokehouse, dairy, stables, and livestock. De Sable remained in Chicago until 1800 when he sold his holdings to a neighbor, Catherine having died sometime previously. He moved himself and his children to St. Charles, Missouri, likely convinced that nothing would come of the swampy land in Chicago, and died insolvent in 1818, but was, as biographer John F. Swenson has noted, "a successful free-born black entrepreneur, advancing through a series of significant careers to a position of prominence in Chicago."[5]

The earliest newspaper accounts of Chicago were largely unfavorable, providing what could be called the first bad press for the future city. An American fur trader named William Ketteltas, traveling from New York to New Orleans through the Chicago portage, complained to the *New York Morning Chronicle* in 1805 of "the injuries and insults he met with in our own waters, from foreign nations, but in particular from the English. . . ." His passage marked the first known direct connection between Chicago and its future trading partner New York, but overall, the Northwest frontier remained largely unknown to early nineteenth-century Americans. American soldiers began garrisoning in what was called Fort Dearborn, located south of the Chicago River at the intersection of present-day Wacker Drive and Michigan Avenue, in 1803 and 1804; need for the fort became apparent in 1807 when the *New York Commercial Advertiser* and other eastern newspapers warned that land travel was becoming unsafe between Chicago and Detroit due to difficulties created by the predominant British traders in the region and their Native People supporters. Visitors warned that the tiny Fort Dearborn was vulnerable to attack. "We have now upwards of 1,000 strange Indians within 30 miles of this place," an anonymous letter writer told a Vermont paper in 1808. "What can be their object, time only will tell."[6]

Leading up to the War of 1812, reports of Native Americans killing the fort's stock of horses and cattle and attacking nearby Euro-American settlers were published in eastern newspapers, helping to dampen settler interest in the area. The first public word of the Fort Dearborn Massacre appeared in the *Alexandria* (Virginia) *Daily Gazette* on September 3, 1812, a short communiqué based on war department correspondence; the newspaper cry "Remember Chicago" in the weeks and months following the attack helped advertise the name if not the prospects of the distant settlement. Details were difficult to come by initially, with the *Buffalo Gazette* blaming the British for attacking and plundering the fort, while the Providence, Rhode Island, *Columbian Phoenix* attributed the attack to an "Anglo-Indian force." The Zanesville, Ohio, *Western Star* sensationalized its coverage, warning readers that "our extreme frontiers are in danger of the tomahawk and scalping knife."

The often-quoted Washington, D.C., *National Intelligencer* published a letter from a St. Louis correspondent stating to the effect that one of the fort's captains had had "his breast cut open and his heart roasted and eaten by the chiefs present," a form of warrior honor in Native American culture. The Exeter, New Hampshire, *Constitutionalist* quoted from a Pittsburgh newspaper that the "Government [had] promised to wage an offensive war, and to lead the youth of our country to glory. Has it been found in the ruins of Chicago and [Fort] Niagra [*sic*]?" while the Georgetown *Federal Republican* complained that "the British have lopped off from the United States the entire ancient territory of Michigan, with the forts of Detroit, Chicago, Michilimachinae, &c." Complete details of the massacre did not emerge until two years later when the *Plattsburgh* (New York) *Republican,* basing its article on recently freed survivor reports, put the final death toll at twenty-six soldiers, two women, and twelve children, with another group of twenty-six soldiers and eleven women and children taken as prisoners, several dying or being killed in British captivity in Canada. According to the paper, eleven children were "massacred and scalped, in one waggon [*sic*]" at the time of the attack, and "the officers who were killed on the 15th of Aug. had their heads cut off and their hearts taken out and broiled in the presence of the prisoners" at a location near modern day Prairie Avenue and Sixteenth Street. The wife of one soldier "in an advanced stage of pregnancy, was tomahawked, scalped, cut open, and had the child taken out and its head cut off" as well, according to the newspaper—details repeated in grizzly recreations of the event that were staged in Chicago throughout the nineteenth and early twentieth centuries.[7]

Early Chicago had limited experience with the fur trade, in contrast to western cities like Detroit, Green Bay, and St. Louis—or even New York, which became the financial center of the fur business during the 1820s. Trading activities were reported as early as 1800: a trading house was established in 1805 with the encouragement of President Thomas Jefferson, and the American Fur Company reported profits from its Chicago post through the 1820s. But the unchallenged capital of the western fur trade was St. Louis. As many as three-fourths of that city's residents were involved in the business, far more ever than in Chicago. The natural elements of weather and water that supported fur trading in other places seemed to make life more unpleasant for early Chicagoans. A 1856 *Putnam's* magazine article based on early eyewitness accounts portrayed the area as "a dead-level stretch of prairie, lying but a few feet above the level of the [Chicago] river, most of it undeniable swamp of that species called wet prairie." "I passed over the ground from the Fort to [Wolf] Point [the corner of Lake Street and Wacker Drive], on horseback, and was up to my stirrups in water the whole distance," a European traveler wrote. "I would not have given sixpence an acre for the whole of it." One Euro-American settler, who eventually located in the vicinity of present-day Archer Avenue, recalled that "no one with common sense would buy such land [as in downtown Chicago], for it was so sandy that one sank up to his knees at every step"; another early settler, when given the opportunity to purchase land where the Auditorium eventually stood, explained, "But mud was more'n knee deep on Water and Lake streets—the only business streets ther wuz then—and the water was so deep and the grass was so high when the fellow and I went out to see the land I couldn't see it when I got there." "The winds here hold an eternal jubilee," visiting New York newspaperman Charles Fenno Hoffmann wrote in 1834, perhaps anticipating the future "Windy City" nickname. "It is the most vicious, chilling, comfortless place I ever visited." "People who are desirous to emigrate to the West should remember that 'all is not gold that glitters,'" the *Litchfield* (Massachusetts) *Enquirer* warned its readers the following year in an effort to keep them from emigrating.[8]

A smallpox outbreak in 1795, which killed an estimated fifty Native Americans, was a precursor of another shortcoming of the future city, a predilection for infectious diseases. Visitors complained of ague or bilious fever (contemporary descriptions of malaria) throughout the Chicago region, spawned by quagmires of standing water and mud; patent medicines for ague were regularly advertised in early newspapers. Writing of the Chicago River, a 1822 traveler noted, "No more than about a dozen boats pass to and from Chicago in a season, as there is an inevitable certainty of a great portion of the hands contracting fever, which is presumed, will be prevented by turning a large current of Michigan water down its channel to increase its motion and sweep away the cause of it." "The fact cannot be controverted that on the streams and wet places the water and air are unwholesome, and the people are sickly," a settler wrote in the summer of 1831. "We called at almost every house, as they are not very near together, but still there is no doubt that this is an uncommonly sickly season." A 1832 cholera outbreak killed fifty-eight Fort Dearborn soldiers, sickened seventy, and induced an estimated three hundred to four hundred to desert. "It is useless to disguise the fact that the present is the most sickly season ever known in the west; owing undoubtedly to the protracted hot and dry weather," the *Chicago Democrat* complained in a story copied throughout the East in 1838. "A large number of people in this city are now complaining" of what was called influenza in 1843 according to the Chicago *Western Citizen,* which noted that the same ailment had struck the area in 1826. "The land is almost one level plain in every direction from Chicago, and for a great part of the year it is mud, mud," a correspondent told the (Concord) *New Hampshire Patriot* in 1850, complaining of another cholera outbreak. With weekday streets as empty as if it were a Sunday, the writer continued, "[Chicago] stands immediately on the shore of the lake, and is not elevated six feet above the water. . . . The thick, greasy water that stands in the streets looks as if it was full of pestilence." Thousands of early Chicagoans would die of water-born infectious diseases up to and including a dysentery outbreak at the Century of Progress World's Fair in 1933.[9]

Spreading the Gospel of Success

In spite of such deterrents, the vast major of Chicago's earliest Euro-American settlers epitomized the economic phenomenon of their day—entrepreneurialism—or the commercial spirit as it was called. Inspired by political philosopher Adam Smith, the quest for personal fortune and fame become the driving force of early nineteenth-century Britains. "The spirit of commercial enterprise by which our countrymen are distinguished above all other people on the globe, is now displaying itself," the *London Times* bragged in 1807, and English poet Samuel Taylor Coleridge called entrepreneurialism "the paramount principle of action" in 1817. "What is it," Thomas Carlyle asked in 1843, "that the modern English soul does, in very truth, dread infinitely, and contemplates with entire despair? What is his Hell? . . . With hesitation, with astonishment, I pronounce it to be: The terror of 'not succeeding.'"[10]

This new ethic or "gospel of success" migrated across the Atlantic in newspapers and among British émigrés to New England, New York, and the Middle Atlantic states, and in turn many of their sons became fanatical advocates. "The Yankee of pure race," the *New-Bedford* (Massachusetts) *Mercury* copied from a British newspaper in 1837, "is discovered by the desire of locomotion; he is under a necessity of coming and going, of agitating his limbs and keeping his muscles in action." The article continued on, noting that tides of emigrants pouring from the Alleghenies chased before them the Native American, the bear, and the buffalo. "Every one for himself. . . . His camp is a flying one, his motto death or conquest; but conquest is the gain of dollars, the creation of a fortune from nothing, the purchase of lots at Chicago, their resale the following year afterwards at Cleveland, or St. Louis at 1000 percent." Newspapers were an important medium for communicating the gospel in America, the *Chicago American* noting in 1837, "In addition . . . to home influence, newspapers have a distant operation of no less importance. They penetrate every where and carry their information into every section of the commercial community. . . ." The Coshocton, Ohio, *Practical Preacher* advised that "every family in the county should take a newspaper" to facilitate such transmissions.[11]

The primarily young, male, Yankee gospel adherents journeyed to settlements such as early Chicago via the new Erie Canal and the Great Lakes beginning in 1825 in pursuit of the personal wealth and social status that they had read about. While all were touched to some degree by the allure of easy money through land speculation, many were practical enough to recognize that there was a better future in mercantilism, establishing stores and other commercial establishments to sell eastern-made goods to speculators. "The immigrants who first settled in Chicago were mostly young men from the eastern states, imbued with that spirit of ambition and enterprise necessary to stimulate one to seek distant fields of activity on the very borders of civilization," a visitor to Chicago in the early 1830s wrote in the *Atlantic Monthly* years later. As remote from London (the seat of the gospel of success) as physically possible, Chicago's pioneering Yankees were its most energetic and outspoken disciples. Chicago literary renaissance author Henry B. Fuller wrote in his 1895 novel *With the Procession* that Chicago was "the only great city in the world to which all its citizens have come for the one common, avowed object of making money." Chicago's earliest Yankee editors waxed about the gospel to their readers, especially through newspaper exchanges (the mailing and copying of articles), an early form of news wire services.

Chicago's first newspaper, the *Democrat,* warned—some would say boasted to—prospective Yankee settlers in 1835 that "nothing is more easy than to grow rich. It is to trust nobody—befriend none—to get every thing, and save all we get—to heap interest upon interest, cent upon cent—to be mean, miserable and despised for some twenty or thirty years." "The floodgates of enterprise seem to be let loose upon us, and multitudes are crowding on to this young land, as if the pestilence were behind, eager to find a better home, where they can build their fortunes and their hopes and enjoy the plenty which our fat fields yield to the hand of industry," the paper explained in another issue. Denying that Chicago's Yankees were forming a new aristocracy, the *Chicago American* declared the following year, "It is true that many among us have become wealthy in a day, and without exertion; but wealth does not necessarily beget what is commonly called 'aristocracy' . . . it is to [our] enterprise that we are mainly indebted for our unexampled prosperity." "Not long since, a young man reached a settlement on Monday," the *Democrat* bragged in 1837, "surveyed his land on Tuesday, built a house on Wednesday, 'went a courting' on Thursday, 'got married' on Friday, moved home on Saturday, and, with his new wife, like the rest of the settlers, went to church on Sunday." "Remember, young man," the *Democrat* admonished readers in 1844, "that your character ought to shine brighter than your boots."[12]

Land speculation was the passion of Chicago's initial Yankee settlers. The sale of former Native People's lands provided the greatest profits to a small group of primarily eastern investors, much as similar out-of-town investors would profit from western mineral deposits later in the century. "As a place of business, [Chicago's] situation at the central head of the Mississippi Valley will make it the New Orleans of the North," *New York American* correspondent Charles Fenno Hoffman predicted in 1834, "its easy and close intercourse with the most flourishing eastern cities, will give it the advantage, as its capital increases, of all their improvements in the mode of living." Noting that Chicago's population had begun with fifty-four Euro-Americans in 1831, the *Cincinnati Mirror* wrote that lots, "partly under water, forty by 200," sold for as much as $7,000 apiece. "The cry is still they come," the *Chicago Democrat* bragged a short time later. "The floodgates of enterprise seem to be let loose upon us." Chicago was "one of the speculating wonders of this wonderful speculating age," the *Pittsfield* (Massachusetts) *Sun* reported in 1835. "I never saw a busier place than Chicago was at the time of our arrival," a correspondent told a New Hampshire newspaper two years later. "The streets were crowded with land speculators, hurrying from one sale to another."[13]

In anticipation of the Chippewas, Ottawas, Potawatomis, and other Native Americans being forced off their lands, a group of twelve Euro-American settlers gathered on August 12, 1833, and signed incorporation papers making Chicago a village of what some said was 400, others 150, residents. "[They were] heroes of a heroic generation," the *Chicago Tribune* romanticized of them years later, "who battled with Indians, smiled at hardship and privation, and opened the new West to the world." As thousands of Native People were pushed to the west, the village's population grew rapidly, climbing officially to 3,265 in 1835 and 4,170 in 1837. But early Chicago's economic and population surges were slowed by the nation's first full-blown recession in 1837. As the bubble in overpriced western lands in places such as Chicago burst, and numerous eastern investors were left penniless, Chicago recovered temporarily as a result of the Illinois and Michigan Canal, which had started in 1836. Built in stages between 1836 and 1848 at an investor cost of $6 million with 284,000 acres of government land grants, the canal was the first (but hardly the last) time that Chicagoans would benefit from federal government largess.[14]

The "state improvement," as the *London Times* called the project, made Chicago a city on March 4, 1837. The first municipal elections were held two months later, with a faction of recently arrived white male Yankees led by William B. Ogden defeating another faction of more settled white male Yankees led by John H. Kinzie, each supported by a different newspaper. Although the two candidates had different national political affiliations, both were members of the same St. James Episcopal Church, both were men of wealth, and both fervent gospel of success advocates. In contrast to the doctrine of individual success, which held that men should not call excessive attention to themselves, a frontier community's success was founded on the advertising and promotion of whatever attributes it could legitimately claim, putting the settlement's name forward if nothing else. Newspapers were considered the most vital tool in such campaigns. "An editor is dangerous, because he is not himself merely; but he is the embodied token, the essence, the tangible representative, of you know not how many thousand other people," a New York newspaper observed in 1830. As such, frontier editors were practitioners of what came to be called "boosterism," the art of "deception and puffery," as a Maine newspaper put it. Boosterism was the collective responsibility of every frontier community settler, and it was through the promotion of early Chicago that the hopeful seeds of its eventual bid to become the nation's most populous city were first planted through the pages of its earliest newspapers.[15]

The *Chicago Democrat*

Despite all of early Chicago's self-enterprise and importance, it was a visitor's lament on the lack of a newspaper that brought the first mass news medium to the village. Sight unseen, twenty-five-year-old John Calhoun dispatched a small Washington hand press (the preeminent printing technology of its day) from his home in New York State aboard a lake schooner and made the four-week journey himself to start Chicago's first paper in 1833. Up to that time, mass communication was rudimentary in the village. The telegraph would not reach Chicago for another fifteen years, and mail service from Michigan was sporadic at best given that it had begun only two years previous and was dependent on road, lake, and weather conditions. Bulletin boards functioned as the city's first newspapers, featuring crude warnings such as "bottomless" to describe roads—a common problem because wooden planking was either stolen for firewood or rotted in the marshy soil. "It was a custom of those early days for Chicagoans, as soon as the weekly postman had galloped from Detroit, to assemble at the post office, there to hear some prominent citizen read at the top of his voice and from the top of a barrel the teachings of the New York papers," an old timer recalled. Under such circumstances, Calhoun faced what the old timer called a "Carthage-must-be-destroyed feeling" to bring a newspaper to Chicago.[16]

Calhoun's initial impressions of his new home, described in a letter to his wife, who would not join him until the following summer, were equally inauspicious. "It is . . . the muddiest place I have ever seen; level—a prairie as back as the eye can see," he wrote to her. Born in New York in 1808 and trained as a printer, he was operating the *Watertown Eagle* when he heard about Chicago in 1833. Described as "a quiet, unassuming man, [and] a practical printer" with a "childlike openness," he was a contrast to the more hardcore gospel-of-success advocates he joined in the village. He found a vacant upstairs office in a three-story hardware-and-stove building on the northwest corner of South Water Street at Clark and issued the first edition of the *Chicago Democrat* on November 26, 1833. Newspaper technology was so new to the settlement that spectators jockeyed to see him operate the platen press and cheered as he peeled the first pages of the newspaper from the sticky type, vying for the "first" first edition as a souvenir. Calhoun was a printer, not a newspaperman by trade, and there was little local news in his initial issues, hardly surprising given that the few Euro-American residents in the village had little need to be apprised of what they already knew. Instead, the *Democrat* reprinted laws and other legal documents, advertisements for Yankee merchants and professionals, and booster editorials. "Situated as Chicago is at the mouth of a fine river, on the shore of the noble lake into which the river empties itself; in a country possessing a soil of extraordinary fertility, with a climate whose clear and salubrious atmosphere is almost unsurpassed, it is a matter of wonder that it should be so eagerly sought by enterprising emigrants," Calhoun (or an anonymous contributor) wrote. Another editorial reiterated the theme of unbridled opportunity in early Chicago. "The floodgates of enterprise seem to be let loose upon us, and multitudes are crowding on to this young land, as if the pestilence were behind," the paper observed, "eager to find a better home, where they can build their fortunes and their hopes and enjoy the plenty which our fat fields yield to the hand of industry."[17]

In comparison to the more timely content that would come later, frontier newspaper boosterism was largely reactive rather than proactive, responding to the demands of paying subscribers and public and private leaders rather than dictating or leading public policy. As Don Harrison Doyle demonstrated in his study of Jacksonville, Illinois, newspaper editors and other boosters defined their priorities based on prevailing local conditions and concerns, even going so far as to recast booster claims retrospectively to reflect newer, revised priorities. Eastern newspapers' notice of the *Democrat* came the following spring when the *Pittsfield* (Massachusetts) *Sun* reprinted an item about the price of potatoes, a staple of early Chicagoans' diets, reaching an exorbitant price of $1.25 a bushel with little left for seed. While not necessarily positive, such notices put Chicago's name in the eastern public's perception and gave Chicagoans an opportunity to see themselves through others' eyes.

The *Pittsfield Sun* reprinted another *Democrat* item in early 1836 to the effect that Chicago's unofficial population had climbed to 3,279, with forty-four stores, nine brick buildings, a county clerk's office, and "the foundations of 2 churches (episcopal and baptist)." "Eastward Ho!" noted another copied *Democrat* article, noting that nearly a thousand Chicago merchants were on their way to the Atlantic cities to obtain supplies and find wives. "The song of the husbandman has taken the place of the war-hoop," the *Democrat* rhapsodized, "and the waters of Lake Michigan are navigated by hundreds of vessels, including ships and steamboats equal in beauty, strength, and size, to any in our country." "The Spring of 1833 may be marked as a new era in the history of Chicago," the *Democrat* noted a few issues later. "At that time Chicago did not contain more than five or six regular stores, and now may be counted from twenty to twenty-five. . . . To describe the want that has been for building materials and mechanics, would be only to incite incredulity."[18]

The *Democrat's* interest in an eastern readership was far from incidental. A review of John Calhoun's circulation books reveals that only one-quarter of his paying subscribers lived in Chicago. Forty percent were in other parts of Illinois with the remainder situated from the competing frontier village of Milwaukee through Michigan, Indiana, and beyond to Vermont, New Hampshire, and New York State, mainly along the water route that carried most of Chicago's goods and information. It was no surprise that early Chicago garnered most of its population and financial support from the East, a fact not lost on Calhoun. Such dedicated self-promotion should have paid well, but in a desperate attempt to get recalcitrant subscribers to pay, Calhoun wrote in 1834:

> What is glory! Ask the *Printer*
> Laboring hard, both night and day;
> Stea[me]d in summer—froze in winter;
> He would tell you for better pay.
> Ask delinquents, What is glory?
> They'll reply, with scoffs and sneers,
> 'Tis like printers—tell a story—
> Promise pay for many years.[19]

Long John Wentworth, Steam Printing, and a Cleansing of Public Morals

Calhoun may have lacked the rough-and-tumble disposition of a frontier editor, but his successor did not. Six-foot, six-inch John Wentworth is best remembered for an offhand remark he made on September 22, 1860 (during his second mayoral term), when the nineteen-year-old Prince of Wales, the future King Edward VII, visited Chicago as part of the first North American tour by a British royal. Standing on the balcony of the Richmond House hotel at the northwest corner of present-day Michigan Avenue and South Wacker Drive, Wentworth introduced the prince to a large crowd gathered below by saying, "Boys, this is the prince. He has come here to see the city and I am going to show him around. Prince, these are the boys." More than any other single event, that comment attached the label of "philistine" to early Chicago, an image that persisted into the twentieth century. "I felt no undue elation and the acclamations of the crowd were intended for me as much as for him," Wentworth rationalized his behavior later. Even the *Tribune* was forced to note at the time that "live princes [are] scarce on this side of the ocean."[20]

In reality, Wentworth was anything but a detractor of his adopted city, but he did have a habit of putting his very large foot into his mouth. Arriving in October 1836, he recalled that "could you have been on the sand hills . . . you would have seen me stretched out like a leather shoe string tied up, just after wading a prairie marsh—all length and no breadth . . . with all my clothes under one arm and a jug of whiskey under the other." The New Hampshire native took control of the *Democrat* the following month, just in time to save it from financial extinction, and made it the personification of Chicago for the next twenty-five years, simultaneously using its pages to birth and catapult his own political career. It was no coincidence that Wentworth's political enemy Stephen A. Douglas commanded his operatives to "make war on Wentworth every good chance you get" and that when the *Chicago Tribune* bought the *Democrat* from Wentworth in 1861, a pivotal element in the sales agreement was a non-competition clause. No one knew better Wentworth's potential than his political and business competitors.

Wentworth's reputation for hyperbole, mudslinging, and unabridged irritability was as large as his physical stature. In print he wrote of politician Daniel Webster, "His talents are like our vast American wildernesses where flourishes and decays a rich and plenteous vegetation, which avails no man anything." Of a competing Whig newspaper, he editorialized, "Before anything emanating in any way from 'the amiable editor of the [Chicago] *Express*' can obtain more than a passing glance from us, he must take daily, full doses of Dr. Duncan's Whig-purgative pills for at least two weeks in succession." In person, Wentworth lived in hotels and spent hours in grogeries, as taverns were called, drinking, eating, and reading aloud from his and other newspapers. He was an ally of early Illinois Governor Thomas Carlin, who named Wentworth an honorary Illinois militia colonel in 1838 at a time when Kentucky governors were adopting a similar practice. Though married, Wentworth's wife and family never moved to Chicago, preferring the more civilized East. Wentworth encouraged his irascible persona in a letter to a friend written after his first election to Congress in 1843:

> This is the same Col. Wentworth—Col. John Wentworth—who . . . whipped his wife, turned five of his children out of doors in a cold winter's night, broke up five married couples, run away three men's wives, was baptized by

> Joe Smith in Nauvoo as a good Mormon . . . took his pay in Virginia slaves, finally fell from a horse and broke his neck, was buried the next day and then arose again, and before he paid his funeral expenses, got elected by 1,621 vote majority to Congress."

There was a modicum of truth to the allusion of Mormonism, for Wentworth had written to church founder Joseph Smith Jr. the preceding year asking Smith to describe "the rise, progress, persecution, and faith" of his Latter-day Saints. Smith's response became the first written account of his vision of his church, and his thirteen statements to Wentworth became the church's formal Articles of Faith in 1880. Wentworth claimed in subsequent years that he lost votes in elections because some thought him a Mormon, "an old bachelor," or "believed the story that he was in the habit of whipping his wife," which he had started himself.[21]

The *Democrat* became Chicago's second daily paper on February 24, 1840 (the first, the *Chicago American,* tried but failed at daily publication in 1837), but Wentworth was forced to abandon his *Morning Democrat* in 1841 because his hand-powered Washington press could not satisfy demand. Long John rectified the problem in 1845 with the purchase of the first Adams printing press to cross Lake Michigan. Invented by New Englander Isaac Adams in 1836, the new press used a steam-powered plate to more than double the number of four-page copies that could be produced. The effect was also one of initial wonder, and it quickly changed the reading habits of Chicagoans. With the press installed, Wentworth's operation needed wood to fire its steam engine. "[The head printer] rushed out into the street and brought back two Norwegians with their saws and bucks on their backs," the *Tribune* later wrote. "They thought [the press] was wood to be sawed. They could not speak a word of English, but [sawed wood was] the motive power needed. After considerable pantomime, [the pressman] got his 'power' to understand what was wanted, and thus it was that machinery was first introduced into the printing business in Chicago." "The number of daily visitors to it is immense and takes up a great deal of our time," the *Democrat* boasted. "But to this we make no objection if every man would bring along a job of work or subscribe for the paper." Resuming its daily edition, the *Democrat* moved into a new, larger office on LaSalle Street in 1847. Built at a cost of $4,000, the building was named Jackson Hall, after the Democratic president, and featured one of Chicago's first public reading rooms so that local politicos could gather and discuss the day's events.

The *Democrat* bragged on large signs painted outside of Jackson Hall that it could print the "latest news" as many as thirty-six hours ahead of the mails, the first time that Chicagoans could expect timely information in their newspapers; with time, Wentworth's new press had an even more dramatic impact on the local culture. Its efficiency led to an overall decline in the price of newspapers, books, and other printed materials, meaning that more residents could afford to buy and read printed materials on a regular basis—immigrants included. The latter became more conscious of their lack of political pull in the growing city as a result of what they read in the English-language newspapers, and a growing consciousness of their limited role contributed to the 1855 Lager Beer riot. With the introduction of the first telegraph to the city, readers became even more accustomed to timely reporting, distant and local. The *Daily Democratic Press*' (a different paper) boast in 1853 that "the press of Chicago has, in a great degree, made the city" was as much a reflection of the changing role of Chicago newspapers from poorly paying political and economic boosters to profitable businesses as it was a plug for those businesses. Ultimately, New Yorker Richard H. Hoe bought Adams's patents and perfected a steam press using cylinders rather than a flat platen. The *Democrat*'s technology was eclipsed by other local papers during the 1850s, including the new *Tribune*, but it was Wentworth who made information cheaper and a more plentiful in Chicago.[22]

First elected mayor in 1857, Wentworth personally championed two civic reforms that inspired the city's lowbrow public image. The first involved gambling, a bane that continued to plague Chicago into the twenty-first century. The connection between Chicago and games of chance began early. The *Democrat*'s second commercial job (before Wentworth bought the paper) had been to print two hundred lottery tickets. British newspaperman Charles J. Latrobe testified to another form of gambling in a 1833 essay, *The Rambler in North America*, when he wrote of Chicago that "[Horse] races occurred frequently on a piece of level sward without the village on which temporary booths afforded the motley multitudes the means of 'stimulating'; and betting and gambling were the order of the day." Not three months later, a *Chicago Democrat* letter writer complained about popular games of chance abounding in the city, and the village council voted to bar them—the first but hardly the last time public officials tried to control the practice. Gaming, saloons, and prostitution began to flourish in the so-called Sands District on the city's near North Side, a neighborhood habituated by sailors and other itinerant visitors, during the 1840s and 1850s. Vice became so commonplace that the *Tribune* maintained that "each morning saw colored Sambo fresh from his penny ante, or the flashy gentry of seals, diamond pins and large patterned waistcoats . . . turning over [his] ill-gotten gains from the bank into the municipal exchequer." With some six hundred liquor purveyors, an estimated 250 gambling establishments, and more than one hundred houses of prostitution, an estimated one of out every ten Chicagoans owed his or her entire livelihood to some form of vice by the 1850s. As one eastern newspaper put it of Chicago, "There you fall at once into the circling tide, and sweep into the very vortex of intense activity and life."[23]

Barely a month after taking office in March 1857, Wentworth advertised a nonexistent dog fight with a $250 purse to be held on the city's outskirts and then personally led a group of Chicago policemen, volunteer firefighters, Sheriff John L. Wilson armed with eviction notices, and a "large posse" of citizens with teams of dray horses, wagons, chains, crowbars, and other tools, and sacked the Sands District. Bystanders cheered when Wentworth allowed them to loot what they could carry away. Tipped in advance, the *Tribune* reported that the event attracted a crowd of thousands. "Yesterday afternoon, about half past four o'clock, six of the remaining buildings, all houses of the worst character, were burned to the ground," the paper wrote. "As the fire broke out in three of the buildings simultaneously, it is probable they were set on fire by the inmates, out of spite to the owner of the property, who had just purchased them."

As the *Tribune* maintained, Wentworth reasoned that vice would be "wiped out" forever in the city as an outcome of his raid—and it was, temporarily. The *Democrat* wrote in November 1857 of a "Decrease of Crime—Moral Improvement of the Age." But his action ultimately had the reverse effect, sowing the seeds of vice throughout the remainder of the city, especially along Randolph Street between State and Dearborn. The Levee, as that area was called, became the city's leading tourist attraction, an integral element in its political, economic, social, and cultural life, and living proof of what the *Tribune* termed "everything that is bad in human nature." "Night after night, and week after week during the administration of John Wentworth," a resident complained to the *Tribune* in 1859, "were the houses of our citizens robbed, while the police were engaged in entering houses of ill fame, and pulling naked from their beds lewd women and paramours." "Probably no event in Chicago's history up to the time of the fire was so much talked about all over the West, and so variously commented upon," a *Chicago Times* reporter wrote years later.[24]

Stunned by criticisms of his raid, Wentworth turned his attention to a different regulatory effort, a beautification of the city's central business district that only furthered Chicago's lowbrow reputation. "There is a surprisingly large class of persons not aware of the practical, daily palpable advantages of advertising," the *Tribune* waxed, and businessmen routinely used early

Chicago's sidewalks and streets to display their goods and services. The city was "disfigured, up to the third story, by large glaring sign-boards, containing the names and occupations of their residents," one visiting Englishwoman wrote. "The side walks are literally encumbered with bales of scarlet flannel, and every other article of an emigrant's outfit." To move about, pedestrians and horses were forced to wind their way through this maze of showcases, boxes, barrels, barbers' poles, saloon signs, advertisements, and other paraphernalia. During the early morning hours of June 19, 1857, Wentworth led another raid, this time to remove the offending obstructions, ordering officers to toss them into one large pile north of State Street near the river.

"Another Brilliant Feat of the Police" was how the *Tribune* headlined its coverage the following morning, noting that "tumbled into the mud were some forty hogsheads of sugar, a lot of grindstones, a number of anchors, piles of heavy iron cables, wooden watches, show cases, signs of every kind, lumber, old chairs, wagons, daguerreotype stands, boxes, pails, auction flags, and hundreds of other articles which were anything but assorted." "We are requested by a subscriber to say to the Mayor, that the barrel missing from the door of No. 115 South Water street, yesterday morning, was not whisky but vinegar," the *Tribune* reported as a public service, suggesting some individual goods such as liquor may have been targeted by police. The paper labeled the raid "too much tyranny for this latitude" and Wentworth's second regulatory campaign went down to failure as well. Within a short decade, advertising signs were spread across entire sides of downtown buildings and huge banners were strung on wires across streets throughout what would become known as the Loop, establishing a model that was imitated in countless other western cities during the remainder of the century.[25]

The *Chicago Tribune*

Unlike the *Chicago Democrat,* which has been preserved from its first issue, the formative years of the *Tribune,* Chicago's longest-lived daily newspaper, will forever be shrouded in mystery. The only complete run of the paper, including all pre-1860 issues, was dropped on the sidewalk in front of the *Tribune* building by panicking employees during the 1871 fire. However, as newspaper historian Franklin William Scott maintained, the genesis of the *Tribune* was a weekly magazine called *Gem of the Prairie.* Founded in 1844 to help a young sporting male named Kiler K. Jones explain his role in a failed duel, the *Gem* evolved from a gossip sheet into a news and literary weekly that exposed a variety of abuses including the 1848 public kidnapping of a fugitive enslaved man named Abram Ross in Chicago, warning fellow African Americans to be wary of "prowling slave catchers in the city." It provided the only illustrated coverage of Chicago's first serious flood in 1849, which caused more than $100,000 in damages to the river area as well, and introduced the city's first novelist, William H. Bushnell, to the reading public. The *Gem* survived under its own name until 1852, when it was renamed the *Chicago Sunday Tribune,* as a journal of "literary, miscellany and general intelligence," burdened, as a later day *Tribune* reporter asserted, with a "Bret Harte flavor [that] has caused it to stick like a bur to the Chicago tradition."[26]

Perhaps because of its name, the *Tribune* has not always been eager to admit its connection to the *Gem.* However, a 1864 *Tribune* article asserted that "to Mr. [James] Kelly belongs the credit of originating, or at least, suggesting the [*Tribune*] publication. He was the owner of the *Gem of the Prairie,* a weekly literary journal. . . . His idea was to start a daily, from which he could make up the weekly *Gem,* regarding the former as in a measure secondary to the latter in point of public interest, and as a financial measure." *Gem* founder Kiler K. Jones agreed in 1879 that "the *Gem of the Prairie* was the foundation-stone of the present *Tribune.*" The proprietors "in order to meet a growing demand for news alone, established the *Chicago Tribune* as an offshoot to the *Gem of the Prairie.*" By contrast, Col. Robert R. McCormick claimed that the *Tribune* "absorbed" the *Gem* in 1847 and even called it a "rival" publication in 1942. In the twenty-first century therefore, while the *Tribune* is technically correct when it prints on its editorial page that it was started on June 10, 1847, it was actually founded March 20, 1844 as the *Gem of the Prairie.*[27]

The *Chicago Democrat* provided another perspective on the *Tribune*'s earliest years in a 1849 article, noting that the *Tribune* was a *Gem* spinoff born as a mouthpiece for the short-lived anti-slavery Free Soil political party. The *Democrat*'s concern at the time was that the *Tribune* was claiming a circulation of 6,765, a figure it did not achieve until the Civil War. Instead, the *Democrat* guessed that its daily circulation was around 1,000 or 1,200 copies and that the *Gem* still had a larger subscriber base. "The *Gem* was started as a literary paper and was so continued until last year when it became a political one," the *Democrat* wrote. "Its subscribers had paid in advance, and had to stand the act of bad faith." Of the *Tribune*'s claim that the *Democrat* had a circulation of only 137, the latter sputtered, "This is hardly magnanimous upon a poor fellow with only 137 subscribers from men who have 6,765! Is it not cruel for them in their elevated position to be thus trampling on us after we are down?" Ill will between the two papers continued until the *Democrat* was purchased by the *Tribune* on July 25, 1861, although the *Democrat* finally forced the *Tribune* to admit to a more accurate circulation of between 1,000 and 2,000 in 1851.[28]

The first issue of the afternoon *Tribune* (it did not become a morning paper until July 1852) had a printing of four hundred copies, produced on an old-fashioned Washington handpress in a one-room office on the third story of a building at the corner of La Salle and Lake streets. The compositors and pressmen cast a lot to see who would get the first printed copy. Its prospectus, printed as was the custom in Chicago's other newspapers, promised, "Our views, in all probability, will sometimes be coincident with the conservatives; sometimes we may be found in the ranks of the radicals; but we shall at all times be faithful to humanity—to the whole of humanity—without regard to race, sectional divisions, party lines, or parallels of latitude or longitude." Not surprisingly given its literary pedigree, the prospectus featured poetry:

> Men of thought! be up and stirring,
> Night and day;
> Sow the seed—withdraw the curtain;
> Clear the way,
> Men of action! aid and cheer them
> As ye may.

As prospectuses went, the early *Tribune*'s was hardly noteworthy. Beginning in 1833, a new breed of newspaper, the penny press, had provided independent, nonpartisan, local news to New York's growing middle class at the previously unheard-of price of one cent per issue. Chicago had a brief incarnation of such a paper, *Quid Nunc* (Latin for "What Now"), said to be the first one-cent daily published west of the Alleghenies, around 1840. By comparison, the first *Tribune* sold for 12½ cents per six-day week (raised to 15 cents in 1852) or $1.50 for three months, in part because it was printed on an old-fashioned press. Instead of espousing the penny-press doctrine of impartiality, the early *Tribune* was fiercely and often embarrassingly partisan, appealing to Chicago's Whig and Free Soil partisans with editorials, commentary, and prewritten telegraphed national and international news. Rather than strong local news coverage, one of the paper's founders bragged that "from the *Tribune* have been uttered dicta that have controlled the destinies of parties and individuals of prominence in the country." Its price did not drop to one cent until 1895.[29]

Still, Chicago could not boast of a real newspaperman until Joseph Meharry Medill arrived and bought a share of the *Tribune* on June 18, 1855. Until his death forty-four years later, Medill reigned as the wealthiest and most influential, if not the most respected, Chicago newspaperman. His legacy persisted through his progeny's iron-fisted control of the paper until the middle of the twentieth century, with grandson Col. Robert R. McCormick noting in 1947 that his grandfather considered his job "the never ending struggle to produce the best, most comprehensive, useful, trenchant, and attractive newspaper, regardless of expense." Medill's name persisted into the twenty-first century as the moniker for the Chicago region's oldest journalism program, Northwestern University's Medill School of Journalism, founded in 1921 and endowed by his family in 1925.[30]

Medill (pronounced mu-dil′) was born in an area of New Brunswick, British North America, that was considered a part of the United States in 1823, but his parents moved to Ohio in 1832 ensuring his American citizenship if not nativity. He studied the law, but distinctions between lawyers, politicians, and journalists were hazy in antebellum America, and men often moved between the professions more for opportunity than education. Medill and his younger brothers purchased a Coshocton, Ohio, newspaper in 1849, learning typesetting and printing, the "art that preserveth all arts" as it was called, in the process. The paper's support of the Whig party helped it overcome a local Democratic majority, and Medill's first taste of political blood remained with him for life. He was obsessed by mass news media technology, from faster printing presses to the introduction of the telegraph during the 1840s, the telephone in the 1880s, and the linotype and telephone in the 1890s, all proof of the "truth of the theory of evolution." "Old men still smile when they think of those times and the mystification the new invention occasioned," Medill wrote of the telegraph.

The Medills sold their paper in 1853 and established a Whig newspaper in Cleveland, eventually consolidating it with another to form the *Cleveland Leader.* In the wake of the Whig election disaster in 1852, Medill later claimed to have written letters to leaders of the disgraced organization asking if they would assist him in the formation of a new party. The written replies were destroyed in Chicago's 1871 fire, but prominent Whigs such as Horace Greeley supposedly replied in encouragement. In March 1854, two months after a similar meeting had been held in Chicago, a collection of anti-slavery Whigs, Democrats, and Free Soilers met with Medill in the *Leader*'s Cleveland office and organized what they called the National Republican Party. In subsequent years, Medill claimed to have created the Republican Party, but evidence suggests otherwise: in particular a group that had gathered in Ripon, Wisconsin, one month before Medill's Cleveland meeting, and a Republican convention held in Jackson, Michigan, in July 1854, meetings which Medill did not attend. Nevertheless "the honor of giving birth to the Republican party ought to be divided between [Democratic Illinois U.S. Senator] Steve Douglas and myself," Medill declared, in reference to Douglas's dismemberment of his Democratic party during the 1850s.[31]

In 1854, the *Tribune* tried unsuccessfully to recruit Medill to become its first managing editor based on his take-no-prisoners partisanship and uninhibited editorial rhetoric. He was described as a quick-to-judge, no-compromise newspaperman, "prone to take either an exaggerated, optimistic view or an extremely gloomy one." Nearly six feet tall, slender and austere, Medill looked perennially angry, with fiery red hair brushed back over a broad, high forehead. Once he was attacked by a downstate congressman in a Washington, D.C., hotel for something printed in the *Tribune.* "I am glad I had no arms or knife," Medill later bragged, "or I should probably have killed [the congressman] on the spot." He was a chronic loner with few friends—not even his wife or children. "I do not recall that Joseph Medill had any close friends," grandson Col. Robert R. McCormick wrote. Near deafness added to his stoic demeanor, and he was egotistical to an extreme in his judgments. "His strongest qualities were his entire devotion to the public interest; his confidence in his own judgment," McCormick recalled. "Such strong traits bring with them the inevitable defect that when their possessor is mistaken, he is just as forceful on the wrong course as he had been on the right course, but Mr. Medill was not frequently wrong, and never, I believe, in any large way." Most significantly, Medill was political to his core. "My grandfather's main interest was politics always," McCormick said. "In that field he wrote countless editorials and read all others late in his house, changing and patching half the night and driving our night editor nearly mad by the delay."[32]

Even though Medill turned down the *Tribune*'s first offer, Chicago intrigued him so much that he sold his share of the *Cleveland Leader* the following year and moved his family to the lake city. There he met Dr. Charles H. Ray, a physician and fellow newspaperman. Ray had cut his teeth in downstate journalism and became involved in the early Illinois Republican Party, serving briefly as the secretary of the Illinois State Senate. A Ray and Medill power meeting at the Tremont House hotel in early 1855 was hardly happenstance, for they had been paired by the nation's leading newspaperman, *New York Tribune* publisher Horace Greeley. Ray wanted to start a penny Republican paper in Chicago like the *New York Tribune* when Greeley learned that the failing *Chicago Tribune* was for sale. It would give Ray and Medill an established mouthpiece if they could come up with the $40,000 asking price. The paper's prospective sale was hot news at the time, and its last sale until 2007. "Rumor hath it," the paper reported on May 4, 1855, "that the *Tribune* has changed hands; that its name is to be altered and its present principles and policies to be abandoned." Medill and Ray officially became partners on June 18, 1855. When former *Gem of the Prairie* editor Thomas A. Stewart retired, Ray was named chief editor and Medill became business manager, a post he held off and on until he seized majority control in 1874. The revitalized paper bought better type and a faster double-cylinder press, merging with the *Daily Democratic Press* for economic reasons in 1858. Shortly before his death in 1899, Medill boasted that the *Tribune* began making a profit for its new owners the first day, "the first month and every other month up to now."[33]

To repay their hefty loans however, Ray, Medill, and co-owners needed an attention-getting gimmick beyond its Republican allegiances. The American Party, dubbed by detractors as the Know-Nothings for their passion for secrecy, flourished briefly in the early and middle 1850s based on its opposition to foreign-born immigrants, especially Catholics. Convinced that a hierarchy of priests, bishops, and archbishops controlled by the Roman papacy was conspiring to undermine native-born, Protestant, American democracy, the Know-Nothings attracted as many as one million members nationwide, experiencing a short-lived but startling political success. Chicago was a promising Know-Nothings hotbed, with dozens of Catholic Germans and so-called "famine" Irish arriving daily aboard numerous railroads. "An emigrant lands on our shores, already reared, and with a strong arm and a willing heart, he is ready to work," the immigrant-supportive *Daily Democratic Press* explained in 1852. "It is a fact . . . that the Irish in this country, particularly those of the 'hewer of wood and drawer of water' class, are imbued with a most remarkable and striking fondness and passion for riots and rows," a xenophobic *Tribune* responded. It defined an Irish wedding as "a row of the most approved and energetic character," and to further impress its immigrant-baiting readers, it told of an Irish woman who petitioned the local, Protestant-funded Relief Society for assistance during the harsh winter of 1856: "In many cases where work has been offered to stout, able bodied and robust Irishmen who have applied for aid from the Society, they have rejected it with the greatest indignation," the *Tribune* wrote.[34]

Medill was no stranger to anti-Catholicism. "[Popery] has landed upon our shores millions of its superstitious instruments who are segregated and clannish and swift to do the will of Rome," he had written two years previous to purchasing his *Tribune* shares. "The tree is known by its fruits; those of the papal tree are noxious and deadly. . . . Crime, pauperism, misery, follow in its footsteps. Intolerance is its temper, ignorance, its cement, inquisitions and duplicity its means, Jesuits its sentinels, and the overthrow of knowledge and liberty its aim." American prisons were full of immigrant Catholics and America's public school system was in danger of being indoctrinated by the Catholic bible, according to Medill. His anti-Catholicism could hardly have been a secret to those who arranged the *Tribune*'s sale, and it was likely a positive attribute on his employment resume.[35]

The 1855 "Lager Beer" Riot

There were a number of characteristics common to foreign-born residents beyond their Catholic religion that angered Yankee Chicagoans, but seemingly none more than their alcoholic consumption habits. Native-born Chicagoans such as Long John Wentworth enjoyed high-alcohol-content beverages such as rye whiskey, bourbon or corn whiskey, and brandy. Whiskey and gin sold for about 40 cents a gallon in early Chicago and a good French brandy could be had for $2 a gallon. Taverns, hotels, and stores featured open liquor barrels with tin dippers so that their male clientele could imbibe freely, and most antebellum business dealings were lubricated with such alcoholic beverages, although on Sundays the drinking stopped or at least was done behind closed doors in deference to Protestant Sabbath customs. By contrast, early Chicago's Germans and Scandinavians brought with them a European taste for ales, stouts, lagers, and wines consumed in saloons or *bierstubes,* outdoor beer gardens, especially on Sundays. "Let any one take a walk down Clark street, any Sunday afternoon, and he will . . . fancy himself in a busy grog shop and gambling den, in full blast," the *Tribune* complained in early 1854. "Beer guzzling, pipe smoking Dutch [Germans] quarreling and swearing, card playing, dice rattling, and one or two fights, are constant occurrences, and not in a corner nor under a bushel, but in broad daylight and with open doors." When Mayor Isaac Miliken issued a proclamation ordering that the Sabbath laws be enforced, the German-language *Illinois Staats Zeitung* was so critical that he was forced to rescind the order. "He caved, and nothing more has been heard from him," the *Tribune* continued. "Have he not the courage to try again?"

Capitalizing on such sentiments, physician Dr. Levi Boone, a great-nephew of frontiersman Daniel Boone, was elected mayor on March 6, 1855, on a Know-Nothing ticket. To appease his native-born supporters, he quickly raised liquor licenses from $50 to $300 and began enforcing Sunday closing laws. A reinvigorated police force, made up of eighty native-born officers, descended on immigrant neighborhoods. More than two hundred primarily German saloon keepers were arrested while Yankee businesses and hostelries like the Tremont House continued to serve on Sundays unmolested. "The *Tribune* says it is a disgrace for our city, that a paper can exist here which continences the establishment and continuance of drinking halls," a letter writer told the *Staats Zeitung* in early 1855. "It is indeed a disgrace for the Germans to suffer their sentiments to be outraged any longer—Let us have another paper representing different principles, and two-thirds of the German population will support it." To make an example, Boone had the courts schedule trials for Saturday, April 21, in the newly constructed county building. As the hearings got underway, a group of immigrant protesters marched from Ogden Park on the north to Courthouse Square under the encouragement of eighth-ward Democratic alderman S. B. La Rue, nicknamed "Rot Gut" by the *Tribune*. In a speech to the protesters, La Rue likened the political disfranchisement of his North Side immigrant constituents to African American enslavement.[36]

Upon its arrival downtown, La Rue's group milled about but was otherwise peaceful except for nine minor arrests. As the day progressed however, a second, larger protest group formed on the North Side and heard from another speaker, a German-born shoemaker named Peter Marsden. Under Marsden's German-language prodding, the second group marched to the courthouse, this time armed with guns, knives, pitchforks, clubs, and bludgeons, and keeping time to a military drum and fife. "The drums were dropping their rat-tat-tat on high-strung nerves of men who are naturally soldiers," *Tribune* co-owner William Bross recalled of the event. "They saw a common purpose in one another's eyes, and a spark was all that was needed to send fire through the whole."

At the encouragement of Boone, an Irish bridge keeper delayed the marchers as they approached the Clark Street drawbridge, stalling them long enough for an armed police force of an estimated fifty native-born officers and sheriff's deputies to assemble around Courthouse Square. More than a dozen musket shots were exchanged between the protesters, police, and armed bystanders in the vicinity of Clark and Randolph streets during the brief encounter. Marsden, at the front of the protesters, was shot and killed by Sheriff James Andrews in an act that earned the latter a lifelong city job; one other policeman lost an arm in the melee. "The scene that ensued was indescribable," the *Chicago Journal* reported. "The streets were densely thronged by our citizens, who fell back from the firing, many of them seeking refuge in the adjoining stores and offices; in one instance carrying away entirely the show-window of a trunk store on Clark-street, as they forced their way in." An unknown number of protesters and bystanders were injured during the confrontation. The local militia restored order by nightfall and cleared Courthouse Square by pointing two old cannons, used formerly by the British to defend Detroit, in a northerly direction. The *New York Times* headlined its page-one coverage "Bloody Riot in Chicago," and numerous eastern newspapers copied the account.

Some fifty-five protesters from the second, more violent group were arrested in what was called the Lager Beer Riot, what a World War I–era German-language publication called "the first invasion of Chicago." None faced serious criminal charges, in sharp contrast to the 1886 Haymarket Square defendants, and only two were convicted, both Irishmen, leading the *Chicago Herald* to lament that "it seemed such a travesty that two Irishmen alone should be martyrs of the cause of beer in which the Germans were the leaders and chief beneficiaries [and] the culprits were afterward released." The confrontation convinced the German community that it needed to become more involved in local politics, and German men joined in defeating Boone in a reelection bid the following year.

Meanwhile, many among the English-language mass news media recognized a responsibility to better report local government news to empower the Germans, Scandinavians, and Irish who were moving to Chicago in large numbers. The latter lesson was lost on the xenophobic *Tribune* however, especially when a splinter group of marchers paraded past the paper's office at 53 Clark Street carrying a black-draped banner mourning "The Chicago *Tribune*." "The ultimate consequences of this deplorable disturbance can hardly fail to be beneficial," the *Tribune* retorted editorially. "Not only will [those arrested] tell with great effect for the cause of Prohibition throughout the state, but they will learn the German population of this city that they must obey the laws." Waving the then-popular banner of Manifest Destiny, the paper also declared that "the crepe may be borne by our door ninety and nine times, but sooner or later the victory will perch on the banner we carry aloft. The Almighty has ordained it."[37]

Although immigrant bashing initially cost the *Tribune* circulation, departing foreign-born readers were replaced by Know-Nothing Yankees who had been subscribing to other, less strident English-language dailies. "Within three months, [the *Tribune*'s] subscription list had greatly changed, having lost several hundred saloon and Catholic subscribers, and obtained a greater number of a more desirable character," the *Tribune* later explained. "Experience, however, proved that while it is much easier to lessen than to increase the number of readers and supporters of a paper, the public will properly appreciate and sustain a journal that is independent in tone, and bold as an advocate of liberty and a conservator of public morals." Preaching to upper-class, white, Protestant men, what it called the "Better Class," became the hallmark of the *Tribune* for the remainder of the nineteenth century, certainly until Medill's death in 1899. As Timothy R. Mahoney noted, a frontier community's social development "results from the complex interaction of the activities and behaviors of those 'on the ground.'" Native-born Chicago men desired to distance their subculture from the foreign-born immigrant subculture. This new, emerging social order, characterized by the *Tribune* as the "five-sixths of the businessmen, of the professional men, of the master mechanics, of the journeymen, of the clerks, the students, the laborers, of American birth" or more simply as "the taxpayers," came to depend on the *Tribune* to explain their social reality and epitomize the gospel of success and culture. From a declining readership base, the daily *Tribune's* circulation climbed to over 3,000 by 1855, with its Sunday edition, the former *Gem of the Prairie,* claiming an estimated circulation of 4,500.

The *Tribune* continued anti-Catholic rhetoric throughout the 1850s. "We appeal to property-holders," it editorialized on Leap Day 1856, "who remember the time when the influence of the Irish Democracy was paramount—when every office was filled by specimens of the most 'illegant pisantry in the world' . . . when it was almost a crime not to be able to speak with a brogue." When Mayor Boone and his Know-Nothings were turned out of office the following month, the *Tribune* openly blamed their loss on what it called "hundreds" of foreign-born Catholics, "the gamblers and those they fleece—the grog-shops and their hangers on—[and the] office seekers and their pimps." "Not a man who believes in the supremacy of the papal Power, that did not go straight out and directly for the triumph of Slavery," the paper wrote. "Not a man who gives up his conscience to the control of the priesthood, that did not use his ballot to beat down freedom." By the end of the decade, the paper was attacking Democratic presidential candidate Stephen Douglas for alleged ties to the Catholic Church through his wife and children.

In an 1891 memoir, *Chicago Times* reporter Franc Wilkie also described a pre-1860 *Tribune* editorial supposedly titled "Nig, Nig, Nigger!" that linked Catholicism to the Democratic Party's opposition to abolitionism, probably in an unpreserved *Tribune* issue. "The Catholics remembered the article when [Dr. Ray] died in 1870, and something of the same class picture that has been painted of the death-bed of Voltaire by a religious body was given of the last moments of Dr. Ray," Wilkie wrote. "It was a picture a trifle less revolting than that of the French infidel, but it was one full of horrible suggestions." With Abraham Lincoln's successful 1860 presidential bid, the *Tribune*'s anti-Catholicism diminished but never disappeared altogether until late in the century. "The press is supposed to be the origin and symbol of public opinion," it quoted a London newspaper in 1877 in an article headlined "Pope and Press." "There is something, we will not say grotesque . . . of the Pope delivering an allocution [*sic*] 'to the Catholic press' on the use and abuse of journalism."[38]

* * *

Mid-nineteenth-century Chicago was a true city compared to the wet prairie that it had been at the beginning of the century. Its boosterism and self-aggrandizement was so thorough that it had earned a place in the American consciousness for speaking and publishing too much of itself. "From your boot-black to your hack-driver all put on real estate airs, and a genuine talent for blowing is the highest Chicago merit," a New York-based letter writer complained to the *Chicago Tribune* in 1856. "Speak to a Chicagoan about any place or any subject other than Chicago, and he knows nothing about it," the *Toledo Blade* wrote the following year. "Chicago, Chicago is the whole theme." A traveling salesman claimed at about the same time to have never seen a Chicago newspaper that did not have "something in it calling the attention of the stranger to some . . . channel of speculation or other advantage to be derived from investing in Chicago." "Chicago is the general headquarters of all the excellence extant among people and things," the *Chicago Times* regaled readers around the start of the Civil War. "No sooner does an individual gain a more than local notoriety than he starts for Chicago. . . ." *Putnam's* magazine put it most succinctly: Chicago had become "a city more full of energy and vitality, as well as 'brag,' than any city in the world." Chicagoans were apparently too busy to mind such criticisms. As new residents streamed into their city each day, the mass news media were already reinventing and rebranding themselves and Chicago in the ultimate bid to be Number One.[39]

2

"Chicago is the Head-Centre, the Mecca, of All Creation"

A crowd of men and women gathered on the chilly morning of January 15, 1848, at the Salon, a large wooden-frame hall at the southeast corner of Lake and Clark streets, to witness history being made. Their attention was riveted to a shining metal-and-wood device connected to a long copper wire running outside of the building. The previous evening, the final leg of the Erie and Michigan telegraph line had been completed between Milwaukee and Chicago. Without fanfare, the device sprang to life, and the city's first telegraph operator began jotting down letters, then words. Sent by William Cramer of the Milwaukee *Evening Wisconsin,* Chicago's first telegraphic message touched on the semidelicate diplomatic affairs between northern Illinois and Wisconsin. "Mr. Cramer sends his cordial greeting to his brethren of the press of Chicago," the operator read aloud, "and hopes that as Milwaukee and Chicago are united in the same chain, the press may never forget that the cities of the Northwest are one in destiny, and should be one in feeling."

A few hours later, what would become a more typical message arrived: "Milwaukee with her 14,000 inhabitants sends greeting to her fair sister Chicago with her 17,000, and requests her to clear the track to allow her to pass." "Chicago with her 17,000 inhabitants will soon have her railroad tracks east to the Atlantic and west to the Mississippi clear," the Chicagoans responded, "so that the 14,000 citizens of their sister city can have every possible facility for passing." "No class of people appreciate the value of the telegraph more than [newspaper] editors," Chicago Mayor Joseph Medill declared years later. "Few of them would know how to get up a paper without the aid of this subtle agency for the presentation of intelligence."[1]

Though at the periphery of the Midwest's communications network in 1848, Chicago was its heart a mere twenty or so years later. This had at least three significant ramifications for the young city. Midcentury Chicagoans encouraged a new kind of newspaper writing, exemplified by the sex and wealth "sensations" of Wilbur F. Storey's *Chicago Times,* which spread to the other papers and inspired the rise of Chicago literary realism by the end of the century. The *Tribune*'s shameless promotion of Abraham Lincoln as the 1860 Republican presidential candidate and Gen. Ambrose Burnside's order to seize the *Times* by military force in 1863 made Chicago a cause célèbre in both the North and South, adding to its national prominence as a city. Most significantly, the city's mass news media came to the realization beginning in the 1850s that open access to timely and truthful information was at least as important as boosterism in advancing Chicago's economic development and growth. Chicago was the first city in the world to give a standardized grade to its leading exportable commodity, wheat, but it was reliable news media reports on the graded wheat that spread the word and helped open new markets to producers. This practice, called signaling, helped establish Chicago as the world's largest wheat export market from 1854 well into the twentieth century. By the late 1860s, Chicago was the Midwest's information center and was maneuvering to surpass St. Louis as the region's most influential city. As the *Chicago Times* put it bombastically, "Chicago is the head-centre, the Mecca, of all creation."[2]

Separating the Wheat from the Chaff

With an official population of 112,172 in 1860, antebellum Chicago's remarkable population growth was enabled in large part by wheat and other foodstuffs. The beginnings of Chicago as a commodities marketplace were as inauspicious as the early city itself. Markets for locally grown produce first appeared in the mid-1820s, although as Perry R. Duis observed, formal markets did not evolve until the 1840s when the city shifted from eastern-produced foodstuffs to local production. "Chicago was still little more than a thriving country town," an *Atlantic Monthly* writer noted of the early city, "which received the products of adjacent farms, and gave in exchange merchandise brought in three weeks from the sea-shore." There was a mutually beneficial relationship for Chicago in working with its agricultural hinterlands. William Cronon has noted that each depended upon the other for survival, arguing that no city played a more important role in establishing the midcontinental American landscape and economy than Chicago.

But it was British social scientist Colin Cherry who observed before Cronon that improved mass communication technologies were invaluable to the process Cronon detailed because they reduced the age-old restraints of time and space. "For endless centuries the mass of people have lived, mentally, in small communities; in farms, villages, or towns," Cherry wrote in 1971. "Societies can develop and advance only as far and fast as they can acquire, use and maintain systems of communication." Chicago's geographic location at the far southwestern edge of the Great Lakes made it a natural gathering place for raw materials from the regions to the west and south. "An erroneous impression generally prevails abroad on the subject of markets in this state," the *Chicago Democrat* observed in 1834. "Many suppose, that on account of our distance from the Atlantic cities, produce will bring nothing, or so little as to render the raising of it of no interest or profit to the farmer, except for the support of his family. This is certainly a great mistake, as regards the northern part of the State."

Beginning in the early 1840s as its technology improved, Chicago's mass news media took increasing notice of its growing agricultural economy. "Every day the streets of our city are filled with teams that have brought in heavy loads of wheat from a distance of fifty to a hundred and a hundred and fifty miles," the *Western Citizen* reported in 1842. "At 65 cents [per bushel] one would hardly think the farmer could be paid for his labor and trouble." "As every team is loaded back, but little specie is taken out of the city," the *Democrat* observed, and the *Chicago American* complained about the clouds of dust hovering over the central business district. "Trains of from 13 to 20 wagons are now familiar spectacles," the paper wrote. "We noticed sixty-two wagons, with their white tops, yesterday afternoon, at one encampment." The adulterating of good wheat with dirt, chaff, or inferior wheat by merchants and grain shippers "has injured our farmers much by keeping prices down," the *Democrat* complained at about the same time. "Our crop is our blood and the man who aims to cut down its price aims to suck that blood—and if he succeeds in doing so, he does suck it," the *Democrat* offered in 1849. "He bleeds us as well."[3]

The completion of the Illinois-Michigan Canal in 1848, connecting Chicago to the Mississippi through the Des Plaines and Illinois rivers, redefined the city's role as an agricultural destination point. "Yesterday was an eventful period in the history of our city," the *Chicago Journal* reported upon the canal's opening. "It was the wedding of the Father of the Rivers to our inland seas—a union of the Mississippi with Lake Michigan . . . Commerce is its first born—Agriculture and general prosperity its increase." Barges soon joined horse carts and ox-drawn wagons as means of bringing ever-increasing quantities of fruits, vegetables, meat, poultry, and grains into the city, making literal Chicago's official motto, "Urbs in Horto" or "Garden City." "For a mile along the [Chicago] river, a continuous forest of masts indicate the extent of its commerce," a visitor remarked the following year, "the puffing of various steam factories adds to the busy activity of the scene."[4]

From the earliest days, most grain was transported to Chicago in two-bushel cloth bags, facilitating movement and limiting spoilage. Although most transactions were settled by actual delivery, some grain was sold "to arrive," meaning after it was harvested, a primitive futures trading market. The bags were unloaded by hand and piled along North Water Street, under present-day Wacker Drive, where sellers and buyers struck deals in makeshift bargaining areas called "switch yards." The process was inefficient, but the volume was small enough that it did not create serious complications. Buyers could open the bags and inspect their grain upon receipt and sellers were paid on the spot, a process called spot pricing. Quality remained the one ongoing glitch. "We all know [the] good quality [of Chicago wheat]," the *Democrat* warned in 1843, "but . . . some farmers are less careful than others to keep their grain clean." "Our western wheat suffers much in the New York market in consequence of the prevailing custom of our merchants in mixing winter with spring wheat," the paper observed the following year. With time, central Illinois' reputation for raising inferior or so-called "stumptail" wheat became almost legendary. The quality was so poor that it could be used only for "third or fourth rate" flour or distillation purposes, a Canadian agricultural book maintained.[5]

The introduction of bulk freight train cars in the early 1850s exacerbated the problem with stumptail and other poor quality wheats even as loading loose grain into freight cars grew Chicago's grain trade exponentially. "There are twelve railroads running directly into Chicago," a visitor wrote in 1855, and one railroad alone received from 50,000 to 100,000 bushels of grain daily. "I went down to the granaries and climbed up into the elevators," English novelist Anthony Trollope wrote of a Chicago visit in the early 1860s. "I saw the wheat running in rivers from one vessel to another, and from the railroad vans up into the huge bins on the top stories of the warehouses; for their rivers of food run up hill as easily as they do down."

The influx of such great quantities strained the existing market infrastructure both for sellers and buyers. The lack of a uniform demand-based market price in lieu of spot pricing made it difficult for sellers to accurately predict what their crop would bring until actual market, too late to turn back. And bulk shipping made it difficult for buyers to ascertain the quality of what they were purchasing. "The piles of grain now [lie] uncovered in our streets, the choked and crowded thoroughfares," the *Daily Democratic Press* complained in 1854. The unhoused piles added to early Chicago's environmental problems, also the result of using the Chicago River as an open sewer, with the consequent situation threatening the city's future as a commodities market, especially in the face of competition from rivals such as Milwaukee, St. Louis, Toledo, and Cincinnati. Clearly, a better system was required or farmers would ship and spend their supplies, services, and entertainment dollars elsewhere.[6]

Part of the solution appeared in the form of a structure invented in Buffalo, New York, but perfected in Chicago. Grain elevators, named for the long, seemingly endless power-driven belts that carry grain into huge vertical bins, became Chicago's first skyscrapers, or "great granaries," "the *entrepôt* for the grain trade of the Northwest" as they were called by *Harper's Weekly* in 1859. Chicago's first elevator, constructed in 1848, was a four-story structure that housed 80,000 bushels. But capacity soon increased so that there was enough room for stored grain in Chicago to feed every man, woman, and child for five years by the time of the Civil War. With a total capital investment of $3 million, grain elevators dominated the city's landscape until the 1871 fire—but the grain they stored was anonymous. In contrast to the days when wheat arrived in individually marked bags, every farmer's wheat now looked more or less the same. "It dawns on the observer's mind that one man's property is by no means kept separate from another man's," *Harper's Weekly* noted in 1859.[7]

Anonymity made adulteration an epidemic. Dishonest producers were able to pass off poor, dirty, and even spoiled wheat with little fear of retribution, and unscrupulous or inattentive elevator operators returned lesser grades or mixed inferior grain and contaminants in their elevator bins. A 1852 *Prairie Farmer* letter writer described four farmers bringing their crops to market. One had malted or sprouted wheat, good for beer but not bread. The second had dirty wheat, harvested with inefficient methods; the third good wheat that had been mixed intentionally with dirt and chaff; and the fourth unadulterated, clean wheat. All sold their produce for virtually the same market price. "There is no wonder then, that our wheat should be thought of so little of in Eastern markets," the writer concluded.

The incentive for dishonesty was intensified by the Crimean War. Fought on the Crimean Peninsula off the southern coast of modern-day Ukraine from 1853 to 1856, more than half a million soldiers and an unknown number of civilians died as a result of disease and famine. European farmers could not meet the demand for foodstuffs, and a vast European market was opened to American producers for the first time, doubling the amount of grain pouring into and out of Chicago. The *Tribune* bragged in 1854 that "small fortunes have been made by citizens of Chicago in the rise in breadstuffs caused by the gradually growing probability of a general European war," and continued demand drove prices ever higher. New Yorkers, who reloaded much of the wheat before sending it to Europe, continued to complain of tainted Chicago wheat shipments. "Wheat must be better cleaned here or in the country, or else rejected here," the *Chicago Commercial Express* warned. The word Chicago virtually came to mean poor or inferior quality wheat.[8]

The solution to this problem was the brainchild of a group of Chicagoans with the active encouragement and assistance of the mass news media. Twenty-five Chicago businessmen had gathered above the Gage and Haines Flour Store at 101 South Water Street in March 1848 to form the Chicago Board of Trade (CBOT). But the group struggled to define itself in its earliest years. "During the last six weeks, we have been endeavoring to collect, from the books of the forwarding and commission merchants, an accurate statement of the receipts and shipments by lake, and yet the work is not near finished," the *Tribune* complained in 1854. "The business community—the merchants, shippers, real estate owners, and, in short, every citizen—has a deep interest in the matter, and it is its duty to adopt some plan by which statistical information of such great value may be preserved."

Motivated by fallout from the Crimean War market, a group of wheat traders seized control of the CBOT in 1856, began establishing more uniform prices and collecting their own statistics, and pressed for self-imposed grades and standards. "The practice of sending wheat to market in a very badly cleaned condition . . . particularly in the vicinity of Chicago, is one of the most suicidal to the farmer's interest that he could possibly adopt," the *New York Tribune* observed. "Boards of Trade protect the buyer as well as the seller they regulate," the *Chicago Tribune* noted. "They regulate business by a strict commercial standard, and make the most approved customs and laws of a business community." Enforced sporadically at first, the CBOT's definitions for grades such as "Club Wheat," "Spring Wheat," "White Winter Wheat," and "Inferior Spring Wheat" eventually made it possible for grain to be better transported, stored, and delivered through Chicago. Such standards were not the first efforts toward market regulation in Chicago. The city had sought to ban loose livestock beginning in the 1830s, and there were rules regarding fair weights and measurements, but these were the strictest marketing requirements to be found in any American city of the day.[9]

In *Nature's Metropolis,* William Cronon details the process that led the State of Illinois to grant the CBOT quasi-judicial powers to enforce its grading system beginning in 1859, but he overlooked the critical role of timely, open, and verifiable information as an element of the process. Chicago's newspapers embraced the new system, educating farmers and grain merchants through their daily market reports. The *Chicago Democrat* began reporting the markets around 1840, limited at first but promising, among other things, that profits from the first load of spring wheat to be brought into Chicago could be used to pay for a subscription. The paper was joined by the *Western Citizen* in 1842, and reports appeared in newer dailies (including the *Chicago Tribune* and *Daily Democratic Press* during the 1850s) based on information garnered through interviews of farmers, traders, brokers, and shippers—the first on-the-scene reporting in Chicago. This was significant because financial information, unlike much of the rest of the news, is one of the few content forms that recipients don't necessarily want to share, with those in the know having an advantage over those who did not. The *Daily Democratic Press* itself was founded in 1852 with a promise to provide reliable business information, pledging in its prospectus that "market reports will be made up carefully by one of the editors, and may always be relied upon as giving the correct state of the market." Coeditor William Bross bragged that "the press of the city was ever the pioneer to spread facts before the people and show their importance to the proper healthful development of the resources of the country."

Not to be outdone, the *Tribune* advertised in 1853 that market "news—accurate, reliable, varied and fresh, is its lifeblood." It also observed that veteran editor Thomas A. Stewart was in charge of its commercial and business columns, and his "established reputation throughout the West, as Commercial Editor, saves the necessity of commendation." Three years later, the paper promised that its new weekly edition for farmers "will contain very full and correct market reports, prepared with scrupulous care and exactness" and editorialized that "grain dealers both East and West would do well to examine [our grain market] summary closely. They may derive hints therefrom, which may be of benefit in shaping their transactions."[10]

Furthering the mass news media's role in the Chicago grain business, the CBOT hired *Daily Democratic Press* business reporter Phelyer L. Wells as its first superintendent in 1859. Wells was a La Porte, Indiana, native who had studied statistics at Wabash College, making him an ideal business reporter in an era when newspapers gathered and calculated their own economic statistics. Wells started with the *Press* in 1852, roaming the city's grain yards, elevators, rail stations, harbors, and commodities markets, filling columns six days a week with prices, trading conditions, commodities information, and weather reports. With his brother Joel, a *Tribune* business reporter, Wells started the *Daily Commercial Letter* in 1856, Chicago's first commodities news publication. In lieu of carriers, the one-page newsletter was distributed to subscribers via the afternoon mail. That publication, and a weekly version called *Wells Commercial Express*, provided breaking news of influential international events such as the 1859 Franco-Austrian war, Board of Trade decisions, national weather information (obtained through a contact with the *Washington Evening Star*), and up-to-the-minute Chicago, Great Lakes, New York, and European pricing and business statistics. Wells used his contacts and experience to promote the complicated grain grading system in its earliest years, returning to his publication shortly before his death in 1862.

Less is known of the extent to which Wells and his fellow newspaper business reporters profited from their access to inside commodities information, a practice sometimes called "stock gambling journalism." Reporters were not required to divulge what the *New York Herald* called advantageous speculation using the "understrappers [*sic*] and connections" of newspapers, but it was common knowledge among nineteenth-century Chicago newspapermen that business reporters were the wealthiest in a profession that otherwise paid fair to poor. Insider information may have been considered repayment for the massive free publicity business reporters provided to the CBOT, its grain regulation system, and early Chicago's commodities markets.[11]

Beyond accessible and timely daily market pricing and conditions, the newspapers provided monthly, quarterly, and yearly reports of Chicago's business activities. The *Tribune* was the first, publishing a trade and commerce report in January 1849. Instead of repeating standard booster rants of unbridled growth and unparalleled prospects, the paper's report extolled financial conservatism, noting, "the experience of the past has led to a commendable degree of prudence on the part of our business men." The *Daily Democratic Press* began issuing business reviews when it started publication in 1852, and took the additional step of reprinting the information in a booklet form that could be distributed by local businessmen and promoters. Authored by copublisher William Bross, the 1852 review admitted that "the press of the city, previous to the year 1849 neglected to publish connected statements of the business of the city." Four years later, the *Press* lamented a lack of cooperation among businessmen at the height of the Crimean War bonanza, but expressed the hope that "all will gladly place at our disposal such evidences of their respective operations as will enable us to arrive at completeness and accuracy in the general aggregate." As well, the Chicago papers served as watchdogs of competing regional grain markets. For instance, the *Tribune* chided the *Milwaukee Sentinel* in 1858 for reprinting inaccurate information from the *Chicago Journal,* noting, "No, no! Messrs. Editors; such miserable shystering will never add a bushel of grain to Milwaukee receipts."[12]

Chicago's mass news media publicized another innovation in commodities trading beginning in the late 1840s. Before that date, only a handful of investors specialized in arbitrage, the buying and selling of commodities at differing prices in different markets. A few profited in the early nineteenth century, but as land and water transportation improved, price spreads between distant markets diminished, and it became increasingly more difficult to make money at the practice—until the invention of the telegraph. "There is now a 'smart chance,' by trying his luck on a cargo of Illinois wheat, and pocketing a cool thousand with very little trouble, if he only watches the telegraph close enough to get half an hour ahead of his co[n]temporaries in the field," the *Democrat* reported in September 1848, only a few months after the telegraph had debuted in Chicago. "A lucky dog . . . came across his man, and immediately struck a bargain for a cargo at 80 cents per bushel, the seller chuckling over his trade. In less than fifteen minutes however, the market rose to 85, and the fortunate possessor of the news by the last flash, pocketed the cool five hundred." The CBOT's first "to arrive" contracts were approved the following year, and the first "forward" contract for 3,000 bushels of corn was recorded in 1851.

In response, the major Chicago papers began publishing overnight market reports in late 1848 to aid those investors who did not have access to their own telegraph line. While it offered speculators a new tool with which to gamble, futures trading also helped level some of the local price fluctuations that hurt farmers who brought their crops to market on a bad day. "They get up at sunrise, bolt their steak and rolls, and rush down to the 'first board,' which meets in a well known corner [called the 'gamblers' corner'] between 8 and 11 o'clock," a Chicago paper reported of this new breed of futures traders, men who neither wanted nor would have known what to do with the tons of grain they bought and sold daily. "There they buy and sell—sell and buy—make contracts—settle differences—open their letters—bolt them as they do their breakfasts—and 'bull' and 'bear,' as it is their interest. . . . Is there any city in the world whose merchants work like ours?" The *New Hampshire Patriot* put it most succinctly: Their lot was to "root, hog, or die." By midcentury, many Chicago investors had switched from land to grain speculation, establishing Chicago as a center for the practice that lasted well into the twentieth century and providing convenient names for two of the cities professional sports teams.[13]

"Chicago is Not One of the Blushing Kind"

The aggregate impact of Chicago's agricultural businesses on the city's economy diminished over the latter nineteenth century as the city became more industrialized. Modernization came to the city's mass news media as well, particularly in the journalism of Wilbur Fisk Storey. Try as he might, even Joseph Medill had limits on the kind of Catholic hate mongering that he inserted into his *Tribune.* Wilbur F. Storey had no moral restrictions, or at least not many. For instance, the most famous Storey anecdote involved his best Civil War correspondent, Franc B. Wilkie. When Wilkie expressed a concern that he would have nothing to report, Storey responded, "Telegraph fully all news, and when there is no news, send rumors." "Any item [article] that would sell ten copies of the paper was always acceptable," Storey told his reporters, although he preferred articles (only New York newspapermen called them stories in the nineteenth century) that his staff called "sensations" because they would sell a hundred or more copies. As such, Storey was the first Chicago editor to encourage aggressive, enterprising, and realistic reporting (the antecedent for what would become known in the twentieth century as literary realism) in lieu of the political partisanship and boosterism present in other Chicago papers.

Upon assuming control of the original *Chicago Times* (not to be confused with the tabloid *Chicago Times,* started in 1929 and merged to form the *Chicago Sun-Times* in 1941), Storey held that it was "a newspaper's duty to print the news and raise Hell!" In his own way, Storey's *Times* helped put Chicago on the American map. "At the time of [Storey's] advent here, in 1861, the city could not boast a newspaper, in the present sense of the term," the Chicago Press Club memorialized of Storey some twenty years later. "He increased his news-gathering service as fast as expansion of facilities would permit, and had no lower aim than to make *The Times* the greatest newspaper in the world." Storey made certain that the *Times* was a newspaper Chicagoans loved or hated as they read it each morning.[14]

The *Times* was born in 1854 as the result of a political feud between *Democrat* editor Long John Wentworth and Illinois Democratic Senator Steven A. Douglas. Originally allies, Douglas forced Wentworth and other antislavery Chicago Democrats out of the party of Jefferson and Jackson with his proslavery positions during the early 1850s. With passage of the Douglas-championed Kansas-Nebraska Act in 1854, Wentworth began attacking Douglas in the *Democrat,* and Douglas responded by starting a new paper that would "make war on Wentworth every good chance you get. He must be beaten at all hazards." The early *Times* struggled financially, going bankrupt in 1860, and it was sold to industrialist Cyrus Hall McCormick to be used in his effort to secure renewal of his valuable grain reaper patents. With the patents renewed through positive publicity provided by the *Times,* McCormick was only too happy to find a pigeon to buy what was left of the paper for the bargain price of $23,000 in May 1861.[15]

Storey was born in Vermont in 1819, learning the newspaper trade as a teenaged printer's devil. He was possibly the victim of some form of childhood physical or sexual abuse, leaving his parents' home at the age of seventeen, never to return or mention them again. He worked as a printer for the New York *Journal of Commerce* where he witnessed rioting between whites and free blacks during the 1830s. These anti-abolition riots convinced Storey of the centrality of white male labor to America and made him a Negrophobe for life. He was exposed to New York's new penny newspaper press as well, watching as hyperbolized or "sensationalized" local news created undreamed-of profits for the publisher of the *New York Herald.* The *Herald's* pathbreaking use of reporters to seek news rather than wait for it to come to them and its exploitation of the city's upper class and its foibles for the titillation of the lower classes (as epitomized by sensationalistic coverage of the 1836 Helen Jewett murder case) made a deep impression on Storey, and he determined to introduce similar news-gathering techniques and standards to Chicago.[16]

Storey moved to Michigan in 1842 and eventually came to own and edit the *Detroit Free Press.* During this time period, he experienced a mental breakdown of sorts, perhaps as a result of youthful abuse, and embarked on a life of personal debauchery, marrying, divorcing, and being estranged from three wives in the process. One of his Chicago reporters later characterized Storey's private doings as a "theater of disgusting orgies in which Storey, whisky, debased women, and occasionally a boon companion or two, played the principal parts." Nevertheless, Storey's theatrics gave him a unique perspective on the private lives and doings of mid-nineteenth-century Chicago's upper class even as they discredited him among those people. Not surprisingly, he contacted syphilis, and in an era before antibiotics experienced a form of paresis that eventually resulted in mental and emotional instability and paralytic attacks, a genius-to-madness pattern that characterized many of the disease's victims. His journalistic intensity and intemperate lifestyle made him an ideal image of the nineteenth-century Chicago newspaperman, a stereotype that with modifications would be immortalized seventy years later in Ben Hecht and Charles A. MacArthur's *The Front Page.*[17]

Storey took control of the *Chicago Times* in June 1861. "The proof of the pudding is in the eating," the tall, muscular, and prematurely white-haired and bearded editor wrote in his first editorial. "The proof of the value of a newspaper is not in promises but in performances." "There are newspapers which have thrived on unpopularity," *Times* editor Willis J. Abbot wrote in 1895, and the *Times* was the personification of Abbot's statement. Storey made a variety of positive changes to the paper, including to its office, typography, circulation, and personnel. He also used Chicago's expanding rail network to speed delivery of his papers beyond the city's limits, increasing the newspaper's influence. In doing so he faced unenviable odds because he had limited financial resources and was opposed by the other Chicago morning dailies, including the *Tribune*. In the end however, Storey was able to remake the *Times* into a leading major market newspaper, a serious competitor to the better-known *Tribune*, with a daily paid readership of more than 32,000 and a weekly circulation in excess of 40,000, more than any other Chicago paper.[18]

Much of Storey's success derived from his expert exploitation of two hitherto underreported Chicago newspaper subjects, sex and scandal. "The Victorians . . . were hypocrites," historian Karen Halttunen has written. "While spending their days professing allegiance to the sexual ideals of purity and self-restraint, Victorian men spent their nights prowling through the underworld of prostitution and sexual deviancy. . . ." The resulting commercialization of sex "exposed the limits and contradictions in the ways nineteenth-century New Yorkers defined freedom," Timothy J. Gilfoyle wrote in *City of Eros*, and the same was true in Chicago. Helen Lefkowitz Horowitz has argued that Victorians categorized sex in a variety of forms or "conversations" ranging from enthusiasts to evangelical Christians' "deep distrust of the flesh." And as the social regulators of the day, many Victorian women believed that any discussion of sexual topics could send men and older boys into an uncontrollable frenzy. Therefore, the slightest reference to heterosexual sex, a mainstay of so-called flash or sporting papers, was unthinkable in the mainstream mass news media. Even private love letters between betrothed couples could only hint at sexual feelings, employing elaborate subterfuges of imagery and metaphor to mask true meanings. "This state of mind lasted in the whole country until the Great War, until 1917," a late nineteenth-century Chicago prostitute wrote in her memoirs, not published until 1970. "[Then] the country club girls were giving it away free."

Under such circumstances, public discussions of topics such as homosexuality, incest, bestiality, prostitution, or abortion were beyond the realm of possibility. Yet "that very considerable male contingent,—now more or less within its pale, which is distinguished as the 'fast set,'" *Times* reporter Frederick Cook wrote of mid-nineteenth-century Chicago, "though outwardly held in strong leash to social *convenances,* would yet covertly associate where it could enjoy a fling for its money." The irony of this state of affairs was not lost on at least one Chicago physician of the day, who likened the behavior of his upper-class Yankee patients to that of the notorious Roman pleasure seeker Petronius. What Victorians of the day considered "unnatural acts" were easily obtainable just blocks from the Chicago's Courthouse Square for prices from ten cents to a dollar.[19]

It was Storey who made the previously private behavior of Chicagoans a subject of public discourse, what social scientists would call social currency or water-cooler conversation. "Mr. Storey's edict [was] to have 'things of that sort written up for all they were worth,'" a *Times* reporter recalled. Within days of assuming the editorial duties, Storey instructed his reporters to begin looking for what he called the "gut-fat" of Chicagoans. The resulting "sensations," often written in the style of narrative fiction, were an early form of literary realism. For instance, "A Woman's Plot to Gain Her Own" was the story of a married Hyde Park woman accused of squatting in the house of her ex-husband and children (married women could not own property in Gilded Age Chicago) that proved "how piquantly the *Times* tells" its tales, as the *Indianapolis Sentinel* explained. Another *Times* sensation had all the elements of Victorian melodrama:

> A woman named Elizabeth Lawrence was brought into the Police Court yesterday as a drunkard and vagrant. She had a little child with her which was bright, intelligent, and more than ordinarily active. . . . She and the man with whom she lived, were habitual drunkards. Not only were they habitual drunkards, but they were doing their best to make the child the same. They gave it whisky until they made it drunk, and then amused themselves with its actions. They stripped it naked, and sent it into the street to wallow in the gutter, with its brain crazed by the spirit, and so inhumanly treated it that the attention of the police was called to the case. The child was a girl five or six years old.

"A Woman's Adventures" described a Southern-born white prostitute who ended up in the same Chicago police court for fighting with her African American, common law, and stepbrother husband. "There is no misery which equals that which is entailed upon unfortunate women," the paper began a 1865 article on a girl who committed suicide in a "Disreputable house."

Another suicide sensation detailed the death of a young Danby, Illinois, woman who threw herself in front of a locomotive because she had been kept from her lover by overly strict parents. "A Young Lady Murdered by Professional Abortionists" touched on a popular Storey cause, male doctors and quacks performing unsafe abortions. Case law suggests that Chicago was a popular center for such procedures, but women were rarely prosecuted before the 1870s. Another *Times* article, published in 1875, detailed the death of a prostitute "from the effects of abortion."

Often written in the style of parables, seduction sensations were a *Times* mainstay. In the East, public opinion had swung from blaming women to men over during the first half of the nineteenth century, but the issue of who best seduced whom remained debatable in the West. "Seduction in the present century in which the woman is not as much to blame as, or more so, than the seducer" was how the paper rationalized its reportage, including an article about a Chicago brewer who seduced and then broke his promise of marriage to "a respectable and accomplished young lady." At the center of an era when women appeared in full dress even on the hottest summer day, the paper even ridiculed a woman observed promenading on State Street wearing nothing but her "Bloomer fashion." "A short skirt, hardly reaching to the knees," the paper described a garment developed in New York during the 1850s. "They were not full and flowing, but on the contrary looked as though their owner desired to economize as much of the raw material as possible."[20]

Storey targeted the upper class as well, but nineteenth-century libel verdicts were typically based on the social status of the plaintiff in the belief that well-known individuals had more of a reputation to protect than those of the lower classes. Storey took a special joy in singling out the upper class in his sensations even though it cost him several unfavorable libel decisions. Early in his ownership of the *Times* for instance he gleefully reported the "attempted suicide" of one Capt. Bond, details said to be too "distasteful" for the other Chicago newspapers to print. Another article covered the attempted suicide and murder of an adulterous couple in Freeport, Illinois. "Both parties were well dressed, and have heretofore borne a good character," the paper related. "All the parties concerned who have been interrogated thus far deny that there is any truth" was how a 1875 *Times* article explained an affair between an ex–Illinois congressman and the wife of a newspaper editor that culminated in an armed attempt by the woman to obtain revealing love letters. The paper accused Chicago Circuit Court Judge Van H. Higgins of stealing from his clients, with Higgins winning a small libel verdict against the *Times,* as did another prominent Chicago attorney whom Storey called a "divorce shyster."

Storey published a report of a prominent Morrison, Illinois, family (said to be abolitionists) alleging that a fugitive slave invited into the home persuaded a daughter to elope. "Jeff. Davis' faithful servant" was how the local paper referred to Storey at his subsequent trial, which the *Times* also lost. "Of course the negro [*sic*] was but a myth . . . but being sandwiched with 'nigger' and 'abolitionist' of course the bait took." A 1874 libel verdict against Storey involved a supposedly adulterous affair between former State Senator Charles H. Crawford and a woman from a prominent area family. "The crime of the *Times*, or rather the series of crimes, was committed not only against the reputation of two innocent persons," the *Springfield Register* complained, "but against society at large and the journalistic profession."[21]

Storey's sensations elicited similar reactions from most editors. "W. F. Storey is a man of talent, but of no principle," Brick Pomeroy, himself blamed for inspiring the assassination of President Abraham Lincoln a year before the actual event, once wrote. "He is cold, selfish, scheming, miserly at heart, unwarmed by generosity, false-hearted, egotistical, domineering, unsocial, illiberal, [and a] pig-headed prostitute. . . ." "A man like Wilbur F. Storey, with a record for morality as vulnerable as that of a Dominican chief, cannot well talk of morality or christianity [*sic*] without causing a smile to flit athwart the countenances of those who know him as well as we," the *Little Rock Daily Republican* wrote." The *Illinois Staats Zeitung* used the German language to mask its designation of the *Times* as "the organ of sodomy, abortion, and prostitution." "Each day 'Fagin' Storey is hounding his 'artful dodger,' Bill Sykes, and other vermin of that ilk to 'pitch into,'" the *Staats Zeitung* wrote. "In any country but America he and his henchmen would be looked upon and treated as vermin." "Mr. W. F. Storey . . . causes to be printed in Chicago a paper which is the most complete specimen of matter without mind which exists in this or any other country," the *Springfield Register* complained.

The *Chicago Tribune* took special pleasure in bashing the *Times*'s "canards," as it called sensations. The *Times* was "an organ which has a marked reputation as a defamer of women," the *Tribune* wrote. "The *Chicago Times* is great on sensation. It is noted for having the news, and not only that, but a great deal more. It gets facts for its corrupt history in the same way that Andrew Jackson Davis procured his facts for the history of creation—by the exercise—of a lively imagination. . . . Anything for a sensation." "Rather than be 'scooped' . . . a *Times* reporter would be torn gently asunder by wild steeds of Tartary, sawn in twain betwixt the ribs, boiled in oil, fried in butter, have his thick hide taken off with clam shells, receive the Catholic curse of excommunication in all his extremities, grilled like a decayed partridge, broiled like a tough beef-steak, hung to a lamp-post, or have a fence rail thrust through his hollow chest, and be buried where four roads meet, or in other words, at the intersection of State Street and Archer Avenue," a *Tribune* reporter maintained in 1872. Even Storey's personal attorney, Wirt Dexter, who represented him in his numerous libel trials, admitted that he was not a *Times* subscriber. "If all decent families would act alike, there would soon be an end of his paper," he said.[22]

Intimating what twentieth-century social scientists would call the social construction of reality, Storey rationalized his sensations as a means of controlling rather than encouraging undesirable social behavior. Readers who recognized the ultimate outcome of deviant social behavior as epitomized by the so-called Victorian double standard would be less willing to duplicate it, according to Storey. In an editorial titled "The Licentiousness in Our Midst" published in 1865, Storey offered that it was the business of newspapers to "furnish an abstract and brief chronicle of the time." "It is only by bringing immorality and crime affecting society to the public gaze that it may know of their existence and take the proper methods to insure against them, and work the reformation of the authors of the offences," Storey wrote. Such labors were not for the faint of heart or pen. Two years later, the *Times* repudiated a claim by a Rockford, Illinois, newspaper that Chicago should be ashamed for the dumping of tramps and other "rascals" outside of its city limits instead of jailing or finding jobs for them. "We desire to inform the elderly maiden lady who perpetuated [the Rockford article] that Chicago is not one of the blushing kind," the paper responded, beginning Chicago's newspaper incarnation of its hometown as a rough-hewn city of brawlers and sinners.[23]

The *Times*'s greatest sensation, involving neither sex or scandal, appeared the day before Valentine's Day 1875. Convinced that local theaters were unsafe in the event of a fire, the paper published a page-one article with eleven individual deckheads beneath the headline "Burned Alive; The Angel of Death Brings Terrible Mourning to Chicago." (Deckheads were typeface smaller than a headline but larger than story type that added information to the headline, and were popular in the late nineteenth century.) Only did the last deckhead, "Description of a Suppositious Holocaust Likely to Occur Any Night," admit that the entire article was fabricated. The article, which appeared three and a half years after the 1871 fire, described a fictitious fire at an unidentified theater (thought by many to be Hooley's), which supposedly broke out just before the curtain on an unidentified play was to rise. With flames and smoke filling the structure, more than two hundred theatergoers were allegedly killed by the blaze; the paper published a list of 108 "victims" containing the real names of prominent residents in the next morning's issue. Even if they had not read the entire deckhead, most careful readers would have deduced from the article that it was fiction by the fourth paragraph—an early form of crusading to alert readers to the unsafe theater construction.

However, most readers were not careful, and they only gleaned that some terrible disaster had occurred the preceding night. The *Inter Ocean* compared the resulting outcry to a panic created by a *New York Herald* article the previous year detailing a fictional escape of dangerous animals from the Central Park Zoo, designed to call attention to dangerous zoo conditions. "Something equally ridiculous . . . was perpetrated by a morning paper yesterday," the *Inter Ocean* wrote. "We leave the public to characterize such journalism as it deserves." The *Tribune* responded with an article headlined "The Fun of Supposing the *Times* a Newspaper" which held that an Evanston woman had been driven into insanity after seeing her husband's name in the hoax fatality list. Angry *Tribune* letter writers decried the *Times*. "We Americans are so proud of the 'freedom of the press' [that] we would not 'gag it by law' even from the utterance of falsehood and indecency," theater owner J. H. McVicker complained, and newspapers across the country joined the *Tribune* in denouncing the article. "A few copies of the *Chicago Times* of last Saturday were received in this city, and read with horror," the *Lansing* (Michigan) *Republican* wrote. "Hundreds of people now refuse to buy the *Times* or even look at it." Storey had crossed a boundary between fact and fiction with the article; he did not repeat the stunt in subsequent sensations. However, twenty-eight years later and after his death in 1884, a fire at Chicago's Iroquois Theater, which started on stage during a performance, killed 571 people and injured another 350. The *Tribune*, unaware of the original *Times* article, published a front-page casualty list much like the *Times*'s in an attempt to dramatize the preventability of the disaster.[24]

"Turbulent and Mischievous Elements of This City"

While the *Times* was providing what some thought was too much information about Chicagoans, the *Tribune* was championing the political prospects of one downstate railroad company lawyer, and in the process making it the best-known local newspaper beyond the city limits. In fact, no other major nineteenth-century American paper sold its journalistic soul so completely in support of a nonnewspaperman political candidate than did the *Tribune*. To Abraham Lincoln historian William Baringer, Joseph Medill was Lincoln's "propaganda agent," and Col. Robert R. McCormick's biographer John Tebbel noted that "there is little doubt that Joseph Medill influenced the course of American history in his use of the *Tribune* as a political weapon."

Lincoln had received only sparse notice in the Chicago papers before the 1850s. In one article headlined with a woodcut of a cock fight, for instance, the *Chicago Democrat* reported in 1842 that the "great whig [*sic*] champion Lincoln" had engaged in a duel with Illinois auditor James Shields over a letter to the editor allegedly written by Lincoln in which neither man was injured or achieved satisfaction. "So the parties sat down on a log and played cards to see who should apologize," the paper said, "and the lot fell to Lincoln." In October 1854, the then forty-five-year-old Lincoln was campaigning for the state legislature and gave what came to be called his Peoria speech, which was noticed by the *Tribune*. "The occasion was a great one and the speaker was in every way equal to it," editor Thomas Stewart wrote. "The effect he produced on his listeners was magnetic." A year later, Lincoln showed up at the *Tribune's* third-floor editorial offices unannounced and paid $4 for a half-year subscription because, as he confessed, he was tired of borrowing his neighbor's copy.[25]

Lincoln gave another speech in Bloomington in May 1856. A number of Chicago newspapermen were present that day, including the *Tribune*'s Dr. Charles Ray and Joseph Medill (it was the first time Medill heard Lincoln speak), and *Daily Democratic Press* editor John Locke Scripps. Few notes were taken as Lincoln explained his position on enslavement in his shrill Kentucky voice. Reporters likely assumed, incorrectly, that Lincoln was speaking from notes and would share the notes at the conclusion of the speech, a common practice of the day. Instead, Lincoln quickly left town at the end of his talk, and the newspapermen were too embarrassed to admit to their mistake. Claims were made later that a mass hypnosis had settled over the crowd in the sultry hall.

That was the genesis of what the *Tribune* and other newspapers came to call Lincoln's "Lost Speech," said to be one of the most compelling statements ever delivered by an American politician. Scripps later wrote "there never was an audience more completely electrified by human eloquence," and Medill compared the address to Patrick Henry's famous 1775 "Liberty or Death" speech. "There stood Lincoln in the forefront . . . hurling thunderbolts at the foes of freedom, while the great convention roared its indorsement," Medill wrote in 1896. "I never witnessed such a scene before or since." Lincoln claimed later that he did not want to be directly quoted or have his speech transcribed out of concern that his words would prove too inflammatory for pro-enslavement voters in central and southern Illinois. "Well, after you fellows had got me into that mess and began tempting me with offers of the presidency, I began to think, and I made up my mind the next president of the United States would need to have a stronger anti-slavery platform than mine," Lincoln confided to Medill in 1862. "So I concluded to say something." The mystique of the Lost Speech put Lincoln at the forefront of the state's newborn Republican party and convinced Medill and Dr. Ray to hook their star to that of the lanky lawyer.[26]

The Republican National Convention, held in Chicago May 16–19, 1860, was a defining moment in the city's history, largely made possible by the *Tribune*'s unfettered support of Lincoln. Chicago's first national gathering, the 1847 River and Harbor Convention, attracted 3,000 national delegates but generated limited public notice because Chicago was then considered little more than a frontier settlement. However, 1860 Chicago was different, a city fit for royalty as the forthcoming visit by the Prince of Wales portended. It was "a merchant's beau ideal of paradise" as theologian Henry Ward Beecher exclaimed, "a great and growing city, worthy to bear the title of Empire City of the West" as the *Sacramento Union* put it. Nearly 1,000 national and international reporters covered the convention, most first-time visitors, along with 500 delegates and an estimated 40,000 spectators, the "very flower of the leaders of the Young Republican party."

Behind closed doors in various hotels and at the Wigwam (the hall hastily assembled at the corner of Lake Street and modern-day Wacker Drive to house the convention), political bosses conspired to give the presidential nomination to New York Senator William H. Seward but faced determined opponents in Lincoln and the *Tribune*. Before the convention officially convened, Medill helped arrange the delegate seating to minimize Seward's strength. New Yorkers were located at one end of the hall, surrounded by other Seward states but far from any undecided delegates such as those from Pennsylvania. In between were placed solid Lincoln delegates from Illinois, Indiana, and New Jersey. "It was the meanest trick I ever did in my life," Medill bragged later. "I have always believed that the way the delegates were seated in that convention had a great deal to do with this nomination." "Such demonstrations as this always have their influence upon doubtful and wavering delegates," *Pomeroy's Democrat* wrote in 1873, "and that was the secret of 'Honest Old Abe's' nomination."

As the convention got underway, Dr. Ray wrote Lincoln that "you need a few trusty friends here to say words for you that may be necessary to be said." A pledge or two, Ray predicted, "may be necessary when the pinch comes." Lincoln's supporters headquartered themselves in the Tremont House and depended upon operatives on the convention floor and throughout the city to tell them when horse trading was necessary. Dr. Ray and Medill labored day and night trading favors for undecided or wavering delegates. As was the custom at that time, Lincoln did not attend or speak at the convention, remaining instead in Springfield and relying on newspaper accounts to keep him abreast of developments. The pressure on him must have been almost unbearable. At one point, he sent a newspaper clipping of a Seward speech with the marginal notation, "make no contracts that will bind me," to *Illinois State Journal* editor Edward Baker with the admonition to pass it on to his team. "Lincoln ain't here, and don't know what we have to meet," campaign manager Judge David Davis told Medill and others when they read the notations. "So we will go ahead, as if we hadn't heard from him, and he must ratify it!"[27]

At 4 P.M. on Friday, May 18, as a third ballot for president was being taken, pro-Lincoln spectators using counterfeited tickets flooded the Wigwam, making movement impossible inside the building. As the roll call neared completion, Dr. Ray promised the Pennsylvania delegation a cabinet appointment in exchange for their support. "O! What is the difference," Ray said later, "we are after a bigger thing than that; we want the presidency, and the treasury department is not a great stake to pay for it!" Meanwhile Medill was seated with his home-state Ohio delegation, counting the votes until Lincoln was 1½ shy of success. "If you throw the Ohio delegation for Lincoln, [Ohio Senator Samuel] Chase can have anything he wants," Medill whispered to state chairman Daniel Carter. "H-how-d-d'ye know," Carter, who would be named an ambassador and federal judge by Lincoln for his support, stuttered. "I know, and you know I wouldn't promise if I didn't know," Medill replied. Carter switched four votes and the nomination was Lincoln's.

"It is absolutely impossible to describe, as it is equally impossible for one who was not present to imagine, the scene in the Wigwam when Mr. Lincoln was nominated," Dr. Ray wrote in the *Tribune* the following morning. "The tumultuous emotions of men all over the platform, who had not closed their eyes during the last forty-eight hours, trembling between hope and fear, laboring for what they deemed the best interests of the noblest cause under the heavens—acted with electrical effect on the immense auditory." One hundred guns were fired at Courthouse Square in downtown Chicago the following day. When Lincoln considered making the short train ride from Springfield to Chicago to meet with delegates and console Seward's supporters, he was advised otherwise. "Our consultation to the Penna [*sic*] folks say do not come here till after New York has gone home," Ray, Medill, and Scripps telegraphed their candidate; he stayed home until after the convention had adjourned. Illinois lined up with other Northern states the following November, guaranteeing Lincoln's election.[28]

In spite of such events, Chicago was home to one of Lincoln's most viciously outspoken detractors. If Lincoln biographer Carl Sandburg is to be taken at his own word, it was Wilbur F. Storey who was most responsible for John Wilkes Booth pulling the trigger of his pistol at Ford's Theater the evening of April 14, 1865—not Jefferson Davis or the rest of the Confederacy. Storey had favored Democratic candidate Stephen Douglas in the 1860 election, dismissing Lincoln as a political accident, but he threw his support behind the new president and the Union as the Southern states seceded and fighting broke out in 1861. However, he warned in a widely reprinted editorial in February 1861 of a "fire in the rear" if Lincoln and his fellow Republicans turned to abolitionism or emancipated enslaved blacks. A few days after he took control of the *Times,* Storey wrote that "abolitionism was never so feeble and execrated as now. Not even in the days when its peripatetic lecturers were greeted with rotten eggs, and made the recipients of all manner of forcible expressions of popular dislike, was it sunk so low." Instead he contended that African Americans were meant as "mere hewers of wood and drawers of water to a superior and dominant race."[29]

Storey supported Lincoln through the early months of the war, explaining that "the alternatives are government or no government . . . Mr. Lincoln is the head of the government, and upon him, as such, devolves the duty of meeting the insurrection and suppressing it if he can." Still, a pro-Southern proclivity for the *Times* under previous publisher and Virginia-born Cyrus McCormick made it an object of contempt among Unionists. In June 1862, Indiana Governor Oliver Morton cited the *Times* along with one Indiana and two Ohio papers for "invidious, malignant, and vituperative attacks upon Union men, [and] by their continued apologies for the crimes committed by the leaders of the rebellion." The following month Illinois Republican Governor Richard Yates asked Secretary of War Edwin M. Stanton to declare martial law in Chicago because "there is an urgent and almost unanimous demand from loyal citizens that the *Chicago Times* should be immediately suppressed for giving aid and comfort to the enemy." Simultaneously, the Chicago Home Guard, a volunteer paramilitary group of men over the age of forty-five who helped guard prisoners at Camp Douglas, a Northern prisoner-of-war camp located just south of the city, threatened to "clean it out good," referring to the *Times* building on Randolph Street. In typical fashion, Storey retaliated by calling the guard "insignificant and cowardly barking dogs" and stockpiled arms and enlisted employees to protect the paper against a potential attack.[30]

The 1863 Emancipation Proclamation forced Storey, by his own admission, to become the North's most radical editor (as he had prophesied in 1861). He held that the Constitution failed to provide for so broad a presidential power as emancipation—a true charge—making Lincoln "a rebel engaged in the destruction of the government." "If these abolition sympathizers go on as they have begun," Storey wrote in September 1862, "hundreds more will ere long be thrown out to beg, to steal, or to starve, for the purpose of making room for the now more than ever 'Almighty nigger' [*sic*]." "A monstrous usurpation, a criminal wrong, and an act of national suicide. . . . The President is sacrificing soldiers' lives without cause," Storey editorialized. The *Times* launched a torrent of criticisms against Lincoln, Republicans, abolitionists, African Americans, and conscription. Storey had an imaginary soldier named Jonathan ask in a "letter" to home, "What are you fighting for? Why not fight for a new Union? Because the old Union had liberty in it as well as slavery, and the new Union may not have liberty at all."

Meanwhile, the *Times* claimed it had uncovered what it called a "startling plot" by several Republican governors, including Illinois Governor Yates, to withhold volunteer troops as a hidden agenda until emancipation became official. Another *Times* editorial asked, "Shall Illinois be Africanized?" warning Chicagoans they "must set their faces against [black] immigration if they would preserve the state to the uses of their children and from the blight and mildew of *Africanization*." The official announcement of the Emancipation Proclamation on January 1, 1863, was labeled "the deed which unites the people of the South forever in their rebellion." "Mr. Lincoln has now deliberately cut loose from all restraint," Storey editorialized, "and has sold himself body and soul (a precious little modicum of the latter he has) and his country so far as he can, to the abolitionists."[31]

The Union military had been drawing a bead on Storey for some time. A *Tribune* correspondent claimed in 1862 that soldiers preferred his paper to the *Times* because "the *Times* ought to be excluded from the army. Its influence is anything but good." But both papers were read by soldiers across the war's western front. "If we had the rotten editor of the [*Times*] here, in these secessh [*sic*] woods, the soldiers would shoot him down without making an attempt to take him prisoner," Capt. Samuel E. Daniel of the 3rd Iowa Infantry wrote, and an Illinois soldier confided in his diary, "Don't think I am much out of the way in saying that . . . the editors of the *Chicago Times* would be hung if caught within the lines of many Illinois regiments in this army." In early 1863, Gen. Stephen A. Hurlbut forbade the sale of the newspaper in his Department of the Tennessee, which spread as far west as the Mississippi River; anyone caught with a copy could be fined and imprisoned. Copies were destroyed and newsboys brought before a provost marshal for punishment. The *Times* retorted, "General Hurlbut and Governor Yates are boon companions; they get drunk together and have the *delirium tremens* together."

Hurlbut's order was revoked by Gen. Ulysses S. Grant, not because Grant liked the *Times* or newspapers in general but because he "admitted [to] the right of anyone to pay for it and read it," as the *Times*'s chief Civil War correspondent was told by the general himself. The paper was said to have "an immense circulation in the armies of the south-west," which included Grant's own troops. By 1863, to protect itself against detractors, Storey had amassed a small armory (including muskets, pistols, ball-cartridges, and grenades) in the *Times* building in Chicago along with a hose attached to a steam boiler. The paper was also said to have a small army of "courageous men who were on watch night and day, and others, well-armed, [who] could be summoned at a certain signal." Storey even bragged to a Union agent that he had "sixty men in his office to protect it."[32]

In April, two months after Hurlbut's unsuccessful suppression order, Gen. Ambrose E. Burnside, commander of the Department of the Ohio (which included the entire state of Illinois), issued General Order No. 38 providing "those who commit acts for the benefit of our enemies will be tried as traitors and spies" and that "the habit of declaring sympathy for the enemy will no longer be tolerated." Burnside was concerned about Confederate sympathizers who were damaging troop morale, but he especially disliked those who attacked President Lincoln and military conscription. Storey had editorialized in February 1863 that "the crusade against freedom of speech, the attempt to fetter the press of this country is as visionary and impracticable as would be an attempt to fetter thought."[33]

The military leaders' concerns were not without foundation. In April 1863, the *Houston Telegraph* lauded the *Times* for helping "widen the breach between the [Union] East and the West" and the *Macon* (Georgia) *Weekly Telegraph* gave the *Times* and another Northern newspaper credit for "having more influence than all others" in encouraging an estimated 150,000 Union desertions. Storey wrote an editorial in late May 1863 comparing the Burnside directive to the 1798 Alien and Sedition Acts, which resulted in prosecution of four of the five leading opposition newspaper editors of the day, and he maintained that the American public of 1863 had discovered that "however disreputable and contemptible [the administration's] measures, our people might be imprisoned or banished for truly, candidly and intelligently discussing them." On June 1, Gen. Burnside issued General Order No. 84 suppressing the *Times* "on account of the repeated expression of disloyal and incendiary statements." Burnside sent a warning telegram to the publisher, advising him to "govern yourself accordingly" the following day; Storey responded by seeking a temporary injunction against the military from Chicago U. S. District Court Judge Thomas Drummond. Drummond's writ ordered the military to wait until the issue could be considered in full in court, but Burnside had already telegraphed nearby Camp Douglas. "I have issued an order suppressing the *Chicago Times,*" he said. "You will see that no more publications of it are made; and, if necessary, you will take military possession of the office."[34]

Two companies of the 65th Illinois Infantry led by Capt. James S. Putnam marched north along the lakefront and seized the *Times* office at 74 Randolph Street at about four o'clock the following morning. The building was locked at the time so the soldiers broke in the doors and took possession of the press room. Eight thousand copies of the day's paper had already been printed and handed over the roofs of neighboring buildings to waiting carriers, as the daughter of the *Times*'s press superintendent recalled fifty-three years later. A few hundred remaining copies were destroyed by the military, and no June 4 paper was ever issued. The action scared even the most loyal Lincoln supporters and made the unlikeable and uniformly detested Storey (as well as his hometown) an instant cause célèbre. Storey's attorney, Wirt Dexter, attacked the action in federal court, warning that "if General Burnside may suppress the *Chicago Times* he may equally suppress every other paper in the country. In the days of Washington and Adams they never dreamed that such a power existed in a military commander." "I desire to give every aid and assistance in my power to the government in restoring the Union," Judge Drummond responded, "[but] I personally have contended and shall always contend, for the right of free discussion, and the right of commenting . . . upon the acts of the officers of the government." In Washington, D.C., Secretary of the Navy and former newspaperman Gideon Welles wrote in his diary, "good men, who wish to support the Administration find it difficult to defend [Burnside's] acts."[35]

Burnside's edict infuriated Chicagoans, many of whom in the previous year had elected Democrat Francis C. Sherman as mayor and a Democratic city council. Angry crowds gathered outside of the *Times* building shortly after sunrise on June 3, and Randolph Street became a "solid pack of humanity" from State to Dearborn by late afternoon. Circuit Court Judge Van H. Higgins convened a group of prominent citizens from both parties to draft a petition asking Lincoln to cancel the order, noting that "the peace of this city and state, if not the general welfare of the country, are likely to be promoted by the suspension or rescinding of the recent order of General Burnside."

Simultaneously, Illinois Republicans U.S. Senator Lyman Trumbull and Congressman Isaac N. Arnold, the latter a war veteran and personal friend of the president, sent Lincoln an urgent telegraph. In Springfield, the General Assembly approved a resolution censuring the seizure by a vote of 47 to 13 while U.S. Supreme Court Associate Justice David Davis, Lincoln's 1860 campaign manager, telegraphed Lincoln and urged him to revoke the order.

As the sun set, a mass meeting in support of the *Times* was held in Courthouse Square, two blocks west of the newspaper's office. Trumball, Arnold, Mayor Sherman, and former Mayor William B. Ogden delivered speeches in favor of free speech and press. An estimated 20,000 people (many described as the "hard-fisted sons of toil" Irish who voted Democratic and were not altogether in favor of the war) were present, most of them *Times* subscribers. A handbill circulated in the crowd calling for a mob to burn down the nearby *Tribune* office in retaliation for the *Times*'s suppression, but a Chicago militia, present in full force, acted as a deterrence, as did a speech from Republican Wirt Dexter. The *Tribune* (probably Dr. Ray) accused the handbill writers of being "full of money, with which the dens and groggeries in which it was left, were made to pour out their fiery additions to the popular excitement." The *Tribune* complained also of "better class" Republicans joining the crowd, writing, "Let us hope that in all future gatherings of the turbulent and mischievous elements of this city, the Union men may not give dignity to the proceedings by their presence."[36]

The threat of violence was not an exaggeration, not only in Chicago but throughout the nation. "The march of despotism is always onward," a *Times* letter writer wrote from Albion, Michigan. "Therefore I expected that the blow would soon fall upon you, and that ultimately all out-spoken democratic papers would be suppressed, and speakers silenced, incarcerated in prisons, or banished, unless the people should rise in their majesty and say, Hold! No farther cans't thou go." "The principle of a 'free press,' despite the military, has triumphed in this case, and thus averted civil war in the West," the Democratic *New York Express* editorialized, "for it is clear (nothing was clearer) that the people of the West would not have submitted to the suppression of their democratic press, without, at least, suppressing all others in opposition to them."

A western rebellion in the immediate weeks before Gettysburg and Vicksburg would have had a dramatic effect on the Union war effort, perhaps altering the war's outcome, but it was another scenario that concerned the *Times*'s Civil War correspondent Franc B. Wilkie. To him, the events of Chicago in June 1863 were a preview of the antidraft riots that rocked New York City the following month, in which more than 1,000 people were killed or injured and damages of more than $1 million occurred. "All over the Northwest, among citizens, there was a tremendous excitement among partisans of both sides," Wilkie wrote later. "In Illinois many secret meetings were held, organizations were formed, and armed insurrection on the one hand, and forcible resistance on the other, were determined on. Had the work of Burnside been persevered in, there would have been an outbreak in hundreds of places, and a neighborhood war would have followed."

Writing in 1865, the acting assistant provost marshal general of Illinois, James Oakes, gave credence to Wilkie's recollection. "But the grand cause—the only really guilty and formidable source of the dangers through which Illinois has passed—is to be found in the steady streams of political poison and arrant treason which have been permitted to flow from the wicked, reckless, and debauched newspaper press of the State," Oakes wrote, revealing the depth of statewide prejudice against the *Times*. "And chief among these instigators of insurrection and treason, the foul and damnable reservoir which supplied the lesser sewers with political filth, falsehood, and treason, has been the *Chicago Times*—a newspaper which would not have needed to change its course an atom if its place of publication had been Richmond or Charleston instead of Chicago."[37]

As was the case with the 1798 Alien and Sedition Acts, the *Times* incident threatened the delicate balance between collective security and individual human rights in the American democracy. Abraham Lincoln had embarked on a collision course with the Constitution in the opening months of the war, ordering wholesale arrests without warrants, detentions and imprisonments without trial, and suspension of the writ of habeas corpus. With his approval, military courts were trying civilians in contested regions and executing them with little or no due process. How far would the powers of the presidency extend in a civil war scenario never envisioned by the country's founding fathers? Would Lincoln suspend the right of free press in a loyal, noncombat area? Observers on both sides waited, breathlessly, for a decision.

His answer, issued in a telegram to Secretary of War Edwin Stanton on June 4, was to countermand Burnside's directive. First Amendment advocates have since portrayed the decision as a victory for free press and speech, but a closer evaluation reveals that Lincoln was motivated more by a concern for his 1864 reelection bid than by any firmly held belief in individual or press freedom. The president never had an opportunity to fully explain himself but he told Congressman Arnold nearly a year later, on May 27, 1864, that it was his and Senator Trumbull's telegram that tipped the scale in favor of his reversal. In their telegram, the two Republicans argued that the suppression order was bad politics for their fledgling party. Other documents reveal that Lincoln was willing to allow soldiers to occupy the *Times* building for as long as a week, waiting until public opinion crystallized either for or against the suppression. Many Lincoln supporters, including the *Tribune,* were disappointed by the decision, the paper writing, "the *Times* has proceeded upon the assumption that nothing can be written or spoken against the Government that is unconstitutional. . . . Yesterday, before the revocation of the order was announced, a clear majority of citizens were in favor of the order and resolved it should be enforced against mob opposition."

It was Congressman Arnold, not President Lincoln, who paid the political price for the *Times* incident. Chicago's Republicans never forgave him for his support of the paper and forced him to abandon his 1864 reelection bid, effectively ending his political career. Arnold was so embittered that he failed to mention the *Times* incident in either of the two Lincoln biographies that he eventually wrote. Lincoln's order did not affect the military suppression of the *Times* either. A *Tribune* correspondent at Vicksburg noted the following month that the *Times* could not be purchased among Union troops due to "*lex non scripta,*" unwritten law among the soldiers. "I do not exaggerate in the least when I say that no act of President Lincoln has caused more pain among the officers and men of this army than the rescinding of Gen. Burnside's order," the correspondent wrote. The paper was banned briefly in the Department of the Missouri in 1864, the ban ending only when Storey wrote a letter of protest; a restriction in the Department of the Kentucky did not cease until March 1865, just days before Appomattox.[38]

The winners in the suppression incident were the *Times* and the city of Chicago. The suppression catapulted the *Times* (which had dwelled in the shadow of the Lincoln-toadying *Tribune* outside of Chicago) into national prominence and made Wilbur F. Storey a wealthy man. As early Chicago historian Alfred T. Andreas observed, "These events proved of great financial benefit to the *Times.* Its circulation and advertising patronage were largely increased." A *Times* letter writer from Oshkosh, Wisconsin, observed that two hundred copies of the restored paper sold out within hours of their arrival, and copies were selling in Springfield, Illinois, for as much as 50 cents apiece, ten times their normal price. Chicago newspaperman Willis J. Abbot wrote in 1895 that Storey was contemplating selling the *Times* and returning to Michigan when Burnside issued his 1863 order. "When [the *Times*] publication was recommenced," Abbot continued, "it was the most widely known newspaper in America and its circulation bounded upward in unprecedented fashion." "The attempt at suppressing the *Times* was an immeasurable benefit to the financial interests to the journal," reporter Franc B. Wilkie wrote.

As well, Chicago became an overnight cause célèbre in the North and South. The *Macon* (Georgia) *Weekly Telegraph* called the Burnside directive "the death order against freedom of speech." A vast "Peace Conference," held in New York's Cooper Union on the day of the suppression, was keynoted by "Copperhead" New York City Mayor Fernando Wood. "And this night, at this moment, the city of Chicago may be in flames," Wood told a supportive audience. "There has been assembled, this night, one of the largest and most resolute and determined gatherings of the people of Chicago, in front of the office of the *Chicago Times,* protesting, with stentorian power, against the military usurpation against the rights of a free press." Editors of the several New York dailies met on June 8 and drafted a resolution condemning the *Times*'s suppression, calling for an end to such orders and an endorsement of a free press even in the direst circumstances of civil war:

> While we emphatically disclaim and deny any right as inhering in journalists or others to invite, advocate, abet, uphold or justify treason or rebellion; we respectfully but firmly assert and maintain the right of the press to criticize freely and fearlessly the acts of those charged with the administration of the Government, also those of all their civil and military subordinates, whether with intent directly to ensure greater energy, efficiency and fidelity in the public service, or in order to achieve the same ends remotely through the substitution of other persons for those now in power.[39]

In the years after the war, retired Gen. Burnside probably came to agree with the New York editors. Reporter Wilkie happened upon the general at an Indianapolis soldiers' and sailors' convention during the 1870s and accosted him, thanking him for "a great service you conferred on some of my friends during the progress of the war." "Please tell me what you refer to," Burnside responded optimistically. "Who is it that says these pleasant things?" Wilkie explained that he was an employee of the *Chicago Times* during the war. "A change flashed over his countenance like that of clouds suddenly obscuring a sunshiny sky," Wilkie recalled. "He glanced at me with a pained sort of look, and brushing swiftly by, went into the street." Even the *Tribune* had to admit grudgingly on its seventy-fifth anniversary in 1922 that the suppression "helped to make the *Times*' fortune, for it brought notoriety."[40]

* * *

In an editorial upon the *Times*'s resumption on June 5, 1863, Storey predicted that his lawsuit would have persevered in the federal courts had it been allowed to continue. One hundred and eight years later, the *New York Times,* the *Washington Post,* and several other newspapers succeeded in ending temporary restraining orders issued against them at the request of President Richard Nixon for publication of passages from a secret government study of the Vietnam War known as the Pentagon Papers. Writing for a sharply divided court, Associate Justice Potter Stewart held that the only effective check on the abuse of presidential power was "an enlightened citizenry—in an informed and critical public opinion which alone can here protect the values of democratic government." "I should suppose," Stewart continued, "that the hallmark of a truly effective internal security system would be the maximum possible disclosure." The willingness with which nineteenth-century Chicagoans such as Storey shared the news and opinions of their city with the rest of the nation signaled Chicago as the new and unchallenged information center of its region. It seemed that nothing could stand in the way of the Garden City becoming the nation's greatest metropolis.[41]

3

The Victory over St. Louis

Among the usual police reports of drunkenness, brawling, and petty mayhem common in mid-nineteenth-century Chicago newspapers, a new type of crime began to appear with greater frequency beginning in the late 1840s. "We warn the farmers and others visiting the city to keep their eyes open for mock-auction sales," the *Gem of the Prairie* cautioned readers in 1848. "Swindling on a wholesale scale has become the order of the day among a class of Hackman [taxi drivers] in this city," the *Chicago Tribune* wrote in 1856. "It appears that he made the acquaintance of a very clever, sociable chap on the cars," the *Tribune* wrote of an unnamed country "greenhorn" who had arrived in the city via a train. "Finally a bet was proposed, and [the confidence man] who had no small money, asked a loan of the countryman of something less than a hundred dollars, and proposed to give him as security a check on the Bank of Commerce in this city for $640, and a $100 bill on a New York bank." Of course, both the check and bank bill were bogus, and the greenhorn was left poorer but wiser. Even in the immediate weeks after Appomattox, the *Times* warned veterans traveling though Chicago that attempts "to grasp [the vets] much loved greenbacks amount almost to open pillaging." "From this inland port the hardy sons of trade are to go forth, to cross seas, to traverse deserts, to explore the arcana of nature, and gather up the riches of continents," the religious *New Englander and Yale Review* warned in 1854, "unless, like Nineveh, and Babylon and old Tyre, its wickedness will antedate its doom, and call down the scourge of God to execute it."[1]

With an ever-increasing number of trains daily depositing new "pigeons," slang for naive or gullible persons, it was only a matter of time before Chicago earned a reputation as a "fast city." As Karen Halttunen observed, in early

American literature—beginning with a young Benjamin Franklin—seduction tales of young country men being victimized in cities were almost as popular as those involving women. "In the nineteenth century, the raw country youth entering the city to seek his fortune was coming to symbolize the American-on-the-make," Halttunen wrote. "And in the central drama of antebellum advice literature, that inexperienced young man had just set foot in the city when he was approached by a confidence man seeking to dupe and destroy him." Tim Gilfoyle described a young New York City man's introduction into the graft of urban life. "As I learned the different systems by which one could earn money easy and with less risk than picking pockets and other rough ways, I started in for myself and was quite successful in making money in 'sure thing graft' as it is called by crook." The *Richmond Examiner* revealed in 1866 that "pocket picking and larceny" were common at Chicago prayer meetings. In 1870 the New York humor magazine *Punchinello* chronicled a Chicago horse who supposedly picked its hostler's pocket and chewed his tobacco. "Well," the magazine sniffed, "that is just what one might expect of a Chicago horse."[2]

Mid-nineteenth-century Chicagoans radiated in their new persona of self-important busyness. "The pavements are so filled that locomotion is attended with difficulty, and, spread out for a hundred yards or more, is a dissolving view of bright eyes, rosy cheeks, whiskers, hats of all kinds, gaily trimmed bonnets of various patterns, gaiter boots, shapely and unshapely ankles, breeches, dresses, and all surroundings and appearances of a crowded street in a great city," the *Times* bragged. In particular, the paper pointed with pride to the short period of time that it had taken for their muddy settlement to become a modern, crime-ridden nineteenth-century city, in decades rather than the century or more required for Paris, London, and New York. With its combination of youthful energy and gospel of success mentality, it was widely believed that postbellum Chicago could not help but become the greatest western city. The speeding locomotive of destiny came to a crashing halt with the 1871 fire, but Chicago's rebirth from its ashes only gave further testimony to its greatness, especially as it accelerated past St. Louis during the 1850s to become the region's largest trading center and, in 1880, to become the Midwest's most populous city. With requisite encouragement from their mass news media, Chicagoans could not help but believe that they were on a collision course with destiny.

Creating a Chicago Mythology and Humor

Post–Civil War Chicago was a far cry from what it had been twenty, ten, or even five years previous, due mostly to the city's energetic and narcissistic overachieving Yankees. This "common band of brotherhood," as it was sometimes called, was slowly relinquishing its numerical predominance by 1870, with the city's overall population totaling 298,977—but it still represented about 20 percent of residents. Nearly all of the city's mayors had been Yankees, businessmen, lawyers, physicians, and land speculators intent on advancing their gospel of success ideology. The average annual income of the twenty-seven candidates who had stood for mayor between 1847 and 1869 was $9,400 compared to a mean annual income for most city residents of less than $1,000. Yankees owned 90 percent of the city's wealth and controlled all of the city's mass news media, with the exception of the *Illinois Staats Zeitung* and a few other foreign-language papers.

The extent of their dominance is evident from the incomes they reported from 1863 to 1867 as part of a wartime law requiring all Northerners having incomes of more than $1,000 to pay a 5 percent tax. At the top of Chicago's list (duly published to the curiosity of thousands in the *Times* and *Tribune*) was real estate speculator, lumber baron, and former Mayor William B. Ogden, who had a 1864 income of $388,455. Banker Samuel Nickerson was second with a reported income of $275,643 the same year; former *Times* publisher and industrialist Cyrus H. McCormick's income increased 35 percent between 1863 and 1864 to a reported $191,399. Future *Chicago Republican* stockholder John V. Farwell made $197,152 in 1863; lawyer and future *Chicago Inter Ocean* publisher John Young Scammon reported an income of $26,689 that year. *Tribune* stockholder Alfred Cowles made $56,268, and Joseph Medill reported incomes of $26,790 in 1863 and $24,430 in 1864.

The *Times* was less profitable, but Wilbur F. Storey still reported incomes of $19,653 in 1863 (the year the military seized his paper) and $15,522 in 1864. Former *Democrat* editor, congressman, and mayor Long John Wentworth reported only $5,354 income in 1863 and $2,260 in 1864—but most of his wealth was invested in real estate, which did not reach its true value until after the war. By comparison, well-known German banker and potential 1872 mayoral candidate Henry Greenebaum reported an income of $5,000 in 1863 and $19,499 in 1864, and *Staats Zeitung* publisher A. C. Hesing made only $4,938 in 1863 and $2,797 in 1864.[3]

Chicago's 1871 fire consumed most of the paper record that these wealthy, self-important, fastidious Yankees had produced, destroying the chronicle of themselves that they had so wanted to leave behind. The damages were especially devastating to members of the newspaper fraternity. Joseph Medill lost not only most of the *Tribune*'s earliest issues but notes from his personal conversations with Abraham Lincoln that he had hoped would form a Lincoln biography. Fellow *Tribune* stockholder William Bross lost volumes of early

Chicago history and statistics and spent his final years attempting to reconstruct the past in speeches and pamphlets based on his often faulty memory. *Chicago Democrat* publisher Long John Wentworth was one of the most generous contributors to the early Chicago Historical Society, donating most of his papers including personal journals of his congressional years. Some 30,000 of the society's books and papers were destroyed in the 1871 fire, and a second, smaller fire in 1874 finished off what had been saved from the first. "The catastrophe that visited this community came near obliterating it," former *Chicago Times* reporter Frederick Francis Cook observed, "and in no respect was the destruction more complete, or so irreparable, as in the matter of records and landmarks. Hence the ante-fire 'Garden City' will exist for the future only as it may be restored from the memories of those who were of it."[4]

So Cook began the process of creating the same kind of mythology for Chicago as could be found in cities such as New York, Boston, Philadelphia, and St. Louis. A native of New York State, he worked as a printer's devil before sailing to Chicago in 1862 aboard a lumber schooner as an impetuous twenty-year-old adventure seeker. Cook worked in the composing rooms of several papers before becoming a *Times* reporter, covering the police and court beat. In the immediate years after the fire, he sought out "old guard" Yankees, "the men who practically constituted the first generation of settlers," and assembled their stories into some eighty *Times* columns that appeared between 1874 and 1879 under the title "Bygone Days."

It was in one of his articles that he labeled John Kinzie, namesake of the modern-day street and railroad bridge, as "Chicago's first *bona fide* settler," furthering the process of negating black Frenchman Jean Baptiste de Sable's contributions—a process initiated by the Kinzie family. Another column described a large painting then being completed for the historical society by artist Samuel Page honoring the 1812 Chicago massacre. It incorrectly showed Kinzie in the midst of the tomahawking fray even though he had been tipped off in advance to the event by Native American friends and had left the settlement with his family. Kinzie was portrayed standing, staring, but otherwise doing nothing while all types of slashing and mayhem were going on around him, contrary to Cook's hero stereotype. "This idea seemed never to have occurred to dear old Page; and when I mooted the point, he looked quite troubled for a moment," Cook wrote in the *Times.* "Then with a happy-thought expression: 'But can't we suppose that he had just *been* doing something?'"

In another column, Cook wrote of a 1868 silver wedding anniversary celebration for early settlers Gurdon and Mary Hubbard, namesakes of the

Kennedy Expressway tunnel. "While of the exclusive North Side set, the Hubbards were by no means confined to it," Cook rhapsodized, "but continued in the neighborly touch with all who could look back to a time when the social life of the city was a primitive solidarity." Cook's observation was at odds with the cultural walls that divided Yankees from their foreign-born and African American neighbors, many living mere blocks from the Hubbards. "The old settlers of Chicago were an exceptionally fine body of men," he wrote instead, "many uniting in their persons the distinction of good breeding with the off-hand manner born of the early free life of the West." "'Long John' . . . was for many years far and away the 'top liner' and 'hero *par excellence,* if not always *sans reproche,*'" Cook wrote of the notoriously antisocial John Wentworth. "[His] doings naturally came in time to include much of which he was wholly innocent; but the story most often retold and redecorated to suit the jaded tastes of *blasé* listeners referred to the way this mayoral giant 'cleaned out' and submerged the 'North Side Sands.'"[5]

Cook romanticized another group of early Chicagoans, albeit for a less auspicious reason. He blamed the growing perfection of Chicago's vice industries on an antebellum influx of white Southerners into the city, "blacklegs" as he called them, "swarthy, long-haired" gamblers and thieves who arrived from the lower Mississippi River regions via the Illinois-Michigan Canal or the early Illinois Central Railroad. "Indeed if the Garden City of the early sixties could in any respect be called 'fast,'" Cook claimed, "it was this contingent that supplied the speed; for the mass of the people, brought together from staid New England or York State, Germany, Ireland, or Scandinavia, found the fullest scope for their gambling propensities in real-estate operations, with at most an occasional 'flyer' on the Board of Trade" rather than games of chance and prostitution. Identified by a unique "toggery and demeanor," Cook explained, "however arrayed, your gambler was never other than a picturesque *poser,* invariably 'on the mash'—a pastime at which he was ably seconded by another unique species."

Within this Southern group were a few of Chicago's earliest African American residents, cryptically identified as "yclept 'burnt-cork artist[s],' a bunch of whom, when not on exhibition at Metropolitan Hall, usually vied with the blackleg in giving 'color' to the panorama of the street." The blacks mingled with and worked for early gambling kingpins such as "Cap." Hyman, George Trussell, and "Jack" Haverly and brothel keepers Mrs. Roger Plant and Mollie McKeever. In recognizing such folks, Cook inaugurated the Chicago literary tradition of celebrating rather than condemning its criminal element. "It was an off-day when [Police] Captain Jack Nelson didn't have a new story about Mrs. P[lant], and her *entourage,*" Cook wrote of the city's most well-known brothel. He was also instrumental in introducing a young Irishman named "Sure Thing" Michael C. McDonald to the city's reading public, a man who would in time become Chicago's first crime boss. Cook returned to his native New York in his later years but published a collection of his memoirs of early Chicago in 1910 using the title *Bygone Days in Chicago* from his newspaper column.[6]

Cook worked alongside another *Times* reporter who became Chicago's first newspaper columnist and its first local humorist. Franc Bangs Wilkie was a fellow New Yorker, born in 1832. He worked as a Civil War correspondent, writing dispatches from the western front for the *New York Times* until he was hired by the *Chicago Times* to take a position left vacant by the death of Wilbur F. Storey's brother-in-law. Wilkie was simultaneously attracted to and repelled by Storey, whom he described on their first meeting as having "the grace of Apollo." Wilkie had a special talent for writing sensations, beginning with a melodramatic piece about abhorrent conditions at a local orphanage and continuing virtually nonstop until his retirement in 1888, four years after Storey's death and with the once-vibrant *Times* tittering on the verge of bankruptcy.

Writing under the pseudonym Poliuto (Storey discouraged reporters from using their own bylines), Wilkie described his adopted city in a series of columns called "Walks about Chicago" during the late 1860s and early 1870s. The columns provided a reconstruction of the reality of a city already grown too large for most of its residents to conceptualize themselves. For instance, "the inhabitants of the Nord Seite consist of men, women, children, dogs, billy-goats, pigs, cats, and fleas," he wrote of the German and Scandinavian communities, where English was still a second language. "In the warm season a Nord-Seiter has a lively time in flea-hunting. In hunting this game the Nord Seiter shuts himself or herself in a tight room and strips to the skin. Then the flea is pursued and captured." Wilkie claimed that the predominantly western Irish neighborhoods had an inordinate number of saloons and butcher shops. "Every other shop on Westside is owned by a butcher, who has always a bloody and half-skinned calf hanging up in his door for a cheerful sign," he wrote. "The thing is so agreeable to Westsiders, that, on every pleasant afternoon, the ladies take their knitting-work, and go and sit in front of the butcher's shop." Acknowledging that Chicago's Yankee residents, many living in the near downtown First Ward, had their share of divorces and similar shortcomings, Wilkie maintained that it was they who supported everyone else in the city:

> Every resident of First Ward, and being tainted with a descent from a family which has lived in the United States more than thirty years, is, together with his descendants, forever debarred from holding any office to which there is attached any profit or emolument. If he have an ancestry of less than thirty years' residence in the country, and cannot speak English well, and is perfect in German, or Celtic, then, if he resides in First Ward, he is allowed a rebate of one per cent. In his assessments both on taxable property and for campaign purposes.

Wilkie's brand of humor was extremely popular among his Yankee readers. His "Walks about Chicago" were republished in book form and considered one of the earliest forms of Chicago's comic spirit by twentieth-century literary scholars Kenny J. Williams and Bernard Duffey.[7]

Voted by readers as one of the most popular Chicago newspapermen of his day, Wilkie was an embodiment of Chicago's fast life in other senses. The *Times* published a 1874 sensation that accused the unmarried daughter of Illinois Lieutenant Governor John Early of a "criminal amour" with a former U.S. senator. The article resulted in a well-publicized libel suit in which Wilbur F. Storey was initially ordered to pay $15,000 damages. But as part of an appeal Wilkie helped arrange to have several local prostitutes testify that the lieutenant governor's daughter had patronized a local brothel. When Wilkie was accused of slander for making the secondary arrangements, Storey initially refused to pay his legal expenses. The slander case was eventually dismissed, and in 1881, the Illinois supreme court reduced the original $15,000 libel verdict to $500. "The *Times* had a libel suit almost constantly in progress," Wilkie wrote in his memoirs, published in 1891. "It became so common a matter that Storey paid little attention to them."

Beyond libel, Wilkie gained notoriety in 1875 when he successfully crusaded to free former first lady Mary Todd Lincoln from the suburban Chicago insane asylum where she had been committed by her son Robert. He made a well-publicized pilgrimage to New Orleans in search of an alleged African American ancestor, writing upon his return, "I was so relieved to find that it was not I who was the nigger [*sic*]." And he was repeatedly conned by his employer into thinking that he would one day own the *Times*. Calling Wilkie one of his most trusted employees, Wilbur Storey made a verbal promise of one-eighth ownership in the *Times* if Wilkie remained with the paper in his earliest years. For years Wilkie cherished the hope that the promise would be consummated and claimed in his memoir to have worked twice as hard accordingly, only to be told one day by Storey, "I have determined never to take another partner." In the end, Wilkie never moved beyond page editor, churning out one sensation after another. His memoir was a tell-all of Storey, making his former employer's antics Wilkie's ultimate sensation.[8]

The Growing Diversity of Chicago

Another *Times* employee lived perhaps the fastest life of a postbellum Chicago newspaperman, attesting to the growing diversity that marked midcentury Chicago. John M. Wing was a native New Yorker who worked for several newspapers in his home state. In 1865 he used a railroad pass given to him in exchange for favorable articles to immigrate to Chicago. Applying at several papers, he had an unsuccessful *Tribune* audition before the *Times* snapped him up. Within a week, he was writing in a diary (not published until 2002) that "things that I never dreamed of have passed before my vision, and I am getting to be quite at home in this great metropolis of the west." "Chicago is awfull [*sic*] full of excitement," he wrote, "but it seldom gets on a tear, like smaller cities."[9]

In particular, Wing's diary reveals an important aspect of mid-century Chicago, its growing homosexual community. French novelists George Sand and Honoré de Balzac, not unknown to upper-class Chicagoans, featured vivid homosexual characters in their mid-nineteenth-century novels; Walt Whitman celebrated male love in his poetry; and men such as Daniel Webster and Ralph Waldo Emerson and women such as Emily Dickinson and Susan B. Anthony wrote freely of thoughts toward their own sex. "You two have taught me to love, and that not selfishly but in a broad, generous way," Wing's Chicago newspaper contemporary Henry Demarest Lloyd wrote to his future wife and a male college friend in the early 1870s. As social historian Peter Gay has observed, "As long as they preserved their appearances, [Victorian-era] bachelors were above suspicion and women sharing quiet establishments gathered only praise for their devoted friendship."[10]

As such, homosexuality was not taboo in early Chicago. A small but noticeable gay subculture had first formed in New York City during the 1840s, identified and ridiculed in flash or "sporting" newspapers but otherwise ignored by the mainstream mass news media. "Rarely considered a sexual issue," Timothy J. Gilfoyle wrote, "homosexuality was not a scapegoat for social problems." The anonymity of a big city attracted "inverts," as they were sometimes called, because they furnished employment, acquaintances, and a social life not available in smaller localities. "Only in a great city," historian George Chauncey quoted a New York man as writing in 1882, could a gay man give "his overwhelming yearnings free rein *incognito* and thus keep the respect of his every-day circle."

A similar community began forming in mid-nineteenth-century Chicago as well. When homosexuals were a topic in the early Chicago newspapers, they were called "dandies" or a "hack man." "A foppish and effeminate youth is called 'a regular Miss Nancy,'" the *Tribune* explained, and "Sweet Williams" were defined as "'nice young men' who . . . smell so sweet, and talk so like gentle waiting women." Lesbianism was discussed rarely, although the papers did have a particular fascination for cross-dressing. For instance, the *Tribune* reported on a seventeen-year-old Rochester, New York, girl who was found in 1862 Chicago by her father, dressed as "a young man of juvenile and effeminate appearance." The *Times* published a lengthy 1874 article on "the most accomplished liar the West ever beheld," a woman who specialized in impersonating men occasionally for criminal reasons; and the famous English vaudeville troop the "British Blondes" scandalized the Chicago clergy during the 1870s by appearing in the city dressed in men's clothing. Otherwise, only in court docket articles were crimes such as sodomy or buggery even referenced, and then in passing. "Would it not be a good thing if the Mayor . . . would call the attention of the police to the night habitues of the regions under some of our bridges," a letter writer complained to the *Tribune* in 1879. "The one at Randolph street is infested with a set of men who would have been cleaned out even in Sodom."[11]

Initially, Wing's sexuality was of little matter to the dissolute *Times* newsroom. "Two of my men are ex-convicts, ten of them are divorced husbands, and not a single one of them is living with his own wife," editor Alexander C. Botkin bragged in the late 1860s. Only such men could provide readers with a "feast fitted only for the tastes and appetites of vultures and carrion-loving vermin," as Franc Wilkie wrote, "to attract attention to the paper, to secure notoriety, advertising and circulation." However, none of Wing's "sensations" were infused with the same kind of homosexual glee as his diary entries: "Saw a boy with whom I fell in love, and chased him up. Found him and got him all right. Engaged a bed and he and I retired. He is a bully fellow. . . . Johnny Maier, my *enamorata* of last night, is a character in truth. Soon after he got up "to get a drink of water," I found him playing billiards and going on a big bum [outing]."

Another entry involved one Billy Bissel, a Detroit man who visited Wing in Chicago: "He agreed to stay over night. Went to the opera, and then to my room. Billy is a brick—a *roue!* How the night passed, let memory only know. It was happiness, bliss. He is my beau-ideal. . . . Billy went away before breakfast, and with him went many joys. I must go to Detroit soon, and enjoy another season with the Hanky [stylish, dashing] boy of the Auditor's office." Another of his lovers, a survivor of the notorious Andersonville, Georgia, Confederate prisoner-of-war camp, passed through Chicago, befriended Wing, and left him with unexpected gifts. "Found to my great horror that my soldier boy had given me crabs, and worse than that, head lice," Wing journaled. "Found my corpus alive with vermin, and shuddered at the thought." As George Chauncey has observed, Victorians believed that some men were so highly sexed that they accepted such kinds of homosexual advances because women, and other men, were unable to satisfy them.[12]

But it was Wing's journalism rather than his lifestyle that ultimately cost him his newspaper career. He had problems reconciling his Yankee abolitionist convictions with those of the "secesh" *Times.* "Wrote an article on 'Negro Immigration' in which I said many things against my belief," he admitted in his diary in July 1865, "now that I am selling my brains to a copperhead paper." His article chronicled the train arrivals of hundreds of newly freed slaves, "dropped down in the streets of Chicago, ragged, hungry and as ignorant of life as so many apes." Wing probably excised his frustrations with such reporting by writing about the near North Side Irish shantytown of Kilgubbin, located not far from present-day Chicago Avenue and Division and Sedgwick streets. Since its founding as a Democratic paper the previous decade, the *Times* had built its circulation on the nickels of Chicago's pro-Democratic Irish community.

Wing's description of their shantytown, which appeared in the paper without Storey's prior knowledge on August 6, 1865, was a drastic departure for its predictable Irish patronage. "Collected data and facts for an article on the 'Squatter Settlements of Chicago,'" Wing noted in his diary. "This article . . . was destined to make more commotion and disturbance in Chicago than any ever printed. . . . [and] it was also destined to make Jack Wing tremble in his boots, and carry a six shooter in his pocket night and day." In the two-column-long article, Wing noted that the First Ward vice district was not the only Chicago locale for "wretchedness, poverty and vice." "There are other sources whence come frequent complaints, to annoy and puzzle the [police]. These are the 'patches' where the sons of the Emerald Isle have 'squatted,' built their seven-by-nine shanties, reared their offspring and bred their extensive droves of geese, hens, cows, dogs and cats." According to Wing, the city's rapid progress meant little to the so-called famine Irish who had immigrated to Chicago during the 1850s and 1860s. "Wherever a block of land, or, perchance, a dreary sandhill along the lake, is in litigation, or of doubtful title, they find it out as if by instinct; up goes the shanty . . . [constructed by] joint proprietors, Paddy and Biddy. This single land-mark having been erected, a village of shanties soon grow up, which can only be displaced by the whole police force united or by some action of the elements."[13]

Reaction to Wing's Kilgubbin article was immediate and forceful. As many as 5,000 of the *Times*' estimated 30,000 subscribers, mostly Irish, canceled their subscriptions, throwing the paper into a financial skid that lasted for months. In response, Storey published a rare retraction, writing, "An article appeared in this paper yesterday entitled 'Squatter Settlements,' which would not have appeared had the manuscript passed through the hands of the responsible editor. Its publication was one of those accidents which sometimes happen in the best regulated newspaper establishments." Meanwhile, the article was a boon to Storey's detractors. "The Copperhead print in this city has long set itself as the organ and special champion of the Emerald element in Chicago," the *Tribune* chuckled the following day, reprinting the entire article without permission. "Strike out the patronage derived from the Irish, and the *Chicago Times* would die as speedily as a rat in an air exhausted receiver." The *Evening Journal* editorialized, "In a sensation article in its issue of Sunday morning, [the *Times*] made a wholesale onslaught upon the Irish residents of this city, ridiculing their ways of living and slandering them socially, morally, and otherwise."

A resolution by the pro–free Ireland Fenian Brotherhood organization criticized the article not "as the production of honest American editors, but as the contemptible work of English adventurers, who come to this country filled with malice toward our countrymen." In a letter addressed to the *Times* and copied to the *Tribune* as well, "An Irishman" complained, "Did you ever hear, or did any of your sensational staff ever hear anything concerning the wrongs which you can so merrily sneer at, of the sufferings of the people you seem so heartily to despise." The resulting outcry even contributed to Irish defections to the Republican Party in the 1866 city elections, and memories of it lingered for years. "Now, fellow-country men, have you no memory," a *Tribune* letter writer identified as an Irish Democrat wrote in 1878. "Do you forget the Killgubin [*sic*] article?" Wing's *Times* employment ended shortly thereafter and, subsequently, he made his small fortune in the trade magazine business, bequeathing much of his estate to the Newberry Library following his death in 1917. Chicago's homosexual community continued to grow throughout the nineteenth century.[14]

Fast Destruction

The topic of Chicagoans' water cooler conversations in the weeks and days before the Great Fire was hardly of impending doom. Instead, an event that the Little Rock, Arkansas, *Morning Republican* called a "painful episode of Chicago life—From Gutter to Grave" probably dominated talk among the middle and upper classes. Chicago Board of Education member and former alderman Dr. John Macalister and his fellow physician father Hugh went "on a spree" of the city's vice district in August 1871 and "wallowed together in beastliness." Taken home with "delirium tremens," the father died days later "suffering all the torments of perdition" as the Arkansas paper put it. The son, when confronted with his father's twisted corpse, retreated to his "crazed with whiskey" ways for several more days "and crying for more liquor . . . finally died in the midst of imaginary reptiles." "This double suicide," the Arkansas paper continued, "has created a profound sensation in all [Chicago] circles where the facts are known." As certain as sermons were preached the following Sunday, ministers all across the city warned their congregations of a similar fate awaiting anyone foolish to follow in the Macalisters' ways, especially members of the younger generation intent on duplicating the events that lead the men's deaths. Chicago's newspaper coverage was predictably lower keyed. In its obituary, the *Tribune* noted that the younger Macalister "was a thoroughly upright, honest, and capable man" who "commanded the unbounded confidence of his patients."[15]

A few newspaper items portended the great fire, especially during the record dry September. The *Evening Journal* complained midmonth that "the dust in [the] La Salle street tunnel this morning was almost impenetrable." A few days later, the *Tribune* noted that "water famines" were predicted for New York, Philadelphia, and Boston, but not in lakeside Chicago. Both reports were symptomatic of a drought that had plagued a large part of the country throughout the summer of 1871. According to *Evening Post* reporter Elias Colbert, only two inches of rain fell on Chicago between July and early October 1871—1.5 inches on July 3, four light sprinkles of one-half inch or less in August, and just three light sprinkles in September. He noted that the summer's rainfall total was only 28 percent of what was considered normal at the time, in an era before modern weather records were kept. More precise records for nearby Milwaukee indicated that that city received only 0.57 inches of rain during September.

There were other, less obvious indications as well. "The street [fire] hydrants are being painted," the *Journal* noted in September. "Forethought and prudence both may insure your life. Take their advice and insure in The Mutual Life Insurance Company of Chicago," a newspaper advertisement read. "The weather, for some time past, has been rather hot and dry," a Cedar Falls, Iowa, correspondent told the *Tribune*. "The streams are all low, and perhaps it is owing to this that there is so much sickness just at present." A September gale created a rare rogue wave that dropped Lake Superior's level five feet, temporarily reversing the flow of the Sault Ste. Marie canal and grounding a number of ships. "Delightful fall weather" the *Evening Journal* waxed only to note a few weeks later that in downstate Illinois "clouds of dust, raised by every passing vehicle, fill the air, and are carried onward with great rapidity by strong currents of the wind." "It is a fact of world-wide observation that clearing a timbered country lessens rain," the Vermillion *Dakota Republican* wrote.

Regional newspapers chronicled a series of devastating wildfires in Minnesota, Wisconsin, and Michigan in late September and early October, fueled by wasteful logging practices and low humidity levels. The *Tribune* called the resulting fires "circumstances which seemed to indicate the near approach of the millennium." "Wisconsin Afire!" the *Columbus* (Georgia) *Enquirer* reported, "flames are lapping up everything, sweeping houses, barns, stores and piers in its course." "The only refuge is the lakes," the *Trenton* (New Jersey) *Gazette* related. "Many people have had to betake themselves to their boats in order to save their lives, while some have perished in the flames." The *Chicago Journal* noted that "the fires which now prevail in the six or seven northeastern counties of Wisconsin have never had a parallel since the settlement of the country."

In Chicago, a railroad warehouse fire caused more than $1 million in damages in late September with undermanned firefighters unable to control the blaze. The *Chicago Journal* reported a few days later that a new piece of firefighting equipment called the Babcock Self-Acting Fire Engine "distinguished itself last night by extinguishing a fire in the Mansard roof on the Honore block, on Dearborn street, without loss worth mentioning." Fire extinguishers were to be left in various parts of the city to aid firefighters, something the newspaper called "a good idea." An arson fire in a building at 300 Mitchell Street pointed to another firefighting problem, Chicago's chaotic system of fire reporting or alarm boxes. "Box No. 297 was struck from sight at ten minutes of 1 o'clock this morning," the *Tribune* reported, "and, as is naturally the case, the fire was about a mile and a half from the place where the [fire] box is located." "The carnival of fires still continues," the *Times* noted four days before the great fire. "Already this month there have been fifteen alarms sounded, of which only two were false."[16]

Chicago fire scholars such as Carl Smith have asserted that the *Tribune*'s "editors throughout the summer and fall [of 1871] exhorted the Common Council to raise the level of fire protection if they wished to avoid . . . disaster." Of the eighty-four editorial articles appearing in the *Tribune* between January 1 and the date of the fire using the phrase "common council" only nine included the word "fire," and only one, on the "smoke nuisance," called on the council to do anything about a fire threat. One editorial did call for the city to increase water pressure so that residents could keep themselves more comfortable in the hot summer months. However, the paper wrote in June, "The fire department has especially become one of the most expensive branches of the public service. We have apparatus enough to serve all of the increased wants of the city for ten years to come"—hardly the sentiment evoked by Smith.

Much too has been made of a *Tribune* editorial on September 10 complaining of the shoddy construction methods used in pre-fire Chicago. "If [Chicagoans] mix up Ionic and Corinthian, Renaissance and Elizabethan . . . their lines of beauty and of strength preserved in everlasting pine and shingle-nails and putty—in doing these and a hundred other things like them quite as shocking," the paper wrote, "we hug ourselves with a comfortable feeling of self-complaisance, and rejoice and possibly boast that if we have not got the real thing itself . . . we have got, at least, the semblance of it." For those who read beyond the editorial's first few paragraphs however, the remainder of the editorial advocated the construction of a new public library using the same pinewood, shingle nails, and putty techniques. "It is, we are afraid, a radical fault in the average Chicagoan of to-day that he cares very little for anything but the present moment," the paper wrote prophetically.

In reality, the city's highly combustible buildings were anything but news in 1871. The New York-based humor magazine *Punchinello* had written of Chicago's notorious building methods in 1870 that "the Garden City seems to be a quiescent state at present. . . . the main portion of the Court House has not yet fallen in." Architect G. P. Randall wrote a letter to the *Tribune* that same year advocating a new method of fireproofing buildings, a call unheeded by the paper or the city. "We have had a good many fires in Chicago and nobody as yet has attempted to use our experience as the base of a theory," the *Times* complained in 1867. Writing in his diary in 1865, new arrival John M. Wing may have put it most succinctly: "Police and Fires—the latter to excess. It seems as if the whole d____d town would burn down."

In contrast to the *Tribune*'s "apparatus enough" assertion, Chicago had fewer than two hundred firefighters in 1871, a ratio of about one for every

1,650 residents. By contrast, New York (a city surrounded by water and having more brick and stone buildings) had one firefighter for every 1,330 residents in 1865, and the department underwent an upgrade in 1868 following several disastrous blazes. Aiding Chicago's firefighters were just seventeen horse-drawn steam engines and only 48,000 feet of fire hose—nine miles placed end-to-end for a city that stretched more than twenty miles. Those meager resources were exhausted fighting a seventeen-hour blaze the night before and day of the great fire. A four-block area bounded by Van Buren, Clinton, and Adams streets and the river was destroyed, and tired firefighters were forced to remain at the scene the following afternoon to hose down hot spots. Contemporary historian Alfred Andreas conjectured that if the fire department had not been so vigilant in battling that blaze it might have been better able to fight the DeKoven Street fire, "but speculation is idle now."

By two o'clock in the afternoon of October 8, Chicago's U.S. Signal Corps observer on La Salle Street was reporting steady south-southwesterly winds of 23 miles per hour. At 5:35 P.M., a rudimentary map prepared by the fledgling U.S. Weather Bureau showed a strong high pressure area centered over the Carolinas, a deep cyclonic low centered over Kansas and Colorado, and a warm front between the two with a deep pressure gradient, ingredients for continued hot, dry, strong winds.[17]

The exact cause of the Chicago Fire, the greatest news story in the city's history, will never be known for certain, but there is no doubt that the mythology of the fire's origin was created by the local mass news media. A one-page *Chicago Evening Journal* extra edition dated October 9, 1871, the first local paper to be published during the fire, noted: "Amid the confusion and general bewilderment, we can only give a few details. The fire broke out on the corner of DeKoven and Twelfth streets, at about 9 o'clock on Sunday evening, being caused by a cow kicking over a lamp in a stable in which a woman was milking. An alarm was immediately given, but owing to the high southwest wind, the building was speedily consumed, and thence the fire spread rapidly."

That explanation was expanded upon in subsequent reports and in newspapermen Elias Colbert and Everett Chamberlin's instant history book, *Chicago and the Great Conflagration,* which observed that "the blame of setting the fire rests on the woman who milked, or else upon the lazy man who allowed her to milk." The Mrs. O'Leary in question never talked about the fire publicly, keeping her role to herself until her death, although the *Journal* claimed that she blamed it on an unidentified incendiary. Dismissing the story as "nothing but a newspaper lie," her son told reporters in 1909, "the first we knew about the cow and the lamp was when we read about it. Father and mother died sad at heart over that monumental world-strewn fake."

In 1921, an Irish-born former *Chicago Republican* reporter named Michael L. Ahern claimed that he and either one or two fellow reporters, the *Times*'s James Haynie and or the *Tribune*'s John English, concocted the cow "kicking over the lamp" explanation because they had found a broken kerosene lamp in the wreckage of the O'Leary's barn at 137 DeKoven Street. Not coincidentally, fifteen horses had been killed in a fire set "by the accidental upsetting of a kerosene lamp in the barn of ex-Alderman Hildreth, at Nos. 597 and 599 South Halsted street" as reported in the *Evening Journal* about a month before the great blaze. Other reporters claimed responsibility for creating the O'Leary myth as well (including one for the *New York Herald*), and even for concocting Ahern's confession.

Regardless of which reporter was responsible, the cow story made Chicago's the best-known urban fire in American history, much in the spirit of Chicago's tradition of self-promotion. An official investigation was inconclusive as the entire blame was centered on the highly flammable wooden structures and shanties used by the poor Irish living in the DeKoven Street area. "There is no proof that any persons had been in the barn after nightfall that evening," the official report noted. More recently, fire historians have speculated on a pipe-smoking itinerant named Dennis "Peg Leg" Sullivan, who placed himself very near to the barn at the time of the fire's origin, perhaps the "unknown incendiary" referred to by the O'Learys.[18]

In his history, Carl Smith used private accounts like H. A. Musham's recollections from his fire marshal father to retell the fire's story, but those remembrances were unavailable to either contemporary Chicagoans or millions of out-of-towners in the fire's wake. Instead, their social reality was based on their personal experiences, what others told them, and what they read in newspapers and instant histories. "Though I at many points rely upon [the newspapers] for more 'factual' descriptions," Karen Sawislak observed in her study of the fire, "it is their partisan and social identities that makes them so critical to my analysis."

However it was ignited, the blaze spread quickly, and within minutes, twenty to thirty small wooden buildings were engulfed, the flames fanned by gusty, dry southwesterly winds. "The buildings were generally of the cheapest character," a Chicago correspondent for the *New York Times* wrote, "embracing saloons, small shops, poor residences, &c." Twenty-year-old *Chicago Evening Post* reporter Joseph Chamberlin arrived at the scene before most of the firefighters. His account, reprinted in his brother's instant history, was colored by his Yankee prejudice against the famine Irish. "The fire had already advanced a distance of about a single square [block] through the frame buildings that covered the ground thickly north of DeKoven Street and east of Jefferson Street—if those miserable alleys shall be dignified by being denominated streets," Chamberlin wrote. "That neighborhood had always been a terra incognita to respectable Chicagoans, and during a residence of three years in the city I had never visited it."

Chamberlin's prejudice was shared to some extent by *Tribune*'s editor-in-chief Horace White. "The district where the fire got its first firm foothold was the Alsatia of Chicago," White wrote in reference to a notorious London neighborhood where "the law cannot reach." Even though he was not near the fire's actual point of origin, Chamberlin continued, "Fleeing before it was a crowd of bleary-eyed, drunken, and diseased wretches, male and female, half naked, ghastly, with painted cheeks, cursing and uttering ribald jests as they drifted along." "Soon . . . casks of whisky appeared, and scores of excited men drank deeply of their contents," Chamberlin wrote. "The result was, of course, that an equal number of drunken men were soon impeding the flight of the fugitives."

Efforts to limit the fire to the near West Side continued until, as Chamberlin noted, "I caught the word, 'across the river,' uttered doubtingly by a bystander. The words passed from mouth to mouth, and there was universal incredulity, although the suggestion was communicated through the crowd with startling rapidity." A shed across the river was the first to catch fire. It was torn down, but within minutes a square block of buildings near it was in flames. By 11 P.M., the keeper of the city's water intake two miles offshore in Lake Michigan "found the sky full of sparks and burning brands." The U.S. Signal Service officer on La Salle Street reported southwesterly winds of 60 miles per hour before his office was destroyed. The fire continued to move in a northeasterly direction toward the central business district. "The roar was terrific; the smoke drifted over me in huge volumes," *Tribune* business manager Joseph Medill recalled. "There was a strong wind blowing, apparently from every direction, into the fire; but the prevailing pressure was from the southwest." Reporter Elias Colbert described the phenomena as "huge balloons of fire . . . [breaking] like a burning water spout." In its first six hours, the fire advanced more than two miles from its point of ignition. The noise was terrific, Chamberlin recalled as he tried to run to his newspaper, his path impeded by scores of spectators watching the transfiguring flames and hundreds of others attempting to flee with what few possessions they could carry."[19]

The courthouse, surrounded by Randolph, Clark, Washington, and La Salle streets, collapsed about 2:30 A.M. Monday, October 9. To spare their lives, Mayor Roswell B. Mason ordered the release of some 150 prisoners confined in a basement jail. Their isolated drinking and looting activities in the immediate area, especially in a nearby jewelry store, inspired a plethora of false reports detailing wanton robbery and murder that circulated outside of Chicago in the mass news media in the days and weeks after the fire. At the same time the courthouse caught fire, the city's corps of telegraph operators were forced to flee their burning structure across the street, cutting Chicago's ties to the outside world. An Associated Press telegraph reporter broke off a dispatch in mid word and escaped the flames in Army Gen. Phillip Sheridan's carriage to a suburban telegraph station, where he resumed his reporting. "Mobs of men and women rushed wildly from street to street, screaming, gesticulating, and shouting, crossing each other's paths, and intercepting each other as if just escaped from a mad house," *Tribune* reporters James W. Sheahan and George P. Upton wrote. "Every few steps along the avenues were little piles of household property, or, perhaps, only a trunk, guarded by children, some of whom were weeping, and other laughing and playing." "Half clad people were running about screaming such things as 'run for your lives' and 'the world's coming to an end,'" a survivor recalled in 1934.[20]

The flames continued in their northeasterly direction, limited to the west by the north branch of the Chicago River and to the east by Lake Michigan. As the fire raged, *Tribune* editor Horace White raced to his paper's four-story structure on the corner of Dearborn and Madison streets, constructed of "fireproof" marble at a cost of $250,000 in 1869. White was another Yankee newspaperman, born in New Hampshire in 1834, who began in Chicago newspapers at the age of nineteen. He covered the police beat for the *Evening Journal* before joining the *Tribune*, where he reported on the 1858 and 1860 Lincoln-Douglas election contests. White became a part owner and editor-in-chief of the *Tribune* in 1865 when another owner sold out his share. White wrote how he took what he thought was the only flammable item from the editorial office, a kerosene lamp, and dumped its contents into a basement drain. Otherwise, the paper's presses were readying to run, preparing for a Monday edition that few would ever see. "We saw the tall buildings on the opposite sides of the two streets melt down in a few moments without scorching ours. . . . After the fire in our neighborhood had spent its force, the editorial and composing rooms did not even smell of smoke. . . . So I supposed [the danger had passed], and in this belief went home to breakfast."

Unfortunately, White's building was anything but fireproof. As with all other newspapers of the day, the *Tribune* used a coal-fired steam engine to power its rotary printing presses, creating an explosive coal-dust hazard within the building. Staff members slept or worked in the *Tribune*'s fourth-floor editorial room and on its roof after White left, writing by candlelight when their gas lighting failed, and watching the flames spread. "Men were sent to get buckets or anything that would hold water to throw on whatever might catch fire," Joseph Medill recalled. "By this time thousands of sparks and bits of burning shingles were falling on the roof. . . . We set to work stamping it out, some using boards, others shovels, and others threw on water, but it didn't seem to do much good, the 'fireproof' roof was constantly catching here and there." Sometime after 3 A.M., reporter Elias Colbert, looking through a telescope, discovered that the flames were redoubling back toward the city center, so he grabbed a copy of the half-printed Monday paper and the bound volumes of the only complete *Tribune* run. When a wall from the next-door McVicker's Theatre fell against the *Tribune,* the "fire proof" building ripped open, with coal dust exploding, and everything Colbert carried was dropped on the sidewalk and left to the flames. The only surviving *Tribune* items were a few financial papers, a linen coat, and a box of matches secured in a vault that could not be opened because their guardian had absentmindedly left the keys at home.[21]

A Merry Christmas for Some

As White hurried his family and possessions out of the stricken city, he apparently had the time to observe how well he thought upper-class Yankee refugees were behaving. "The only quarrelsome person I saw was a German laborer (a noted exception to his race), who was protesting that he had lost everything, and that he would not get out of the middle of the road although he was on foot," White wrote. "My driver was preparing to knock him down with the butt end of his whip, when two men seized the insolent Teuton and dragged him to the water's edge, where it is hoped he was ducked." Hastened by worsening winds and the destruction of the city's waterworks, the blaze moved fastest through the largely immigrant North Side on Monday morning, destroying nearly a dozen blocks of wooden houses in less than an hour. The Sands District and surrounding lakeside, made famous by Long John Wentworth's two decades previous raid, was the only refuge for those who could not escape the flames. "This is the day of judgment," a number of survivors told a *New York Sun* correspondent. "This must be the end of the world!"

As many as 5,000 West Side and North Side working class families were left homeless and destitute by the fire, and in its wake, most nonprofit fraternal or mutual fire insurance companies were bankrupted, paying pennies on their claims. By contrast, many of the city's most affluent Yankees insured themselves through eastern firms, and although it was argued that those with the most lost the most, they were quickly able to resume their comfortable lives. "Despite the many assertions of universal spiritual awakening inspired by the fire, the authors of the fire commemorative and instant histories reserved their sympathies mainly for the plight of 'the landlord and aristocrat,'" Carl Smith wrote. "Anybody was has had a house on the North Side, with a brick basement, and does not intend to rebuild it before next Summer should put his lot unconditionally at the disposal of those fire victims who would like to erect a hut on it," the *Staats Zeitung* noted on October 14. "Basement walls are always better than none at all." "Much as every person's identity and location had a major effect upon any Chicagoan's experience of the Great Fire itself, such a range of particularities ultimately determined the sort of hardships later suffered by an individual or a family," Karen Sawislak wrote.[22]

The mass news media's sensationalization of fire-related crimes obsessed survivors and out-of-towners alike. In constructing their reality of the otherwise unimaginable event, people had to devise some explanation for its devastation, and unknown and threatening incendiaries and criminals were the ideal scapegoats. Rumors quickly spread as previously scheduled trains arrived in the devastated city, and each survivor or tourist had his or her own story to tell, with flourishes. For instance, according to the *Philadelphia Inquirer,* a prominent Chicago banker was said to have been found murdered in the ruins of his bank, curiously still with "money and valuables in his arms." "Two men, caught in the act of firing houses on the west side, were arrested and immediately hanged to lamp-posts," the *Baltimore Sun* reported. "Another dispatch says seven or eight men have been shot or hung at sight—a fit fate for such devils," the *New Hampshire Patriot* wrote. Other outside newspaper reports indicated that hundreds had been trampled to death in a panic to escape the flames, 800 had been smothered in the Washington Street tunnel, 1,300 inmates burned to death in a prison not even located in Chicago, and Lake Michigan was said to be strewn with an estimated 9,000 to 10,000 "dead bodies, oil, filth, etc."

The fire "awakened a large underclass to follow its base nature in ways that threatened the 'better' elements in the city" in the minds of the Yankees, as Carl Smith explained. "Before daybreak, the thieving horror had culminated in scenes of daring robbery, unparalleled in the annals of any similar disaster," the upper-class *Lakeside Monthly* magazine reported. "Villainous . . . flitted through the crowd collarless, dirty, unkempt," the *Evening Post* wrote a week after the blaze, "these negroes [*sic*] with stolid faces and white men who fat-ten on the wages of shame, glided through the masses like vultures in search of prey." In reality, most of 1871 Chicago's small African American population had been burned out by the fire and were living with other blacks. Few had reason or the mind to walk about the burned-out city except perhaps in search of work. "My coachman filled my buggy with some harness, a bag of coffee, and other articles, and left it with his friends on the lake shore," *Tribune* publisher William Bross complained. "That was the last I ever heard of the buggy or anything that was in it."

Such mass behaviors were even more unlikely in the wake of the fire because many businessmen hired Chicagoan Allan Pinkerton to guard what valuables they had left. To transgressors Pinkerton warned that "no mercy shall be shown to them, but death shall be their fate." Major Gen. Phillip Sheridan was already stationed in Chicago, and he ordered his troops to join Pinkerton's patrols. "Another sleepless night," Bross wrote, "and in the morning as I sat sipping my coffee over some cold ham, I saw Sheridan's boys, with knapsack and musket, march proudly by. . . . *Had it not been for General Sheridan's prompt, bold, and patriotic action,* I verily believe what was left of the city would have been nearly, if not entirely, destroyed by the cutthroats and vagabonds who flocked here like vultures from every point of the compass." "All the rumors of incendiarism, murder, and lynching exist[ed] only in the imagination of the frightened population," State Militia Commander Adjutant General Henry Dilger wrote in his eventual official report. Chicago Police Commissioner Thomas B. Brown admitted that "during the fire and the two weeks succeeding it, there were remarkably few cases of crime." Regardless of such findings, "no sort of factual reportage could dissuade these readers from their ready made vision of a city gone completely awry," Karen Sawislak wrote.[23]

The six major English-language daily newspapers suffered combined loses of $575,000 in the fire, but all resumed publication. The *Evening Journal* produced the first post-fire edition, a single-page Monday afternoon extra that called the fire "The Great Calamity of the Age." The paper issued a four-page edition the following day listing several St. Louis residents who had pledged toward Chicago's eventual recovery. Advertisements included real estate agent William D. Kerfoot's famous "All gone, but wife, children and energy" remark. In its first post-fire edition, which appeared October 9, the *Daily Commercial Bulletin* reported that $1.2 million worth of grain was destroyed; it assured its business readers that option contracts arrived at before the fire would be resolved. The first *Tribune* post-fire issue, printed on the *Journal*'s press, featured the well known "Cheer Up" editorial, erroneously attributed to Joseph Medill. "In the midst of a calamity without parallel in the world's history, looking upon the ashes of thirty years' accumulations, the people of this once beautiful city have resolved that CHICAGO SHALL RISE AGAIN," editor Horace White actually wrote. Chicago songwriter George F. Root used White's phrase as the hook for a piano song he wrote about the fire, "From the Ruins Our City Shall Rise," and the line became the unofficial slogan of the city's recovery.

Like the *Tribune*, the *Times*'s five-story office building on Dearborn Street, at the northwest corner of an alley between Madison and Washington, was destroyed. As the fire ravaged the city late Sunday night, Wilbur Storey wrote an editorial appealing to other cities for help, an editorial that never appeared. A witness saw the paper's presses spinning out a Monday edition at midnight, and a final bulletin, "The Very Latest—The entire business portion of the city is burning up, and the *Times* building appears doomed," was inserted about 2 A.M. Reporter Franc Wilkie found Storey sitting dejectedly in front of his undamaged South Side house the following afternoon. "I saw three men sitting on the piazza," he wrote, one "an elderly man who leaned forward in his chair in an attitude of dejection, whose mouth was pinched, and about whose eyes there were innumerable wrinkles. It took a second glance to recognize in this third person Mr. Storey, who seemed ten years older than when I had left him Saturday afternoon." According to Wilkie, Storey announced "The city is destroyed. Everything is played out. I am now an old man (He was only fifty-one)." But like his competitors, the inscrutable Storey resumed his paper within a few weeks using old type stored in his garage.

The authors and publishers of paperback instant histories, advertisers, novelists including the Rev. E. P. Roe, and hardcover publishers all profited from the fire, as did out-of-town newspapers, which were shipped to eager Chicago readers. "You see, Boss, the Shecargo [*sic*] fire has been a fat thing for all of us," a New York newsboy explained, and he and other "little fellows" raised ten dollars to aid Chicago fire victims in gratitude for their increased business. The fire even produced its own form of humor. The *Tribune* observed a signboard, stuck in the ruins of a Madison Street business, which read, "Owing to circumstances over which we had no control, we have removed." Another sign read, "Moore & Goe, House and Sign Painters . . . Capital $000,000.30." Writing years after the fact, Franc Wilkie spun a couple of even taller tales about the fire. In one, basements left by the hungry flames were inverted and used "for shops for business till they could get lumber to build something else." Or the waters of Lake Michigan were said to be so overheated by the fire that Chicagoans feasted on boiled trout and catfish for months. "Everything was favorable to building operations that winter," Wilkie wrote. "The water in the lake kept at the boiling point for two or three months, and the masons used the hot water to mix the mortar with."[24]

The Race Against St. Louis

Wilkie's tales of the Great Fire made reference to Chicago's dramatic population growth as well. Census takers were never able to entirely complete their duties because the city's boundaries kept expanding—or so Wilkie held. "Most of them are now so far from home that they send in their returns by mail; several have died, and not one of them has seen his family for over two years." Chicagoans withstood challenges for the title of "most populous city" from a host of competitors beginning with its establishment as a city in 1837. Early on, river-town rivals such as Joliet, Aurora, and Geneva cherished hopes of outdistancing early Chicago. The Chicago area's oldest newspaper, the *Juliet Herald News* [*sic*], was founded in 1839, eight years before the *Chicago Tribune*, with an eye toward boosting what it considered to be the area's settlement of the future. Only upon completion of the Illinois-Michigan Canal in 1848 did Joliet and its like gave up their hopes of surpassing Chicago.

Chicago also had to beat back another tenacious early competitor, Galena. Located in the northwestern corner of Illinois and situated on a Mississippi tributary with the unfortunate name of the Fever River, Galena was the first major settlement in Illinois north of Springfield. Named for the Latin word for lead oxide, its leading export, the *Miner's Journal* was founded in 1826, seven years before the *Chicago Democrat*. A 1829 article in the *Galena Enterprise*, named for the town's aspirations, noted that a test load of lead had been shipped successfully via an oxen-drawn wagon through Chicago; the paper applauded the tiny lake settlement as a future transshipment point for the more prosperous Galena. However, that affluence disappeared during the 1850s, due in part to flooding, some of the same water-born diseases that plagued Chicago, the advent of the railroads, and a declining price for lead. But the original Illinois Central Railroad mainline was routed to Galena—not Chicago—by the State Legislature in the early 1850s based on the strength of the former's legislative contingent. Chicago's line, which ran along the lakeshore to the center city, was considered a branch.[25]

With the implementation of the Illinois-Michigan Canal, Chicago's mass news media set its sights on larger prey: Detroit, Milwaukee, Cincinnati, Cleveland, and Toledo. Most of what was printed was provided by what the *Milwaukee Sentinel* called "croakers," boosters intent on creating an advantage for their particular city. When a Boston correspondent asked in 1846, "Which shall be greatest, Milwaukee or Chicago?" the *Chicago Journal* retorted that Milwaukee had no harbor, only a "mere indentation of the land . . . two miles deep and fifteen wide." The *Chicago Democrat* employed its own statistics three years later to prove that its city was second only to Cleveland in wheat shipments; that same year the *Chicago Tribune* bragged that Chicago was the "beef market of the West as Cincinnati is the Pork Market."

Such rhetoric took on serious overtones occasionally. For instance, the *Chicago Democrat* alleged in 1850 that at least fifty people had died in Milwaukee due to cholera—a "shameful falsehood" from "our loving neighbors" according to a Milwaukee paper. But most of the sparring was on the lighter side. The *Tribune* scuffed at the outmoded business practices of 1852 Detroit, bragging, "Chicago has continued to make herself in the age of Railroads . . . while Detroit, as of old, is content to be somewhere on the side." "Chicago is 'all in all' to Chicago people," the *Cleveland Herald* mocked in 1853, the same year a Toledo-based writer claimed that nature had destined his city for greatness. "Toledo . . . at no distant date will go ahead of Chicago, and equal if not surpass St. Louis," he predicted, to which the *Chicago Tribune* agreed that businesses were springing up in Toledo, but largely "where the mud banks [had] raised their ragged heads" just a few weeks previous. In a 1857 editorial titled "Great Cry and Little Wool," the *Tribune* mocked the *Milwaukee Sentinel* for using what it considered deceptive statistics to promote its city. "Mr. *Sentinel*, never 'hollar' until you are out of 'the woods,'" the *Tribune* scolded. In return, the *Sentinel* called Chicago "our gaseous neighbors at the head of the Lake."

The verbiage was out-and-out humorous at times. The *Detroit Free Press* joked that Chicagoans were selling "40 lots lying directly East of the city limits, for $2,000 per lot—'Water lots' of course," to which the Chicago *Daily Democratic Press* replied that "some jealous sprite has administered a little of the *pure* juice of 'sour grapes'" to the Detroit paper's editor. In another article, the *Free Press* maintained that the Chicago city council had voted "to extend the limits of that city, so as to take in all east of the Rocky Mountains; all south of fifty-four degrees of Latitude, and all north of Pasigonia." "Whether we shall afterwards admit Detroit depends upon your good behavior," the *Tribune* rejoined. A Chicago newspaper claimed that grass was growing in the streets of 1856 Milwaukee and its "citizens are to be seen drunk at every corner," which prompted a Milwaukee paper to protest that its residents weren't intoxicated "all of the time." "The *Detroit Advertiser* calls the editor of the [Detroit] *Free Press* a 'measureless liar,'" the *Chicago Journal* wrote, to which the latter responded that the greatest liar was indeed measurable at six feet four inches in length, a reference to Long John Wentworth.[26]

In spite of such exchanges, it was clear that by 1850, Chicagoans had drawn a serious bead on one competitor in particular, a city to their south that dared call itself the "Gateway to the West." "In the early competition for regional dominance, St. Louis was an unlikely winner," historian Jeffrey S. Adler wrote, and in spite of prolonged stagnation and frequent crises, it was the first major urban center in the trans-Mississippi region. St. Louis drew what vitality it had from the same Yankee gospel of success advocates as Chicago; although Chicago had stronger ties to New York City and State, St. Louis had ties to Massachusetts.

However, unlike Chicago, which was at the center of a vast nineteenth-century cultural region dubbed "Yankeeland" by historian Lois K. Mathews, St. Louis was a tiny island of Yankees in a sea of immigrants from Tennessee, Kentucky, and Virginia. Southerners, who dominated Missouri State politics, straitjacketed St. Louis's development and growth through a series of restrictive banking, investment, and business regulations unknown to Chicagoans. In particular, Chicago and Illinois borrowed from the banking and infrastructure traditions of New York while Missouri's rural-dominated legislature looked to South Carolina, Kentucky, and Tennessee as models. Illinois paid for the Illinois-Michigan Canal through state-backed bonds, nearly going bankrupt in the process. In contrast, in 1841, "Missouri has not one single mile of railroad, turnpike or canal, not a single bridge, lock or dam, not a single improved road or river, not a single school, academy or college, built or endowed by the State," the *Missouri Republican* bragged. Such narrow-minded thinking did not deter St. Louis's proponents however. "The progress of this city continues to be wondrous," future Civil War Gen. William T. Sherman wrote of St. Louis to his Ohio brother in 1851. "The future prospects of it are certainly as fair as that of any city on the continent."[27]

Since early Chicago was tied to river commerce through its canal, newspaper coverage of St. Louis was supportive initially, with vestiges lingering throughout the century. "The people of St. Louis, for a long time, and in fact, until they began to perceive the benefits to them, opposed the Illinois and Michigan Canal," the *Chicago Democrat* noted in 1849. "So soon, however . . . their opposition was turned into a strenuous support, and their papers are daily filled with statements of the immense benefit derived and in prospect from this important work." The Chicago papers published water levels with their St. Louis and New Orleans market reports along with related Mississippi River news during the 1840s. A visiting *New York Tribune* correspondent called

Chicago the "young metropolis of the Northwest" in a 1856 article but continued that "St. Louis has no superior west of the Alleghenies . . . and she also is the centre of a vast region which is bound to contribute to her prosperity."

When a St. Louis delegation met their Chicago Board of Trade counterparts in 1857, they were warmly received and won a unanimous pledge of support from the Chicagoans to promote river navigation against a plethora of new railroad bridges then under construction over the Mississippi. In 1860, the *Tribune* disagreed with the contention that another canal project would automatically "build up St. Louis" to Chicago's disadvantage. "St. Louis will reap advantages from it . . . but it by no means follows that Chicago would suffer on that account." As late as 1884, a *St. Louis Globe-Democrat* letter writer renewed a call first made fifty years previous for a Lake Michigan to Mississippi River canal cutting across the entire state of Illinois, overcoming the seasonal closings of the Des Planes and Illinois rivers. "The great interests of [St. Louis] and of the whole [Mississippi River] valley lies in maintaining the power between the river interest and the railroads," the writer wrote.[28]

The mass news media was not in itself responsible for Chicago's population success over St. Louis, and never made that claim. Differing railroad shipping rates, supplies of investment capital, the Civil War, and other factors were all more influential on businessmen, politicians, residents, and perspective settlers. But the newspapers were the accelerants in the process, the noisy kid in the back of the classroom always saying "look at me." Long John Wentworth probably fired the first shot in the contest between the two cities when he announced in his *Democrat* in 1850 that "we have but just entered on our life as a city," the same kind of threshold that St. Louis had crossed some twenty years previous. The *Chicago Tribune,* noting that Illinois River trade was "immense, furnishing St. Louis with more than a fourth of her commerce," reasoned that "there is nothing wanting to prevent our city from controlling it."

With the construction of four rail lines leading into Chicago between 1850 and 1855, however, a growing arrogance toward St. Louis manifested itself in Chicago's mass news media. A 1896 *Tribune* article thought the animosity had commenced in 1856 with the construction of the first Mississippi River railroad bridge, but feuding was underway when the *Daily Democratic Press* declared in 1853 that "the days of canal traveling are about over." "The merchant of the interior, too, will soon divest himself of his partiality for St. Louis, and he will go wherever his interest leads him—to Chicago," the paper wrote. "Merchants, like all other men, will trade where they can do so to the best advantage."

The following year, the Rock Island Railroad bypassed St. Louis in its westerly run, forever linking the rich north and westerly agricultural regions to Chicago, not St. Louis. As in St. Louis during the early 1840s, a self-perpetuating process commenced in Chicago that would make it an economic stronghold. In 1855, the *Pittsfield* (Massachusetts) *Sun* observed that St. Louis had processed 600,000 bushels of wheat in the month of September; Chicago 3,190,000. "It cannot be doubted that Chicago is destined to a proud eminence among our cities," the paper predicted. "The fact is, rivers are voted 'old fogeys' when they no longer are the only available thoroughfares," the *Chicago Democrat* wrote the same year. "The hand of 'manifest destiny' is upon them, and they must yield to their fate—even the mighty 'Father of Waters' must yield to the attractions of the iron way."

St. Louis's residents initially took a magnanimous view toward their upstart rival, with a *Missouri Republican* letter writer maintaining in 1851 that a majority of his friends favored a transcontinental railroad that included a connection to Chicago, built on principles of "empire," "nationality," and "a revolution in the commerce of the civilized world." But all a *St. Louis Intelligencer* reporter could do four years later was to lament the indignities being heaped upon his city by pretentious Chicago. "We found all through Wisconsin, Minnesota, and Iowa, the drummers and traders of Chicago," he wrote. "We can call to mind having met but one business man of St. Louis. We wait for the apples to fall. Chicago picks all she can reach, and then shakes the tree for the balance."[29]

Nearly all of St. Louis's failings in its economic competition with Chicago were attributable to its rural-dominated state legislature. Starting in the 1830s, rural Missourians began blaming fiscal woes on "foreign" Yankee sharpers in St. Louis, whom they accused of employing financial slight of hand to cheat them, and they flexed their political clout in Jefferson City to prevent any economic development that would directly benefit St. Louis. Chicagoans had their political problems with so-called rural "downstaters" and their competitors in Galena, but the Yankee-populated northern third of the state gave them a proportionately stronger (although never dominant) representation in Springfield.

German and Irish immigrants streaming into St. Louis during the 1850s changed the demographics of the city, to the further derision of native-born rural Missourians. Cholera and yellow fever, said to have been brought by the immigrants, "carried away hundreds of prominent citizens and thousands of newcomers, and the municipal 'dead cart was continually engaged' during the [St. Louis] boom years," Jeffrey Adler wrote. Chicago's sudden success in the 1850s made it the *saveur de jour* of out-of-town newspapers and national publications such as *Hunt's Merchants' Magazine*—a position formerly occupied by St. Louis. "St. Louis merchants have failed to advertise in our State Journals, and have lost that vast and valuable trade which she once had in this state," the *Davenport* (Iowa) *Daily State Democrat* complained in 1857, "while Chicago merchants have observed the correct rule, of letting the world know who and what they are and what they have to sell."

St. Louis has been incorrectly faulted for failing to embrace railroads the way that Chicagoans did. The former city's business community solicited the construction of a railroad as early as 1848, the same year as the first railroad construction in Chicago, but Missouri's rural interests demanded that they be served, to the financial determent of the line, and they opposed any public financing for the project. Such recalcitrance gave St. Louis an image of Southern-style complacency, of always being behind the times. The *Chicago Journal* told the story in 1854 of a Missouri man who traveled by train to Chicago for a vacation only to discover that the city's hustle and bustle was too disquieting for him. Returning to St. Louis, his sleep was disturbed again, this time by a group of noisy Chicago speculators intent on buying St. Louis as a southerly addition to Chicago.

As the balance of regional trade shifted from St. Louis to Chicago, the *Daily Democratic Press* joked about a proposal to connect the Mississippi River to Lake Michigan. "We would hate to see our neighbor city of St. Louis washed away in thirty-six hours' time," the paper predicted. The *Chicago Democrat* declared that the primary difference between the two cities was that St. Louis businessmen wore "their pantaloons out sitting and waiting for trade to come to them" while Chicago businessmen "wore their shoes out running after it." The 1854 Kansas-Nebraska Act cinched the shift, polarizing eastern businessmen in St. Louis by reminding them that they were doing business in a slave state. A Massachusetts manufacturer told the *Missouri Democrat* in 1857 that he was being denigrated as "a Yankee and abolitionist" when all he wanted to do was conduct business.[30]

St. Louis's larger population number annoyed Chicagoans. The 1860 census put St. Louis at 143,920 residents and Chicago at 112,172, even as the *Tribune* was complaining of chronic undercounting in Chicago, especially in boardinghouses during working hours, and a "somewhat imperfect" overcount in St. Louis. But it was the image of slaves unloading steamboats in St. Louis as their drowsy owners looked on that hurt it the most in the North, almost as much as the Union blockade of the Mississippi River during the Civil War, separating it from its natural trading partner of New Orleans.

In studying western railroads, the *New York Herald* noted that Chicago was a "natural depot of Western produce," while St. Louis was a tributary with "prospects less promising than those of the roads leading to Chicago." "If St. Louis had ever shown a tithe of the energy which Chicago is continually exhibiting, [railroad] cars would be daily running from this place to that," the *Iowa State Register* complained, "and it would now be receiving the vast Iowa trade which naturally belongs to it, but which Chicago has diverted away." St. Louis newspapers tried to deflect such criticisms, but with limited success. The *St. Louis Democrat* held that no matter which way a railroad ran, no matter how much Chicago expected to profit by it, "St. Louis would still rejoice at its construction," and the *Missouri Republican* cherished the hope that newer western cities such as Omaha, St. Paul, and Duluth would "set up for themselves, and no longer be regarded as the outposts of Chicago." "Judas Iscariot could be properly at home in Chicago," a St. Louis supporter wrote to a newspaper, "and would think he had at least reached his own place." "Our newspapers have no St. Louis in them," the *St. Louis Democrat* complained.[31]

Chicago's 1871 fire put a different spin on the rivalry, but passions had deepened the previous year when St. Louis again overcounted itself. St. Louis's residents took a vicarious pleasure in Chicago's fiery misfortune. The *St. Louis Times* reported that "poor people, all color and shades, and every nationality, *from Europe, China and Africa,* mad with excitement, struggled with each other to get away" from the fire. The report, an AP dispatch, added the italicized portion as a sensation not seen in any other papers, overlooking the fact that 1870s Chicago had almost no Chinese or African immigrants. "We with some public display sent money for the homeless and provisions for the hungry, and even resolutions of sympathy for the unfortunate city—all of which was of right appearances," a St. Louis resident wrote after the fire. The city's contributions were duly and gratefully noted in Chicago's post-fire newspapers.

Yet, a *Missouri Republican* editorial five days after the fire declared that Chicago should be rebuilt only with an appropriate "pay the piper" mentality. "It will be some years to come before Chicago can again be a center of opulence, luxury, and extravagance," the paper predicted, "but it will be a good place for an industrious man to go, if he desires to find profitable employment, and to grow up with its growth." "The pious spiritual ejaculation: 'Again the fire of heaven has fallen on Sodom and Gomorrah'" was a popular private saying among St. Louis's residents. "Even the richest Chicago firms are pushed so closely to the edge of precipice," the *St. Louis Republican* glowed, "that a single additional touch will plunge them into irretrievable ruin." St. Louis's newspapers created subsequent sensations when they accused Chicagoans of mishandling relief money, agreeing with the *Detroit Free Press* that Chicago had become a "beggar city." The *Missouri Republican* noted in 1872 that the date of Chicago's fire coincided with the seventh anniversary of Union Gen. Philip H. Sheridan's "Red October" burning of the Shenandoah Valley, fired in part by Illinois troops.[32]

Ironically, St. Louis's moral character had come into question the previous year when "by a curious mistake in the census of 1870, or the act of enumerators driven to unscrupulous lengths by morbid ambition in the race with rivals, about 100,000 names too many were added to the [St. Louis] list" as *Harper's Magazine* explained. The falsification—St. Louis County reported a population of 351,189 compared to Cook County's 349,966—gave St. Louis's newspapers bragging rights for another decade even though Chicago's unofficial city directory listed 100,555 family names compared to St. Louis's 71,925. "Brooklyn and St. Louis exhibit an unexpected increase," the Columbus, Georgia, *Ledger-Enquirer* noted of the census reports. The *San Francisco Bulletin* chided that "with all the noise and clatter Chicago falls behind St. Louis more than 12,000 in the enumeration."

The *Chicago Journal* reported that an unnamed visitor to St. Louis claimed that a quota of inhabitants was assigned to each city block corresponding with street numbers, adding extra population. "The Quincy [Illinois] *Whig* hits the nail squarely on the head, when it attributes the figures arrived at in the recent census in St. Louis to two facts, first, that Chicago and Cincinnati had already made up their returns, and the St. Louis [census] Marshals knew exactly what figures they must cover," the *Chicago Tribune* reported, "and secondly, that they had summoned thirty or forty thousand of the agricultural population of the rural districts into the city to attend a State Fair, and counted as many of them as were necessary to 'fill the bill.'" According to the paper, "No sane man believes the result arrived at is *true*."

Angered at what was called an "odious" numerical manipulation, Chicago's mass news media intensified its crusade against St. Louis in the 1870s. The *Lakeside Monthly* magazine likened Chicago's growing railroad network to natural transportation routes, the modern equivalents of lakes, rivers, and streams, in an obvious bid to downplay St. Louis. A *Chicago Tribune* reporter warned in late 1871 that the River City was endeavoring to acquire Chicago's trade in the wake of the fire, "but lacking the vim and go-aheaditiveness which has marked the career of Chicago," the reporter noted that chronic rail car shortages had failed to change the shipping preferences of northern Missouri and southern Iowa farmers. In their best-selling *Chicago and the Great Conflagration,* newspapermen Elias Colbert and Everett Chamberlin published a table of railroad mileage in nine western states, including Missouri, with the observation that "almost every mile of which is a tributary to Chicago." Identifying St. Louis as a smallpox hotspot, the *Tribune* claimed that "Chicago has enjoyed the best record as to small-pox of any large city in the Union, and promises to maintain the same through the present flurry" even as it was experiencing a devastating post-fire cholera outbreak. "So matters have gone on from one thing to another," the Little Rock, Arkansas, *Morning Republican* summarized of the deepening competition, "somewhat in the spirit of the boy revenged himself upon his bigger rival by making faces at his sister."[33]

The rivalry reached its peak in the immediate years before the date of the 1880 census. "Ask a St. Louis man about Chicago, and he will admit there is such a place in Illinois," the Connecticut *Daily Constitution* wrote, "but will add, it is all mortgaged to Boston." "If authorities don't suppress the Chicago directory man," the *St. Louis Globe-Democrat* wrote in 1874, "he'll have as many people in Chicago as there are frogs in the Chicago River." "Important to St. Louis," the *St. Louis Globe-Democrat* headlined in 1875, "Chicago Wide Awake." "And St. Louis has only just now awakened to a realization of it?" the *Inter Ocean* responded. Writing to a national *Scribner's Monthly* audience, *Tribune* editor James W. Sheahan reported that Chicago's 1875 population had been calculated at 420,000, well ahead of St. Louis's.

The *Chicago Tribune* reprinted a 1875 article by a French visitor to Chicago and St. Louis predicting that Chicago's population would top one million in ten years, but "there is no use in saying what the population of such a city may be." "You must know that to get out a [city] directory is a dangerous business," a *Tribune* letter writer explained of St. Louis in 1878. "Few publishers can hit the happy medium and know where to draw the line between a population sufficiently large enough to beat that of Chicago and yet not so extravagantly large as to carry its contradictions on its own face." The *Tribune* wrote of another St. Louis city directory that "like most works of fiction, it is pleasant reading." "Wicked St. Louis," the *Inter Ocean* complained in a 1878 article reporting that women carried Southern-style stilettos for self-protection in the city. "Possibly the half has not been told us." "If poverty gives enterprise, spirit, and business activity, Chicago is poor," the *Inter Ocean* wrote in 1879, "and St. Louis is—well she is not like Chicago, and she is welcome to all that sort of 'richness' that produces business stagnation." The inhabitants of Chicago were using more water, the *New York Times* reported in 1879. "Envious St. Louis will say that the extra gallons have gone into the whisky which Chicago's enervated citizens can no longer drink 'straight.'"[34]

Chicagoans literally danced in the streets in early July 1880 when the census finally proved them victors, with an officially enumerated population of 503,298 just forty-three years after becoming a city. "The report that St. Louis has only 375,000 inhabitants sets everybody crazy, and the cry of sham and fraud is immediately raised," the *St. Louis Post-Dispatch* observed of what was called the "census infamy." "The census enumerators of Chicago are still at the melancholy task of copying names off the graveyard tombstones," the *St. Louis Republican* charged. "The hotel registers and ancient directories were exhausted very early in the action." "The wild romance of arithmetic known as the Chicago census should be dramatized," the *St. Louis Globe-Democrat* declared.

But as the totals were calculated, the *St. Louis Post-Dispatch* was forced to admit that "there is no longer the slightest doubt that Chicago will have at least 150,000 more people than St. Louis." Wiser to the game than they had been in 1870, Chicagoans waited for St. Louis to release its number first before divulging theirs. On July 2, 1870, the *Times* teased that "it is remarked that in a general way, the cities on the lakes like Buffalo, Cleveland, Milwaukee, and Chicago, grow much faster than those on the great rivers adjacent to the southern territory. The path of empire follows a cool climate." "Say 'youens, down thar' in St. Louis," the *Chicago Journal* gushed. "Chicago is now the fourth city in the Union. D'ye hear? First comes New York, then Philadelphia, then Brooklyn, then Chicago, and then—St. Louis. Chicago 495,000—St. Louis 375,000. Oh! ah! aha!"

There were a host of reasons for Chicago's ultimate success, but one overlooked factor was that postbellum St. Louis voluntarily limited its physical size, stifling population growth. In 1876, St. Louis City seceded from its county and established a 61.37-square-mile area in an effort to avoid paying county property taxes, ending any chance of suburban annexations and creating a noose around itself much like Manhattan Island did to New York City. In contrast, Chicago's aggressive annexation of its suburbs (especially during the 1880s and early 1890s) created a city of 185 square miles by 1893 and kept it vital until the 1898 New York City consolidation. Chicago met a similar fate as St. Louis when, in the early twentieth century, home-rule suburbs stopped it from further annexations, thus preventing it from ever catching up to New York. Even after construction of the famed Gateway Arch in 1965, a bit of nostalgia more fitting for Chicago given its greater role in the development of the West, a St. Louis academic told the *Chicago Tribune* that secession "was the most fateful and wrong decision. To be forever frozen by the boundaries left [St. Louis] too small for real growth."[35]

News of Chicago's victory spread quickly. "Chicago has been making a tremendous struggle to outdo other ambitious cities," the *Wisconsin State Journal* reported, "and with her press consistently urging the inhabitants to be sure and see to it that none of their names be left out by the enumerators." "Chicago at Last Foots Up Her Half a Million," the *Philadelphia Inquirer* noted while the *San Francisco Bulletin* headlined its story on Chicago's victory simply "The Fourth City." The *Idaho Statesman* observed that Chicago's population was ahead of St. Louis's because "St. Louis . . . enumerators were so indiscreet as to publish their figures first," while the *Idaho Avalanche* reported that the census superintendent was right when "saying that the trouble in St. Louis and some other places, is that there are not as many people as had been supposed." Only when Chicago's victory was a certainty did the *Chicago Tribune* pronounce that "this time Chicago . . . ranks as the fourth city in the Union and the FIRST IN THE INTERIOR."[36]

* * *

In the aftermath of Chicago's victory in its angry contest with St. Louis, rational minds struggled to make sense of the accomplishment. For instance, the Duluth *Lake Superior News* reasoned that "the jam and rush are more intense. The rich are richer and the poor poorer. The struggle for life is more difficult" in a larger Chicago, so why bother? But with St. Louis safely behind them, Chicagoans ignored such naysayers and girded themselves for their next challenge. One of Chicago's earliest boosters, magazinist John S. Wright, had predicted before his death in 1874 that the city's population would top one million by 1885, and the Chicago Building and Loan Association optimistically asserted in 1869 that Chicago's 1890 population would number 10,936,540. The only late-nineteenth-century American city that could aspire to such dream numbers was the same city Franc Wilkie satirized as part of a fictional conversation in an 1881 *Chicago Times* "Walk About Chicago" column:

> "Where is Chicago? Is it near New York?"
>
> "Yes, it is near New York; that is to say, too near for the comfort of New York."
>
> "I beg pardon!"
>
> "What I mean is, that Chicago, although a thousand miles from New York, is still so near that city that the trade of New York is gradually dropping off, its streets are becoming pasturage for stray cows and pigs, and the most of its once happy residents have become paupers. Why, they take up a collection every Sabbath in the churches of [Chicago] for the poor of New York, those who have been made paupers owing to the rivalry with Chicago."

"Whatever else Chicago may do, she will never be behind," the *Chicago Tribune* had written in 1871. Late-nineteenth-century Chicagoans radiated in such manifestations of their self-importantness. With requisite encouragement from the mass news media, they believed they were on a collision course with destiny. Before that could occur however, Chicago had to deal with some of its own demons, not the least of which were "incendiaries scattering the seeds of conflagrations in our alleys" as the *Tribune* described them.[37]

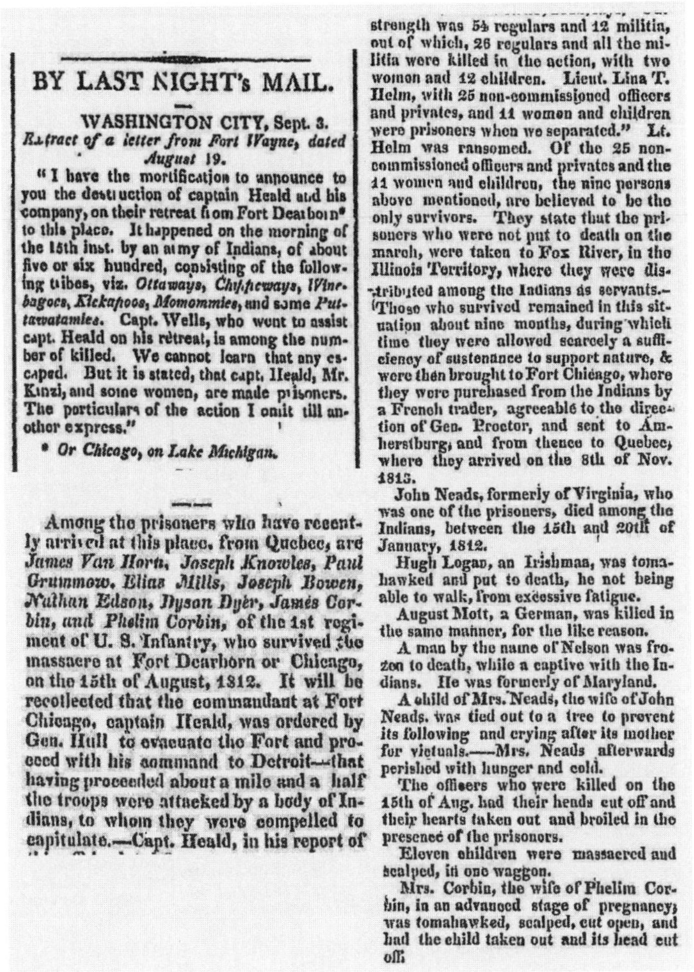

BY LAST NIGHT's MAIL.

WASHINGTON CITY, Sept. 3.

Extract of a letter from Fort Wayne, dated August 19.

"I have the mortification to announce to you the destruction of captain Heald and his company, on their retreat from Fort Dearborn* to this place. It happened on the morning of the 15th inst. by an army of Indians, of about five or six hundred, consisting of the following tribes, viz. *Ottaways, Chippeways, Winebagoes, Kickapoos, Momommies,* and some *Puttawatamies.* Capt. Wells, who went to assist capt. Heald on his retreat, is among the number of killed. We cannot learn that any escaped. But it is stated, that capt. Heald, Mr. Kinzi, and some women, are made prisoners. The particulars of the action I omit till another express."

* *Or Chicago, on Lake Michigan.*

Among the prisoners who have recently arrived at this place, from Quebec, are *James Van Horn, Joseph Knowles, Paul Grummow, Elias Mills, Joseph Bowen, Nathan Edson, Dyson Dyer, James Corbin, and Phelim Corbin,* of the 1st regiment of U. S. Infantry, who survived the massacre at Fort Dearborn or Chicago, on the 15th of August, 1812. It will be recollected that the commandant at Fort Chicago, captain Heald, was ordered by Gen. Hull to evacuate the Fort and proceed with his command to Detroit—that having proceeded about a mile and a half the troops were attacked by a body of Indians, to whom they were compelled to capitulate.—Capt. Heald, in his report of ... strength was 54 regulars and 12 militia, out of which, 26 regulars and all the militia were killed in the action, with two women and 12 children. Lieut. Lina T. Helm, with 25 non-commissioned officers and privates, and 11 women and children were prisoners when we separated." Lt. Helm was ransomed. Of the 25 non-commissioned officers and privates and the 11 women and children, the nine persons above mentioned, are believed to be the only survivors. They state that the prisoners who were not put to death on the march, were taken to Fox River, in the Illinois Territory, where they were distributed among the Indians as servants.—Those who survived remained in this situation about nine months, during which time they were allowed scarcely a sufficiency of sustenance to support nature, & were then brought to Fort Chicago, where they were purchased from the Indians by a French trader, agreeable to the direction of Gen. Proctor, and sent to Amherstburg, and from thence to Quebec, where they arrived on the 8th of Nov. 1813.

John Neads, formerly of Virginia, who was one of the prisoners, died among the Indians, between the 15th and 20th of January, 1812.

Hugh Logan, an Irishman, was tomahawked and put to death, he not being able to walk, from excessive fatigue.

August Mott, a German, was killed in the same manner, for the like reason.

A man by the name of Nelson was frozen to death, while a captive with the Indians. He was formerly of Maryland.

A child of Mrs. Neads, the wife of John Neads, was tied out to a tree to prevent its following and crying after its mother for victuals.——Mrs. Neads afterwards perished with hunger and cold.

The officers who were killed on the 15th of Aug. had their heads cut off and their hearts taken out and broiled in the presence of the prisoners.

Eleven children were massacred and scalped, in one waggon.

Mrs. Corbin, the wife of Phelim Corbin, in an advanced stage of pregnancy, was tomahawked, scalped, cut open, and had the child taken out and its head cut off.

Top left: The first published account of the 1812 Chicago massacre, in an Alexandria, Virginia, newspaper, which helped to instigate the "Remember Chicago" battle cry used during the War of 1812. The remainder is the first survivor account of the massacre as published in a Plattsburgh, New York, newspaper two years later. The two articles, republished in other newspapers, were the first references to Chicago for many eastern readers.

extended this communication much further then I originally intended, I shall, therefore, only add, that it is confidently hoped Congress will give to the subject all the consideration its importance merits.

With great respect, I remain
Your most ob't serv't.
WM. L. MAY.

CHICAGO DEMOCRAT.

We regret to learn, that a man was found frozen to death, during the intense cold weather of last week, on the prairie between this place and Blue Island. He was in all probability devoured by wolves, as a few mangled remains of the body and some remnents of clothing was found at the place where he is supposed to have fallen.

There is a rumor afloat that a woman residing near Blue Island was also frozen to death, last week on the same prarie, while on her way home from this place. We trust it is without foundation.

No one is more gratified than ourselves, in witnessing the increasing prosperity of the West. Not a building is enclosed, but it adds to the high expectations we have already formed of the future destiny, power and resources of this section of our country. Sanguine as we are in our calculations of the wealth, industry and enterprise that will soon be the distinguishing features of our own town of Chicago, we are

The first breaking news to be published in a Chicago newspaper, sandwiched between numerous booster articles, attesting to the difficulty of life in the early settlement. The woman referred to in the second paragraph did freeze to death, as was reported in the following week's issue.

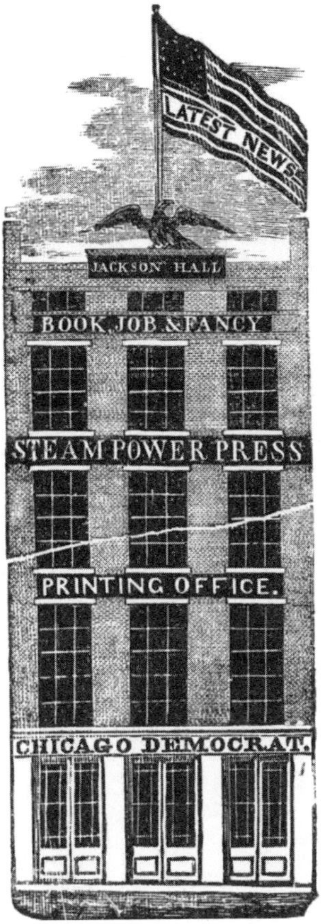

Constructed in 1847, Jackson Hall was Chicago's first building made exclusively to house a newspaper. The *Democrat*'s steam-powered press increased literacy by reducing the cost of printing. With the introduction of the telegraph into the city the following year, it also influenced journalists to turn to local news gathering rather than political partisanship in their papers.

A FLURRY IN WHEAT.

Chicago futures traders as pictured in *Harper's New Monthly Magazine*. "There is nothing to be heard among the crowd but 'No. 1 Red,' 'Standard,' 'My option all next week,'" the *Chicago Tribune* wrote of the traders.

The *Chicago Tribune* building as rebuilt after the 1871 fire, located at the southern edge of the city's newspaper district. Situated at the corner of Dearborn and Monroe streets on property leased from the Board of Education, the rent was said to "cheat the schools," evidence of the paper's importance to the city.

PROTECTION AGAINST TRAMPS.

A suburban correspondent wants THE TRIBUNE to inform its readers in the outlying districts how to get rid of tramps, some of whom, the writer says, are still prowling around, barefooted and ragged, begging for one thing and another, and stealing what they can lay their hands on. The correspondent believes that the law which went into effect on the 1st inst., on the subject of vagabonds, will give him some relief, and asks to be informed just what consolation he can get from that source. This law, concerning which he asks, makes it the duty of the Constables or police to arrest all [illegible] sentenced to a long term in [illegible] jail, calaboose, or other building.

The law, while an improvement on the old one, is not of much use for suburban districts, where officers are scarce and Justices of the Peace hard to find. The simplest plan probably, where one is not a member of the Humane Society, is to put a little strychnine or arsenic in the meat and other supplies furnished the tramp. This produces death within a comparatively short period of time, is a warning to other tramps to keep out of the neighborhood, puts the Coroner in good humor, and saves one's chickens and other portable property from constant depredation.

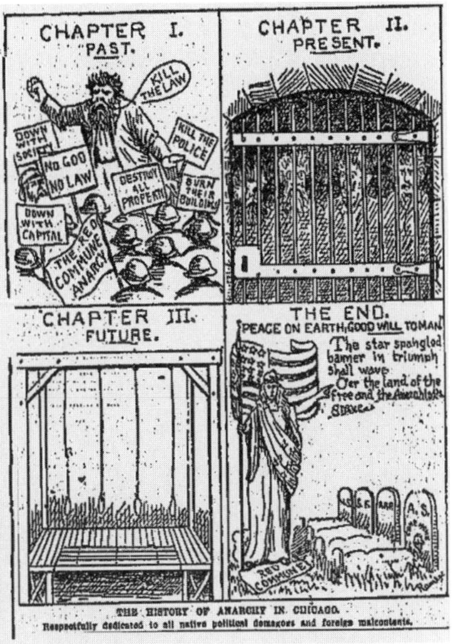

Left: This condensed *Chicago Tribune* clipping instructed readers on how to poison unemployed and homeless immigrant "tramps," published days before the 1877 railroad strike. Right: A *Tribune* editorial cartoon, with images and grave markers of the Haymarket Square defendants, which appeared just before jury selection in 1886. Both clippings were used by the Haymarket defendants as proof of "anarchism" in the city's mass news media.

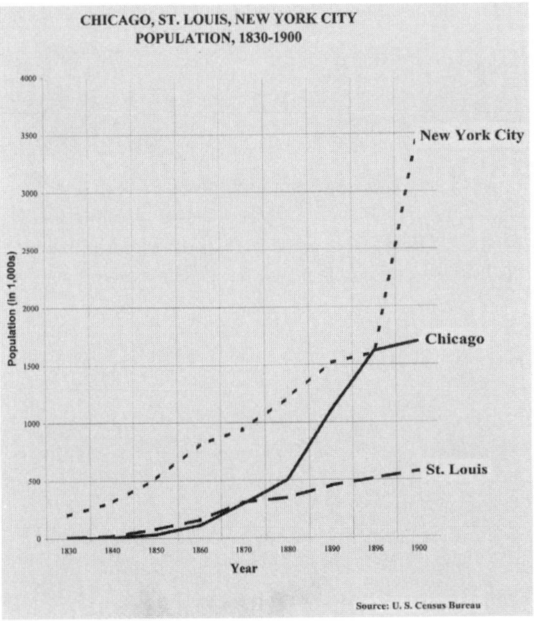

The 1898 New York consolidation nearly doubled the city's population overnight, going from a virtual tie with Chicago. Without the consolidation, Chicago would have likely surpassed New York in the 1900 census.

A goddess-like figure representing Chicago and welcoming refugees from the "dark city" to the 1893 World's Fair "white city" as depicted in *Puck*, a magazine edited and published at the fair. The insert right is a detail from another *Puck* drawing satirizing the popularity among men of the "Streets of Cairo" Midway belly dancing exhibit.

Top left: A newspaper drawing of Michael "Hinky Dink" Kenna's saloon in 1894, including its notorious second-story flophouse. The remainder is an 1897 *Chicago Tribune* representation of what downtown Chicago would look like one hundred years in the future, once again the nation's First City. The streets in front of the sixty-story skyscraper (which vaguely resembles the Empire State Building) were filled with commuters from the city's pneumatic subway system without benefit of horses or vehicular transportation.

A postcard produced a decade after the Greater New York consolidation to extol the pedestrian congestion of downtown Chicago. The former Marshall Field clock, located above the corner of State and Washington streets, was installed in 1897 as a meeting place for shoppers and made famous in a 1945 Norman Rockwell magazine cover.

4

Chicago Radicalism, Nineteenth-Century Style

The Haymarket Square bombing, the first major domestic bombing in American history, touched the lives of many Chicagoans, but none more intimately than one Nina Van Zandt. Born of affluent Yankee parents, Van Zandt was one of Chicago's earliest young socialites. An attractive woman, she was a graduate of Vassar College who played music, was well traveled, spoke French, German, and Italian, and stood to inherit a goodly fortune. *New York World* reporter Charles Edward Russell described her as "slenderly fashioned, handsome, always exquisitely gowned," and *Chicago Daily News* newspaperman Charles H. Dennis considered her "intensely romantic, self-willed and adventurous." The twenty-four-year-old Van Zandt attended the Haymarket legal proceedings during the summer of 1886. "I wanted to see the men who are on trial," she wrote, attracted by the prejudiced newspaper coverage of the event. "I thought they must be brutal and savage-looking. But I was astonished to see how mild-appearing they were."[1]

She quickly fell for the romantic, blond-haired *Chicagoer Arbeiter Zeitung* editor August Spies, one of the eight defendants, who found "Miss Nina" an attentive listener as they conversed in German in his jail cell. With the cooperation of the Cook County civil court, Van Zandt and Spies were married *in absentia* on January 29, 1887. "Nina Van Zandt, the mad bride of an anarchist was successful at last to become last Sunday evening the lawful wife of August Spies by proxy," the *Illinois Staats Zeitung* reported. "The 'dignified' ceremony was performed by the anarchist sympathizer Judge Engelhardt, at which Henry W. Spies acted as proxy for August Spies, his brother."

The new Mrs. Van Zandt-Spies joined with her sister-in-law Gretchen and Lucy Parsons, the wife of fellow newspaperman and defendant Albert Parsons, writing and publishing instant biographies of their loved ones to raise funds for a new trial. On the day that Spies was hanged in November 1887, Van Zandt-Spies was turned away from the proceedings and secluded herself in her near North Side home, displaying a draped picture of her husband in the front window. She carried the Spies name with her for most of the rest of her life, even after she remarried and divorced an Italian magazine editor. When she died in 1936, the erstwhile socialite left an estate of $3,000 to eight dogs and a cat and was buried in Forest Home Cemetery near the husband she barely knew.[2]

Many Chicagoans expressed concerns of a similar bandwagon or third-person effect on other equally unsophisticated individuals they knew in connection with the bombing and the radicalism that inspired it, although none as dramatically as Van Zandt-Spies's transformation. "Violent speeches have been made on the lake front to small squads of listeners, and the next morning the newspapers, for the purpose of selling papers, have spread broadcast over the land the utterances of these nihilists and law-breakers," Mayor Carter Harrison Sr. charged in 1886. Improvements made the mass transmission of such persuasive information more efficient, setting rather than following public opinion in controversies such as Haymarket. "Socialism in American is an anomaly, and Chicago is the last place on the continent it would exist were it not for the dregs of foreign immigration which find lodgement here," the *Daily News* warned in early 1886. No one—least of all the newspapers—knew for certain what hysteria a mass news medium like a daily urban newspaper could inspire, at least not until Haymarket. As *Inter Ocean* editor William Penn Nixon lamented eleven years after the event, "The Haymarket square massacre was the direct result of too much newspaper."[3]

New Mass News Media Technology

Several important changes occurred in Chicago's mass news media during the mid to late nineteenth century. The most noticeable was a growing number of titles. Four mass circulation English-language dailies and one foreign daily in 1870 grew to eight English and five foreign language dailies around 1880, and to a dozen English and more than a dozen foreign language papers by 1890. Titles such as the *Arbeiter Zeitung, Chronicle, Daily News, Die Fackel, Globe, Evening Mail, Evening Post, Herald, Record, Staats Zeitung, Telegraph,* and *Times,* along with the Western News Company (the city's largest newspaper distribution agency), most of the city's wire service offices, and the Chicago Press Club, were located in an area bounded by Randolph, Franklin, Madison, and Clark streets. A secondary media district developed along the southeastern edge of the downtown, centered around Dearborn and Madison streets, that included the *Chicago Journal,* the city's oldest daily; the *Inter Ocean,* known for its clock-tower building; and the *Tribune,* which had been moved to property leased at a bargain basement price for ninety-nine years courtesy of the property owner, the Chicago Board of Education.

As well, the number of pages per issue increased dramatically. Before 1867, Chicago papers were generally four pages long, the most that flatbed and early cylinder printing presses could produce. Moving the flat-type forms onto spinning cylinders, a process called stereotyping, accelerated printing speed. The *Tribune* and the other Chicago papers invested in large multiple-deck cylinder presses after the Civil War that could produce as many as 20,000 impressions per hour. The morning papers, including the *Times,* which relocated to the corner of Washington and Fifth Avenue (now Wells), belched their products into the waiting hands of drivers and distributors gathered behind their building in what was known as "newsboys" alley. With gas and eventually electric lighting, Chicago's late-nineteenth-century newspaper buildings were some of the few places in the city where darkness never got "an inning," as one observer put it. "The great half-cylinder shaped rolls of lead laden with news" would spin and produce 80,000 pages per hour of what "all Chicagoans and thousands upon thousands throughout the Northwest know and like so well." "As the weary [press] workmen step out of the office, they find the building environed by newsboys, eagerly watching for the first copies from the press." Half a day later, the afternoon papers repeated the process, so that newsboys could again "grub our hash sellin' papers," as one put it.[4]

Less obvious was an increasing competition between the growing number of papers. "Scoops," breaking news stories that no other paper had, evolved from accidents to common occurrences during the latter 1860s and 1870s. The afternoon *Chicago Daily News,* which first appeared in late 1875, exploited scoops, updating sports and other breaking day stories in as many as five hourly editions by 1880. Scooping increased with the implementation of the local telegraph and telephone in Chicago. "The Cincinnati *Enquirer* wants to know if the telephone is going to be of any service when a man wants to tellephony story," the *Chicago Tribune* joked in 1877, but it lined up with the other Chicago newspapers when phone lines were first installed in 1879. "The imagination is free to count up what will be the result when a man in Chicago can go to his telephone and call up by a simple 'hello' any person he wishes," the *Tribune* reported. A 1882 *Tribune* letter writer suggested that Chicago be renamed the "garden and mast or forest city" for the growing number of utility poles that were popping up along streets to hold a growing number of telegraph, telephone, and electric lines, suggesting that "the pole companies might be required . . . to nail evergreens and boughs to the poles in order to adorn and beautify the same."[5]

With the increasing content competition, publishers began casting about in search of new revenue sources to meet added expenses. In a sense, newspaper advertising was an indirect result of Long John Wentworth's June 1857 good government raid to clear downtown Chicago streets of hanging signs and sidewalk impediments. As Colin Cherry documented in 1860s London, increasing regulations forced paper "bill-stickers" and similar outdoor advertisers to concentrate their announcements in centralized locations where they could be seen together. Newspaper advertising was a natural progression of that practice. In 1854, Charles Woollett's Northwestern Advertising Agency was the first in Chicago to buy newspaper space wholesale and resell it to individual clients.

Chicago became a regional advertising center in the 1860s as agents moved from wholesaling newspaper space to providing more comprehensive services to publications and advertisers. In the wake of the 1871 fire, mail order retailer Aaron Montgomery Ward began producing illustrated advertising, and within a decade his catalogs had more than 280 pages of copy with 10,000 illustrations with enticing rather than simple descriptive copy. Ward was joined in the mail order business by Richard W. Sears, who began producing his illustrated mail order catalogs in 1887. The first full-page display advertising to appear in a Chicago newspaper, an ad for the Chapin and Gore restaurant, was published in the *Times* in 1875. Within the decade, most of Chicago's larger department stores and other retailers had in-house advertising managers who set and illustrated partial and full-page newspaper display ads.

Advertising was considered a form of gambling by many late-nineteenth-century Chicago businessmen; firms who advertised were downgraded by bankers and investors, considered at the verge of bankruptcy. Nevertheless, "Chicago is the greatest advertising city in the world," the *Tribune* boasted in 1890, noting that "an advertising expert ranks as an artist and commands a corresponding salary." As advertising revenues flowed into newspapers, editors and reporters were freed from the tyranny of obeying the political partisanship of subscribers. In turn, as growing numbers of shoppers flocked to Chicago's "Loop," a term for its central shopping and business district that first appeared in Chicago's papers in 1882, department stores needed the newspapers to support and build their businesses. To meet their demand for greater circulations, newspapers sought to provide more mainstream content. Details of foreign political radicalism and the events that led up to the 1886 Haymarket Square bombing sold more papers to English-language readers.[6]

Chicago's Working Class

Chicago's first middle class had little to fear from nihilism, communism, radicalism, or even socialism because the gospel of success, to which all espoused, ruled the city. In contrast to Europe, early Chicago had an abundance of natural resources and a shortage of human labor, ordaining higher wages and better working conditions for laborers. Industrialization, especially new production techniques, helped compensate for some of the shortages of human capital and skills, but the city suffered periodic labor shortages until the mid-1840s. Famine Irish and "Forty-eighters," well-educated Germans escaping persecution for democratic political radicalism in their home provinces, created the city's first labor surplus by the end of the decade.

To produce a growing number of newspapers and other publications, large numbers of printers and typographers were attracted to Chicago, and they formed the city's first trade union in 1850. In turn, Chicago's first nationally recognized union, Typographical Union Local 16, was chartered in 1852 and boasted nearly 150 members by 1860. The 1857 recession eliminated the jobs of many skilled tradesmen, including wagonmakers, carpenters, tailors, and printers, as numerous Chicago businesses went bankrupt or were forced to merge, including the *Daily Democratic Press* and the *Tribune*. Between 1855 and 1857, German workingmen formed the Chicagoer Arbeitor Verein (Chicago Workers Organization) in response to the weakening economy and Know-Nothing political movement. The Arbeitor Verein became the most powerful immigrant organization in the city; by 1865 it had more than one thousand members. It was the center of political radicalism in the city and included Germans, Scandinavians, Poles, and even a few Frenchmen. "These men are not yet educated up to the ideas of Socialists, and joined [the organization] for no other purpose than to secure bread for their starving families," a briefly supportive *Chicago Tribune* wrote in 1873. Beyond organizations, Chicago was a popular site for national labor conventions during the 1860s. Among the groups that met in the Garden City were printers, cigarmakers, bricklayers, and general organizations such as the National Labor Union and the National Labor Congress.[7]

Rampant inflation made it difficult for many of Chicago's skilled workers to support their families or even themselves during the Civil War, but unionization efforts were stymied when thousands of wage workers left to join the Northern armies. The Chicago General Trades Assembly was organized in 1864 to address declining real wages and spending power, comprising twenty-four local and national unions from around the city. Although there is anecdotal evidence of small strikes within individual industries such as printing before 1850, the Trades Assembly was influenced by a series of strikes against the railroads and the McCormick Reaper Works around the time of the war. The success of the strikes made iron molders Chicago's preeminent labor union during the decade. President William H. Sylvis hosted his union's first national convention in Chicago in 1865, criticizing employers for taking advantage of the war emergency. "What would it profit us, as a nation, if the greasy mechanics and horny-handed sons of toil became slaves themselves?" he asked.[8]

The *Chicago Times* was the object of the next organized labor action in the city. Chicago's earliest newspapers typically had good relationships with their printing employees, better than with their more easily replaceable editorial staff members. *Democrat* founder John Calhoun, *Tribune* business manager Joseph Medill, and the *Times*'s Wilbur F. Storey were only three of several mass news media employers who had learned typesetting and printing as youths. However, Storey had fought unionization at his *Detroit Free Press* before moving to Chicago in 1861 and considered unions a form of "obnoxious despotism," especially when his typesetters argued that they should be paid for an average amount of daily work rather than by piecemeal rates. In his editorials and related pronouncements, Storey labeled union typesetters and printers "rats" and "vermin," and he routinely fired employees who joined the local typographical union.[9]

His intransigence forced Local 16, which represented about one-third of the printing room employees in the city, to strike the *Times* in April 1864. Storey was angered at first, but within days he appeared to relent and allowed other employees to join the union. Unknown at the time however, he had set up a carbon copy of his composing room in an empty building on Randolph Street and hired forty women to learn typography. On September 9, Storey marched his female army to the *Times* and locked his union men out. "A dispatch from Chicago says the movement caused great sensation among the printers," the *Macon* (Georgia) *Weekly Telegraph* reported. The Chicago General Trades Assembly called a mass demonstration for the following evening at Courthouse Square, where Storey was denounced as "a traitor to his country, to his God, and to the workingmen of Chicago." A resolution condemning the use of women as "instruments of a base plot . . . to overthrow and crush the manly independence and dignity of labor" was approved, as was a call to the local Democratic Party, generally supported by the *Times*, to repudiate the paper for its anti-labor actions or "stand in danger of losing both prestige and support with the masses of laboring men."

The other papers, all members of a short-lived, loosely organized trade group called the Northwestern Publishers' Association, tacitly supported the *Times* by refusing to print anything about the strike. "Legitimately conducted, the Trades Assembly may become a powerful engine to accomplish the purposes to which it was organized," the *Tribune* editorialized. In one of its earliest issues, the *Workingman's Advocate* wrote of the *Tribune*, "Oh! You hypocritical, unprincipled and lying sheet, how you blister your lips with the lying declaration that you are the friend of the Labor cause." Ultimately, as Storey recounted, his women refused to consider themselves as anything other than temporary workers, being more interested in searching for "a husband in the future" than in having a career, and were not up to working grueling all-night shifts in a chemical-filled, poorly ventilated composing room. Additionally, Storey paid them only $5 per week, about two-thirds that of his striking men. As Storey could, they were replaced by nonunion typographers who drifted into the city; the strike ended with workers repudiating their union.[10]

Three years later, Chicago laborers tried to force employers to adopt an eight-hour workday. From fifteen or more hours per day in the city's earliest years, Chicagoans had settled on a ten-hour, six-day work week by the time of the Civil War with the exception of typesetters, who won a concession of a nine-hour rather than a ten-hour Saturday. Workers pointed to the eight-hour day as a means of improving their social and intellectual well-being and efficiency, while employers held that ten hours' pay for eight hours' work would increase the cost of living and consumer prices as well as cut into their profits. In 1865, a loosely organized group called the Eight-Hour League successfully lobbied the city council for an ordinance mandating a reduced workday. "The real object of this movement is to force employers to pay a whole day's wages for four-fifths of a day's work," the *Tribune* complained. The state legislature enacted a similar provision in 1866, but neither law mandated an eight-hour day or provided that workers doing eight hours of work should be paid the same as those doing ten hours. As a result, both laws were largely ignored by employers.

Beginning a practice of May Day marches that would become international in 1889, thousands of workers representing forty-four trade unions marched through Chicago in a "grand civic procession" on May 1, 1867, to press for better enforcement of the new laws. "A very deep feeling pervades the entire community . . . in reference to the eight-hour system of labor," a Chicago correspondent told the *Daily Iowa State Register* the day before the march. "The programme of the celebration included a procession of the various trade-Unions through the principal streets of each division of the city," the *Tribune* reported, "involving a fatiguing march of fully 7½ miles, being in itself a good day's work." Speeches were made in both English and German. "A man can do as much work in eight, or even six hours of skilled labor, cheerfully rendered and intelligently applied, as he does (mark the word, *does*) now in ten hours as at present rendered and applied," a letter writer named "Mechanic" told the *Tribune*. "It is not always an easy thing for labor to ascertain what proportion of the capital properly belongs to the labor fund," the *Tribune* replied.[11]

The unions called a general strike for the following day, and the newly founded *Chicago Republican* joined in the effort to force the hand of non-compliant employers. "The day for starting new dailies in American cities, we regard as practically past," the *Tribune* had written in 1860. But the *Republican*, founded on an investment of $500,000 to counter a perceived wavering in the *Tribune* of Radical Republican ideology that included worker rights, argued that "on [the workers'] side a kind of capital is invested which employers ought not to seek to control, viz., the souls of men." Gangs of mainly Irish and German youths and men fanned out across the city's North Side and Bridgeport sections, setting fire to buildings and confronting the police, who were armed only with hickory clubs. "On [May 2nd] the workmen of Chicago to the number of several hundred, visited various factories, lumber yards, shops, [grain] elevators, etc., and compelled them to close," the *New Hampshire Sentinel* reported. "It was the voice of the slave power," the *Tribune* wrote using a metaphor applied by both sides in the controversy, "crying out, 'you shall work only when, where and on such terms as we dictate.'"

An unknown number of workers were injured or jailed by the end of the strike's first day. Noting that "a good many of the 'strikers' in this city behaved badly, yesterday," the *Times* predicted that continued labor agitation would "bring an influx of mechanics [workers] from other places. Probably there never were so many mechanics in Chicago, of all kinds, as there are at this time." The following day, the paper noted, "A large majority of the workingmen of the city express themselves ready to go to work, and they would if not prevented by intimidation."

A nearly total cessation of labor was not the desire of the "great majority of workmen" the *Tribune* wrote. "It was rather the work of a few lawless ones who formed in mobs, and, visiting the different workshops, drove out those who were peacefully following their avocations." "Shall mobs rule Chicago?" Wilbur Storey demanded, employing rhetoric that the radical press would be criticized for two decades hence. "If rioters are to rule Chicago, law-abiding citizens must leave it. If the city and its prosperity are not to be destroyed, the rioters must be put down. In such an emergency, the shortest way is always the best."

The *Memphis Daily Avalanche* observed that Chicago's workingmen had lost face by rioting, and the *New York Sun* wrote, "It is unfortunate . . . that a spirit of opposition has been aroused between the two classes." Many of the striking workers were replaced and those who had won shorter workdays found their wages reduced proportionally. Workers who typically made less than $10 per week lost an estimated $125,000 in real wages among them. "Such crude notions of social and political economy as these may provoke a smile upon the faces of intelligent men," the *Times* wrote, and the paper blamed the *Republican* for inflaming the strike. "What businessman reads the *Chicago Republican?*" the *Times* demanded. It would take Chicago's unions and working men another twenty years to rekindle the needed momentum for an eight-hour workday. The *Republican* would be reborn, in a sense, in 1872 as the *Chicago Inter Ocean,* certainly the most appropriately named Chicago newspaper.[12]

Wilbur F. Storey's intransigence against his employees was the inspiration for Chicago's first labor newspaper, the weekly *Workingman's Advocate.* Named after a pioneering antebellum New York labor paper, a group of disgruntled *Times* employees led by Andrew Carr Cameron started the *Advocate* during their 1864 strike. The son of a Scottish printer, Cameron emigrated to Chicago in 1851 and eventually found work as a *Times'* printer. Because Cameron was a Scotsman, the *Advocate* was printed in English. A German-language supplement was attempted in 1864 but failed to generate enough readers or revenue. Cameron was a Chartist, an adherent of the first mass working class movement in world history, but he refused to embrace newer and more foreign ideologies such as socialism or Marxism that arrived with subsequent German, Bohemian, and other immigrants.

Rather than radical political and economic change, the *Advocate* championed universal male suffrage and the eight-hour workday, noting in 1866 that "it is a fact not to be denied, that the American is the hardest working quadruped in the world." Cameron was involved intimately in the 1867 May Day rally and strike, but its subsequent failure disheartened him toward the use of violence as a tool for social change. "The country is ripe for such a [mass] movement," he wrote in 1866, "[but] the chicanery and corruption of professional politicians have convinced the great masses of workingmen, that no dependence can be placed on their profession, and that it is about time [workers] were beginning to think and act for themselves." When the *Times* asserted that all men wish someday to become capitalists, the *Advocate* responded that the era of pure entrepreneurial opportunity was already over in mid-nineteenth-century Chicago. "No, the workingmen do not expect to become capitalists themselves," Cameron wrote. "You might as well encourage the laborer with the hope that he might one day become president of the United States because Lincoln was a forester and a boatman."

The *Advocate* achieved an estimated circulation of 3,500 during the 1870s, but a large portion of its readership included women interested in serialized weekly fiction, "replete with thrilling incidents, telling points and illustrations in the life of a workingman." The paper crusaded for an end to the convict labor system in Illinois, in which prisoners were forced to perform backbreaking labor without compensation. It endorsed pro-labor candidates in both local and state elections but became increasingly more out of step when growing numbers of foreign-born workers began entering Chicago's labor system during the 1870s. It lashed out at the English-language dailies for misleading the working class with "falsehood, ridicule and misrepresentation . . . to intimidate the doubting and mislead the public mind." "Why is it that we see men and women asking vainly for work when work is the only support of the community?" Cameron asked during the 1873 Bread Riot. "Why is it we see men and women asking for bread, hungry, starving, in the midst of plenty?" The *Advocate* ceased publication in 1879, oblivious in the end to the growing radicalization of labor in the city. It even accepted advertising in its final years from one of the Gilded Age Chicago workingman's greatest antagonists, department store magnate Marshall Field.[13]

Bread Riots and Mayor Medill

As the ashes of the 1871 Great Fire cooled, Chicago's surviving working class members were reminded of where they truly stood within the city's social and economic structure. The *Times* had observed in 1867 that the streets of Chicago were the only place where all classes met on one universal level. "It is not uncommon to see the courtezan sandwiched between high-toned ladies of the patrician order, and the pious clergyman jostled by profligates and thieves," the paper wrote. "Society places a wall as high as heaven between them in every place except on the street." As flames devoured the city, all of the classes briefly found themselves homeless. Survivor accounts attested to a camaraderie that briefly flourished, or as *Tribune* editor Horace White put it, "the poor helped the rich, and the rich helped the poor."

But reconstruction quickly renewed and even strengthened Chicago's preexisting social order, and indigent immigrants were forced to relocate to cities such as St. Louis, Milwaukee, and Cincinnati, or return to their native countries for lack of support networks that existed for the native born. For those who remained, social service agencies such as the Yankee-administered Chicago Relief and Aid Society did all they could to remind the poor of their inferior position. Of the nearly 19,000 families who requested post-fire assistance, only 1,965 were native born according to official records. And in a primitive version of trickle-down economics, a vastly disproportionate share of aid went to the native born. None was provided to "vagabonds," a term used by the papers to describe what they considered the "great, lazy, able-bodied hulks of men . . . sitting and lounging about" the relief shelters. The assumption was that the propertied were the most valuable economically, and aiding them would more efficiently restore Chicago to its former greatness. "Every man who can pay wages will render himself and the public great service by hiring all the labor he can use," the *Tribune* explained. "The money thus distributed will be grateful to the recipients, and will be a great relief to the committees charge with providing for the destitute poor."[14]

Those who could not find work, in particular those who could not provide a pre-fire street address or city directory listing, quickly learned what charity workers called "St. Paul's rule": "He who does not work, neither shall he eat." More than two thousand women and children refugees subsisted entirely on salted meat—no fruits, vegetables, or milk—at a shelter for five weeks after the fire. Male workers who found jobs were cut off from welfare immediately, before their first post-fire wages could be paid to them, leaving their families temporarily impoverished. "It is not uncommon thing to see children crying and begging for bread merely because their fathers have found work," a *Tribune* letter writer complained. "These people should be fed until they are able to feed themselves." Workers attracted to the city by the lure of reconstruction jobs, many of them illiterate immigrants, were often cheated out of wages by their employers. After terminating aid to almost all fire victims in spring 1872, the Chicago Relief and Aid Society used its remaining $600,000 in funds donated from cities such as St. Louis and Detroit to pay administrative costs, money that lasted until 1885. The *Tribune* applauded this parsimony, noting of the privileged few who received aid, "with this plan 30,000 people, hitherto householders, will still be in their homes . . . which are so immense a moral force in the community."[15]

Instead of crusading for the afflicted, most of Chicago's mass news media joined with the *New York Tribune* in warning that "a starving, discontented, turbulent population" would become riotous if public assistance were given too freely. The one partial exception was the *Chicago Tribune,* temporarily edited by a sympathetic Horace White. Angered by the Radical Republicans in Congress, White liberalized his paper during the latter 1860s and early 1870s, supporting civil service reform and free trade, and attacking the corruptions of the Grant administration as it advocated some working-class issues. The *Times* chided the *Tribune* for its apparent defection from the party of Lincoln. "Republican newspapers in this section of the country say the 'protective policy' as now managed is simply villainous," the paper wrote. "Yet their partisan malevolence, and the blindness caused by 'nigger on the brain,' bind them fast to the party in power." White created national headlines in 1870 when he and Republican House Speaker and future presidential candidate James G. Blaine laid out the foundations for a new Liberal Republican party for the upcoming 1872 election. For its heresy, on June 20, 1872, the *Tribune* was read out of the party that it had helped found during the 1850s.[16]

Joseph Medill had been demoted to *Tribune* business manager as a result of the White management reshuffle. He helped return the *Tribune* to publication following the 1871 fire, but angered by the paper's liberal swing, he quit and threw his hat into Chicago's tempestuous political arena. Medill had long opposed immigrant shantytowns and ramshackle neighborhoods such as that of the O'Learys, and in the wake of the 1871 fire he politicked for strengthened fire codes that would effectively force much of the city's working class into European-style tenement housing. His fire code platform attracted broad support among other Yankees rebuilding their city from a disaster they believed had been brought upon them by immigrants. Even Wilbur F. Storey admitted that an "upright and honest Medill would maintain and strengthen the credit of Chicago." Only the *Republican* demurred, protesting that "a few men who happened to control a few newspapers" were foisting Medill on an unsuspecting electorate.[17]

The socially and politically inept Medill won an uncontested election as mayor in late 1871, and used the fire emergency to induce the state legislature to expand his powers, revising the city's traditional weak-mayor/strong-council system. He also effected an organizational and fiscal overhaul of the city's highly decentralized and patronage-riddled government. But the remainder of what Medill called his "good government" reforms blatantly benefitted the city's Yankee business community. "Republicanism is somewhat puritanical in a good sense—in its best sense," Lincoln's law partner

William Herndon had told Medill in a 1861 letter, and Mayor Medill embodied that advice. The city's new fire code had little impact on downtown property owners, who were already rebuilding with stone and brick, but it was a unique hardship on burned-out Northsiders and Westsiders who faced the impossibility of replacing their cheaply built wooden houses with brick. "This is no joke," *Illinois Staats Zeitung* editor Anton Hesing told a mass meeting on the night of January 14, 1872. "If [sixty thousand inhabitants of the North Side] are forbidden to build wooden shacks they will be forced to throw their property away at fifty percent or seventy-five percent less than it was worth before the fire."

The following night, more than 10,000 German and Scandinavian protestors, some carrying torches and signs reading "No tenement houses" and "Leave the worker his home," marched to a temporary city hall on Illinois and Market streets and disrupted a council meeting, reminiscent of the 1855 Lager Beer Riot. "Communism," dismissed the *Tribune* the following morning. "It was a noisy mob, and nothing else, being composed principally of the scum of the community—men who spend most of their time in saloons and in idleness—and half-grown boys, who created the essential 'enthusiasm,' by yelling without any justification."

The *Staats Zeitung* responded that naturalized Northsiders only wanted Chicago to remain a city where wage workers could live in their own houses, "better Americans than the insolent money-bags who demand that the laboring classes should be squeezed into large dirty barracks, in order to sink to the level of the European proletariat." Incensed by what he considered "mob dictation," Medill made arrangements for a police, or if needed state militia, response if the protesters returned or persevered. "Is civil government a failure in Chicago?" the *Times* provoked Medill. The council approved a watered-down fire code the following month, extending protection from the downtown to a narrow strip of northern lakefront property already in industrial use. Northsiders were allowed to rebuild with wood, even if that raised the specter of another large-scale fire.[18]

Meanwhile, instigated by rumors that some of the $5 million in relief money donated to the city was being embezzled by society employees, dozens of angry immigrant aid recipients protested in front of the Chicago Relief and Aid Society offices on La Salle Street in April 1872. "One instance is given," the *New York Times* reported, "in a case of four families occupying a single house, of three receiving an abundance of everything by paying [a society inspector] $5 each, while the other, the most needy, received nothing, because it refused, or was unable to bribe the visitor." Instead of investigating the charges, Mayor

Medill and the city council passed a resolution in favor of the relief agency's decision to strike an additional eight hundred families from its roles.

Anger boiled over into violence when Medill sided with pro-temperance Yankees and cracked down on violators of the city's detested Sunday saloon closing law in 1872, the same laws that had instigated the 1855 riot. "For some time Mayor Medill has justified his actions concerning the Sunday law by claiming that he had the support of prominent Germans," the *Staats Zeitung* noted. "To disseminate dissension among the Germans is now the main purpose of the knownothings [*sic*]." "To depend on policemen and constables . . . to be sober and cure them of their appetite for stimulants is to lean on a broken reed," Medill admitted years later. But his police force went after errant saloon keepers at the time, jailing them as Mayor Boone had done in 1855. A national recession in 1873 only intensified the poverty that Chicago's working class had been experiencing since the fire, creating the worst hunger the city had yet seen. "Shall the majority of people submit to such a system?" the newly founded Chicago *Freie Presse* challenged its German-language readers. "A horde of Puritanical nativists and Know Nothings . . . [have] sought since they were natives of this country, to force out those who thought differently from themselves, through laws and forcible measures, their special customs and limited views."[19]

As many as seven thousand unemployed workingmen, many curious, gathered outside of the Turner Hall at Twelfth Street and Halsted on December 21, 1873, to listen to German, French, Polish, and English-language speakers talk of "work or bread" and blame the mass news media for attracting surplus workers to Chicago, depressing local wages and employment conditions. "The press never told the truth," one speaker told the crowd, "but always tried to blind the poor workingman." Two days later, as many as five thousand workers marched along Adams Street demanding assistance. Unreported in the city's English-language papers, an unknown number of marchers were injured or killed when police trapped and clubbed them inside the dark, narrow Washington Street tunnel. Tales of what was called the 1873 Bread Riot caught the attention of a newly hired *Times* reporter two years later. "I began to examine into this subject [of the corrupt use of the money]," future Haymarket defendant Albert Parsons wrote, "and I found that the complaints of the working people against the society were just and proper."[20]

Chicago's Yankees had not seen such displays of civil disobedience since the 1867 eight-hour protests or the 1855 beer riot. From the beginning of his mayoralty it was clear that Medill's newspaper background made him unsuited to be a mayor. In Medill's personal papers is an unsigned letter, dated

March 16, 1872 (just three months after taking office), in which he proposes that another *Tribune* stockholder buy him out so that he could "purchase the *Times* and convert it to a Republican paper while the *Tribune* can take its place as a Democratic paper." "I don't care a button about the mayoralty," the letter continued, "and am ready to resign if you accept my offer."

In the face of growing civil disobedience, Medill resigned as mayor in August 1873, citing physical and emotional stress. However, his heavy-handed autocratic behavior reminded aldermen that they had only recently yielded much of their power to him, and by a vote of 34 to 2 they resolved upon his departure never to be subservient to a mayor again, beginning the most corrupt period in Chicago politics, the so-called Gray Wolves era. According to political journalist David L. Protess, Medill's failure to effectively employ the broad powers granted to him weakened Chicago mayors for years to come. Medill's only justification of his mayoralty and resignation came in 1893 when he wrote that "from the day of the fire I worked 16 to 18 hours a day and had things in pretty good shape [at the *Tribune*] when I was snatched away and thrust into the mayor's office, much to my dislike and pecuniary loss."[21]

The 1877 Railroad Strike

Fears of continued unrest festered among Yankees and other upper-class members in the aftermath of the Bread Riot, again fanned by the English-language mass news media. For instance, from 1872 to 1909, Chicago socialists commemorated the 1871 Fall of Paris each year on March 28 with speeches, dances, songs, and other festivities. The *Illinois Staats Zeitung* considered the fall "the most glorious feat of arms recorded in modern history," but unwilling to share in the vicarious glory, the *Tribune* labeled the local celebrators "a regular German-Scandinavian-Bohemian-American crowd, that tramples over one another . . . such as only a Socialistic community could bring out or would tolerate." "I thank God there are no communists among us," Chicago civil rights leader John Jones told an African American audience in 1874.

The *Tribune* reported that the Chicago Relief and Aid society dispersed only $23,980 in December 1874 and January 1875, compared to $112,124 for the previous October and November when it was acting "under threats against their lives and property . . . afraid of the Communist mob." "To Arms! To Arms! Chicago To-Day Expects Every Man to Do His Duty," the *Times* headlined in 1875 as it exploited fears of rioting. "Be ready at the Signal to Cut, Slash, Shoot, and Boot Communists." In reality, fear and anxiety forced a few workers to desperation, but not revolution. "August Hielank, a lumber shover," committed suicide in 1876 following an extended strike. "No cause, except despondency, caused by poverty, is assigned," the *Evening Journal* noted. While they attended meetings and speeches, the vast majority of workers remained loyal to the prevailing economic order.[22]

Unemployment returned to 1873 recessionary levels during the summer of 1877, affecting an estimated 3 million in a nation of only 45 million. Chicagoans were angered by a litany of seemingly endless strikes and bank runs and another cholera outbreak, while the English-language dailies added to their misery by continuing to sensationalize communism. In particular, and as dictated by new editor and publisher Joseph Medill, the *Tribune* had embarked upon a course of communist-baiting reminiscent of its antebellum crusade against Catholics. The disgraced mayor had returned from a European vacation in early 1864, borrowed $500,000 at 10 percent interest from retailer Marshall Field, and bought controlling interest in the *Tribune,* an event he considered the most important day in his life. He quickly returned the paper to rigid mainstream Republicanism, serving again the same upper-class, male, Yankee, businessman readership that it had first embraced during the 1850s.

Speaking on behalf of the city's "Best Men," Medill lashed out at the unemployed, whom he saw as idle, indolent men shifting about without shame. "Of the many fallacies that have encouraged the strikers, the rabble, and the Communists," he wrote, "the most dangerous and delusive is this: 'The world owes us a living.'" In a widely reprinted article that probably was not written but certainly influenced by Medill, the *Tribune* provided some free advice to a rural reader troubled by "bare footed and ragged . . . tramps." "The simplest plan probably, where one is not a member of the Humane Society, is to put a little strychnine or arsenic in the meat and other supplies furnished to tramps," the paper counseled. "This produces death within a comparatively short period of time, is a warning to other tramps to keep out of the neighborhood, puts the Coroner in 'good' humor, and saves ones chickens and portable property from constant depredation." Not to be outdone, the *Times* held that "hand grenades should be thrown among those union sailors who are striving to obtain higher wages, as by such treatment they would be taught a valuable lesson, and either strikers could take warning from their fate." Such statements were cited as prima facie evidence of anarchism in the English-language mass news media by the Haymarket defendants in their trial.[23]

The worst (or perhaps best) fears of the newspapers came to pass in late July 1877. As social scientist George Gerbner postulated, audience members participate in a social process in which they internalize the messages of social elites when they consume something like the mass news media over a period of time. As well, psychologist Paul Slovic found that bad news headlines have a far greater negative impact on risk perception than good headlines. Therefore, a steady diet of negative messages about "tramps," "communists," and "rabble" in the Chicago papers after the 1871 fire may not have proved to readers that they were in any personal danger, but certainly gave that implication. The perceptions became real, especially to less sophisticated readers, during the third week of July 1877 when a strike on the Baltimore and Ohio Railroad in the wake of a 10 percent across-the-board wage cut grew in scope and spread to the rail hub of Chicago.

For days, the city's news media inflamed readers with sensationalistic reports of radicalism and worker-sponsored violence. At least one newspaper recognized this fact, and tried to make it known. The *Chicago Daily News,* founded in late 1875 in part by former *Tribune* newsboy and copy editor and Yankee Melville E. Stone, took Joseph Medill and Wilbur F. Storey to task for inflaming the labor situation in an editorial titled "The Two Old Men." "Smut is not smart . . . vilification is not argument . . . vulgarity is not wit . . . billingsgate is not humor," the *Daily News* wrote. "While they are engaged in the filthy business [of cutting each other's throats] we would advise those who have families, to find some other reading matter for the home circle, than that which appears in the *Times* and *Tribune.*"

Two days later, the *Daily News* editorialized in favor of the workingmen, noting that while violence had to be prevented, the railroads "must employ good men at good wages or else the public will suffer the consequences." However, when violence erupted, the paper cast its lot with the propertied class, featuring headlines such as "Great Loss of Life and Goods," "Fires Raging Everywhere," and "Insurrection." Meanwhile, the *Tribune* evoked images of European-style anarchy with headlines such as "Guns-shops Gutted for Arms, and Artillery Seized by the Crowd," "Gangs of Half-grown Boys Closing Up All of the Factories," and "Red War"; the *Times* was not far behind with headlines such as "Lawless Labor," "Red Sunday," and "Wild War." Such rhetoric was even more threatening because the trade publication *Railway Age* had calculated that one-twelfth of the Illinois population was supported either directly or indirectly by the more than fifty railroads then doing business in the state. "Employers are suffering as well as employees, and all classes of laboring men must expect to feel the gripe of the pressure," the paper wrote.[24]

On Sunday, July 22, a number of labor speakers attacked the callousness of the *Tribune* and the *Times* at a rally held at Sack's Hall, 20th and Brown streets. One of the speakers was twenty-nine-year-old *Times* typesetter Albert Parsons. The *Tribune* commented the following day on Parsons's "popularity" at the rally, as "he commenced his haranguing." "If the proprietor has a right to fix the wages and say what labor is worth," Parsons was quoted as saying, "we should be perfectly happy; content with a bowl of rice and a rat a week apiece." "He also read an editorial from the *Sunday Times* which he treated with contempt as far as its logic was concerned," the *Tribune* commented. Parsons attacked the railroads again in a speech the following day, and was quoted in the newspapers in telling some 10,000 at a rally near the intersection of Market and Madison streets that it was incredulous that the railroads expected their employees to feed and clothe their wives and families for less than one dollar a day. "Virtue on ninety cents a day!" he exclaimed. "What shall we do with the capitalists?" Portions of the crowd allegedly responded, "We'll hang them."[25]

The strike intensified on July 23 when workers walked off their jobs at the Michigan Central yard at Randolph Street and Michigan Avenue. The nation's rail network quickly ground to a halt as the strike spread in Chicago, proving how integral the city had become to the railroads. Freight cars were left standing on tracks, passenger service was disrupted, and workers attempted to sabotage the few locomotives moving that were manned by supervisors. Most other industries were closed or affected as a general strike spread throughout the city. The *Tribune* labeled the strikers "idlers, thieves and ruffians" again, accusing them of being eager to riot and loot, and warned, "When the contest comes, if a contest be insisted upon, there will be no firing over the heads of the mob. The orders are to aim low." Tensions increased when German furniture workers fought with police at the Turner Hall near Roosevelt and Halsted.

State militia and federal troops were dispatched, and the *Daily News* began providing coverage in hourly extra editions. Chicago's first newspaper extras had appeared during the Civil War, but no paper had yet attempted the depth of coverage provided by the *Daily News* during the 1877 railroad strike. "A corps of reporters, mounted on horseback, went through the riotous districts and telegraphed or telephoned the situation hour by hour, almost minute by minute," Melville E. Stone later explained. "Some of them were even disguised as rioters; and one at least fell into the hands of the police because he was in the front ranks of the mob." Circulation increased to over 70,000 copies a day, double previous levels. Businessmen led by Marshall Field department store partner Levi Z. Leiter threatened Stone and his new partner, Norwegian newspaperman Victor Lawson, with a cessation to their lucrative department store advertising contracts, claiming that the paper's coverage was inciting the violence. Stone and Lawson refused the businessmen's demands largely because their paper, just more than a year old at the time, was achieving the highest circulation of any Chicago daily paper to date. "We say there are two sides to this question and the workingman's side of it should not and cannot be ignored," the paper responded.[26]

On the morning of July 26, 1877, a group of some 10,000 strikers challenged police lines at a viaduct over several railroad tracks that ran perpendicular to Halsted near 16th Street. Mayor Monroe Heath had called the strikers "ragged Commune wretches," akin to the *Times*'s characterization of them as "an uncombed, unwashed mob of gutter-snipes and loafers." "Their numbers seemed to inspire them with the valor of savages," a *New York Times* correspondent wrote. Two regiments of state militias, a battery of artillery, five thousand special deputies, and members of several patriotic organizations (including the famous Civil War Col. Elmer Ellsworth's Zouave militia) were dispatched to the scene to assist police; they were joined later in the day by six companies of the 22nd U.S. Army Infantry Regiment (ordered to Chicago by President Rutherford B. Hayes), fresh from seeking revenge against Native Americans in the Dakotas for the massacre of Gen. George Custer.

The *Daily News*'s Elwyn Barron was the only reporter to witness the resulting combat firsthand, in what came to be called the Battle of the Viaduct. Secreting himself in a railroad switchman's box below the viaduct, Barron watched as police and troops charged the strikers repeatedly. "Thousands of idlers and roughs were within distance of two blocks from the bridge, but not in any organized body," he wrote. "Suddenly a shower of small stones fell upon. . . . This was a signal for a general fight. . . . Shot after shot was fired, while clubs and stones were freely used." The fighting subsided only when the Army arrived; when strikers fled, troops marched back toward the central business district in formation along Michigan Avenue in a very visible show of force. As the blood flowed, Chicago Symphony Orchestra founder Theodore Thomas led musicians in a loud rendition of Wagner in Exposition Hall, on the site of the present-day Art Institute, in an effort to drown out the noise and ignore the chaos. A businessman attending the concert recalled that for at least a few hours, he felt that his world had returned to normalcy.[27]

Disheartened by the show of force against them, most of the striking workers returned to their jobs over the following days, and freight trains began leaving Chicago on Saturday, July 28, with military protection. Between twenty-five and fifty strikers were killed, some two hundred were seriously injured, and nearly four hundred arrested during the railroad strike. No police officers or soldiers were killed or seriously injured. "The *Tribune* is in favor of one more strike, and it ought to be made today," the paper reported at the end of the week. "This strike should be against the villainous scoundrels who have incited the mob and who at the same time have been too cowardly to lead or take part in it." The Chicago's Citizens' Association, a group of prominent members of the propertied class led by Marshall Field, bought four 12-pound Napoleon cannons, several light artillery pieces, and a Gatling gun, donating them to the police department in 1878. As twentieth-century journalist Floyd Dell observed, "the need of a Gatling quick-firing gun which could sweep a street from side to side and mow down a thousand men in a few seconds" was apparently the upper-class's only solution to Chicago's labor troubles.[28]

Haymarket Square

Chicago's English-language dailies heated up their rhetoric against communists and other political radicals even more in the aftermath of the 1877 strike. "There is distrust, dissatisfaction, discontent about us everywhere," the *Inter Ocean* reported and warned readers, "the socialist element are sowing seed daily which they, no doubt, hope will bear fruit directly." Influenced by a different press philosophy and tradition, most of Chicago's postbellum foreign-language newspapers followed a different course. Karl Marx had worked on a number of Prussian and other European radical papers during the 1840s before he took up book writing and other pursuits. To his way of thinking, political opponents were not to be humored or baited as they were in the English-language press but treated with extreme disdain and denigrated as lifelong enemies. Radical Germans had a passionate faith in press freedom in contrast to the more laissez-faire attitude of nineteenth-century American mainstream newspapermen. The "German [mainstream] daily press is the weakest, most lethargic and timid institution under the sun," Marx wrote, an attitude that characterized Chicago's dailies in the eyes of their more radical foreign-language competitors. For Marx, newspapers were necessary to reinforce and interpret political certainties that did not sway in the winds of current events. "The investigation of truth must be honest itself," he wrote, "the real investigation is the unfolded truth whose disconnected parts are combined in the results."[29]

During the 1870s and 1880s, several German-language labor newspapers sought to fill the shoes of the *Workingman's Advocate,* especially within Chicago's growing foreign-language immigrant community. *Der Vorbote* (The Herald) had been founded in 1874 as a mouthpiece of the Illinois Labor Party, and for a few issues it had advocated a mild form of social democracy. Within a few months however, Swiss-born typographer Conrad Conzett became editor and radicalized the paper, developing an estimated paid circulation of 7,115 by 1884. Conzett had been fired from the *Illinois Staats Zeitung* for radical ideals such as support of worker militias, armed self-defense units called *Lehr-und Wehr-Verein* (study and resistance associations)—the same type of organizations that would aid the growth of Adolf Hitler's National Socialist Party during the 1920s. The resulting success of the eight-page weekly *Der Vorbote* inspired a tri-weekly called the *Chicagoer Arbeiter Zeitung* (Chicago Labor News) in 1876, which became a daily in 1878 with a Sunday edition called *Die Fäckel* (The Torch).

All three papers came under the editorial control of August Spies in 1884. Spies was a German immigrant who had arrived in Chicago in 1873 to work in the upholstery business. His interest in socialism, as was that of the American-born Albert Parsons, was strongly influenced by the growth in the number of Chicago's needy and disinherited in the years after the Civil War. Another immigrant socialist, twenty-seven-year-old German Michael Schwab, served as assistant editor of all three papers. The revamped *Arbeiter Zeitung* had little love for its less radical competitors, noting in 1880 that "the masses are slowly awakening. . . . The only way to avenge yourselves is to kill the serpent which you have fed on your bosom. . . . Out with the *Staats Zeitung, Freie Presse, Volksfreund, Tribune,* and *Inter Ocean.*" For the next six years, all three German-language publications built a combined circulation of perhaps 25,000, bearing witness to the growing numbers of foreign-born immigrants in Chicago and their influence in the city's labor movement. Available by subscription, most readers bought their papers at German businesses or retailers; saloons in particular advertised in them to promote business.[30]

A lack of success in the local political arena during the late 1870s convinced some of the radicals, including Parsons and Spies, that stronger measures were necessary to achieve their goals. In the wake of the 1877 strike, Chicago's police department had engaged in paramilitary training, adopting uniforms similar to the U.S. Army, complete with shoulder straps showing rank. Officers were marched in close order drills and learned the use of the cannons, artillery, and Gatling gun purchased for them by the Citizens' Association. In response, worker militias became more conspicuous in immigrant neighborhoods. The city council approved an ordinance in 1881 making it unlawful to carry concealed weapons within city limits, but reports persisted of armed militias' drills and parades, sometimes in the dark. By the early 1880s, the choice of weaponry and tactics was becoming apparent between the two sides. The police practiced frontal assaults with breach-loading rifles, grenades, and cannons while the radicals favored more surreptitious tactics with revolvers, dynamite, nitroglycerine, and "czar" bombs, the latter patterned after a bomb that killed Russian Czar Alexander II in 1881. "Though everybody now-a-days speaks of dynamite," the English-language *Alarm,* founded in 1879 by former *Times* printer Albert Parsons, maintained, "it may be said that but few have any knowledge of the general character and nature of this explosive."[31]

Tensions between the opposing sides mounted during the early 1880s. On Thanksgiving Day 1884, a "Poor People's March" wound its way through the Yankee neighborhood of Prairie Avenue; participants were encouraged to ring doorbells and ask for jobs among the wealthy. The following April, Parsons, Samuel Fielden, a stone hauler and Methodist lay-preacher from Lancashire, England, and Oscar Neebe, a beer wagon drivers' union organizer, staged a "March Against the Board of Trade" that coincided with a $20 a plate CBOT banquet. "The *Daily News* says America is a marvel of universal happiness; that the prosperity of the people is wonderful, and the 'content phenomenal,'" the *Alarm* editorialized a month later. "When we read of men willing to work, freezing to death under the open sky, living on stray crusts and charity soup, of women and children dying of fever induced by starvation and want . . . of the places, Board of Trade temples, and magnificent clubhouses built for the accommodation of the robber classes; when we know these things and that the masses do not rise in tempestuous rebellion, we may well pronounce the 'content' of the American people 'phenomenal.'"[32]

In January 1886, an explosive device in the shape of a coffee flask was found on the Cass Street doorstep of a Cook County circuit court judge, and a similar device was discovered at the general offices of the Chicago, Burlington & Quincy Railroad at Michigan Avenue and Randolph Street a few days later. Neither exploded but in the aftermath of the discoveries, *Daily News* reporter M. H. Wilkinson was invited to interview August Spies largely because Spies and his colleagues wanted the public to know that they had nothing to do with either of the bombs. In a January 14 page one article, the *Daily News* showed the differences between the radicals' bombs and the bombs that were found, including detailed line drawings, and brainstormed on the best bombing locations in the city. "The principle [locations] are the lake front, [Hay] Market square, and West Randolph street, between Desplaines and Halsted streets," the paper reported. "The point upon which the socialists seem to place most reliance in the point of military advantage is the Market square, between Madison and Randolph streets."

The *Daily News* offered no sympathy to the radicals or what was called the social question of the day, namely what to do with the growing legions of poor and unemployed. "Ninety-nine times in every hundred the man who will boast of blowing up a city with a dynamite bomb," the *Inter Ocean* wrote, "is a lunatic or a coward, who could be scared into fits by pointing a hollow corn-cob at him." "The *Tribune* refuses to accept the fact, that there are at least 1,000,000 men in the United States, who would be willing to work for a small wage, if employment could be found," the *Arbeiter Zeitung* responded. "The proverb 'none is as blind as the one who refuses to see' could be properly applied to the *Tribune*." Instead of offering a solution, the *Daily News* argued against the same open spigot of immigration that had given Chicago its population victory over St. Louis in 1880 and was helping threaten New York as the nation's most populous city. "[They are] scum and dregs of countries where despotism has made paupers and tyranny has bred conspirators," the paper complained. "So in the thousands of immigrants who come to Chicago . . . there remain an insignificant number who do not appreciate the new civilization to which they have come and into which they should assimilate."[33]

The English-language dailies' rhetoric intensified in the weeks and days before Haymarket, inflamed by a strike and lockout at the McCormick Harvester Works. On March 2, 1886, police shot at a group of strikers, killing at least four. "Speaking of the police protection, Mr. McCormick said that the presence of the police was immaterial to him," the *Tribune* rationalized a few days later. "It was the men who worked in the shop who needed it." As the strike and lockout continued, the Federation of Organized Trades and Labor Assemblies scheduled a rally for May Day 1886, the nineteenth anniversary of the city's first bid for an eight-hour workday, to demonstrate continued support for the strikers. "The eight-hour day has been argued for twenty years," August Spies told supporters. "We at last can hope to realize it." "There are some dangerous ruffians at large in this city. . . . One of them is named Parsons. The other is named Spies," the *Evening Mail* warned. "What modest demand, the introduction of the eight-hour day," Spies wrote in the *Arbeiter Zeitung* days before the bombing. "And yet a corps of madmen could not demean themselves worse than the capitalistic extortioners." "Clean your guns, complete your ammunition," the same newspaper warned in its May Day edition. "The hired murderers of the capitalists, the police and militia, are ready to murder."[34]

Parsons, his wife Lucy, and their two children marched at the head of 80,000 workers in a parade along Michigan Avenue on Saturday, May 1, 1886, in support of an eight-hour workday. The English-language dailies ignored the event largely, with the *Tribune* editorializing, "In this important direction, as in some others, the striker for ten hours' pay for eight hours' work will soon find himself in the dilemma of the engineer told of by Shakespeare, who was hoist with his own petard." "We are rapidly drifting into a state of disorder," a native-born march participant confessed to the Associated Press. "The majority of [strikers] are law abiding citizens who know that Chicago's business prosperity means their prosperity," Mayor Carter Harrison Sr. told reporters. "I hope, therefore, that there will be no trouble, but a great deal depends upon how the employers meet the men."

Another gathering two days later featured Spies as a speaker; following his address, about two hundred policemen clubbed and shot into a crowd of some 6,000. The *Daily News* put the resulting death toll at six even though only two actually died, but Spies used the newspaper's estimate in a dodger (a handbill calling for further action) known subsequently as the "revenge" circular. "Attention, workingmen! Great mass meeting to-night, at 7:30 o'clock, at the Haymarket, Randolph street, between Desplaines and Halsted," Spies wrote in German. "Good speakers will be present to denounce the latest atrocious act of the police—the shooting of our fellow workmen yesterday afternoon." "Blood has flowed. It had to be, and it was," Spies editorialized, cryptically, in the Monday, May 3, *Arbeiter Zeitung*. "Do you know what that means? You soon will know."[35]

"Words on Trial"

The Haymarket rally itself occurred without incident, principally because Mayor Harrison had issued a permit to participants, had ordered the police not to interfere, and was present to see that his orders were obeyed. Typographer Adolph Fischer, in charge of publicity, left at 7:30 P.M., shortly after the rally was supposed to have started, and went to a clubroom bar. Another organizing committee member, painter George Engel, stayed home to play cards and drink beer with his wife and friends. The youngest of the defendants, German-born carpenter Louis Lingg, stayed in his North Side apartment and made bombs, but was not present at the time of the Haymarket bombing. An hour later, Spies mounted the back of an empty wagon and spoke to a crowd of perhaps 1,500. He was followed by Parsons, who claimed that Chicago's workingmen were being driven by employers into a condition lower than the Chinese. Samuel Fielden then told the crowd that the socialists intended to prove to the English-language dailies that they were willing to risk their lives for their cause, that it was unhealthy for the upper class to live among so many discontented workers.

Around 10 P.M., a light rain started to fall and the mayor, assuming the rally was over, ordered the few police officers present to leave and went home himself. Certain that Harrison had gone, the police reassembled a force of between 150 and 200 and returned to attack the remaining crowd. Earlier in the day, some of the same policemen had allowed a mob of three thousand to loot a drug store owned by an alleged police spy in the hope that the disturbance would provoke the evening meeting. When that failed to occur, the police marched in military formation toward the speakers' wagon and ordered the crowd to disperse. At about 10:30 P.M., a single dynamite bomb was thrown from the vicinity of the wagon toward police. "A red spark is seen in the air—a point of fire moving in a slow arch. . . . It drops down among the silent cohorts of police between the first and second divisions," Dr. Francis W. McNamara (eventually the Cook County jail's chief physician but a medical student aiding victims that night) told the *Tribune* in 1936. "After it disappears one may count, perhaps, three. Then there is a burst of flame and a shattering explosion, more vicious than that of any shell which veterans of the civil war—there are many present—have heard." Seven policemen eventually died, all but one the victim of resulting police gunfire, along with an unknown number of participants, perhaps dozens, who no one bothered to count.[36]

Haymarket was not the first time in Chicago's history that the mass news media had created a similar wide-ranging hysteria. In addition to the 1875 *Chicago Times* hoax of the theater fire discussed in chapter 2, one of the publishers of the *Chicago Tribune* claimed to have heard, during a street car ride in late 1864, details of a conspiracy to release thousands of desperate Confederate soldiers being held prisoner in Camp Douglas, located just north of the present-day University of Chicago. With the full cooperation of Union officers, the paper detailed a supposed plot in which four hundred Knights of the Golden Circle, a pro-Confederate organization, and various "bushwhackers and guerillas" were to liberate the camp, arm the prisoners, and invade downtown Chicago. "A general sack of the city intended—plunder, rapine—fire—bloodshed in the streets of Chicago," the paper reported on November 8, 1864. "The city to be laid in ruins." More than one hundred people were arrested in military and police sweeps throughout the city in response to the article. Streets were empty as panicked *Tribune* readers stayed away from the central business district, many arming themselves as they hid in their homes awaiting an attack that never came. In reality, the entire story had been created to advance the career of the camp's commanding officer and the political interests of the same publisher at the *Tribune* who had supposedly first heard the details. The *Tribune* refused to admit complicity in the hoax, and as late as 1959 the paper treated the report as a genuine threat to the city in a history of itself.[37]

In his discussion of the cultivation theory, George Gerbner observed of such hysterical news reporting that "most of what we know, or think we know, we have never personally experienced." In the days, weeks, and months after Haymarket, Chicagoans of all classes talked about the bombing as they had in the wake of the Camp Douglas conspiracy, basing their beliefs almost entirely on what they had read in the mass news media or were told by others reading the same reports. That such was the case cannot be doubted because the bombing was witnessed by only a few hundred people, and few of those actually saw anything of note, just as Gerbner theorized one hundred years later. Given such circumstances, the newspapers and their makers were only too well aware of the powerful role they played in controlling public opinion regarding that night. Writing in his 1921 autobiography, *Daily News* editor Melville E. Stone claimed that it was his suggested wording that Cook County State Attorney Julius S. Grinnell used in his indictments against the eight so-called anarchists—especially the idea of charging them with conspiracy rather than more difficult-to-prove murder. Stone was an intimate of Grinnell as the president of the good government Citizen's Association; Stone and the other Chicago newspaper editors would go on to win a labor case in front of Judge Joseph E. Gary just days before the Haymarket trial began.

Many Haymarket historians have misunderstood the role that mass communications can play in creating public hysteria in the aftermath of an event like the Haymarket bombing. For instance, Bruce Nelson in *Beyond the Martyrs* discussed the role of the immigrant press but noted only that Stone and the *Daily News* paid for Pinkerton agents to search for the bomber, typical of a paper that practiced what it called "detective journalism." Paul Avrich referenced the newspapers only in passing, almost like props, in a drama called *The Haymarket Tragedy*. In a chapter titled "Words on Trial," Carl Smith focused on dime novels, "instant" histories, and autobiographies in his *Urban Disorder and the Shape of Belief* but diminished the mass news media, admitting only to "the centrality of the press' role in Haymarket and of the influence of Stone and the *Daily News* in particular" in one footnote. At that, Stone's remembrance was "suspect" according to Smith.

However, social psychologist Carl Hovland and others have observed that the higher intensity a fear appeal is, the greater the expected attitude and opinion change that can be expected. "Pretrial publicity often influenced juries in murder cases," James Green wrote in his 2006 *Death in the Haymarket*. "Your venomous attacks condemned us in advance," Albert Parsons told Stone in his jail cell two nights before the executions. Stone admitted in his Haymarket remembrance that "words can kill." Nine-year-old Carl Sandburg, future poet and *Daily News* reporter, remembered the glee that met word of the executions in his distant downstate home of Galesburg. "The feeling grew on me," only later, Sandburg wrote, "that I had been a little crazy, 'off my nut,' along with millions of people like yourself gone somewhat crazy."[38]

The English-language news media was at high pitch in the wake of Haymarket. When a police captain was "reported in one of the afternoon papers as having said that the press of Chicago has been derelict in its duty," the *Tribune, Daily News,* and most of the other English-language dailies practically fell over themselves to appease the "manly and courageous" policeman. "A hellish deed" was how the *Tribune* characterized the event. "Immediately after the explosion the police pulled their revolvers and fired on the crowd," reporter Henry Heineman, who was present, wrote. "An incessant fire was kept up for nearly two minutes, and at least 250 shots were fired. The air was filled with bullets." The *Tribune* thought it significant that one dead crowd member had only 12 cents on his person, proof that the crowd was itinerants and not real citizens. "One howling Anarchist is the cause of greater evil in this country than a hundred Chinamen," it editorialized. The *Daily News* was the only other paper with a reporter present at the bombing. "A Gatling gun could not have cut a wider swathe," Paul Hull wrote. "In an instant every [police]man's revolver was in action, and every man shot to kill."

Attention shifted quickly to finding the guilty parties. Two days after the bombing "the arrest of Spies and the other anarchist leaders and followers was the principal theme of talk in the city both yesterday and this morning," the *Evening Journal* wrote. The *Daily News* called the anarchists "a pack of fiends" and noted that "that bomb which exploded on Desplaines street Tuesday night should be the last utterance of anarchy tolerated in Chicago." The *Tribune* called for the death penalty even if an actual thrower could not be found. "Is it not time to muzzle those already here and . . . [to forbid] any more of the scum to land on our shores?" The *Daily News* noted that "the man who threw the bomb deserves some special recognition for having knocked the whole bottom out of Chicago anarchism." Repeatedly, the English-language newspapers were on the verge of calling for mob violence, reminiscent of western-style vigilantism. The *Tribune* published a chillingly prophetic editorial cartoon on May 16 showing four nooses and four grave stones marked "M. S." for Michael Schwab, "S. F." for Samuel Fielden, "A. S." for August Spies, and "A. R. P." for Albert R. Parsons, with the notation, "The star-spangled banner in triumph shall wave, o'er the land of the free and the Anarchists slaves."[39]

Emotions intensified as a grand jury considered indictments. The *Daily News* related a conversation allegedly overheard among anarchists on the day of the bombing that included the threat to police: "If they come we will give it to them." "The testimony introduced tended to show the incendiary utterances of the arch anarchists, and that there had been preparation on their part for the work of May 4," the *Daily News* wrote of the supposedly secret proceedings, not surprisingly since *Tribune, Times, Inter Ocean,* and *Daily News* reporters all testified voluntarily as part of the proceedings. During jury selection, the *Daily News* noted that in Milwaukee, the scene of a less deadly encounter between striking workers and police at about the same time, a jury had been impaneled, the case heard, and guilty verdicts returned all within a week. "The contrast presented by the proceedings in [presiding] Judge Gary's court is too humiliatingly familiar to our readers to justify its rehearsal," the paper complained. When jury selection was completed in mid-July, the *Daily News* published a complete list of its members, including home addresses, individual biographies and drawings having been provided during voir dire. It was revealed only with time that perspective jurors had been initially screened for their compliance by bailiff Henry Ryce, and only those who professed guilt based on information obtained from the newspapers were allowed to go forward.[40]

The dailies competed with each other in reconfirming the defendants' guilt each day, coverage freely available to the nonsequestered jury. For instance, the *Tribune* printed a letter to the editor (probably instigated by a staff member) on the day jury selection began, positing that "no matter how much [the jury members] may have read in the newspapers, no matter now much they may have talked over the subject, no matter how indignant they may feel towards Anarchism . . . they are then simply to decide the question of guilt or innocence according to the law and evidence." "Many Dynamite Bombs," the *Daily News* contended in a late July multi-deck headline. "Did Fielden Shoot?" the *Inter Ocean* asked at the same time that it was trying to connect the defendants to other criminal activities in the city. "The laws are only formed to protect those that are rich," the *Daily News* contended Fielden had once said. "There is no law anywhere in this land that will permit a person to advise or encourage the commission of crime by speech or by printing," the *Tribune* maintained just days before the case went to the jury.[41]

The predictable guilty verdict returned against the "Chicago bomb-throwers," reached after less than four hours of deliberation, received crowing praise in the English-language mass news media. "An eye for an eye. A righteous verdict," was the *Inter Ocean*'s response. "The law 'throttles' them," announced the *Tribune.* "Justice Reigns / Seven Must Swing," the *Times* wrote, and it editorialized that "the case was tried throughout with remarkable ability, carefulness, and legal accuracy." "It is with perfect satisfaction, unalloyed with any sentiment of triumph over the convicted anarchists, that the *Daily News* congratulates Chicago and civilization on the verdict that condemns Spies, Parsons, Fielden, Lingg, Fischer, Engel, and Schwab to the gallows and Neebe to prison." Only *The Current,* a short-lived Chicago literary and political weekly, differed, noting at the time that "their one chance to live (outside of Lingg, the actual bomb-maker) lies in outlasting the present cruel humor of the people."[42]

Reports of the executions, which took place November 11 the following year, reinforced the malice harbored by the English-language newspapers toward the Haymarket defendants. More than fifty reporters witnessed the hangings. When the executions were finished (all four men died of slow strangulation rather than broken necks), runners posted word on newspaper office windows along Dearborn Street. "Triumph of the Law" read the *Daily News.* The *Evening Journal* reported "Spies, Parsons, Engel and Fischer Meet Their Doom on the Gallows," while the *Inter Ocean* thumped, "Justice is Done." The *Tribune* proclaimed, "Dropped to Eternity." Even the German language *Illinois Staats Zeitung* wrote, "The four executed men were under the delusion of being martyrs to a good cause and walked stoically to their death."[43]

Six years later, German-born Democratic Illinois Governor John Peter Altgeld pardoned the three surviving defendants, Fielden, Schwab, and Neebe (Lingg had committed suicide in jail the day before the hangings). English-language mass news media criticism was swift and mostly vicious. "Anarchists Freed" proclaimed the *Tribune,* noting in an editorial, "by letting Fielden and Schwab go free, instead of commuting their sentences to a term of years, the Governor indicates that he disapproves in toto of the verdict of the jury. The patriotic people of Chicago do not." "Gov. Altgeld has rendered the state a poor service in accompanying his pardon of Fielden, Schwab and Neebe with a controversial manifesto," the *Daily News* wrote. In his 1921 autobiography, the *Daily News*'s Melville E. Stone retreated from such a position but still refused to apologize for his hand in the executions, writing, "Then, at the appointed hour, four men were hanged. The announcement went out, and as by the wind of the morning, the cloud lifted and business of the great city moved on its wonted way. The tragedy was over. And it was a tragedy."

In contrast to 1886 however, some of Chicago's mass news media took issue with the *Tribune* and *Daily News.* The *Globe* predicted that time would prove the "righteousness and justice" of Altgeld's decision, the *Herald* was saddened that the pardons would still not remove "the stain of guilt from the memories of the Anarchists," and the *Times* and *Inter Ocean* published Altgeld's pardon statement verbatim in a show of support. "Gov. Altgeld, in giving them freedom for the rest of their days, has performed an act which appeals to every heart imbued with a love of mercy," the latter paper wrote, and *Inter Ocean* editor William Penn Nixon editorialized four years after the pardons:

> The Haymarket square massacre was the direct result of too much newspaper. . . . A sensation was wanted, and the blatherskite's talk was printed. Some other blatherskite read the printed speech, and being ambitious to appear in type, he also made a speech, and so it went on, and gathered until every one of these creatures had been heard in the press a dozen times. . . . Every incident was magnified, every speech exaggerated; sensation was piled on sensation, and in this way, step by step, Haymarket square was reached. . . . Chicago outside of her limits, is the recognized headquarters and hot bed of these vagabonds, and for this our citizens can either thank or damn her newspapers.

Doubt about the guilt of the executed anarchists continued to grow in subsequent years, with the Chicago papers eventually seizing upon a lesser-known anarchist named Rudolph Schnaubelt as the actual thrower. Schnaubelt was Michael Schwab's brother-in-law, was near the wagon at the time of the bombing, was arrested twice by police in the aftermath, and indicted, but never tried. He died in Honduras in 1895. A century later, Paul Avrich identified another local anarchist, George Meng, as the true bomber. Meng was also arrested and released by police. He died in a 1895 saloon fire, never revealing his actual role if any.[44]

The 1894 Pullman Strike

The native-born reporters and editors who covered and wrote about the Haymarket bombing and trial had no empathy for the largely foreign-born anarchists and their supporters, but Chicago's last major nineteenth-century labor event produced a different response. Passions had cooled somewhat in the months after the Haymarket pardons when some 4,000 members of Eugene V. Debs's American Railway Union (ARU) staged a wildcat strike in Chicago. Their job action began when railroad-car maven George Pullman cut wages 28 percent while keeping rents the same in his Pullman company town, located south of Chicago, in the wake of the 1893 recession. Some workers took home as little as 7 cents per week after deductions, and others went into debt literally by working.

On May 11, 1894, Pullman workers voted to strike even when Pullman promised to let them see his accounting books to prove that he was losing money. "Big Strike at Pullman" the *Daily News* reported, and it included an interview with one of the striking workers along with a prepared statement from Pullman. In subsequent days, the *Daily News* published articles such as "Pullman and Its Features," "Debs Set Them Cheering," and "Life With the Soldiers," a description of a lakeside encampment built by Army soldiers sent to monitor the strike. "This is the workingman's country. Here he has more rights, privileges, opportunities than in any other land under the sun," the paper wrote in contrast to its Haymarket coverage. Some 125,000 rail workers in other states joined the strike, refusing to handle Pullman cars that were operated by the Pullman Company independent of the railroads. As tensions flared, the *Daily News* reported "Beef Train Now Stalled / Trouble at the Stock Yards Increases and Trouble is Feared Before Nightfall." "The infantry troops are armed with carbines and bayonets and each man is supplied with 100 rounds of ammunition," the *Herald* reported. "Rifles and pistols are carried by the calvary."[45]

At its peak, the boycott crippled traffic on twenty-nine national lines. In early July, the federal government obtained an injunction against the workers under the pretext of protecting the U.S. mail, and rioting ensued. "Mob Attacks the Police," the *Daily News* wrote, but it also reported the deaths of strikers (in contrast to the unknown civilian victims of the Haymarket bombing). "There are more anarchists in Chicago than St. Petersburg," the *Tribune* quoted a New York minister as saying in early July. "They are not fit to live beneath the American flag." The *Tribune* noted that the disorganized condition of train service was having an effect upon other branches of labor as well, writing that thousands of Chicago stockyard workers had nothing to do but "hang around the railroad depots and yards and 'see the fun.'" A *Daily News* editorial complained that "with apprehensive eyes glued on the scattered seats of riotous excitement in this Chicago community, our hurtled citizens go stumbling about the down-town streets and with stoicism born of necessity."

On July 7, the *Daily News* reported in a late extra edition, "Shot Down by Soldiers / Militia Obeys Orders and Fires Upon a Mob at 49th and Loomis Streets / Twelve People Severely Wounded," and in a rare Sunday extra edition (it was a Monday through Saturday paper otherwise), it noted, "A young lady named Miss Martha Bach was standing on the roof of a house near by watching the conflict when she was shot and instantly killed by a bullet from the revolver of a policeman." Only when troops gained control of the railyards and the strikers disbanded did the *Daily News* observe that "the Storm is Past." An estimated thirteen strikers were killed, another fifty wounded, and some $340,000 worth of property damage was reported. No policemen or soldiers were killed or seriously injured.[46]

Still biting at times, the English-language mass news media's coverage of the Pullman strike was milder than it had been during Haymarket, perhaps moderated by their previous rush to judgment. One paper even took a supportive position toward the strikers. Following Wilbur F. Storey's death in 1884, ownership of the *Times* had been contested by his three wives until a final court ruling in 1888. As that controversy simmered, employees stole from and betrayed the good name of the paper and even started a short-lived imitation, the *Globe*.

The last issue of the *Times* with Storey's name on it appeared on April 18, 1888, and after that it went through the hands of two ineffectual owners, who employed at least two editors with criminal records, before it was sold to Carter H. Harrison Sr. in 1891. The former mayor was planning another run for office to coincide with the 1893 World's Columbian Exposition and needed a mouthpiece to tout his bid. He put his two sons, William and Carter Junior, in charge of the paper and adopted a pro-labor position previously unknown in Chicago journalism outside of labor and foreign-language papers. "Pullman Seeks a Good Way Out / He Requests a Conference with Debs and Howard to Discuss the Terms of a Lifting of the Embargo" was how a conciliatory article on the strike was headlined in the *Times* at the same time that the *Tribune* was demanding Debs' imprisonment. "No newspaper nor any public man can deplore the existing strike and its consequences more than does the *Times*," the paper wrote. "But to denounce the strike while ignoring the conditions which led up to it is demagogy—the demagogy which appeals to the rich and powerful and which they miscall patriotism. It is perfectly certain that the strike could be suppressed by the regular and volunteer military forces. . . . But what then? Are the working people of this country to be driven to work henceforth at the point of the bayonet?"

On July 4, the *Times* printed a lengthy article labeled the "True History of One George Mortimer Pullman / How He Made Money." Union president Debs had agreed to be interviewed by editor Willis J. Abbot, a first for a mainstream Chicago paper. Abbot recalled, "I had occasion to meet Debs several times at his headquarters or in my office, for the *Times* was frankly friendly to the strikers. . . . No man ever strove more earnestly to keep violence and lawlessness out of a strike than he. I was present on two occasions when he put lieutenants on the carpet for having permitted something of the sort, and well recall the bitterness of his rebuke and his clear discernment that resort to riot was the surest way of defeating the ends he and the Union sought."

The Chicago police had a somewhat similar view of the 1894 strikers as well. Police Superintendent Michael Brennan later admitted "to the charge made that the police sympathized with the strikers, I would say that such is probably the fact. Most of the police as well as most of the [U.S. Army] troops came from the same class of society from which the working men come, and their sympathies were naturally with the men who were striving to better their conditions." In contrast to immigrant participants in the 1877 and 1886 events, most of the 1894 strikers were native born and belonged to patriotic societies such as the Grand Army of the Republic. Not surprisingly, the average Chicago newspaper reporter supported the strikers as well, even if their management did not, because most were paid roughly the same $10 to $12 per week as trained industrial or railroad workers. Their salaries proved the adage that "writing was the cheapest commodity purchased by newspaper publishers."[47]

In spite of—or perhaps because of—its more humane treatment of strikers, the *Times*'s days were numbered. Its circulation climbed during the strike but advertising disappeared as businessmen, especially department store owners, sought more appreciative publications. In particular, the *Times* lost the advertising patronage of Marshall Field in 1891 for publishing a series of articles on the inequities of tax assessments for Loop properties such as Field's compared to residential owners. Nearing bankruptcy, the Harrisons sold the paper to the *Herald* in 1895. In turn, the combined *Times-Herald* was purchased by the *Daily News* in 1901 and sold to *Tribune* editor James L. Keeley in 1914, only to fail altogether in 1917. The last physical vestige of Chicago's most colorful daily newspaper disappeared with the demolition of its old office building at the corner of Washington and Wells streets in 1964.[48]

* * *

As the most important defining moment in nineteenth-century Chicago history other than the Great Fire, Haymarket Square remained as a presence into the twenty-first century, in the form of one final, grizzly artifact. The wooden gallows, built hastily within the walls of the Cook County jail to keep the defendants from any last-minute escapes, were used for eighty-six more hangings before electrocution became the state's preferred execution method in 1927. However, when convicted gangster hit man "Terrible" Tommy O'Connor escaped from the jail two days before his scheduled 1921 execution, authorities were forced to keep the gallows as his legal means of execution if he was ever recaptured.

Stored dissembled in the basement of the Hubbard Street criminal courts building, it was not until 1977 that Circuit Court Judge Richard Fitzgerald ruled that O'Connor had finally escaped justice and the gallows could be disposed of. They were sold to a suburban McHenry County Wild West theme park where they were neglected but remained on public view during the remainder of the century. In 2006, the theme park owners decided they no longer fit in with a new, more family-style motif, and the gallows were auctioned online to Ripley's Believe It or Not museums for $68,300 in a bidding war with the Chicago History Museum. In the possession of Ripley's, the gallows will likely be available for public view for years to come, a final grim testament to the mass news media's hysteria over Haymarket Square. Regardless of the gallows ultimate fate however, Haymarket faded from the consciousness of late-nineteenth-century Chicagoans in fairly short order as they prepared their city to become the world's *grande dame* for the 1893 World's Columbian Exposition and to press their case to be Number One.[49]

5

The Beauty

The Haymarket executions emboldened a new generation of American newspapermen and reformers, but none quite like twenty-seven-year-old *Chicago Evening Post* columnist and second-generation Irishman Finley Peter Dunne. Writing under the guise of a fictional Bridgeport saloon keeper named Martin J. (or Mr.) Dooley, Dunne called anarchism a "humbug" or unproven political philosophy, hardly a threat to the American democracy. To Dunne, the anarchist's mentality was surprisingly similar to that of the mainly Irish Chicago policemen they were supposedly trying to kill. "Did ye iver see an American or an Irishman an arnychist?" Dunne had Mr. Dooley ask his saloon regulars in an Irish brogue. "Naw, an' ye niver will. Whin an Irishman thinks th' way iv thim la-ads he goes on th' polis force an' draws his eighty-three-thirty-three f'r throwin' lodg-in'-house bums into th' patrol wagon." Instead, Dunne sought to humanize the anarchists, something the generation of older newspapermen refused to do. He called one Casey, as Mr. Dooley related:

> "Be that as it may . . . [Casey] was a most ferocious man. Manny's th' time I've heerd him lecture to little Matt Doolan asleep like a log behind th' shtove [in Dooley's saloon]. 'What ar-re we comin' to?' he'd say. . . . Pretty soon in come a little woman with a shawl over her head—a little German lady. Says she: 'Where's me hoosband,' in a German brogue ye cud cut with an ax. . . . [Meanwhile] 'Ar-re ye min or ar-re ye slaves,' [Casey] says to Doolan [in the back of the saloon]. 'Julius,' says his wife, 'vat ye doin' here, ye blackguard . . . coomin' ze, or be hivens I'll break ye'er jaw,' she says. Well, sir, [Casey] turned

> white an' come over as meek as a lamb. . . . Afther a while Doolan woke up an' says he: 'Where's me frin'?' 'Gone [with his wife],' says I. . . . 'Well,' says Doolan, 'tis on'y another victhry iv th' rulin' classes.'"[1]

Few other topics were off limits to the irrepressible Mr. Dooley as well. As temperance advocates were gathering strength in Gilded Age Chicago, Mr. Dooley claimed that he had read in a newspaper that "liquor is food." "D'ye think [whisky] sustains life?" one of Dooley's patrons asked. "It has sustained mine f'r many years" was the reply. Dooley also spoke of another Chicago institution, the World's Fair "hootchy-kootchy" belly dancers:

> They'll be mountains iv infant food an' canned prunes, an' pickle casters, an' pants, an' boots, an' shoes an' paintin's. They'll be all th' wondhers iv modhern science. Ye can see how shirts ar-re made, an' what gives life to th' sody fountain. The' man that makes th' glue that binds'll be wearin' more medals thin an officer iv th' English ar-my. . . . Where did I bring up, says ye? In th' fr-ront seat iv a playhouse with me eye glued on a lady iv th' sultan's coort . . . thryin' to twisht out iv hersilf.[2]

The 1893 World's Columbian Exposition remains the most celebrated entertainment event in Chicago history. First publicly proposed in a letter to the *Chicago Times,* the World's Fair was a shining moment that defied the corruption, pollution, social disorder, disease, and poverty that was rampant in late-nineteenth-century Chicago. Such an incongruity caught the attention of the *Puck* humor magazine, which portrayed Chicago's beauty and beast personas in a 1893 cartoon that showed a goddesslike figure labeled "Beneficence" directing residents from the dark, smoke-choked city to the fair's pristine garden setting. The fair was awarded to Chicago through an unprecedented and bitterly fought war with New York City and its newspapers. With Chicago's selection as the location, the World's Fair Department of Publicity created one of the first public relations agencies in the world, working closely with the mass news media to make the fair a success. The fair itself came to be defined through its portrayal in the mass news media, newspapers, magazines, and newspaper guide books as a softly focused, surrealistic black-and-white utopian image. And underneath it all percolated Chicago's crusade to be Number One.[3]

The World Comes to Chicago

The movement to stage a world's fair in Chicago began in 1882 when the *Chicago Times* published a letter from a Chicago dental surgeon, Dr. Allison W. Harlan, advocating "an international exhibition in Chicago in 1892" to celebrate the 400th anniversary of Christopher Columbus's first voyage to the New World. "It seems that such an event might very appropriately be celebrated in this manner," Harlan wrote. His brief letter, which also included a prediction that Chicago's population would reach one million by 1892, was buried in the middle of page seven and attracted little notice at the time. Recognized at the fair eleven years later, Harlan died in 1909 uncelebrated for his suggestion. The *Chicago Inter Ocean* observed in an 1883 editorial titled "Why Not?" that "this western world ought to celebrate the year 1892 with a grand fete" and, ignoring the fact that Columbus never once set foot on what came to be known as North America, the paper continued, "Of course Chicago is the most central large city of the western continent, and the only suitable place for the celebration." "Nine years from now," the paper predicted, "our literary and artistic status among the cities of the western world will go as far toward attracting visitors as our present and future commercial greatness."[4]

Two years later, officials of Chicago's leading exposition venue began agitating for a world's fair in an effort to foil a threatened St. Louis bid. In the wake of the 1871 fire, Chicagoans had constructed a multi-pagoda-topped structure between the lake shore and Michigan Avenue at Adams Street that came to be known as the Inter-State Industrial Exposition Building (located on the early twenty-first-century site of the Chicago Art Institute). For nearly two decades, the building hosted fairs, displays, operas, and traveling theatrical productions along with Theodore Thomas's early Chicago Symphony Orchestra concerts. It served also as the scene of the 1880 Republican National Convention and both Republican and Democratic national conventions four years later. In 1885, some 100,000 spectators jammed the venue over a twelve-day period to hear the most popular coloratura soprano of the latter nineteenth century, Adelina Patti. In response to Patti's success in what many outsiders considered to be a still-uncultured city (Chicagoans had been enjoying operas since the late 1850s), concert promoter Ferdinand W. Peck originated an idea that led to Dankmar Adler and Louis H. Sullivan's Auditorium building, completed in 1890 on Congress Street between Wabash and Michigan avenues. It was Patti who headlined that structure's gala opening in December 1889 to a standing ovation for her performance of "Home, Sweet Home" in a full house that included President Benjamin Harrison.[5]

With word of a potential St. Louis proposal, Exposition Board Secretary John P. Reynolds and board members Edwin Lee Brown and George Mason suggested in November 1885 that Chicago try to become the site of a world recognition of the impending 400th anniversary of Columbus's first landing. Ignoring South America and Central America all together, Mason proclaimed that "Chicago is in the centre of the continent. . . . It is the middle between China, Japan, and India on one side and Europe on the other." St. Louis supporters discounted Chicago's proposal, with the *Chicago Daily News* reporting "Old St. Louis in a Huff." Chicago's newspapers sneered that "there are some reasons why St. Louis would be a capital place to celebrate an event . . . [for] she is practically in the same condition she was when Mr. Columbus discovered the continent."

The *Chicago Herald* demanded the formation of a commission to study a Chicago application "from the most active, energetic and enterprising of our citizens in every walk of life—from trade unions as well as the Board of Trade." To head such a commission, the *Herald* advised against any "pent-up Utica" men, a reference to exposition bureaucrats, instead suggesting solid Yankees such as retailer Marshall Field, former Relief and Aid Society director Wirt Dexter, banker Lyman J. Gage, and hotelier Potter Palmer. "Like London, Paris and New York, Chicago is cosmopolitan in its population, and of the nations which, under proper invitation, would send hither evidences of their ingenuity, wealth and progress, none would find itself actually among strangers," the paper proclaimed.[6]

Any enthusiasm for a Chicago fair quickly evaporated however. The *Chicago Tribune* was in standard booster mode when it reported that an evangelist was bringing his revival to St. Louis in December 1885. "Such testimony from a Southern star preacher goes to show that poor, foolish, wicked old St. Louis is gangrened with sin all through," the paper exclaimed. Exposition Secretary Reynolds told the *Tribune* that he had been misquoted with an estimated fair price tag of $5.2 million or that one of the city's suburbs might be a more suitable location for such an event. Responding to an item in the *Cincinnati Times-Star* that Cincinnati might have an interest in a fair, *Chicago Daily News* columnist Eugene Field challenged, "What can Cincinnati, the toothless, witless old dotard of American civilization, accomplish?" "Nothing has been heard for nearly a year of the proposition to hold a world's exposition in Chicago in 1892 to commemorate the 400th anniversary of the landing of Columbus," the *Tribune* complained. "There are six years in which to work, and, although the scheme may be slumbering at present, interest may be taken in it after awhile and the proposition carried out."[7]

The 1889 Paris World's Fair induced some Chicagoans to renew their efforts. American newspapers and magazines were filled with dispatches from the French capital extolling that fair's wonders months before its gates opened. In particular, details of the Palais de Machines, the largest enclosed building constructed to date, and the Tour Eiffel, the fair's official symbol, captivated readers. The *Boston Journal* mocked a Chicago visitor to the fair when she pronounced it as "toot sweet." In May 1888, the Iroquois Club, Chicago's most influential Democratic political organization, resolved that a celebration of Columbus's first landing should be held in Chicago, "the latest and best illustration of American civilization." Soon thereafter a group called the Christopher Columbus Celebration Committee organized; the *Tribune* reported that a few thought it in bad taste that Chicago would act so quickly in the wake of a House of Representatives report that Washington, D.C., should be the fair's rightful location. The group approved the formation of a committee to create a plan for a fair using Columbus as its unifying theme.

As the Paris exposition attracted record crowds, New York residents were mobilized into action. On July 17, New York Mayor Hugh J. Grant called on his city's business, industrial, and trade leaders to work together "in response to a manifest feeling on the part of the community that the time had come when the initiatory step should be taken in the preparation for the occasion which had already been discussed." Apart from other considerations "the chief commercial city of the American continent would be the proper place for such an exhibition," the *New York Times* wrote. Former *Chicago Republican* and later *New York Sun* editor Charles A. Dana donated $10,000 of his own money to help cover initial expenses, and New Yorkers were said to be displaying "unmistakable interest" in a fair. With such broad-based support, New York's bid was viewed as inevitable. By early August, the New York-based *Harper's Weekly* declared, "Everything conspires to make the World's Fair of 1892 at New York what it purports to be—a thoroughly representative occasion . . . in the chief city of the Western hemisphere." The magazine even went so far as to suggest potential fairs sites in its city, arguing that "New York city apparently labors under an embarrassment of riches."[8]

The Great New York–Chicago Newspaper War

New York's new-found interest in the next world's fair was the final motivation to push Chicago politicians and newspapermen into action. What followed was one of the most extensive and acrimonious examples of intercity competition in American history, a propaganda war of words and images. The resulting fray also provided pundits with an unparalleled opportunity to lambast the provincialism of America and its two largest cities. The comic magazine *Puck* mocked New York's newspapers with names such as the *Daily Stabber, Fault Finder,* and *Daily Bigot* for "shaky editorials," "pig-headed hostility," and "ape-like malice" toward Chicago. *Scribner's* called the newspaper warfare an "extraordinary exhibition of indecorum . . . with the brutal acrimony of an English parliamentary campaign and the sputtering hysteria of an interpellation in the French Chamber of Deputies." British newspaperman and novelist Rudyard Kipling, then on an American tour, called it a "dispute between New York and Chicago as to which town shall give an exhibition of products, and through the medium of their most dignified journals the two cities are ya-hooing and hi-yi-ing at each other like newsboys."

To Europeans, the hostilities proved that America had advanced little from the continent of squabbling colonies that it had been in the previous century. As with the St. Louis rivalry, the mass news media never claimed exclusive credit for winning the fair for Chicago—a variety of factors influenced the ultimate decision. But politicians, businessmen, and residents could hardly have ignored the incessant drum beat for the fair in the daily Chicago newspapers, especially as the proposal moved toward a decisive Congressional vote in February 1890.[9]

Four cities began as contenders when Congress authorized a Columbian "Quadro-Centennial" exposition in late 1889—the weakest was Washington, D.C. As the nation's capital, Washington shared a pedigree with Paris and London, the latter the scene of the first World's Fair in 1851, and already standing government buildings could serve fair duty. Regardless, there seemed to be little inclination within and without Washington toward hosting a fair, the Washington press complaining at one point that "the Nation's Capital is no more mentioned than a frontier town of the Pacific Slope." Some of the Chicago papers initially suggested Washington if a more permanent structure such as a new Smithsonian Institute were constructed. The *Tribune* even defended Washington's sultry summers, complaining that New York residents were said to "disport themselves upon housetops [at night], gasping for a breath of air."

As Chicagoans came closer to making a bid of their own, however, the *Tribune* changed its tune, citing mosquitoes, flies, snakes, and sunstroke as but a few of the hazards present during an average Washington summer, observing that even "Congress leaves Washington with pleasure in summer, and returns to it only when the first frost has made life there endurable." "Were [the fair] held in Washington it would be necessary to store there the world's largest stock of quinine and so build extra hospitals for the sufferers from malaria and sunstroke," the *Tribune* wrote. Even with the support of nearby Baltimore, Washington lacked enough private capital to stage an international event, unable to "furnish accommodations for the crowds that would be drawn there, and it would fleece those it could accommodate." In the end, "Washington wants the exposition," the *Tribune* surmised, "because appropriations from Congress would go on for several years." Or as the paper put it less eloquently, "To hold the Fair in Washington by the Federal Government would be to make it a merely Government Fair for the exhibition of government stuff."[10]

The next weakest bid was from St. Louis. Its newspapers maintained that the River City was not only the "logical location" for a world's fair but for a new seat of national government "if the question were reopened." "Chicago is, we presume, only joking in her wild talk about getting the World's Fair of 1892," the *St. Louis Globe-Democrat* wrote in 1889. "That particular enterprise belongs of right to St. Louis, and there should be no reason to doubt that it will come here."

In response, Chicagoans attacked St. Louis on a variety of fronts, including climate and boosterism. As the *Tribune* noted misleadingly, "[Chicago] has a delicious summer climate; St. Louis a hot, sickly one," and it reminded readers of St. Louis's problems with malaria and "an intolerable sun." "Northern people do not mean to go to the infernal regions when they die, and do not see why they should voluntarily visit that American city which most closely resembles them." St. Louis's apparent inability to grow and promote itself was cited as another mark against it, if for no other reason that it needed to get its name "before the public so it may be a successful candidate for some future exposition." That strategy worked, for St. Louis hosted the 1904 Louisiana Purchase Exposition, made famous in the 1944 Judy Garland film *Meet Me in St. Louis.* The *Tribune* chided that "St. Louis is foolish to cry out that her material prosperity will be greatly retarded if Chicago secures the World's Fair. Before long she will be yelling herself hoarse in trying to prove she never said it." Their old rivalry still colored perceptions of Chicago and St. Louis elsewhere. "If Chicago, instead of Cincinnati, had been honored with the nativity of the first giraffe born in this country she would have stretched her neck out over the prairies and said: 'Ah, there St. Louis,'" the *New Orleans Picayune* predicted.[11]

Most significantly, however, St. Louis was counted out of the competition by the Chicago newspapers because it was said to personify the discredited antebellum culture of sectionalism, a major factor in the race between Chicago and St. Louis only a few years previous. In particular, St. Louis published and distributed a pamphlet "to people in the [S]outh whom it wishes to gain over" which contended "if the fair is held in the [N]orth or [E]ast the young people of the [S]outh who visit it will be brought under the influence of northern spirit and become infected with northern ideas, a danger they would not suffer if the fair were held in St. Louis." Such rhetoric, reminiscent of the Civil War and slavery, indicated to the *Tribune* that St. Louis was "trying to make capital out of an alleged sympathy on the part of St. Louis for the old lost cause and spirit of treason and rebellion that were once so potent in the South." According to the paper, St. Louis was "trying to breathe life into hates and fears that this nation had hoped were dead in the seceded states beyond the possibility of resurrection."

Ironically, even as it accused St. Louis of refighting the Civil War, the *Tribune* was employing Civil War–style rhetoric to discount its competitor. In particular the paper criticized the South's demographics, which did not count as many affluent, educated whites as Chicago or New York but did have a larger percentage of African Americans. "Six millions of colored men in the South who are mainly field hands and who do not belong to the fair-going element in the cotton season," the *Tribune* wrote, along with a "large proportion of whites . . . whom poverty will keep at home" would not be expected to attend a prospective fair, which was for "white men only" according to the *Tribune.* "Plantation negroes [*sic*] will have neither the time nor money to attend [the fair]."

As Robert Rydell observed in *All the World's A Fair,* Euro-American racism was an integral element of the 1893 Chicago fair, clearly from the fair's earliest conception. Third-world ethnic groups were minimized and African Americans were excluded altogether from almost every aspect of the fair. *Puck* magazine, which was written and published at the fair, even belittled "Colored People's" or "Jubilee Day," calling the event "Darkies' Day," and fair officials gave away two thousand watermelons to visitors that day to further the racist stereotype. Under such circumstances, St. Louis and Washington, with their larger African American populations, had little chance of selection, and St. Louis had been counted out of the competition by its larger competitors by January 1890. As the *Washington Post* observed, it remained stubbornly "in the field [only] to prevent Chicago from having it."[12]

With St. Louis discounted, World's Columbian Exposition scholar Reid Badger considered a June 1889 *Chicago Tribune* editorial, "The World's Fair of 1892," as the opening salvo in Chicago's ultimate crusade against New York City. But the city's newspapers had been spoiling for a fight for years. As early as 1871, the *Chicago Tribune* chided a Peoria paper for accusing Chicago of having "engaged in a newspaper warfare with New York city" to which the *Tribune* replied, "There have been columns written . . . at the East for every paragraph which has appeared from Chicago." In the immediate wake of the 1871 fire and in reference to the corrupt Boss William M. Tweed and Tammany Hall political machines, the *Tribune* wrote, "while Chicago burned and the people of New York were reading the account of the tempest of flames and work of devastation, they forgot their own local grief over the huge robberies perpetrated by the "four Caesars" (seizers), which had trebled the city debt." By 1875, "It was New York upon which Chicago now turned its guns. . . . New York was its business adversary," as Chicago newspaper reporters Lloyd Lewis and Henry Justin Smith wrote in their 1929 history of the city.

In 1885 the *Chicago Herald* predicted that by 1892 Chicago "having passed Philadelphia in populousness" would be prepared "to challenge the commercial supremacy of New York; at least there would be no chance, if there be the disposition in any quarter, to dispute the commanding position of Chicago as the great central metropolis of the North American Continent." According to the *Chicago Tribune,* the fatal obstacle that would stand in the way of New York was its lack of public spirit and generosity in money matters. "There has never been a public event of any description in that city where its people have not gone begging all over the country for money instead of putting their hands into their own pockets to help it along," the *Tribune* said. More to the point, the *Tribune* reported that a man who was learning how to ride a high-wheeled bicycle sent some money to a New York publisher for a book titled *How to Get On.* "When the work arrived he was disgusted to find that it contained no instructions for mounting the wheel," the paper reported. And when a New York man, who was engaged in lobbying the Board of Aldermen, was asked if he had persuaded the aldermen to pass his bill, he replied, "Yes. I purse-swayed them."[13]

It was hardly unexpected then when the *Tribune* attacked New York in late June 1889 as a city unable to take "a broad, National view of any subject" or even in its "attitude toward the government during the War of the Revolution and Rebellion." "Be it remembered this is not only to be a world's fair but an all-America exposition, and New York is the smallest and least conspicuous element in American life, habits, responsibility, and loyalty," the paper wrote. In succeeding days, the *Tribune* asked, "Why not have it at New York? Because it would be a failure. The city has not the public spirit to make a success of such an undertaking." "The fact that the Chicago press has said little upon the subject [of a fair] so far is no criterion of the true state of feeling on the matter in this city," the *Chicago Herald* explained in countering what it called the "booming of the ancient Dutch town on the Hudson." New York, the *Tribune* contended, "is not a patriotic city and never was," and conjuring an empiric metaphor the paper noted that "as all roads go to Rome, so all railroads go to Chicago."

When the *New York Sun* asked "If the strangers within the walls of Paris leave this year behind them $500,000,000, why shall not the strangers of 1892 leave a like sum in New York?" the *Chicago Tribune* mocked, "The fair in [New York's] hands would be but a money-making scheme. But for the chance of making a good thing out of it that city would never touch it." When the *New York World* alleged that Chicago's "citizens have been educated as 'boomers' and 'hustlers,'" the *Tribune* countered, "Chicago slaughters and packs its hogs. New York puts them on committees." "Does Mary Minkum, who went to school with me, move in the best society in Chicago?" Miss Gotham supposedly asked Mrs. Lakeside of Chicago in the *New York Weekly*. "Dear me, yes. All of her husbands have been pork packers."

On July 22, 1889, Mayor DeWitt C. Cregier directed the Chicago City Council to bid officially for the 1892 World's Fair. Within a week, aldermen authorized the mayor to enlarge an existing exploratory committee and undertake serious planning efforts. The enlarged committee was authorized "to appoint subcommittees and solicit subscriptions to a guaranty fund, the amount of which the committee should determine." "Chicago is the most convenient centre in this country for a gathering of a large number of people," the *Chicago Economist* wrote in support of the council's action. Ultimately, thirty-five businessmen were named to the executive section of the committee, including newspapermen: *Daily News* publisher Victor F. Lawson, *Inter Ocean* business manager William Penn Nixon, *Tribune* managing editor Robert W. Patterson, and *Herald* publisher James W. Scott. All exercised considerable influence on committee decisions.[14]

With the gauntlet thrown down, the tone of the newspaper rhetoric intensified. When the New York papers characterized Chicago as being "too young to be hampered by traditions," and even mislocated the city in southeastern Illinois at one point, the *Chicago Tribune* labeled New York "the greatest and meanest of American cities." "Ignorant of the fact that Chicago, like the good boy in the nursery rhyme, has decided to stick in its thumb and to pull out the plum, the hawks, buzzards, vultures, and other unclean beasts, creeping, crawling, and flying, of New York are reaching out to get the control of the fair," the *Tribune* asserted. "If the New-Yorkers want to reap part of the profits of the fair there is an easy method to do it—shake off the dust of a greedy, unprogressive city from their feet and come and settle in Chicago." The *Daily News* reasoned that "if Manhattan Island is the best place to hold the World's Fair because it is easily accessible from Europe, what is the matter with the Bermudas?"

The New Year papers complained of the propaganda thunderbolts hurled back and forth. "The New York *Tribune* says the Chicago papers are 'conducting a campaign of defamation against New York.' What an unjust remark," the *Chicago Tribune* wrote. The same New York paper noted a few days later that "there is no conceivable reason why in some future year Chicago should not hold a great fair. It would probably be national rather than international." "I want to talk to the spirit of Christopher Columbus," a man told a spiritualist according to the *New York Sun.* "You can't. He's sick," was the reply. "What has made him sick?" "Somebody has told him the World's Fair was going to be held in Chicago."

The *New York World* wondered why any other western town would support Chicago, "the arrogant rival of them all. Her merchants prey upon their trade and her newspapers taint and malign them." The *New York Mail* reported that "Chicago ladies have formed an association and hired a lawyer to prosecute gamblers and rid the city of them. The men wouldn't take the trouble. They're busy attending baseball games and blowing about the world's fair." The *Chicago Herald* asserted that a Chicago world's fair would ascertain Joseph Medill's lifelong ambition of the Midwest as the nation's center of politics, business, and culture. "Every one that has thought about the matter must see that the balance of political power in this country is in the West, and in the great Mississippi Valley," the paper wrote. "The holding of the world's fair in this great valley, whether in Chicago, St. Louis, Kansas City, or Omaha, would do more to show the West what its real strength is, whereas that strength lies, and what its real interests are." "An Indiana corporation is to 'pipe natural gas' to Chicago," the *New York World* replied in kind. "Is not a case of 'sending coals to Newcastle'?" "Ah! Chicago people are not the wild Western creatures you Easterners imagine," a Western Man told the *New York Weekly.* "Shouldn't wonder," an Eastern Man rejoined. "Now I think of it, I saw by the papers only a few months ago that the city had established public baths."[15]

Beyond name calling, out-of-town papers played up Chicago's well-known affliction for infectious waterborne diseases. An extraordinarily heavy rainfall in early August 1889 further increased the flow of the polluted Chicago River into Lake Michigan; the *Evening Journal* reported "an epidemic" of typhoid fever in the Cottage Grove area in the aftermath. Within a few weeks, the New York papers had seized upon the report and were telling readers that Chicago city officials were "seeking to induce people to stay away from Chicago" to protect their health. The *Chicago Tribune* dismissed the allegations as "an unfortunate and sensational and ill-advised report some time since in one of our decrepit evening contemporaries" and countered "there is no typhoid fever here. There is no epidemic of any kind here, and there has been none."

To further deflect damage, the paper faulted New York for being the "distributor general of disease" for the thousands of foreign immigrants who passed through its portals each year. The *Washington Post* complained of the "joining of the foul, inky, Satanic Chicago River to the pure, sweet waters of Lake Michigan" and continued, "The offspring of this terrible miscegenation has to be boiled before citizens dare indulge in its use, but this fact cannot prove any drawback to the World's Fair, for it will only stimulate millions of palates for more 'lager.'" "It is not apparent that the people of Chicago care for any information on the subject of water," the *Memphis Avalanche* continued. "It is beer that interests them." The *Lincoln Journal* reported that "it is considered the proper thing now to stab Chicago water with a knife before drinking it."

Out-of-town papers attacked Chicago for its omnipresent air pollution as well, especially in the wake of a number of smog incidents that briefly reduced day visibility in the Loop to zero. The *New York Times* thumped in September 1889 that "a pall of smoke constantly hangs over [Chicago]," and warning of "unholy smoke," the *New York Sun* asserted that "some of [Chicago's] statesmen have prepared a bill which is to be submitted to the Fifty-first Congress in the hope of bamboozling that body into believing that the Big Smoke is a good place in which to hold the World's Fair." "A man died in Chicago the other day at the age of 110," the *New York Sun* reported. "What a fierce hold upon life he must have had."

Even the otherwise optimistic *Chicago Tribune* could not ignore the smoke, editorializing in October, "the people must choose between the smoke and the Exposition. Which shall it be?" "No one appreciates or admires the enterprise and energy of our great Western cities more than I do," legendary smoke-and-mirrors showman P. T. Barnum wrote in a New York publication shortly before his death in 1891, "but I am sure their populations will consent to put aside selfish considerations in order to make the exhibition of '92 a credit to our republic in the highest degree." "Hullo, my jolly tar, where away?" a railroad conductor joked with a passenger according to the *New York Sun* at a time when the haze had cleared. "Steering to wind'ard, sir," was the reply. "But your ticket reads Chicago." "Aye, aye, sir, same thing, sir."[16]

"Chicago Patriotism"

To battle such evil, Chicagoans rallied around their city and its newspaper warriors as the decision date of February 24, 1890, approached. When the

New York Sun chided, "Where is this progress of which Western people are so proud?" the *Tribune* replied, "[Chicago] cannot afford to be lazy so long as the parvenu New York is still sunk in the slough of provincialism."

In the wake of the grand opening of the Chicago Auditorium in December 1889, the *New York Sun* launched a campaign against what it considered Chicago's cultural shallowness, beginning with a metaphor delivered in a speech by Illinois Gov. Joseph W. Fifer. A wounded Vicksburg veteran, "Private Joe," as he was called, had complained somewhat cryptically that "the diamond of Chicago's civilization has not been lost in the dust of the warehouse nor trampled beneath the mire of the slaughterhouse pen." "We regret that there have been, if there have been, any vulgar disparagements and comments respecting Chicago in any newspapers of this town," the *Sun* wrote of jibes directed at Fifer's statement. "What a miserable commonplace name the Chicago philologers chose for their tremendous new Auditorium, as they call it!" the paper mocked, and it aimed a barbed reference at *Chicago Record* columnist Eugene Field, then first experiencing fame for his writings beyond Chicago. "The Panprytaneion, or the Synaulliothryon, or better still the Cholropolagora, would have filled the bill. But Prof. Eugene Field was in Europe at the time, and there's no other Chicago genius that knows Greek."[17]

In reply, Chicago's newspapers reframed the final weeks of the war as a battle between Chicago's "common sense" businessmen—a concept which would come to denote the fair itself—and New York's corrupt Tammany Hall politics. "Chicago was not compelled to go upon the defensive and pledge that the fair would be non-partisan, while each speaker in favor of New York seemed to think it was necessary to remove the impression the Gotham scheme was thoroughly Tammanyized, " the *Tribune* wrote. The paper editorialized two weeks later that "the game-cock of the West has fairly thrashed the big dunghill bird of the East," and noted that "a fair at New York means one in a city which cannot house a crowd of strangers and cannot daily transport them to or from the inconvenient narrow site which has been chosen."

In an effort to stir readers it feared were becoming too complacent, the *New York Sun* pretended to throw its last-minute support toward Chicago, writing of the Windy City in February 1890, "It is a noteworthy and enterprise-loving town. If it undertakes to hold a Fair it may be relied upon to put it through with all the energy and all the resources of a people not accustomed to failure." Simultaneously, the *New York Tribune* reported the prediction of a California man that Chicago would inexplicably be swept away by a tidal wave on April 19, 1890, two years before the fair was scheduled to open. "Mr.

Erickson's prophecy was promptly telegraphed to Chicago, yet she is paying no attention to it, but going on eating and drinking and marrying and getting divorced just as if there was no danger. Our advice to Chicago is to wake up and move to Waukegan and Kenosha." "New York is just 'humping' herself now for the World's fair," the *Knoxville* (Tennessee) *Journal* observed. "Chicago is not asleep."

As the deciding vote neared, the House Committee on the World's Fair reported two bills, one specifying Washington, D.C., as a site and the other leaving the location blank. An "uninterrupted flow of oratory about the greatness of our country, and especially of the importance of each of the four competing cities" followed on Capital Hill in what the *Chicago Tribune* called the "battle of the talkers." The speakers "wanted their constituents to know that they had taken active part in behalf of their favorite city." "As the arguments for this city were notably strong," the *Tribune* editorialized, "so were those for other places notably weak," a comment the *Tribune* conceded was a form of what it called "Chicago patriotism."

To add to the competition, all of the contenders including Chicago personified themselves as classical goddesses, a practice that began as newspaper art reproduction technology was perfected during the 1880s. Editorial cartoonists strived to portray their home cities as tightly corseted beauty queens or "May Day" queens vying for the favor of a bearded Uncle Sam figure, greeting foreigners, or just standing, staring, and being beautiful. The *Inter Ocean* called its representation, complete with the post-fire motto "I will" emblazoned on her breast, "Miss Chicago"—an image that represented the city until the practice was abandoned in the twentieth century. "Chicago at the Head," the *Herald* wrote a few days before the final vote. "It was a battle of wit and eloquence, of reason and fact, and it is conceded by all sides that the representatives of Chicago have carried off the honors." The goddesses were fair game in the propaganda war. "Don't you have trouble in keeping track of your city limits," a Mr. York is shown telling Miss Chicago in the magazine *Truth*. "Yes, but there is a strong movement on foot to abolish them altogether," was the reply. "My hair reaches down to my feet," Miss Chicago bragged as related in the *Cincinnati Porcupine*. "Doesn't it recoil when it sees them?" Miss Ohio responded.[18]

Going into the actual vote on February 24, bookmakers placed Washington's odds at 40-to-1, St. Louis 8-to-1, Chicago even, and New York 4-to-5. Proving to be the accelerant that it had been throughout the contest, the *Chicago Daily News* thumped the day before the vote, "New York does not want the world's fair in 1892," and that evening it predicted, "Again, let us remark that we think New York is beaten." The paper's prediction was correct, for on the day of the vote, Chicago persevered in eight ballots (over a determined, if unspirited, last-minute push for New York) by a House vote of 157 for Chicago, 107 for New York, 25 for St. Louis, and 18 for Washington. New York drew its strength from its own large legislative contingent and a coalition of New England and Southern Democrats while Chicago had nearly unanimous support from Republican lawmakers west of the Alleghenies. A front-page *Chicago Tribune* editorial cartoon showed a fainted classical female figure labeled St. Louis, a crying woman denoted as Washington, a perplexed elderly woman wearing a gown with dollar signs marked New York, and Uncle Sam tipping his hat and handing a bouquet to a fair-haired, youthful Miss Chicago. "Chicago Wins" declared the paper in an uncharacteristic 36-point page one, column one headline. "Hurrah for Chicago," echoed the *Bismarck Tribune*. "The wonderful Western Metropolis Secures the World's Fair on the Eighth Ballot." "World's Fair Awarded to the Windy City," the *Albuquerque Morning Democrat* wrote.

In response, New York newsboys complained that the fair had been "Chicagoed." Descriptions of the actual festivities were downplayed in the Chicago papers, but in a story headlined "Chicago All Torn Up," a *New York Sun* correspondent described the local reaction:

> A wild prairie yell, a long ringing roar, which is seldom heard in the East, reverberated through the streets as the result of the final ballot was announced. A moment later cannon were booming on the lake front. Such a crazy demonstration was never seen in Chicago.... At 8 o'clock, when the final vote was announced, Madison street, from Halsted to Ogden avenue were ablaze with Greek fire.... Over on the north side the enthusiasm was of the most riotous character. Men paraded the streets with horns and castanets, and bands of music played in front of the Palace Hotel.

Lamenting the failure of New York's "dignified, businesslike way," a *New York Times* correspondent reported that when news of the victory reached Chicago, "there began a session of wild enthusiasm and drinks, particularly the latter. Chicago enthusiasm has a way of showing itself by resort to convenient bars."

In their celebrating, Chicagoans again overlooked the lack of any historical connection between their city and Columbus, booming instead about attributes such as infrastructure. "The greatest railroad center of the country, [Chicago] can give the cheapest passenger and freight rates," the *Tribune* exclaimed. The paper downplayed its own efforts in the war, repeating that it had been the "deadly provincialism" of New York that accounted for the latter's downfall, lamenting, "the inability of that city to look over the Alleghenies and see that there was anything there or to understand that those who lived beyond these mountains had any rights when the comfort or convenience of New York was concerned." "In New England, a thousand miles away, Chicago got ten out of twenty-three [Republican Congressional] votes, with New York right at their door, showing that the New Englanders understand and appreciate the provincialism of New York."

In jubilation, another *Tribune* editorial cartoon showed a threadbare old man labeled "New York" and an equally haggard old woman marked "St. Louis" mourning over a grave presumably containing the remnants of their world's fair aspirations. Behind them in the distance was a big-top tent labeled "Chicago World's Fair," and behind it a structure reminiscent of the Eiffel Tower but topped with a bell, the first precursor to Chicago's famous Ferris Wheel. Forgotten in the excitement of the subsequent fair, the Great New York–Chicago newspaper war was strong evidence that a nineteenth-century city's mass news media, while never the dog, could certainly be its wagging tail.[19]

Marketing the Fair

Construction of the Chicago World's Columbian Exposition, built on "a treacherous morass, liable to frequent overflow," land on the city's far southern border otherwise known as Jackson Park, began on July 2, 1891. "It is in no way suitable for a site for an exposition, even of the indifferent character that the Chicago fair will possess," the *New York Times* sniffed. But the paper noted that there were hundreds of acres of unimproved land surrounding the park "and more money can be made by putting the fair there [by real estate agents and contractors] than by selecting the [downtown] lake front." The opening date of the fair was delayed one year to May 1, 1893, because of local controversy in determining the site, and as the *Tribune* observed unabashedly, "a World's Fair is not a thing with the planning of which Chicagoans are as yet thoroughly accustomed." As early as 1890, *Tribune* publisher Joseph Medill had maintained that since Columbus's landing did not occur until October 1492 according to legend, a delay of an additional six or seven months "when the climate had gotten pretty well regulated in the matter of good weather" would not represent a serious anachronism.

The exposition's main design was developed by a retinue of architects led by Chicagoans Daniel Burnham and John Root (before his death in 1891) with contributions by Chicagoans Louis Sullivan, Dankmar Adler, and others. Beyond design and construction, the major task of organizers was marketing. Described in twenty-first-century terms, late-nineteenth-century Chicago suffered from an extreme image problem, due largely to the same braggadocio and puffery that had helped put it in the public eye fifty years earlier. The city's egocentric persona was at the heart of an oft-told joke by popular New York orator Chauncey M. Depew: "[A] Chicago man was . . . a guest at the Eagle Hotel in Poughkeepsie. After the [huge] dinner was over he said, 'What have you got for dessert?' The waiter said, 'Pie.' 'What kind?' 'Mince, apple, lemon, custard, and pumpkin.' 'Well,' said the Chicago man, 'bring me mince, lemon, apple, and pumpkin.' The waiter: 'What the thunder is the matter with the custard?'"

Such a larger-than-life representation was difficult for even the most fervent late–Gilded Age Chicagoan to stomach. A *Chicago Tribune* real estate writer stated the obvious in 1890 when he asked, "Has the Chicago man . . . after having earned a reputation which made the name of a Chicagoan synonymous with every attribute of self-appreciation, at last come to a point where his dreams of Chicago's future greatness are laughed at by the outside world?" "When Chicago learns that ancient Greek women had longer feet than men of the present day," the *New York World* wrote, "Boston will have a hard tussle to keep her name of Modern Athens."[20]

As well, disgruntled Chicago editors added fuel by criticizing their own city and the forthcoming fair in dispatches copied by out-of-town newspapers. One Chicago newspaper predicted that foreign governments would boycott the forthcoming fair in protest of high American tariffs. Another claimed that Chicago's streets were crowded with beggars and homeless people, that "every pedestrian is importuned by unfortunate strangers, the majority of them of a much higher order of appearance than the genus tramp." The *Chicago Herald* expressed a concern that Chicago would be personified by "a vulgar and fanatical old man" during the upcoming fair, a reference to Mayor "Cahtah" Harrison. The *Chicago Tribune* complained of the high salaries paid fair managers, including $10,000 for the director of foreign affairs "for doing nothing except to look important" and a $5,000 payment made to the choral director. Illinois Gov. John P. Altgeld thought it a "malicious libel" on all of the Chicago newspapers for fanning fears of an anarchist revolt during the fair in the aftermath of his Haymarket pardons. The *Inter Ocean* wrote that "in no city has the press been more open in its criticism of the defects of street cleaning, the smoke nuisance, and other sanitary affairs. There is a bureau of opposition. . . . Having committed these openly it will not be strange if it be found to have secretly plotted against the success of the great event of the century."[21]

Beyond overkill and self-inflicted wounds, Chicago's image had been sullied by the out-of-town mass news media for years, culminating with the 1889–1890 New York–Chicago newspaper war. This was troublesome because much of what the European news media reported about Chicago had been copied verbatim from eastern American newspapers. The *Philadelphia Press* mocked in 1890 that "Chicago isn't bothering much about a World's Fair, but she is doing the very best she knows how to get up a credible Chicago Fair," a sentiment that spread throughout Europe. "A Chicagoan is merely a transplanted New-Yorker or Bostonian," *Harper's Weekly* maintained in 1892, "if he had less veneration for neckties, and a more natural sympathy with a brilliant collar button." "The Chicago anarchists are to boycott the World's Fair," the *Philadelphia Inquirer* reported. "The bureau of publicity should get in some very active work with this bit of news." An offhand and self-admitted incorrect statement that there were 30,000 starving people in Chicago was repeated throughout Europe and induced a rare apology and correction from a Chicago socialist who otherwise opposed the exposition.[22]

In an era before the awareness of psychology contributed to the rise of professional public relations, many Chicagoans nevertheless recognized a need to improve their city's public image. Writing in 1892, fair marketing director Moses P. Handy summarized the challenge he and his staff faced:

> As Europe had long been accustomed to receive American views and to gain its expression of American affairs from New York it was not surprising that Europe was led to believe that the American government had made a great mistake locating the Fair at Chicago, and that the exposition, in all probability, as an International or even National affair, would be a failure. . . . A much more favorable vision of Chicago and of the prospects of the Exposition was brought about. . . . [through] carefully prepared arguments showing why it is to the advantage to foreign countries to exhibit at Chicago were put forth with good effect.

In particular, Handy wanted to avoid the traditional "hard sell" form of boostersism that had gotten Chicago into its image problem in the first place. Instead, he counseled a softer, more dignified, more psychological approach, enabling rather than browbeating potential fairgoers to pay for an event they had already decided they wanted to see. This distinction between the needs of the producer and the needs of the consumer, the genesis of the psychological soft sell, was part of the new late-nineteenth-century practice of mass marketing. In Chicago's case, potential visitors who had never before seen a world's fair—a market that included most of the western United States and anyone too young to have attended Philadelphia's 1876 World's Fair—had to be gently prodded into thinking that this was a once-in-a-lifetime not-to-be-missed event in a way sensitive to their needs and in a manner that made them think that it had been their decision rather than some command.[23]

Late-nineteenth-century Chicagoans were familiar with mass marketing. Montgomery Wards and Sears, Roebuck, and Company were household names, and the Quaker Oats man was born in Chicago in 1888 with the formation of the American Cereal Company. The fair's first semi-soft-sell pitch came in a 1889 *Harper's Weekly* advertising supplement that featured doubtful advertising claims such as Chicago's temperate summer weather, with an "average temperature for the months of June, July, and August" of an alleged 64 degrees, and that the mineral wells of the one-time city cemetery renamed Lincoln Park were "the resort of thousands who drink health and strength from their depths." Bordering on traditional boosterism, the supplement set a standard for future appeals and created a kind of word-of-mouth excitement that author Hamlin Garland epitomized best when he wrote his Dakota parents in 1893, "sell the cook stove if necessary and come. You *must* see this fair."[24]

The public relations process began in the summer of 1889 as the larger battle over a location raged. Chief of construction Daniel Burnham had an extraordinary eye for detail, even to the point of designing the fair's official seal, and it was only logical that his obsession be carried over to other image aspects. "It was moved and carried that wrappers [prewritten news stories] be sent to the papers of the United States," the *Tribune* reported in August 1889, "and that they be asked to send the committee marked copies of all papers containing reference to the world's fair." The publicity committee suggested that "a competent newspaper man be sent through the towns of the West to arouse enthusiasm and awaken interest in Chicago." Richard J. Murphy, a native Chicagoan who had worked on the *Mail, Journal,* and *Herald,* was hired for the job, but it was clear from the beginning that his task involved more than the redrumming of Chicago's name. "The establishment of [a Department of Publicity and Promotion] is an immediate and imperative necessity," the committee reported. "The lack of interest and information in regard to the Fair, not only abroad but in our own country, shows that the work devolving on this Department cannot be commenced too soon, and that the vigor and intelligence with which it is prosecuted will have a most important bearing upon the success of the Fair."

The following December, Moses Handy was hired as the publicity chief executive at a munificent salary of $10,000—more than the U.S. president made, as one newspaper reported. Handy was a Missouri native, an ex-Confederate army officer, former *New York Tribune* reporter, and *Philadelphia Times* editor who understood the news business intimately and made himself likeable to an extreme—both attributes of a good public relations practitioner. One newspaper described him as "one of the princes of good fellows" while the *Tribune* lauded him for having "few equals in the art of presiding at a public dinner."

Handy was different than a press agent, "the only man in the world proud of being a liar," as *Collier's* explained in 1911. Instead, a public relations practitioner was a graduate newspaper man, an expert on public opinion, and "a useful counsel to his employers," according to the magazine. Beyond those skills, Handy possessed a talent for organizing complicated undertakings such as a world's fair, complete with an "expenses be hanged" attitude that got things done as it irritated accountants. "Handy was committed to his own vision however and saw his mission as one that extended beyond press agentry, paying for favorable publicity in newspapers and a practice made common for lesser fairs, museums, circuses, and other traveling exhibitions by P. T. Barnum," the *Tribune* wrote of him. Advancing the fair would come through the legitimate use of the "news columns of the newspapers," not what Handy called "paid advertising" or "plants," fake stories passed off as real news. "Authentic information regarding the Exposition is becoming necessary because of the rumors that have been from time to time set afloat," Handy told reporters soon after his appointment. "This seems to be particularly noticeable in Europe."[25]

The publicity department set to work in the new Rand McNally building on Adams and Quincy streets in early 1891, home to the fair's growing bureaucracy before its administration building was completed in late 1892. Handy hired a staff of experienced news writers, reporters, stenographers, typewriter operators, translators, artists, and photographers, many drawn from the Chicago mass news media. "The most careful scrutiny of the press of the world is necessary in order to ascertain where unfavorable opinion or indifference exists," he told them in March 1891. "This means that everything appearing in print in relation to the Exposition, no matter in what section of the world, must find its way into this department and upon the nature of such publication the Department must regulate its action."

Among the department's most important tools were "boilerplate" (prewritten and stereotyped) newspaper articles and illustrations that could be inserted into an existing newspaper page, and ready prints or "patent insides," preprinted newspaper pages or sections that could be inserted into newspapers so as to appear that they had been produced locally. The nation's largest Gilded Age boilerplate and ready print manufacturer, A.N. Kellogg Newspaper Company, was located in Chicago, and newsmakers from politicians to preachers as well as national advertisers such as the patent medicine industry knew they had a larger readership than any lone American newspaper. At the time of the fair, more the half of the nation's weekly newspapers and significant numbers of dailies used such preprepared materials and were eager for quality feature articles and illustrations on interesting subjects such as a world's fair. In turn, boilerplate gave the publicity department total editorial control over what appeared in print about the fair. As Handy explained on Dedication Day in October 1892, "The articles sent out explained why the time was especially opportune for the holding of a World's Fair in America, and why the choice of Chicago as its location was a wise one."

To win over recalcitrant Europeans, foreign-language writers were hired and boilerplate created in French, German, Spanish, Portuguese, Swedish, Danish, Dutch, and Italian. Writers could customize specific articles and illustrations for major newspapers that would not use boilerplate themselves. The department created an unprecedented mailing list of 30,000 North American and 15,000 foreign newspapers and magazines along with influential local, state, national, and international opinion leaders. Visitors to Chicago were invited to browse the department's scrapbook library, which featured articles clipped from thousands of world newspapers. Handy created a special press reception room at the fair featuring newspaper mastheads from six different continents papered on the walls to impress media visitors.[26]

Control of the fair's image included visual representations as well. The department produced boilerplate line drawings, lithographs, maps, and photographs for media clients. In particular, construction chief Burnham hired a Buffalo, New York, photographer named Charles Dudley Arnold to photograph the fair's construction phase; Arnold stayed on with colleague William Henry Jackson to take pictures of the fair to its conclusion. Arnold's platinum-process photographs had a slightly fuzzy appearance that gave them an unreal, dreamlike, almost utopian quality that created the fair's image as a "White City." He was careful to capture only well-dressed, upper-class white visitors in his photographs to create an "anecdote to social disorder" portrait in contrast to the reality of post-Haymarket Chicago. Regulations for all other photographers contributed to the fair's image by limiting their representations. Private picture taking was still in its infancy at the time of the fair: amateurs were charged $2 a day for the right to bring their Kodak pocket cameras onto the grounds, and professional photographers with larger format cameras were required to pay a $10 fee. Some of those images survive, but most of what the twenty-first century knows and sees of the 1893 World's Fair are the same Arnold and Jackson images that created the original White City mystique.[27]

In turn, the surrealism of the authorized photography inspired the fair's commercial artists, lithographers, and engravers. As with the printed word, the guiding principle was to avoid the excesses of everyday graphical images such as cluttered newspaper advertising or the then commonplace practice of plastering signboards, posters, broadsides, and fliers on the urban landscape. Instead, the illustrators were inspired to imitate high art, using representational imagery such as Louis Sullivan's latticework designs for the polychromatic Transportation Building and Arnold's photography to create stylistic impressions of sophistication and aestheticism that were pleasing rather than jarring to the senses. The department hired artists such as Charles C. Graham, who portrayed the fair's scenery in the manner of European landscape art, and Will H. Bradley, whose artwork brought the soft sell theme of sophistication to brochures, stationary, catalogs, labels, and other everyday articles. Combined with the first-time ever sale of picture postcards and other licensed commercial souvenirs, the department helped create a cultural event that "forming in its entirety [was] the most significant and grandest spectacle of modern times."[28]

Beyond positive imagery, the department acted to correct popular misrepresentations about the fair, a practice modern public relations practitioners call spin or damage control. For instance, in March 1892, inspired by eastern American newspaper reports, the London *Times* reported what it considered to be a greater-than-normal typhoid death rate in Chicago. "It seems now to be admitted that there has in truth been alarming prevalence of enteric [typhoid] fever [in Chicago]," the paper wrote. "Extraordinary stories published in London papers about an epidemic of typhoid fever in Chicago," read an internal correspondence sent to the department in Chicago. "Measures taken by the department to correct an impression so injurious to the exhibition." Sure enough, a letter to the *Times* written by Robert McCormick, the department's London representative, appeared two weeks later. "Two years ago the city limits of Chicago were extended to take in three or four towns," McCormick explained. "This extension led to an enormous increase in the demands made upon the water supply," a situation that he asserted would be rectified by the time of the fair.

"Special attention was given at this time to cultivation of public opinion favoring national aid through Congress for the exposition," another internal document reported, indicating the department was involved in lobbying as well as spin control. Department officials also acted to refute a telegram sent to a number of French newspapers indicating that Germany would be more favorably treated at the forthcoming event. "Reporters from all the leading [French] papers kept the commissioners busy with interviews on the subject," a newspaper reporter noted.

The department did not seek to cleanse all "libels of Chicago" as they were called. English author Oscar Wilde had written in his 1891 novel *The Picture of Dorian Gray* that "there is only one thing in the world worse than being talked about, and that is not being talked about," and Handy and his staff subscribed to that sentiment. "The report that gamblers of Chicago are preparing for the World's Fair is superfluous," the *Milwaukee Wisconsin* joked. "They wouldn't be Chicagoans if they neglected 'the opportunity of a lifetime.'" Handy's staff knew only too well that Chicago's First Ward vice district was as much if not more of a draw to the city than the fair. "Perhaps the currency has all been going to the World's Fair," the *Kansas City Journal* complained about a banknote shortage, "and been hoarded in the Chicago girl's stocking," a reference to Chicago prostitutes. "Chicago didn't really need the World's Fair for advertising purposes," the *St. Paul News* wrote. "Her divorce courts and street railway accidents are amply sufficient to impart notoriety, such as it is." "A new asteroid has been named 'Chicago,'" the neighboring *Minneapolis Tribune* reported. "Board of Trade men are inquiring whether it is in the constellation Taurus [the Bull] or Ursa Major [the Big Dipper]." In contrast to previous Chicago boosters, who jumped on such slights, Handy held that department-generated publicity at least neutralized such jibes over time, to the advantage of Chicago.[29]

The department filled more than one hundred scrapbooks of published material during its first year alone; Handy ultimately claimed that it produced or influenced more than 24 million fair-related news articles. "It is now recognized that one of the most important of the multitude of executive bureaus of the World's Fair is that curiously but appropriately titled bureau called 'The Department of Promotion and Publicity,'" the *Inter Ocean* observed in 1892. "To promote is one thing, to impart a knowledge of it to the world is another."

The department was so busy that leading up to opening day it averaged more than 100,000 words, 4,000 pieces of literature, and 2,000 to 3,000 pieces of mail daily in an era before photocopying machines, word processing, or the Internet. It supported a monthly magazine called the *World Columbian Exposition Illustrated,* which detailed the fair's progress through photography, one of the first Chicago publications to use the halftone reproduction process.

Once the fair opened, the department published an eight-page newspaper, *The Daily Columbian,* which was typeset on one of Chicago's first linotype machines and printed in the fair's Machinery Hall. The paper reproduced the front pages of the five major morning Chicago newspapers, the *Herald, Inter Ocean, Record, Times,* and *Tribune,* along with three pages of internally produced information. No other papers were allowed to be sold within the fair complex although newsboys were stationed outside all of the gates throughout the event.

By the fair's end, the department estimated that fully one-third of all that had been printed about it in the United States had been produced by the department—an unprecedented accomplishment for its day. "The tide of sentiment [against Chicago] turned gradually [in] the press of the world, and nearly every public agency having influence with the people became friends to the Fair and did excellent in its behalf," Handy claimed in late 1892. "Now Chicago and the World's Columbian Exposition are known and favorably talked of in almost every city, town and hamlet on earth." "For two years back the bureau of publicity has eagerly stuffed the mails with requests to the press to advertise the exposition and promised to take good care of us when we knocked at the gates," a Wisconsin newspaper editor recalled. "History will recognize a fact which unfair critics presently ignore," former newspaperman J. P. Holland wrote Handy in 1893, "that among the grandest achievements of the World's Columbian Exposition, few will compare favorably with the work well done by the Department of Publicity and Promotion."[30]

The White City

The fair received unprecedented coverage in Chicago's mass news media. Although the newspapers did not exert any direct influence over its construction or operation, they had everything to do with its perception, to the smallest detail. Not surprisingly, most coverage accentuated the positive and overlooked or downplayed the negative, alternating between contrasting paradigms. The first was as the "everyman's" fair, founded on the belief that it had been financed through the common man's purchase of individual $1 and $5 stock subscriptions. "Every man in Chicago who is not already a subscriber should walk right up to headquarters and put down his little name," a *Tribune* letter writer declared in 1891, and in *Mr. Salt,* his 1903 novel of late-nineteenth-century Chicago, *Daily News* reporter Will Payne declared, "It's the Chicago business man's fair. The business man—he did this!"

More lasting was the Charles Dudley Arnold–fairy image recreated in *Evening Post* reporter Frank L. Baum's 1900 *The Wizard of Oz,* with the Emerald City patterned after the White City, the wizard as one of the fair's many scientific geniuses, and hinterland visitors as portrayed by Dorothy and her gang. A Canadian-born fair construction worker named Elias Disney so enthralled his young son Walter with fairytale descriptions of the fair that they inspired the grown Disney's theme parks. All of the city's dailies designated beat reporters or hired freelancers to chronicle the White City's activities during its May 1 to October 30, 1893, run; many staffed the fair twenty-four hours a day. The resulting coverage alternated between the two views and a third of mental and physical overload. "I find two things are necessary in going to the World's Fair," *Inter Ocean* freelance reporter Teresa Dean admitted, "a level compass and a level head."[31]

There was very much about the fair to impress Chicago's mass news media. In spite of oft-stated concerns, it opened on schedule after a Herculean last-minute effort to finish construction and organize the grounds. "The veil of mist was lifted from over the White City and the World's Columbian Exposition was opened under fair skies," the *Chicago Tribune* proclaimed, proof that Chicago had finally arrived as a world-class metropolis. "On the threshold of a new century, it was not beyond the mental stretch to see the time when the city in which all the products of all the nations were gathered should be the center of population and the center of influence as well which would dominate the whole continent." Not above the hoopla itself, the *Tribune*'s opening day commemorative issue was proclaimed a "triumph of modern journalism" and sold for as much as $3.50 for a forty-eight-page issue, compared to its normal nickel price. The increased number of passenger trains routed to Chicago to carry fair passengers allowed the *Tribune* and other Chicago papers to be transported beyond their normal circulation area, and the *Tribune* bragged that a Buffalo, New York, reader could buy a *Tribune* forty minutes before the New York papers arrived in Chicago. "Now that the time between New York and Chicago is so short," the *Detroit Free Press* noted, "the breezy city will soon be advertising Gotham as one of her many suburbs."[32]

Built at a total cost of $22 million, the fair featured 65,000 exhibits and attractions contained in 220 buildings and outdoor locations stretching over more than 6,000 acres. With so many sights, Chicago's newspapers (in tandem with map and guidebook publishers) sought to define the event for time-strapped visitors. Instead of industrial production, the theme of the 1876 Philadelphia exposition, the Columbian fair celebrated consumerism through products ranging from live music delivered over long-distance telephone, Thomas Edison's Kinetoscope, and the zipper, to curiosity exhibits such as a 1,500-pound chocolate Venus de Milo, a 22,000-pound brick of Wisconsin cheese, and a United States map made of pickles. Among the lasting mass-marketed consumer products introduced at the fair were Cracker Jacks, Aunt Jemima syrup (advertised with the stereotyped face of an African American mammy), Shredded Wheat cereal, Juicy Fruit gum (developed by a thirty-one-year-old Chicago soap and baking soda salesman named William Wrigley Jr.) and Pabst (known henceforth as the Blue Ribbon beer). Oddly, such products received scant mention in the press of the day, their fame coming in future years. Instead, the *Tribune* reported that "connoisseurs of beer while visiting the Fair this year will . . . find it just the proper thing to pay a visit to 'Old Vienna' and . . . quaff the cool and delicious Seipp's Salvator Beer, and they will undoubtedly approve of the choice of the commission [as the fair's best beer] in this regard."[33]

When the whirlwind of senses became too much, the mass news media stepped in to provide context. Perhaps the most comprehensive of the many fair guidebooks was *The Time-Saver: A Book Which Names and Locates 5,000 Things at the World's Fair that Visitors Should Not Fail to See.* Compiled by an anonymous team of "bright newspaper men," the guide introduced a rating system, copied in subsequent travel and restaurant guides such as Michelin. The guns that fired the first and last shots of the Civil War, a manuscript copy of the Declaration of Independence, and the chair used by Gen. Ulysses S. Grant at Appomattox Court House were among top-rated exhibits. So was the Fine Arts Building, which contained nine thousand works, mostly by Europeans, and the Ferris Wheel, an attraction twice rejected by fair officials for safety concerns. The newspapers were responsible for designating the wheel as the fair's symbol, as the Eiffel Tower had represented the 1889 Paris event. "The neighborhood of the mechanical wonder is always filled with curious throngs of persons who, after watching the safe and interesting journeys made through space by the hundreds of passengers that fill its coaches on every trip, never leave the plaisance without making several revolutions themselves," a paper wrote.

At twilight, fairgoers watched as some 200,000 incandescent bulbs, 5,000 arc lights, and 20,000 glow lights were switched on slowly so as to appear that "the flying spark flew" from one building to another, as if "the lightning flash [was] held captive." "So the darkness became light and the glory of the evening was surpassed and eclipsed by the brilliancy of the night," the *Evening Post* wrote of this first large-scale demonstration of electric lighting. The outlines of the buildings were "etched in fire against the blackness of the night" and "the lagoons were made bright by the Chinese lanterns which were strung from stem to stern of the gay gondolas and by the bright lights which burned at the prows of the electric launches."[34]

Out-of-town papers echoed the *Inter Ocean*'s sentiments that "every man, woman, and child who visits the World's Fair goes out of the gates as a living advertisement." "It is interesting to hear returning visitors to the World's Fair try to tell how big and beautiful a thing it is," the *Utica* (New York) *Observer* wrote. "They simply can't do it—in one language." The *Tacoma Daily News* gushed that the greatest world's fair was in the city in which it was held. "Chicago the big and blustering, Chicago the windy and wonderful." "The [*Charlotte,* North Carolina] *News* yesterday published that the attendance at the World's Fair the previous day was 713,646," the same paper reported. "It was the greatest crowd ever gathered together in the history of this country, eclipsing the Paris [World's Fair] record." As the fair drew to a conclusion, the *Worcester Daily Spy* lamented about the marvel of the generation, the grandest exposition of the ages as another newspaper laughed at a mythological man who supposedly "saw the fair and lived well on a dollar a day." "He'd qualify for a dime show on the Bowery, as understudy to the Living Skeleton."[35]

But the most written-about fair attraction was not on the fairgrounds proper. The "Columbus Caravels," or Midway Plaisance, as it came to be called, a land bridge connecting lakeside Jackson Park to interior Washington Park and located near the twenty-first-century University of Chicago campus, generated curiosity from its beginning. The *Tribune* called it a "kaleidoscope" and observed of its crowds, "where they came from, nobody knew, but they were there, men, women, and children, and an occasional baby" even before it officially opened. Because it was not part of the main fair admission fee, the Midway evolved into the equivalent of a large-scale circus sideshow or dime museum, each exhibit charging its own admission price thinly disguised as moral or anthropological displays to justify its presence at the otherwise "scientific" fair. In such a free-market atmosphere, lowest common denominators predominated. For instance, primitive ethnological groups were treated like petting zoo animals. New York journalist Richard Harding Davis insisted that the Javanese village was "so odd and dainty and simple, and the little people so like children masquerading in grown-up people's clothes." The *Chicago Globe* noted of the Dahomeyan Village, "covered with paint, savage in appearance and this barbarous aspect enhanced by their weapons . . . the big negroes [*sic*] will be a conspicuous object for sightseers."

The most popular Plaisance attractions however were the semi-transparent-skirted *danse du ventre,* oriental, stomach, or belly dancers from the "Streets of Cairo" exhibit. Visitors to Chicago could and did see more skin walking the streets of the First Ward but the "hootchy-kootchy" dancers revealed sensuous motions and bare midriffs in an era when middle- and upper-class women rarely exposed more than shoulders and arms. "The basic notions of the dance—tossing the head from side to side, gesturing smoothly with the arms, 'fluttering' the belly by deep and shallow breathing and shimmying the hips by changing weight distribution over the legs—appear relatively simple until you try it," advised the *Illustrated American. Chicago Daily News* columnist Eugene Field celebrated the belly dancers in his specialty, something he called a deadline poem:

> Come boys, let's away to the Midway Plaisance
> There are visions of loveliness there to behold.
> Oh, the lithe Moorish maidens with bangles of gold
> And eyes that will set you afire at a glance . . .
> Why the half of the charms of that place can't be told
> And hush, we will see that Algerian dance—
> Come boys, let's away to the Midway Plaisance.

"A Chicago woman has procured an injunction to prevent her husband eloping with a Midway Plaisance beauty," the *Washington Post* reported. "This is undoubtedly the dawn of another Chicago industry."[36]

Not everything about the fair was as idyllic. Chicago's Chemical National Bank failed and was followed by its fair branch, the Columbian National, barely a week after the fair opened, taking with them the deposits of many fair exhibitors and portending the Depression of 1893. Those failures and others, soft pedaled by the local news media, created an atmosphere of financial uneasiness throughout the fair. On July 10, the Cold Storage Building, built to produce ice for refreshments and food preservation, caught fire and burned during the middle of a busy Monday. Clinging to a 440-foot central tower that masked a smoke stack, seventeen members of the Chicago Fire Department were trapped by the flames and were forced to either leap or fall to their deaths as an estimated 130,000 spectators watched in horror. "When the committee of [insurance] underwriters was examining into the character of the [building's] risk last June, Acting Fire Marshal Murphy made the prediction that the cold storage warehouse would be destroyed within a month," the *Evening Journal* wrote. "Within a month that white palace is a blackened sepulcher and with the smoke and flame."

As well, out-of-town newspapers complained about confidence men and women, thieves, pickpockets, muggers, and other assorted criminals who practiced their arts with little interference inside and outside the fair's walls. The *New York Herald* may have been exaggerating only slightly when it noted, "Latest reports indicate an improvement in the almost incredible conditions of disorder [in Chicago]. . . . Murder, burglary and highway robbery are still of nightly and daily occurrence." "I had plenty [of money] to go [to Chicago]," the *Detroit Free Press* quoted a Detroit man as saying, "but not enough to get away with." "Sharks of the confidence, sandbagging variety are once more plying their trade in the neighborhood of the World's Fair grounds," the *Tribune* and the *Inter Ocean* warned in February 1893.

But crime reports all but disappeared from the local papers during the event, even when social worker Jane Addams's purse was stolen during opening day activities. "Many people have an idea that 'fleecing' is the watchword that controls the White City," an *Inter Ocean* reporter wrote. Only twenty "official" arrests for pickpocketing were reported during the entire run. Instead, fair records revealed more arrests for drunkenness and fence jumping than personal crimes or crimes of force. The *Detroit Tribune* joked that a distracted mother complained to a fair official that "my child is lost. I fear it is stolen." "I will have the Columbian [fair] police searched at once," the official supposedly responded.[37]

The October 30 (rather than 31) ending to the fair, the result of a government clerical error, was reported in the press with sadness and expressions of hope for the future. The growing Depression had induced thousands of unemployed workers to demonstrate outside the fairgrounds, in front of the Board of Trade building, and at massive downtown lakefront rallies that included labor leader Samuel Gompers, reformer Henry George, and a young Chicago lawyer named Clarence Darrow. Soup kitchens were springing up around the city. Speaking at the fair on October 26, Chicago Mayor Carter Harrison Sr. sought to soften the economic impact by promising to try to keep the fair open longer as an employment source. Later that day, Harrison was assassinated at the front door of his home by an unemployed "crank" whom reporters, including the *News Record's* Ray Stannard Baker, knew. "His name is Pendergast," Baker was told at a reform club meeting, "we can't keep him out."

Historians have cited fair eulogies given by eastern intelligentsia such as Charles Eliot Norton and Henry Adams, but Chicago's mass news media was equal to the task. "No promises will be made," the *Daily News* wrote, "but if Chicago ever undertakes another enterprise of the kind the world will know what to expect." "For six months the eyes of the people have been gladdened with a vision of beauty which has surpassed their most sanguine expectations," the *Tribune* explained. The *Inter Ocean* published a drawing by Charles W. Saalburg memorializing the late fair as the "Vanishing City," which sold out several editions of the paper. *News Record* columnist George

Ade observed that "the world's greatest achievement of the departing century was pulled off in Chicago. The Columbian Exposition was the most stupendous, interesting and significant show ever spread out for the public." Perhaps the most fitting obituary came in a *Globe* editorial published following the fair's opening ceremony. Referring to a brief moment in the program when all of the foreign dignitaries and spectators stood and watched together as the various flags of the world's nations were raised, the paper wrote:

> In all the pages of history there is no event recorded so fraught with greatness as this simple act. The mighty tread of armies, the battle's charge, not even the coup d'état which made a French Republic, is to be written upon the same page with it. They are of war—this was of peace. This day there has dawned that golden age of peace, plenty and prosperity of which poets have sung and prophets foretold all down the ages. From the night of the past we have stepped in one moment into the sunburst glory of the great future.

"Do you think you would have had over 700,000 people to gaze at you on Chicago day if the press had been silent?" the *Inter Ocean*'s Teresa Dean demanded of fair officials in a column published on October 27, 1893. "Do you think the visitors to this Exposition would have discovered all of the beauties and wonders of the White City if they had not been educated to it by our newspapers before coming? No magazine in the world—whose writers have months to prepare their articles—has ever printed more beautiful descriptions nor more perfect English than has been dashed off daily by some of the press workers of Chicago."[38]

* * *

There was another, albeit at the time lesser known event that coincided with the World's Columbian Exposition in Chicago. As newspaperman Finis Farr observed, it was common knowledge that a tiny percentage of fairgoers "got the overdose of knockout powders, or the knife in the ribs, and then the drop in the lake, or a prairie grave." Newspapers referred to such victims as the "mysteriously disappeared." Officially, the Chicago Police Department admitted to some two hundred such persons during fair time. Unofficially, the estimates of the vanishment, as the process was called, ranged much higher. Only after the fair was over was it revealed that at least some may have been secretly participating in a popular downstate alcoholism treatment program.[39]

But in Chicago's most horrific murder case ever (the *New York World* called its perpetrator "the first criminal of the [19th] century"), a thirty-three-year-old psychopath known as Dr. H. H. Holmes, an alias for Herman Webster Mudgett, may have killed as few as nine or as many as one hundred fairgoers, mostly young women, who checked into his lodging and retail establishment situated about two miles from the fair at the intersection of 63rd and Wallace streets. Holmes and his activities were allegedly unknown to Chicago police at the time of the fair and remained so, except among a select group of lawyers, private detectives, and out-of-town police, until November 1894 when he was arrested for insurance fraud in Philadelphia. As details of his crimes were revealed, the *Tribune* labeled him a "fiend," perhaps the strongest word the late nineteenth century had for a serial killer.

Holmes's building was destroyed by an arson fire on August 18, 1895, not long after most of the fair buildings were torched, destroying critical evidence in the investigation, so he was convicted of a single Philadelphia murder and executed in Pennsylvania the following year. In his only known confession he detailed a few murders, but the precise number of his Chicago victims will never be known. "Had it not been for the exertions of the insurance companies which Holmes swindled," the *Inter Ocean* wrote, "he might yet be at large, preying upon society." The *New York Times* stated the obvious when it reported that Chicagoans "must be amazed at the failure of the municipal police department and the local prosecuting officers not only to prevent those awful crimes, but even to procure any knowledge of them." "Chicago would make a better appearance," the *New York World* wrote in reference to Haymarket, "if she quit arresting innocent men and hanged guilty ones."

As it turned out, another group of swindlers, extortionists, and blackmailers were equally at work while Holmes was prosecuted and went unpunished by an equally oblivious Chicago Police Department. Nicknamed the Gray Wolves, this group of Chicago aldermen enriched themselves at the expense of taxpayers as never before in Chicago's corruption-riddled history. In combination with Dr. Holmes and the city's notorious vice industries, late-1890s Chicago once again found its public image tarnished as it hurtled toward its ultimate goal of becoming the First City.[40]

6

Second City

Chicagoans have long associated the emergence of their world-class city with the timing of the 1893 World's Fair, for it was that event which brought together the diverse talents, energies, and ideas then percolating within and without the city. "That first year in Chicago [in 1893] was a picture so kaleidoscopic, so extravagant, so ridiculous," journalist and author Edna Ferber wrote in her 1924 novel *Showboat.* "Magnolia [her main character] had her first real evening dress, cut décolleté; tasted champagne; went to the races at the Washington Park race track; sat in a box at Hooley's [theater]; was horrified at witnessing the hootchie-kootchie dance on the Midway Plaisance at the World's Fair." Lyricist Oscar Hammerstein 2nd elaborated on Ferber's imagery in his and Jerome Kern's 1928 musical version of the novel:

When the sports of gay Chicago,
Pay a visit to the Fair.
You can tell every swell,
By his dashing air.
They do credit to Chicago,
With their clothes all tailor made.
All their Country Cousins gape and stare,
When they see the dandies on Parade.[1]

However, the accomplishments of "the most marvelous city on earth," as the *Kansas City Times* characterized Fair-era Chicago, were mitigated by a colder, darker, more insensate side of the city. "Chicago is one of the most conglomerate of all cosmopolitan cities," English reform journalist William

T. Stead wrote in his 1894 best seller *If Christ Came to Chicago!* "Mammon holds high carnival in its gilded palaces, while little children hunger, mothers grow faint for food and die, and strong men weep for want of work." "It doesn't seem human," naturalist author Frank Norris put it more simply in his 1902 *The Pit*. "It's all very well for the individual just so long as he can keep afloat, but once fallen, how horribly quick it would crush him, annihilate him, how horribly quick, and with such horrible indifference!"

The mass news media was part and parcel to this darker side of Chicago and its rampant vice, corruption, and inhumanity, contributing what the radical *Arbeiter Zeitung* called the "insane noise of the boodle press." From an ever increasing number of dailies, the late-nineteenth-century Chicago mass news media celebrated what sociologist Herbert Gans would label a century later "responsible capitalism," the myth that capitalists operated for the benefit of all. Most Chicago journalists sought to avoid biting the hands that fed them and promoted rather than criticized the private sector, especially the city's captains of industry. When they did challenge the status quo, especially younger newspapermen (like Theodore Dreiser) who hailed from small hinterland towns, their reporting tended to simplify the conflict as a struggle between the purity and simplicity of country life and the depravity and confusion of the big city—or what Gans called "pastoralism."

Communications technology was on their side. By the very late nineteenth century, newspapers could produce timely forty-eight-page editions, compared to the four-page papers of early Chicago, and had the manpower and financial resources to imitate early muckraker Stead and crusade against such notorious representatives of "responsible" capitalism as prostitution madams Lizzie Allen, Vina Fields, and Carrie Watson, gambling kingpin "Sure Thing" Michael C. McDonald, monopolist Charles T. Yerkes, and Grey Wolves Michael "Hinky Dink" Kenna and "Bathhouse" John J. Coughlin. By the end of the century however, it was more the avarice of Chicago's vice purveyors and corrupt politicians and less the crusading of newspapers that contributed to their downfalls. And it was an equally helpless local press that stood and gaped as New York snatched victory from defeat and forever cast Chicago as America's Second City.[2]

"Abandoned Creatures"

When the precursor to the Chicago Police Department reported in late 1854 that 194 women had been arrested for prostitution during the second half of the year—information duly copied in out-of-town papers—it was really publicizing the fact that Chicago had a significant number of prostitutes in the first place (assuming the same woman was not arrested 194 times). There were certainly more prostitutes three years later when Mayor Long John Wentworth staged his famous Sands raid, sending them packing to other neighborhoods around the city.

By the time of the Civil War, the city's new and improved vice districts had become a must-see attraction for soldiers passing through town, and in turn they provided valuable word-of-mouth advertising of Chicago's attractions. They were so effective that legitimate businesses such as hotels, rooming houses, saloons, restaurants, and railroad stations began situating themselves near or within the vice areas to capitalize on Chicago's growing fame as the "wickedest city in the United States." When one newspaper complained that the downtown's vice areas were "so contaminated by these execrable vagabonds that respectable persons avoid them as they would a cesspool," it could have been more brag than complaint. "Our gamblers . . . have plenty of money to spare, and are not burdened with good taste," a local art seller boasted to the *Times*. "The wickedness and piety of Chicago are in their way marvelous," *Scribner's* wrote.[3]

Modern urban scholars are as ambivalent about prostitution as was Chicago's Gilded Age mass news media. For instance, "Prostitution blurred neat and easy distinctions between good and evil," Timothy J. Gilfoyle wrote in *City of Eros*. Not only was sex a profit-making industry in big nineteenth-century cities such as New York and Chicago, it was a "part of the public culture, structured by the market, organized into institutions, ranging from the brothel to the theater, that guaranteed commercial efficiency, ostentation, and publicity." Interestingly, Gilfoyle differentiated between paid prostitutes and "women who provided sex for other forms of payment: rent, food, clothing, or entertainment." "'Treating' was not the same as prostitution," according to Gilfoyle. Karen Halttunen, in *Confidence Men and Painted Women*, wrote, "Advice books, fashion magazines, and etiquette manuals cautioned young women against emulating the arts of the painted women [both women of fashion and prostitutes] who poisoned polite society with deception and betrayal by dressing extravagantly and practicing the empty forms of false etiquette." Marilyn Wood Hill claimed that those nineteenth-century women who chose prostitution as an occupation did so because they lacked other options, even in prosperous times. "In addition to economic rewards unavailable in other female occupations, prostitution offered social freedoms that traditional employments and familial restrictions did not allow."[4]

There was no question that prostitution was considered a mortal sin, the worst abasement imaginable for women, by Chicago's mid-nineteenth-century newspapers, but there was an element of voyeurism in their concern, embodiment of the Victorian era's famous double sexual standard. For instance, an 1861 *Chicago Tribune* reporter who characterized a Wells Street brothel as a "resort of the most abandoned creatures of both sexes in the city and the nightly scene of disgusting carouses and affrays verging upon murder, where only the force, not the will, was wanting" had to investigate it in person. That same year the *Times* published a sensation chronicling a "young girl rescued from a bagnio [brothel] on State Street" with the observation that "if the experiences which she obtained will excite in her mind that abhorrence of crime which should exist, a good end will have been obtained, and a soul saved from the worst of degradation," a claim that excused revealing details in the rest of the article. As self-appointed moral judges, male newspaper editors were only too happy to chastise obvious moral failings like prostitution through such rationalizations.

In particular it was Wilbur F. Storey's 1865 editorial, "The Licentiousness in Our Midst," which maintained that it was considered a newspaper's business to bring "immorality and crime affecting society to the public gaze [so] that it may know of their existence and take the proper methods to insure against them, and work the reformation of the authors of the offences" that introduced reporting as a form of social control. Storey's justification set the standard for prostitution reporting for the remainder of the century. "A great public scandal is like an enema," a Gilded Age Chicago prostitute wrote in her memoirs. "The result is newspapers sell more copies and there is talk of reform." A 1866 *Tribune* editorial titled "The Social Evil" held that "it is not to be wondered at that . . . good men should occasionally despair of Christianity . . . [at the] unwelcome and disgusting truth that prostitution is inseparable from modern civilization." "It is more and more coming to be understood that this entire problem is at once the most important and the most mysterious of any that vex the social system," the same paper wrote in 1870. "It is no longer sensible to dispose of it in a bigoted aphorisms, as if there were but some thing to be said, done, or availed, and that were plain."

Behind the public posturing, mid- and late-nineteenth-century Chicago newspapermen believed, as Herbert Gans would have predicted, that capitalists somehow operated for the benefit of all, even those involved in otherwise unconscionable businesses such as prostitution. Vice income represented a significant segment of Chicago's gross domestic product during the Gilded Age, and any large-scale closings of brothels, gambling houses, or related vice businesses created an immediate economic hardship throughout the city. "There is no objection to gambling here [in Chicago] so long as it is conducted with a trifling regard for the police," a gambling operator told a

Tribune reporter in 1885. In fact, Chicago businessmen made the best faro and poker dealers because "they learn it as they would learn bookkeeping or anything else in their business." As increasing property taxes shifted vice operations to the South Loop area during the 1880s and 1890s, a *Tribune* reporter waxed nostalgically of the original State Street vice district. "Many a giddy Chicagoan has squandered his money there," the paper noted, "and many a countryman has there paid in money, reputation, and home ties the price of 'seeing the elephant.'"

Vice was an integral element of latter nineteenth-century Chicago politics, law enforcement, and journalism. "The pimps who hang about brothels, the gamblers who keep open dens for luring the innocent and young . . . if courted and flattered while a canvas is going on, expect no active interference with their pursuits when the canvas has come to an end and the officers of their choice are installed," the *Tribune* wrote during the 1860 municipal elections. Twenty-five years later, the same paper maintained that the small number of police raids and slight fines levied on most of Chicago's houses of prostitution represented a public "co-partnership of Chicago with harlotry."

Reporters routinely joined policemen, politicians, and government officials at VIP holiday parties hosted by the city's better brothels, which included free food, liquor, dancing, and run of the house. Many reporters, especially those assigned to a police beat, were on a first-name basis with Chicago's better-known brothel operators and protected them from newspaper publicity for the price of a payoff. Prostitutes and newspapermen viewed each other as fellow professionals, with the same professional detachment from the foibles and follies of the rest of society. "You are never fully engaged, all of you," a Chicago prostitute's customer once complained to her. "You stand aside and watch what is going on like an onlooker." "The idea of establishing a religious daily newspaper at Chicago is a most ridiculous one from a business standpoint," the *Detroit News* said. "The field isn't there to make such a venture successful."[5]

Economic crises, such as occurred during and immediately after the Civil War, enlarged Chicago's prostitution trade, as Timothy Gilfoyle chronicled in New York. Rather than hard-to-find money, war widows traded sexual favors for rent, food, and other necessities of life. "Starvation, prostitution, suicide threaten us largely, unless [this] matter be taken in hand," the *Chicago Tribune* warned in 1864. "The little weekly stipend which at first barely sufficed to keep body and soul together will be totally inadequate to that poor purpose the coming winter, even it if do not cease altogether." Two years later, there were so many war widow prostitutes that the police raided their brothels and cribs only when the city's coffers were empty and their pay wanting. By the *Tribune*'s reckoning in 1870, one woman in every thirty-seven in the city was "an adulteress," a prostitute of some form.

When the occasional raid was publicized in the papers, it often had the opposite effect of adding to the allure of prostitution and its profitability. News articles detailed elegant brothel decorations such as French mirrors, expensive wallpapers, oriental rugs, and otherwise unknown indoor plumbing, along with amenities such as expensive wines, liquors, and cigars. Elaborate escape mechanisms such as trapdoors, secret passages, and double doors added to the romance as they protected upper-class clientele, giving brothels an aura of invincibility. Public supporters spoke of what was called the "St. Louis system" for regulating bordellos, requiring periodic health exams for prostitutes but otherwise allowing the business. "The licensing system does not, on the whole, diminish the diseases which have been affixed by Nature to the social evil," the *Tribune* warned. "On the other had, it does hold out a false hope to the vicious and unwary that they may sin without punishment." Such reform efforts helped elevated prostitution to the status of a semi-legitimate occupation and engendered an attitude toward it as a "victimless" crime that persisted in the press throughout the nineteenth century until Chicago's white slavery scare in the early twentieth century.[6]

Not surprisingly, a select segment of the mass news media sought to cater to the Gilded Age Chicago prostitution and vice industries. The *Chicago Tribune* decried what it called "obscene handbills" posted on buildings, fences, and any other static object during the late 1850s, and the city passed a 1872 ordinance at the urging of Mayor Joseph Medill to suppress "obscene" publications in general and in particular a newspaper called *Town and Criminal Talk*. A few years later, the male-only Chapin and Gore saloon on Monroe Street was forced to remove a large painting of a naked woman from behind its bar (artwork commonplace in nearly every city saloon) during a brief reform period.

Still, a genre of publication known as the flash or sporting paper became a fixture in Gilded Age Chicago. Nicknamed after a popular slang term for communications among criminals, flash was also defined as "fast, roguish, and sometimes infers counterfeit or deceptive," all attributes of its press. "The New York flash papers actually did not have much obscure slang in them, but they described a world of deceit and counterfeit, where attractively innocent young women turn out to be sexually available, where respectable young and old lead double lives . . . where things, in short, are seldom what they seem," as Patricia Cline Cohen, Timothy J. Gilfoyle, and Helen Lefkowitz Horowitz explained in *The Flash Press: Sporting Male Weeklies in 1840s New York*.

From New York, flash newspapers spread to Chicago after the Civil War in titles such as *Chicago Sporting Gazette, Chicago Street Gazette, Chicago Life,* and *Chicago Sporting Life.* Most were the creation of Ransom H. Andrews, known professionally as "Shang," described as a "literary Ishmaelite whose pen was against every man, while every man's pen was against him." Born in Detroit around 1835, Andrews was hired by Wilbur F. Storey to write for his *Detroit Free Press* and moved to Chicago with his boss in 1861. Andrews was a devotee of the sporting life: one story had him playing billiards when he should have been covering an important political event in 1867. Blessed with a talent to "create news with great faculty out of nothing," Andrews returned to the *Times* and fabricated an entire sensation detailing how a rabid dog had attacked and possibly killed a family living in a remote prairie area outside of the city. The thought of missing such a scoop so inflamed the competing *Tribune* that the following morning the paper dispatched a reporter and its managing editor to the scene of the alleged attack only to discover that the nearest building was two miles away. "The 'managing editor' of the *Times* has either been shamefully imposed upon by his local reporters, or he is a party himself to a shameful fraud on the readers of his paper," the *Tribune* complained. When Storey confronted his recalcitrant reporter, Andrews confessed and countered, "I can make more writing for the other paper." Storey relented and kept Andrews.

Nevertheless, Andrews fabricated himself out of his *Times* job by 1873, and he spent his remaining years in legitimate journalism as an *Evening Post* police reporter and was employed briefly by the *Omaha Herald.* Beginning around 1864, however, he began publishing *Sporting Life,* which featured news, shoptalk, and related items of interest to prostitutes, gamblers, sporting men, social outcasts, and voyeurs of various stripes. His publications survived largely on street and mail circulation with some advertising, mainly for baseball, candy, liquor, cigarettes, contraception, and patent medicines for venereal disease and opium addiction—many ads that the mainstream publications would not accept.

He specialized in news of the trade. "There are two strawberry blondes at the Hotel de Goodrich," Andrews reported in one issue. "Ada Hunter has a new lover—Miss Fresh from Pittsburgh," explained another along with news that "the circus house, 70 Wells street, is drawing crowded houses, and performances take place any hour of the day or night." Copies of Andrews's publications found their way to other cities in spite of Anthony Comstock's postal regulations against obscenity, thus furthering Chicago's reputation. "Two of the best [Indianapolis] has," a reference to police officers, "amuses [*sic*] themselves every evening for an hour reading the *Chicago Street Gazette*," the *Indianapolis Sentinel* wrote in 1876, and the *New Orleans Times* confessed that "the *Chicago Street Gazette* continues to circulate in New Orleans. Of course, it would be an easy matter to choke it off, provided the police authorities cared to do so."

While such newspapers had a devoted readership, authorities periodically sought to suppress them as "lewd, wicked, and obscene." Joining them were book-length productions such as Andrews's 1889 *Sporting and Club House Directory*, which detailed the best and worst in the city, and the 1892 *Chicago by Day and Night: The Pleasure Seekers Guide to the Paris of America*, a less titillating survey of Chicago's entertainments written by an anonymous newspaper reporter. Both were sold at selected newsstands and book stores where visitors could find them. They provided reviews of restaurants, saloons, brothels, gambling houses, and related amenities for the middle and upper classes. For instance, "Miss Watson's is the HOUSE of the West," Andrews's 1889 directory reported, "no living human being ever went away dissatisfied."

They also furnished information on how the uninitiated could avoid being fleeced by Chicago's armies of confidence men and women. "Beware! O sportive young gentleman in search of a little diversion, of the young woman who on the shortest term of acquaintance invites you to accompany her to her flat or her boudoir," *Chicago by Day and Night* counseled. "It may be that she has a pair of sharp scissors in her pocket with which she deftly snips off your money pocket." "Every night there may be found . . . any number of 'sporty-looking' gentry," the book advised men, "who will be only too glad to guide the inquirer to a secluded spot where he can be accommodated with as large or as small a game as his inclination may dictate or his means allow." Voyeurs into Chicago's dark side who were traveling on a budget did not have to spend money to find their way around town. Religious tracts, some created by prominent evangelist Dwight L. Moody ostensibly to dissuade visitors from the sin districts, were free for the price of a sermon. And daily newspaper reports of police activities could provide useful clues.

With his penchant for fiction, Andrews penned four of the earliest Chicago crime novels, pairing fictional characters with living people and actual locations to sensationalize gambling, alcoholism, prostitution, and procurement in Chicago. For instance, the 1878 *Wicked Nell; A Gay Girl of the Town* featured as a leading character Police Captain Michael C. Hickey, who in real life was convicted of accepting cash and gift bribes from brothel operators while employed as police superintendent from 1875 to 1878. "'I have heard of this Wicked Nell before,' the "Captain" says in the book, 'but I thought she was one of the old settlers—something like the girls on Wells, Griswold or Sherman streets,'" a reference to some of downtown Chicago's earliest brothel houses. "All the policemen in Chicago couldn't make me cry," a defiant and ostensibly fictional prostitute Nell declares as she is arrested at the end of the novel; Andrews's other prostitutes were equally independently minded and self-sufficient. "I am a child of fate—a creature of destiny—an outcast—a deceiver—a wretch who decoys and entraps and ruins men without conscience and without mercy," Andrews's leading character in *Cranky Ann, the Street Walker* declares. Andrews died uncelebrated in 1887, leaving his wife and children. "An outcast he may have been, but many a worse man than old Shang has died in the last few years," wrote an *Inter Ocean* reporter who obviously knew him. "All I can say is 'Peace to his ashes.'"[7]

Visitors who did not necessarily want to experience Chicago vice in the form of a Shang Andrews novel could participate in a tamer version known as the masquerade. Popularized in the Andrew Lloyd Webber musical *The Phantom of the Opera,* masked social events were common in Paris and New York, and they were carried over into Chicago beginning in the 1850s. "Through fantasies of dress, New Yorkers temporarily dropped their standard conceptions of proper, 'respectable' behavior," Timothy Gilfoyle wrote. From mere socializing, select masquerade balls evolved into whirling male and female dances, exercises that challenged the limits of public sexual behavior.

Chicago's most notorious masquerade was the Lame Jimmy Ball. Beginning around 1880, brothel operator Carrie Watson staged the annual event at Freiberg's Hall on East 22nd Street (ostensibly in the honor of a piano and fiddle player named Lame Jimmy) that became the preeminent Levee society event during the remainder of the century. The gatherings included public officials, politicians, police officers, and reporters and continued at the hall until 1895 when a police officer was fatally shot by another, drawing undue attention. The event was moved the following year to the Seventh Regiment Armory building and eventually the Auditorium, where it was conducted by the First Ward Aldermen Hinky Dink Kenna and Bathhouse John Coughlin until public criticism finally brought it to an end to it in 1908.

The Lame Jimmy Ball was not the only city masquerade. The *Chicago Tribune* reported of another where "better order than usually attends affairs of this kind was maintained." Organizers "did their best to keep out improper characters," it said. "Dancing of women with men they never saw before is bad business," the *Tribune* quoted a minister as warning in 1888. "I hurl an anathema against promiscuous dancing and denounce these public masquerade balls as thoroughfares to perdition." The anonymous newspaperman author of *Chicago by Day and Night* described what he called "a masquerade of the lowest order" organized by the Chicago Board of Trade in 1890 in which the "young 'chippie' of the cheap dry goods shops and her red-necked escort" appeared in costume and danced until noon the next day. "After midnight, when the musicians as well as the maskers found themselves vinously [*sic*] fortified to sufficient extent, all formality was dispensed with and care thrown to the winds," the writer explained. Prizes were awarded to a variety of participants including a female impersonator "with a pair of shoulders exposed that Atlas might have envied." Subject to less social approbation than hard-core Levee entertainments, nineteenth-century Chicago masquerades were still equated with a loss of reputation for women and opportunity for men to practice the sexual double standard.[8]

"Reeking, Stinking Fleshpot"

The 1893 World's Columbian Exposition elevated prostitution to a major Chicago industry. In spite of more than forty years of social disapproval and sporadic law enforcement, Chicago had thousands of prostitutes along with more than two thousand brothels, massage parlors, and "bath" houses in the early 1890s, some charging as little as 25 cents a visit. They competed with freak-show museums, burlesque theaters, so-called "free [sex] shows," and twenty-four-hour sexually related "circus houses," the latter featuring bawdy entertainments, "companionship" of women, nude dancing, and "exhibitions" of women, men, and animals. "Here were the negro [*sic*], the prostitute, the blackleg, the gambler, the romantic adventurer par excellence," former *Chicago Globe* reporter Theodore Dreiser (who arrived in Chicago from Terre Haute, Indiana, in 1890) wrote in his 1914 novel *The Titan*. "Flaring were the lights of the bagnio; tinkling the banjos, zithers, mandolins of the so-called gin mill; all the dreams and the brutality of the day seemed gathered to rejoice (and rejoice they did) in this newfound wonder of a metropolitan life in the West." Chicago was "wide open," the *Tribune* complained or bragged. "The great bulk of Chicago crime is hatched in these resorts. They form the nucleus for the worst phases of urban dissipation and vice." "Chicago people are just now congratulating themselves," the *Bismarck Tribune* reported, "over the fact that the lake at least will remain with them 'after the fair.'"

For such reasons, the First Ward was the ultimate World's Fair attraction, a cacophony of chanting barkers, confidence men and women, street games of thimblerig and three-card monte, clicking beer mugs, flickering lights, and women advertising themselves in windows and doors mixed with the comings and goings of sporting men, pimps, prostitutes, drunks, greenhorns, and a few police. Interspersed were the sounds of tinkling pianos and strumming banjos playing Stephen Foster tunes or German, French, and Irish folk songs. Centered in the vicinity of 18th and 22nd streets and around Custom House Place (an alley in the vicinity of Harrison and 12th streets), the First Ward was a sexual and gambling superstore, serving visitors twenty-four hours a day, seven days a week.

"The World's Fair was a gold mine for me and my friends during the years 1892 and 1893," prostitute and badger or confidence woman May Churchill, known as Chicago May, wrote in her 1928 memoirs. "The first of those years we nicked the builders, the second the visitors." "Confidence men, shell workers, and sand-baggers followed like wolves after a lone prairie traveler," plainclothes police detective Clifton Wooldridge wrote of the First Ward. When one streetwalker put her hand into his coat pocket, "Wooldridge opened his coat and displayed his star, to the astonishment of the woman who expected 'ready money.'" Regardless, Wooldridge and his fellow police specialized in antagonizing only the most egregious of Chicago's vice purveyors for the most part, leaving the less greedy and more politically connected unscathed.

The *Chicago Daily News* half warned, half advertised "the gilded dens of infamy along the avenue with marble steps and brazen door-plates" and "the polluting presence of abandoned women who wandered through the streets." The *Tribune* noted nostalgically forty years later that "the fair itself was a boon to the [vice] business; never before had the city held so many visitors with money and sportive inclinations. Chicago was wide open in the most unpleasant sense of the term—perhaps this was because its citizens, in addition to being busy, were too close to see the situation from a proper point of view." At the time, the magazine *Truth* wrote of a man who bought a Chicago clock that tolled on the quarter hour. "Doesn't it?" a friend asked. "Yes, but you have to wind it every fifteen minutes."[9]

Beyond the street-level attractions were the brothels. As Marilyn Wood Hill observed in *Their Sisters' Keepers,* later nineteenth-century prostitution was created by a complex combination of factors including poverty and destitution as well as economic opportunity and social advancement for women. "Statistics of the social evil seem to show that it diminishes in proportion as the means of employment are opened to women, in a manner to render them capable of supporting themselves by work," the *Tribune* editorialized in 1873.

A select group of women benefitted directly from prostitution during the 1890s. For instance, Ellen Williams, better known as Lizzie Allen, opened a tastefully decorated "parlor house" in 1865 and employed dozens of women in what was reputed to operate the city's most expensive bordello, at 2131 South Dearborn Street, until her death in 1896 of syphilitic-induced paralysis at the age of fifty-six. Her final estate, as reported by the *Tribune*, was valued at between $300,000 and $1 million, and she was buried in Rosehill Cemetery, final resting place of prominent early Chicagoans such as Long John Wentworth.

African American Vina Fields operated the city's largest brothel at 138–140 Fourth Avenue, in Custom House Place; she ran her business as a cooperative with her African American employees catering exclusively to white patrons. Fields was arrested at least once, for procuring a seventeen-year-old New Orleans girl on the pretense of employment as a maid, but operated unmolested for the most part. She employed sixty women during the 1893 fair, and talked openly about her business with a visiting British newspaperman, William T. Stead. "She is bringing up her daughter who knows nothing of the life of her mother in the virginal seclusion of a convent school, and she contributes of her bounty to maintain her unfortunate sisters whose husbands down south are among the hosts of the unemployed," Stead reported. "Every day this whole winter through she has fed a hungry, ragged regiment of out-of-works. The day before I called, 201 men had free dinners of her providing."[10]

And there was Caroline Victoria (known professionally as Carrie Watson) who owned a brothel at 441 South Clark Street, not far from gambling kingpin Michael McDonald's headquarters, "The Store." Watson preferred a New Orleans-style "resort" with French-style decor for her upper-class clientele. She made the newspapers in 1875, described by the *Inter Ocean* as "a well known member of the demi-monde," for gifting a horse and buggy to the same Police Superintendent Michael Hickey (who figured in "Shang" Andrews's novels) not long before she was accused of robbing a patron of $1,600. Watson acknowledged the hardships faced by Gilded Age women without husbands or other means of support, noting that prostitution was the "natural result of poverty on the part of the woman and passion on the part of the man." She staged the famed Lame Jimmy masquerade ball, which was reported in the same manner as society events in newspapers during the 1880s.

Watson's bordello was the Levee showplace during the World's Fair, with some sixty women dressed in silk available twenty-four hours a day, seven days a week. A parrot by the open front door welcomed patrons with "Carrie Watson. Come in gentlemen." Watson was criticized by the *Daily News* in 1893 for a social event staged at the Washington Park horse racing track described as "the greatest Mardi Gras of dissolute sporting ever witnessed in Chicago or any other city." Nevertheless, Watson, too, was applauded for feeding the unemployed during the 1893–94 Depression. "She is the exploiteur [*sic*], the capitalist of her class, for the same conditions reproduced themselves everywhere," William T. Stead wrote. "Carrie Watson is a smart woman, said to be liberal in her gifts to the churches in her neighbourhood, one a Catholic just across the way and the other a Jewish synagogue which local rumor asserts is run rent free owing to Carrie's pious munificence." In the wake of her death in the late 1890s, a newspaperman eulogized that "in all the world, there is not another Carrie Watson."

For the rest of the nameless women who earned $3 a week or less in Chicago prostitution and were regarded, as Theodore Dreiser maintained, as "sows and termagants—wretched, filthy greasy, swining things," there were the fortunate few like Williams, Fields, and Victoria, who proved that it was possible for a Gilded Age Chicago woman to be independent and financially successful. "I don't say—never did—that whoring is the best way of life," a Chicago prostitute recalled, "but it's better than going blind in a sweat shop sewing, or twenty hours work as a kitchen drudge, or housemaid, with the old man and the sons always laying for you in the hallway with their flies open."[11]

If Christ Came to Chicago!

Given its economic impact, inherent secretiveness, and the closeness of reporters to the business and its operators, it was not surprising that the most detailed exposé of late-nineteenth-century Chicago prostitution was provided by an out-of-town journalist. British newspaperman William T. Stead (who claimed to have first heard about Lizze Allen's brothel on the streets of London) created a sensation in 1885 with a crusading series in his *Pall Mall Gazette* on the procurement of girls and women for prostitution titled "The Maiden Tribute of Modern Babylon." Some of the streetwalkers interviewed for his articles were as young as twelve. A detective hired by Stead carried his investigative techniques too far, abducting a thirteen-year-old girl solely so that Stead could interview her—Stead spent three months in a London prison for the kidnapping, but his journalism led to the implementation of laws reducing procurement in the British empire. "Mr. Stead of the *Pall Mall Gazette* should move to Chicago if he wants to be appreciated," the *Washington Critic* mocked in 1886, and true to the jibe, Stead decided to investigate the Windy City eight years later.

What he saw appalled him, especially how Chicago's so-called Best Men had allowed their new city to become as sordid as centuries-old Europe. "The really disreputable in Chicago are not those who are supposed to be disreputable," Stead wrote, "but those who are clothed in purple and fine linen and occupy the high places in the synagogue and the Board of Trade, etc." The result of his investigations, *If Christ Came to Chicago!* was published in 1894 by the tiny Chicago printing house of Laird & Lee. William H. Lee was the first African American book publisher in Chicago, said to be Gen. Robert E. Lee's last enslaved valet.

Stead focused on what he considered to be the sinfulness and Mammonism of Gilded Age America's second-largest city, epitomized in a front-cover lithographic parody of a well-known painting by Danish artist Carl Heinrich Bloch titled "Christ Driving the Money Changers Out of the Temple." In Stead's version, faces were altered to resemble well-known Chicago figures such as traction magnate Charles T. Yerkes, gas trust executive C. K. G. Billings, Alderman John "Johnny de Pow" Powers, and gambling kingpin Michael McDonald, all pictured around a templelike building reminiscent of the Chicago Board of Trade. "The first impression which a stranger receives on arriving in Chicago is that of the dirt, the danger, and the inconveniences of the streets," Stead wrote. "If a stranger's first impression of Chicago is that of the barbarous gridironed streets, his second is that of the multitude of mutilated people whom he meets. . . . I have never seen so many mutilated fragments of humanity as one finds in Chicago." Stead chronicled so-called "streets of sin" where property owners bribed the police up to $100 a week, local elections were bought with whiskey and free lunches, and gambling operated freely, "invisible" to city and police officials. "Editor Stead says there are two honest Aldermen out of sixty-eight," the *Peoria Mirror* observed, "and all the papers up there are howling for proof."

Beyond such observations, the major selling point of the book was a colored foldout map of all the vice businesses in the area surrounded by Clark, Dearborn, Harrison, and Polk streets. Brothels, pawnbrokers, saloons, assignation houses, and related businesses were identified and color coded, making it the best guide for the curious yet published in Chicago. The map was so successful it was imitated by Jane Addams and University of Chicago sociologists in subsequent studies, along with appendixes of information (Stead listed the proprietors and owners of vice properties) as gleaned from public records. Of the various brothels, saloons, pool halls, gambling rooms, and theaters, Stead borrowed a metaphor popular around the time of the 1871 fire in writing that their "vulgarity and obscenity . . . would be more in place in Sodom and Gomorrah than in Chicago."

His solution to Chicago's rampant vice was better government, not the city's mass news media. "To unearth such scandals, to bring them to light, to clear out the Augean stable of the City Hall seems to be an enterprise peculiarly inviting to the indomitable genius of an American newspaper," Stead wrote. "Unfortunately, whether it be, as I am frequently assured, because there are so many in it whom the newspapers dare not offend, or because of simple lethargy of conscience and indifference to the welfare of the town, which seems hardly less credible, or to some other cause, there is no doubt as to the fact." "A Chicago woman laughed herself to death the other day," the *St. Paul Globe* said. "She had just been reading the concluding chapters of Editor Stead's book, in which he predicted that Chicago would yet awake to a sense of her wickedness and reform." "Mr. Stead has not done Chicago justice in his book," the *Kansas City Journal* wrote. "No man can give an adequate idea of Chicago wickedness in a mere pamphlet."[12]

If Christ Came to Chicago! was an instant best seller, going through 70,000 volumes in its first day of publication and hundreds of thousands subsequently, but it faced vigorous opposition from many in Chicago's mass news media for what was considered its "grotesquely unfair" obsession with Chicago's underworld. "The young man with the small, flat head, is the British idiot, Editor Stead," the *Inter Ocean* rhymed of his name. "Mr. Stead thinks that Mayor Hopkins can run the city almost as well as Mr. Stead could," the *Daily News* sniffed, and the *Tribune* editorialized that Stead's book belonged to a class of literature called "denominated obscene." Only the short-lived *Chicago Chronicle* seemed amused by Stead's criticisms of the upper class, joking that "Chicago millionaires are trembling" and predicting that it would eventually be "bought up or otherwise suppressed."

The newspapers were especially critical of Stead for hiring a low-level Chicago political operative named Edmund G. Browne as his guide rather than a seasoned reporter. Browne conducted Stead about the First Ward to the sneers of the regular reporters, at least some of whom were being paid to keep the vice businesses out of the papers. Only a few Chicago newspapermen including former *Tribune* editorial writer Henry Demarest Lloyd (whose 1893 expose *Wealth Against Commonwealth* had failed to sell nearly as well) applauded the book, Lloyd singling out its overt moralization as its solitary shortcoming.

Stead's epistle was sold throughout the English-speaking world, creating another public relations nightmare for a Chicago that had only recently overcome pre–World's Fair libels. "And now Mr. W. T. Stead comes out with the most terrible exposé of Chicago's moral corruption that could be imagined," the *Macon* (Georgia) *Weekly Telegraph* wrote. The *Duluth News Tribune* observed that the book "is true and we need not shut our eyes to unpleasant truths." "Stead was right when he told the Chicago women that the rich, selfish and idle among them might well beware lest their sins were more heinous . . . than the sins of the wayward women, from whom they all drew back their skirts," the *Omaha World Herald* wrote, edited by future Democratic presidential candidate William Jennings Bryan. "Some people complain that Editor Stead's book is worse than Chicago," the *Washington Star* related; the *Kansas City Journal* reported that the American News company would not handle the book because it was a "directory of sin." "What kind of a book on Chicago does the company want?"

The *New York World* cheerfully published excerpts of the book and the *New York Times* crowed that many of Chicago's "millionaires who pose as philanthropists and men of exalted and pious aims of their sets" owned the brothels, saloons, gambling houses, and other vice businesses described in the book. Stead returned to England and died aboard the *Titanic* on a return trip in 1912—still something of a pariah in Chicago, the *Tribune* called him a "moral surgeon. . . . [who] amputated without anesthetics" in its obituary.[13]

The "Bath" and the "Dink"

Chicago's dailies were abuzz with details of a raid on a gambling house at 119 Clark Street on September 18, 1894. As the *Tribune* reported however, this foray was different in one critical respect. Rather than the police parade of "usual suspects" and the sham destruction of broken and unusable gambling equipment, a force of several dozen armed Chicago Pinkertons engaged in what the paper called a "free-for-all fisticuff fight" with some 250 gamblers and employees. "Bloody war waged in the gambling-room upstairs, gamblers and [Pinkerton] agents fought furiously in the Calhoun place, but not a finger did any [Chicago] policeman raise to end the conflict," the *Tribune* reported. "For a full hour the battle went on in alley and gambling-room until the invading army had been put to complete route and Matt Pinkerton and several of his minions had fallen into the clutches of other constables sent to the scene with 'riot' warrants." Constables were neighborhood law enforcement officers independent of the Chicago Police Department and usually on the gamblers' payrolls. They arrested the Pinkertons on trumped-up charges, ending the raid. The event was significant, however, because for the first time in the city's history a citizens' organization had used a private police force to harass the vice industry.

Founded just days after the assassination of Mayor Carter Harrison Sr. the previous October, the Civic Federation of Chicago's inspiration for the raid had been *If Christ Came to Chicago!* William Stead's "indictment of

Chicago," as Jane Addams called the book, had convinced a constituency of middle-class reformers (including Addams, trade unionists, lower-level businessmen, socially prominent women, and tax reform advocates) that only an empowered middle class could bring about governmental honesty and efficiency in Chicago. "The Civic Federation, just organized, has a distinct mission," the *Daily News* editorialized in early 1894. "Its purpose is to promote the general welfare of the city by correcting municipal abuses, as far as possible"; the paper argued that an informed electorate was the best and only guarantee against corruption.

Daily News publisher Victor Lawson was an early Federation member and financial supporter as was Ralph M. Easley, an *Inter Ocean* city hall reporter who went on to organize a national civic federation based on the Chicago model. "The need of these minor organizations is evident," the *Tribune* responded. "The work of reform, to be most effectual, must be localized as much as possible." By design, the group was largely middle class (with the exception of a few upper-class members such as Mrs. Potter Palmer), and it was also Protestant, Republican, and white, counting few if any immigrants, workers, rank-and-file unionists, Catholics, Jews, or Democrats as members. "It may be soon that no man will accept the Mayoralty unless to make money out of the office of when he has some ax to grind," the *Tribune* warned in 1895.[14]

The September raid also marked the beginning of the end of Chicago's first crime boss. "Sure Thing" Michael McDonald was probably the best-known Chicagoan of the 1880s, better recognized than Mayor Harrison or business leaders such as Marshall Field or Potter Palmer. An expert at getting his name into or keeping it out of the papers, McDonald published his own newspaper for a time, the same *Chicago Globe* that first employed Theodore Dreiser. "If you could have looked into the capacious but balanced temperament," Dreiser wrote of a McDonald-like character in his *The Titan*, "you would have seen a strange wisdom there, and stranger memories—whole worlds of brutalities, tendernesses, errors, immoralities suffered, endured, even rejoiced in—the handy, eager life of the animal that has nothing but its perceptions, instincts, appetites to guide it."

McDonald's base of operation was The Store, a four-story saloon and casino located at 176 Clark Street, near Monroe. Gambling was frowned upon on the first floors of businesses even in Chicago, so a saloon occupied that part of The Store, with card, ferro, and roulette rooms on the second floor. The top two floors housed some of the leading sharpers and bunko men of the day including "Hungry" Joe Lewis (who reputedly bilked English bon vivant Oscar Wilde of thousands of dollars during Wilde's 1882 visit to the

United States), Tom O'Brien (who, it was said, grossed $500,000 during the World's Fair), and Charles and Frederick Gondorf (the World's Fair "fixers" who inspired the 1973 Paul Newman and Robert Redford motion picture *The Sting*). McDonald maintained that his vice superstore eliminated much of the petty saloon, restaurant, and back alley gambling that contributed to other crime in the city, therefore performing a useful public service. With time, other gambling operations fell under his "protection," and his profits were so large that one newspaper estimated that his confidence men alone took in $1 million a year.

McDonald was "pards," as the papers put it, with Mayor Carter Harrison Sr., a Kentucky native and relation to President William Henry Harrison, who had arrived in Chicago the same year as Joseph Medill. He worked his way through the Chicago Democratic political machine as did McDonald, the two becoming confederates when Harrison first ran for mayor in 1879 and remaining so until Harrison's assassination in 1893. Allegedly The Store was the real seat of power during Harrison's mayoral tenure in the 1880s—the place one went to conduct real city business. Harrison once wrote a "polite note" to McDonald asking him to return $310 to a man swindled in one of McDonald's gambling houses, a request to which McDonald acquiesced. "Mr. McDonald has the reputation of being a very ubiquitous man," Harrison told reporters, "and if there is a gambling place started in the city he has a finger in it, it is said."[15]

McDonald's political power evaporated with Harrison's death in 1893. The other "Boss Gamblers" held a summit the day following the September 1894 Civic Federation raid to establish a new combine and name a successor. The stakes were high, for as the *Tribune* estimated, some 2,000 professional and 5,000 amateur habitués depended on Chicago's gambling industry for at least a part of their livelihood along with the "blackmailing police force" that relied on payoffs. "Despite this lack of harmony the gamblers determined on united action, and will fight the Civic Federation to the end," the *Tribune* reported. "They claim all the victories are theirs so far, and believe that by dragging the cases through all the legal avenues open to sharp lawyers they will be able to win." As part of its article, the *Tribune* published a list of participating gaming houses, a "description of the kinds of gambling practiced there, and the names of the reputed managers and proprietors of the business." Among the "must-see" establishments were the raided marble palace at 116 Clark Street and "Big Jim" O'Leary's (operated by the son of Patrick and Catherine O'Leary of Chicago's Great Fire), located near 61st and State streets. One "James [*sic*] Kenna (Hinky Dink)" establishment at Clark and Van Buren streets received scant notice but was included on the list.[16]

However, it was Hinky Dink Kenna's saloon, better known as the Workingman's Exchange, that became the next de facto city hall with the active cooperation of fellow First Ward alderman Bathhouse John Coughlin. Kenna was born in 1857 in a frame shack located where Polk and Carpenter streets meet just east of Halsted, while Coughlin entered the world three years later in the Connelly's Patch, just east of the river at Harrison and Franklin streets. Their birthplaces were described by the *Times* in 1865 as ones of "wretchedness, poverty and vice. . . . 'patches' where the sons of the Emerald Isle have 'squatted.'" Raised with a near-fanatical faith in personal democracy, individualism, and a belief that anyone could become part of the American political system, the two became living embodiments of the dream that drove millions of their countrymen to emigrate to America. Kenna's five-foot-four-inch stature and Coughlin's corpulent appearance (complete with bowler hat and omnipresent cigar) also served as models for the late-nineteenth-century's stereotype of success, the "barrel-house alderman." "They were success stories in their own peculiar way," the *Tribune* admitted following Coughlin's death in 1946.[17]

The younger Coughlin was the first to attract the newspapers' attention. Twentieth-century Illinois Democratic U.S. Senator Paul Douglas, who met the elderly Coughlin while serving as a young Chicago alderman, remembered him as "the bumbling and none too bright extrovert" who "with his gaily colored waistcoats, his inability to speak a coherent sentence, his penchant for owning race horses which couldn't or wouldn't run" was "as irresistibly funny as the Keystone Cops." Others described Coughlin as bluff, hearty, and an accomplished backslapper, a man who laughed at everyone's jokes. After dropping out of a Catholic elementary school, he worked at a variety of Levee jobs, befriending gamblers and horsemen. "I never got much schooling after I was 11, but I learned something I still think was better," he explained. "I learned that life is always interesting and that the dough one makes is good to help the fellow out of luck."[18]

Of all of his early pursuits, Coughlin excelled the most at rubbing. Few Gilded Age Chicagoans had indoor plumbing, bathtubs in particular, and a host of commercial bath houses, some patterned after exquisite "Turkish" bathhouses, flourished in the city during the mid- and late-nineteenth century. "[Chicago businessmen] should render the city metropolitan by giving it a public park . . . [and] public libraries and reading-rooms," the *Tribune* wrote on a hot July day in 1868, "but, first of all and above all, public baths . . . and the conveniences necessary to cleanliness and a healthy life." Free public bathhouses did not become a reality until 1894 however, so Gilded Age men and women bathed, steamed, showered, and socialized in privately owned houses, many receiving stimulating rubdowns with salt or sand provided by muscular "rubbers." A rubdown from an experienced rubber was considered one of the finest amenities available in Gilded Age Chicago, the perfect end to a big night on the town.[19]

Young "Bathhouse," the sobriquet given Coughlin, worked his way through a variety of his namesakes until he reached the top of the career ladder as the Palmer House's head rubber. The Palmer, at the same State and Monroe street location as it was in the early twenty-first century, was one of the premier bathhouses in the nation, featuring Russian medicated vapor, and electric thermal as well as Turkish and other baths, beginning in 1877. "There are fourteen twenty-ounce copper bath-tubs, with tubular showers, with hot and cold water operations," the *Tribune* bragged. Coughlin mingled with the city's financial and political elite, including the likes of Marshall Field and other business titans, as part of his Palmer House employment. "I met 'em all, big and little, from La Salle Street to Armour Avenue," he would say. "Ain't much difference between the big man and the little man. One's lucky, that's all." Coughlin opened his own bathhouse at 143 East Madison Street in 1882 and eventually operated several establishments with the slogan "There's health in Coughlin's baths!" Coughlin's "soon became 'The Bathhouse' for the horsemen and gamblers and men-about-town who in those days drank their liquor standing up and drank it hard and long," as the *Daily News* explained.[20]

Bathhouse joined the Chicago Democratic machine during the 1884 Mugwump presidential campaign that saw a host of Republican defections to Democratic President Grover Cleveland. He was put in charge of the Cook County Democratic Marching Club, a group that paraded at political events wearing uniforms of white woolen fatigues, hats, and dark blue pants. From such a modest sartorial beginning, his tastes evolved to loud checks, bright colors, Prince Albert vests, kid-leather gloves, high-button shoes, and bowlers and silk hats. "Straw hats were not officially in season until 'Bathhouse' John Coughlin donned his air-conditioned tropical helmet," the *Daily News* reported. A lifelong Catholic, Coughlin enjoyed horse racing but never indulged in other First Ward entertainments. "I wear good clothes," he told friends, "and you can't wear good clothes unless you're clean on the inside."

Beyond his nattily dressed exterior he impressed political operatives with his honesty, ambition, and complete lack of original thought. "John's not very bright," a friend noted, "but once he gives his word you can count on him." Coughlin was convincing enough that Michael McDonald put him on the First Ward aldermanic ballot in 1892, and he won with McDonald's political and financial support, serving a record forty-six continuous years on the council. Coughlin also operated the Silver Dollar saloon on Clark Street at Madison, promising the council when he assumed his aldermanic seat to "run an orderly house [and] not permit women into the saloon." There was a tradition of politics and saloons in nineteenth-century Chicago, the *St. Paul Dispatch* remarking in 1894 that "only eleven of the Chicago candidates for Aldermen are saloonkeepers." As indoor plumbing became more common in Chicago, Coughlin sold his saloon and bathhouse establishments, concentrating on an "insurance" business that shook down First Ward vice constituents for protection money and political contributions. He remained the consummate Chicago machine politician until his death in 1938.[21]

Kenna's formative years were equally colorful. A diminutive yet energetic youth who considered his birth place "no sissy town," his formal education ended at the age of ten when he entered the workforce in Calhoun Place, also known as Gambler's Alley, a pathway located west of Dearborn Street between Randolph and Washington streets. There Kenna supported himself selling newspapers with a blond-haired English-born youth named William "Billy" Lorimer, the future Republican "Boss" of Illinois. At age twelve, Kenna bought the newspaper rights to the lucrative Monroe and Dearborn street corner, just outside of the *Tribune* building. There he supposedly received his "Hinky Dink" nickname from publisher Joseph Medill, who liked to talk with the newsboys to see what they and their customers thought of his paper. When told Kenna's real name, Medill allegedly said that it was a good Irish name, "but I'm going to call you Hinky Dink because you are such a little fellow." Medill associates later denied the story, and Kenna himself said he got his moniker at "th' old swimming hole," then located at the foot of Van Buren Street. From such a modest beginning, Kenna prospered in the news business, buying the rights to other corners around the city in his teens. Any newsboy who trespassed on his corners was beaten and chased out of the area.[22]

Kenna opened a saloon and gambling parlor at 120 East Van Buren, on the southwest corner of Clark, during the mid-1880s, promoting what he called a "two-handed schooner," a 3½ pound glass that held twenty-five ounces of watered-down beer. When business was slow, Kenna distributed dimes to the unemployed loafing about his saloon and invited them inside to drink and game. As discreet and frugal in business as he was addicted to chewing large, black cigars, Kenna was drawn into the Democratic machine during the same 1884 presidential campaign as Coughlin. Applying himself to ward work, he was described as "the glummest little man in the entire [First] ward organization," "a man of few words" but "who always kept his word." When an important political job needed to be done, he was a man of "silence and action," as associates recalled. Senator Douglas remembered Kenna as somebody "who knew the price of everything and, his opponents alleged, the value of nothing."[23]

Republican Chicago newspapers had exposed Democratic electoral fraud as early as 1856, the first year that foreign-born immigrants became involved in local politics. Incriminations increased with the election of Mayor Harvey Colvin in 1873 and continued during the Carter Harrison Sr. years. When Kenna was named ward captain by Coughlin in 1893, he quickly excelled in getting the vote out for what the papers called the same machine "City Hall crowd." "Though small in stature," Coughlin was quoted as saying, "Mr. Dink is one of us." Carter Harrison Sr. claimed that he was unacquainted with "Mr. Dink," the *Tribune* reported, "but Chicago's Mayor surely cannot have overlooked the personality of this individual who has for many years been a factor in Democratic politics in the First Ward." While others characterized Coughlin as a "personal coward" and Kenna "a rascal," Harrison's namesake and future mayor son admired Kenna for a "marvelous finesse as an organizer of the strange flotsam and jetsam gathered into the First Ward."

With the assistance of "pluggers," lieutenants assigned to seek out itinerants, Kenna and Coughlin "stuffed soap boxes, barrels, tubs, and anything else handy full of votes" as the papers put it. "About 11 o-clock in the morning 300 [itinerants] were lined up in front of the polling-place," a *Tribune* reporter observed in 1893, noting that Coughlin "assisted in making the formation. Of the whole bunch not twenty were legal voters, and it is extremely doubtful if one-tenth of the number could read the names on the tickets thrust into their hands by 'Bath-house' John." "What's your name?" a polling worker demanded of one older man as related by the *Inter Ocean*. "John Bowles." "Resident of this ward?" the worker asked. "No, am not. I live in Vincennes, Ind." "No, he don't any such thing," a plugger jumped in. "His name is Jim Smith and he lives at No. 126 Pacific Ave." "The old man, crestfallen, passed the ticket which was pushed into his hand through the window. His vote was accepted and deposited. Without looking back, the old man fled for the depot and Indiana."

A 1894 *Inter Ocean* illustration showed Kenna's saloon: "The polling-place" of the First Ward's notorious Ninth Precinct "is a barber shop with a door opening into Hinky Dink's barroom," the *Tribune* reported. "A polling-place in the vicinity of a groggery becomes a source of profit for the groggery-keeper." "Several earnest workers for reform, who have lately taken up their abode in the district of the Hon. Mr. Dink in the 1st," the *Daily News* complained in 1895, "entered so thoroughly into the spirit of the hour yesterday as to register in four or five different precincts."

With Kenna's 1897 aldermanic election (Chicago wards had two aldermen until the 1920s), he moved his saloon into a larger building at 311 S. Clark Street, just south of Van Buren, with the name Workingman's Exchange and a giant "bowl" of foaming beer painted on the windows. The structure's top floors were used as a flop house for as many as three hundred itinerants (six hundred the night before an election); Kenna provided his "guests" with free room and 50 cents apiece as long as they voted the next day, a practice the newspapers called "colonization." The Chicago political caveat to "vote early and often" (incorrectly attributed to twentieth-century Mayor William Hale Thompson) likely originated with the Kenna and Coughlin organization during the 1890s, a reflection of the growing affluence of public service. "It now turns out that the Chicago Alderman who resigned was not insane," the *Memphis Avalanche* reported. "He has secured a softer official snap [job]." "The Statement that Chicago's Board of Aldermen decided by a vote of 58 to 4 not to give up their World's Fair passes is hardly credible," the *Kansas City Journal* observed. "The minority is too large."[24]

Despised by Civic Federation reformers such as Jane Addams, Kenna was the champion of his poverty-stricken First Ward constituents, people who otherwise could expect to receive little more than the "old shoe" from wealthier residents, according to the *New York Herald.* Never a public speaker or flashy dresser like Coughlin, Kenna reveled in his common-man image. "Youse fellers don't want a man what you have to put on your Sunday clothes and read on extra diction'ry to see," Coughlin once said of his colleague. "You don't want a man who lives on a bullyvard." Kenna sold his beer schooners, "the Largest and Coolest in the City," for a nickel apiece and featured a huge counter of free food for customers, vagrants, hobos, and the curious that cost him a reported $30 a day to stock. "Almost everyone there seemed to be at this counter, as it was a free lunch and they helped themselves to whatever they desired," a visitor recalled years later. "I dashed in and helped myself to several slices of fresh rye bread, packed them with ham, cheese, and bologna." During the 1893 Depression, Kenna supported thousands of constituents on nickel beers and free lunch. "We sold twenty-five barrels of beer a day over the counter, and gave away a truck-load of lunch," one of his bartenders recalled. "We gave 'em soup, hot stew, fried liver, and all the bread they could stow away."[25]

As Kenna harvested the First Ward vote, Coughlin served as the pair's front man, and his efforts helped make him and Kenna household names. He incorrectly backed *Staats Zeitung* editor Washington Hesing over Carter Harrison Sr. in the 1893 mayoral election, and for his disloyalty his Democratic council colleagues denied him any of a reputed $100,000 boodle in the granting of a dummy West Side cable streetcar company franchise. "Coughlin . . . and the others are well known," the *Daily News* observed of several aldermen that year. "Nothing good is expected of them at any time."

Coughlin lost out on another boodle for the failed Hygeia Mineral Springs Company, which proposed to supply spring water during Chicago's 1893 typhoid outbreak. *Evening Post* columnist Finley Peter Dunne mocked the scheme when he had Mr. Dooley speak of "'an ordinance givin' th' Inter-naytional Mickrobe Company a right to lay pipes and pump mi-crobes' throughout Chicago." However, Mayor Harrison forgave Coughlin and put his glad-handing skills, tailcoat, and top hat to good use when he named him a member of the city's official 1893 World's Fair reception committee. Visitors pointed to him at the fair and exclaimed, "There's the Bathhouse!"

Three men were shot and numerous fights broke out between Coughlin supporters and detractors during the 1894 municipal elections, attracting more attention to the pair. "Of the twenty-nine Aldermen nominated by the Democrats not less than nine are dispensers of grog," the *Tribune* wrote. "It is the experience of the city that the groggerykeepers make the worst alderman." A Coughlin and Kenna tour of New York in 1897 was the talk of that town, the *New York Journal* bragging that Kenna had been fined $100 for operating a newfangled slot machine in his saloon. "Alderman Hinky Dink of Chicago insists on keeping Cuba," the *Tacoma* (Washington) *Daily News* wrote the following year. "Aldermen want to keep everything they can get hold of."[26]

Coughlin was at his best on the council floor. For publicity purposes, he crafted an ordinance raising the fine for opium houses from $3 to $100 even though there was only "a small band of men" and women who were addicted to the drug in 1890s Chicago. "I was born and brought up in the 1st ward," he told a *Daily News* reporter in an article that featured his likeness for the first of countless times. "Every Sunday I used to see our young American girls going in and out on the arms of Chinamen whom I knew to be as degraded as any human beings ever become." "We welcome this amiable statesman to the army of reformers," the *Evening Post* replied, "but we should be more enthusiastic in our applause if we were sure that the statesman was unselfish in his undertaking." Another campaign by the cigar-chomping Coughlin sought to prohibit the sale of cigarettes within two hundred yards of schools, much to the amusement of fellow tobacco-consuming aldermen. "You think it rather funny, do you, to hear a man who deals in cigarettes to say they are harmful," Coughlin told a doubting council in reference to the tobacco products he sold in his saloon. "I think [a cigarette] is one of the greatest evils that boys and young men of the present day have to meet." The *Washington Star* noted of the legislation that "Chicago doesn't prohibit a great many other things that should be prohibited by ordinance, even if the police do not read the ordinances."

In the interest of keeping females from wearing what he considered to be male clothing, Coughlin also drafted a 1895 ordinance banning women from riding bicycles "while dressed or arrayed in costumes commonly known as bloomers, knickerbockers, baseball attire, or trousers." "Immersed in ward affairs, keeping his 'pull' in order and speeding the growler in its holy work, Alderman Coughlin has missed a point or two in social development," the *New York Times* laughed at him. Coughlin crusaded for a citywide nine o'clock curfew as well, to be announced by one thousand bell ringers hired, not surprisingly, at public expense. "Adults cause more trouble in the streets than do children," he told a reporter. "If the home is a good place for children, it should be all right for adults." Doubtless, such good government initiatives were designed to deflect public attention from his primary political interests (election frauds and boodling), but as the *Macon* (Georgia) *Weekly Telegraph* reported in 1899, "Carter Harrison [Jr.] carried by a rousing majority. Doubtless Hinky Dink, Bath-house John and the balance of the 'gang' in the Windy City saw to it that there was a 'hot time in the old town' Tuesday night."[27]

The Gray Wolves

As much as they enjoyed the notoriety that resulted from such gimmicks, it was the promise of boodle, a word that first appeared in the Chicago newspapers in 1882, that attracted and kept Bathhouse, Hinky Dink, and most other Gilded Age aldermen in public service. Reporters used the jargon of late-nineteenth-century politicians, slang terms such a "machine" and "boodle," in their articles to demonstrate the vulgarity of the typically immigrant politicians. "Journalists, who were aligned with genteel, middle- and upper-class readers, stood against the supposedly ethically deficient, lower-class denizens who had captured politics," Richard Kaplan wrote in *Politics and the American Press: The Rise of Objectivity*. "The pragmatic actions of newspapers as crusading protagonists of the Democratic party and the narratives of republican exposure worked together to forge a new political universe." However, like dozens of other American cities, the hegemonical aspects of Gilded Age Chicago politics were overstated, even in the press of the day. Citywide "machine" politics, as were most boodle schemes, was short-lived as factions, personalities, and issues shifted from election to election and between, as M. Craig Brown and Charles N. Halaby observed in a study of thirty Gilded Age American cities.

Instead, a number of factors not only made boodling possible but likely in 1890s Chicago. In part, an improving local economy provided opportunities, especially with the introduction into the city of the new and highly profitable monopolistic technologies of telephones, electricity, and mass transit. Journalists steeped in the belief that responsible capitalists did what they did for the good of everybody failed to consider the potential for corruption in natural monopolies.

The same newspapermen failed to grasp the emergence full-time, professional politicians in the 1880s and 1890s. As William T. Stead explained in *If Christ Came to Chicago!* "the average crooked Alderman has made $15,000 to $20,000," a sizeable improvement over an official $200 a year salary. That pay scale was a carryover from the early 1870s administration of Mayor Joseph Medill, a time when part-time aldermen were paid per diem for a part-time job. By the 1890s, only the wealthy could afford to run for public office, and they were too busy making more money. In their place, immigrants and the lower middle class took control of city hall. In a hypothetical list of reforms he would enact as mayor, a *Tribune* reader named Mike suggested that he would "pay aldermen a fair salary, and have them shot for bribery."

Terrence McDonald observed that ethnic groups such as the Irish generally opposed the expansion of municipal government while at the same time they sought entrée. Instead, Irish ward bosses such as Kenna, Coughlin, and John Powers preferred private philanthropy to municipal welfare, as a means of ensuring their constituent support if for no other reason. The *Chicago Daily News* estimated upon Coughlin's death in 1938 that he and Kenna had performed as many as 200,000 individual acts of charity during their aldermanic years, from patronage jobs to clothing and money for their First Ward constituents.[28]

Late-nineteenth-century reporters had a personal interest in the new monopolistic technologies. First installed in Chicago in 1879, older reporters initially distrusted the accuracy of telephones, preferring personal contact; but as younger reporters began using phones their improved productivity won over most doubters. "For the pulse of the people, literally, is in the pulse of the telephone business," the *Tribune* wrote in 1906. Resourceful fact-finding reporters, known as "legmen," teamed up with talented storytellers, called "rewritemen," to provide timely, informative, and well-written news copy using the telephone.

As well, late-nineteenth-century news was written on a device first perfected by a Milwaukee newspaperman in 1867 but not widely used in Chicago newsrooms until the 1890s—the typewriter. Again, cub reporters were the first to employ typewriters, but they produced more copy than their more experienced elders who were still writing longhand. And typewritten copy was preferred by linotype operators, working on newly perfected machinery that automated the centuries-old hand typesetting process. The *Chicago Daily News* began testing an electrical-powered linotype machine in 1886, linotype machines set the entire World's Fair *Columbian* paper in front of fairgoers in 1893, and most newspapers were using them by 1895. Added to new continuous roll or web-printing presses, which produced as many as 70,000 front-and-back impressions per hour and often were powered by electricity, a typical Chicago newspaper averaged more than forty pages per copy by the end of the century, to the chagrin of some older newspaperman. "There is too much of the forty-eight page newspapers for the good and substantial readers," one editor complained in 1893.[29]

Late-nineteenth-century Chicago reporters had a greater appetite for exposé as well, especially in the wake of *If Christ Came to Chicago!* and aldermen were easy prey. When it came to mass transit, knowledgeable boodling Chicago aldermen preferred partnering with a convicted Philadelphia municipal bond fund swindler named Charles T. Yerkes. "Here was life; he saw it at a flash. Here was a seething city in the making," Theodore Dreiser wrote in *The Titan,* his fictional account of Yerkes. "There was something dynamic in the very air which appealed to his fancy. . . . This raw, dirty town seemed naturally to compose itself into stirring artistic pictures. Why, it fairly sang!" New York newspaperman Lincoln Steffens claimed in his muckraking book, *The Shame of the Cities,* that Yerkes was singularly responsible for raising Chicago's political corruption to an art. "With his large experience of Philadelphia methods, [Yerkes] first made boodling a serious business," Steffens wrote. "The aldermanic combine was fast selling out the city to its 'best citizens,' when some decent men spoke up and called upon the people to stop it, the people who alone can stop such things."

Yerkes was dishonest and greedy, but he wanted to be treated as one of Chicago's Best Men and complained of what he thought was unfair coverage given him in the *Daily News* in 1889. Publisher Victor F. Lawson replied that he had given personal directions to his *Morning* and *Evening News* editors "to be careful that in our criticisms of your cable system [that] we commit no exaggerations and that you and your roads are treated with impartiality. The difficulty is that in this case impartiality is just what you can't stand—hence your complaint."[30]

From an inauspicious beginning with borrowed money in 1882, Yerkes leveraged his holdings through a myriad of real and fictional companies to develop, own, and operate much of Chicago's public transportation infrastructure by the late 1890s, to the financial detriment of riders and the city itself. At the height of the 1893 Depression, the *Daily News* calculated that the entire Chicago street railway system returned only $50,000 to the city. "There is no doubt the sum now paid is too small," the paper editorialized. As well, the construction of new lines gave the "traction magnate" (for his San Francisco–style cable or traction cars) near total control over Chicago's residential and industrial development, which had dramatic implications on its competition with New York City.

That Yerkes excelled in pursuing his responsible capitalism greed to the disadvantage of nearly everyone else was common knowledge in 1890s Chicago. "Unlike the late William H. Vanderbilt, he does not accord the public even the small notice of wishing them damned," the *Daily News* complained in 1890. "They can be that of course, if they choose, but it is a matter of supremest indifference to Child of the Stars Yerkes." "Yesterday was not much of a day for Mr. Yerkes' patent juggernaut," the *Daily News* wrote in another story of the traction system. "Only one boy was fatally injured by the cable cars." "Mr. Yerkes asserts that his companies cannot afford to pay 20 per cent [rent to the city]," the *Tribune* observed. "So say all the owners of his watered stock." Yerkes refused entreaties from the city to construct new tracks unless the requests came with franchises guaranteeing him virtually all profits. "On the whole," the *Daily News* noted of a rare common council rejection, "the baron is somewhat disappointed that the council frustrated his generous intention by demanding some compensation for the streets."[31]

Though supposedly coined by Lincoln Steffens, municipal reformer Edward L. Cole was actually the first to label the most corrupt Chicago aldermen "gray wolves" for their hair color, cunning, and appetite for boodle. "The battle at the polls was something of a defeat for the candidates branded as 'gray wolves,'" the *Tribune* reported a full year before Steffens first used the term.

The Wolves' unofficial leader was Alderman John Powers, an Irish-born grocer and saloon keeper who was otherwise known as the "chief mourner" for the many constituent funerals he attended. Nicknamed "Johnny de Pow" for his political clout, he provided free Christmas dinners for his largely Irish constituents as a form of private charity so that "nobody ever went hungry" at least one day of the year. "Powers has piloted, either openly or covertly, nearly every boodle ordinance in the city council since the embodiment of the pernicious influence that has dictated municipal legislation for many years," the *Times-Herald* reported. Powers invented the practice of selling utility franchises on a block-by-block rather than citywide basis (increasing kickbacks exponentially) and the reselling of franchises whenever a minor technological change occurred; he also arranged outrageously low property tax assessments for supporters such as Yerkes. Powers was the originator of a threat repeated by generations of Chicago aldermen, "Either you go along with us or you won't get a can of garbage moved out of your ward till hell freezes over."[32]

The Big Grab

Bathhouse Coughlin was on the right side of Powers and the Democratic machine on a coal and natural gas franchise boodle in 1894, but received nothing but kudos for his support. However, his efforts paid off the following year with another fictitious project called the Cosmopolitan Electric ordinance. The plan, if real, would have constructed generating stations and underground electrical, heat, telephone, and telegraph conduits throughout the city, making the utilities universally available and removing unsightly utility poles. "A fairly good fight was made," the *Tribune* reported the following morning. "At the proper time the leaders cracked the whip and their supporters stood up to the rack and were brought is as easily as the Southern slave-driver before the war would line up a gang of slaves." Major players such as Democratic Mayor John P. Hopkins and Democratic Governor John Peter Altgeld netted an estimated $100,000 to $400,000 each for their support, with smaller payouts going to lesser figures such as Coughlin. The conduits were never constructed.

The following January, the council approved the so-called General Electric Company ordinance, which provided for a streetcar franchise in Chicago's southwestern side, including an overhead electric trolley that was beginning to be called the "L." Coughlin made an estimated $300,000 brokering the deal with the cooperation of Powers. The lines were eventually purchased by Yerkes, negating the franchise, but the plan inspired Yerkes to propose another that would have given him control over all mass transit lines for a thirty-year period, and at the bargain price of $1,000 to $2,000 per aldermanic vote. "'Tis not [right] . . . that this man Yerkuss goes up to an aldherman an says out sthraight, 'Here, Bill, take this bundle, an' be an infamyous scoundhrel,'" Finley Peter Dunne's Mr. Dooley told *Evening Post* readers. "That's th' way th' man in Mitchigan Avnoo sees it, but 'tis not sthraight." Even Coughlin avoided the Yerkes boodle, telling Mayor Carter Harrison Jr. that he preferred to "stick to the' small stuff; there's little risk and in the long run it pays a damned sight more," an admonition he preached to Republican First District

Chicago Congressman William "Billy" Mason and other political disciples. When the proposal came up on the council floor, Yerkes lost by Coughlin's vote, 32–31, even with the endorsement of "Johnny de Pow" Powers.[33]

With his profitable behind-the-scene machinations Coughlin had become a council stalwart by the late 1890s, and there were calls for him to run for mayor. The newly elected Kenna was not far behind. "In putting forth the claim that he was the best alderman the 1st Ward ever had," the *Daily News* noted, "the Hon. Dinky Hink may be actuated merely by a desire to remind thoughtless people that he who bloweth not his own horn for him his horn shall not be blown." Nevertheless, Yerkes was disenchanted with the escalating demands of Coughlin's colleagues and determined to put his case for control of Chicago's entire seven-hundred-mile transportation system before the state legislature. "As long as it was possible to deal with one or two representatives of the whole [council] crowd it was not so bad," the *New York Times* explained, "but since a lot of individual [council] members have taken to doing business, each on his own account, the thing evidently has become unendurable to the [Yerkes' Chicago City Railway Company]."

To his pleasant surprise, Yerkes discovered that the average state lawmaker was willing to settle for a smaller bribe than the average Chicago alderman. Chicago State Senator John Humphrey introduced a number of measures designed to rob Chicago of its limited home rule authority, creating a state commission to determine city franchises and establish reduced royalties for franchise holders, and allowing the state to grant franchises for up to ninety-nine years. This time Coughlin and Kenna found themselves on the side of reformers such as the *Daily News* and the Civic Federation since the Humphrey laws would have eliminated not just Yerkes' but most of their other aldermanic boodling along with much of the authority of the Chicago City Council. Yerkes spent an estimated $190,000 lobbying for his proposals in Springfield, but an outcry from Chicago's mass news media helped bring about their defeat. "The most important aspect of [the loss] is not that Chicago has escaped the ruin which these infamous bills would have brought upon it," a Yerkes opponent told reporters. "Yerkes had unwisely announced that he cared nothing for the newspapers, and it is particularly gratifying to have him knocked out by the press."

Not to be denied, Yerkes convinced another state lawmaker to introduce a redesigned proposal; this time he lucked out when it was passed by the legislature and signed in June 1897 by Gov. John R. Tanner, "Blond Boss" Billy Lorimer's personal designee. The new law, which allegedly cost Yerkes $1,000,000 in payoffs, provided that Chicago aldermen could issue franchises, but only for a minimum of fifty years, and eliminated any compensation to the city, a provision that would have cost Chicago hundreds of millions of dollars. A *Tribune* editorial cartoon portrayed the Yerkes' bills as a rolled-up piece of paper armed with a knife and revolver and a face resembling that of Yerkes. "The newspapers do not express the sentiments of the people in Chicago, and I defy anybody to prove that they did," Yerkes maintained. "There is at the present time a perfect disgust for the opinions of the newspapers in Chicago." "The press of Chicago has no sense of regard or respect for a fellow who treats Chicago as a milch cow," the *Tribune* countered. "The Civic Federation leaders, who are without doubt frauds," Yerkes retorted, "have stooped to all manner of deceit and trickery for the purposed of gaining their ends and deceiving the people."[34]

To build support for his ultimate grab, Yerkes purchased the 700,000 circulation *Chicago Inter Ocean* from owner William Penn Nixon in November 1897. To manage what the *Tribune* immediately dubbed the *Daily Yerkes,* Yerkes hired *New York Sun* editor George Wheeler Hinman at the unheard-of salary of $10,000. Hinman was an experienced newspaperman with the added, unusual qualification of a Ph.D. in history and political economy from the University of Heidelberg. One employee wrote that "he wielded a pen that was like a Damascus blade. There had not for years, if ever, been anything equal to it in Chicago's newspaper world."

Hinman immediately went to bat for Yerkes, attacking what he called the city's "trust press," and in a bizarre reversal of the mass news media's traditional watchdog role of government, Hinman accused the "monopoly" Chicago papers of seeking to control municipal government and the political parties. "Moved by a petty ambition to become the bosses of the bosses," he wrote, "[the newspaper trust] have denounced and slandered all who would not become their vassals." The *Inter Ocean*'s defense of Yerkes cost it money, subscribers, and advertisers, but as an extension of Yerkes' lobbying and propaganda operation it was not expected to make money. Another newspaper advertising salesman later recalled that when he approached the owner of a State Street department store, the owner pointed to broken streetcars and asked, "Do you think there is anyone under the sun who would place any advertising in a blankety-blank sheet owned by a blankety-blank-blank man who tolerates such transportation as you see out there?"[35]

Rumors circulated during the summer of 1898 that Yerkes was readying any day to make his grab. Council votes were said to be selling for as much as $75,000 apiece, and according to the *Tribune,* Yerkes was ready to spend up to $1.5 million in payoffs. In December, he officially filed for a fifty-year franchise that, with other arrangements, would have guaranteed Yerkes and his successors control of the city's entire mass transportation system until 1953. The proposed ordinance also specified that Yerkes would pay the city less than 2 percent of his gross receipts, guaranteeing him an annual profit in excess of 20 percent. Uncertain of their votes even with the possibility of bribes, the *Inter Ocean* unloosened a verbal onslaught against Coughlin and Kenna, accusing them of controlling "a vast illicit empire of 400 opium resorts, 100 gambling dens, 7,000 saloons and other haunts of sin and over a population which is 18 percent criminal." Yerkes also accused the *Tribune* and *Chicago Record* of trying to extort money from him—to the tune of $50,000—for positive news coverage. "Perhaps Mr. Yerkes believes that he can divert the press from its course, but he is mistaken," an aged Joseph Medill told the *New York World*. "If he thinks he can further the interest of his corporations by attacking the proprietors of other newspapers he is at liberty to do so."[36]

As the two sides stared down each other, Coughlin and Kenna remained uncharacteristically quiet, unwilling to reveal their inclinations perhaps to allow for a better or last-minute deal. While Yerkes did not count them as in his pocket, neither did the papers consider them reformers. There were newspaper predictions of hangings and related violence, a Chicago civil war it was said, if the franchise was granted. "I hope that 150,000 persons will descend upon the city hall when the ordinance is being considered and show the aldermen they mean business!" Mayor Carter Harrison Jr. told reporters. "Harrison and the anarchistic Trust Press," replied the *Inter Ocean,* "want blood to flow in Chicago streets!" When rumors surfaced that the state militia was to be called out, downstate Illinois residents protested that "we will not send our sons to die for an ambitious Chicago mayor who wants to be president."

During the final week of negotiations, streetcar conductors handed out pro-Yerkes pamphlets to tired "straphangers." "It's the only time a Chicago street car company ever gave something for nothing," one passenger remarked. The *Tribune* estimated that Yerkes and the streetcar operators had made a profit of between one and two cents on every nickel fare paid since the introduction of the first horsecar line in Chicago in 1859. "By the time the charters [franchises] expire," the paper wrote, "the profit bagged would not be less than 50 millions." On the Sunday before the vote, ministers preached against Yerkes in their pulpits, warning that "to hand over our streets to the railroad corporations for fifty years to come would be a disgrace to our citizenship, and a dire injustice to the next generation."[37]

Near pandemonium reigned when the first council roll was called the following night. Mayor Harrison had ordered that a German band and a drum and bugle corps march through the council chambers playing the "Battle Hymn of the Republic" and other patriotic songs to defuse the tension, creating a circuslike atmosphere. Anti-Yerkes Alderman Michael McInerney blamed the resulting chaos on the mass news media, complaining, "I say to you that all this claptrap is brought about by the newspapers of Chicago."

When it came to the critical vote, Coughlin and Kenna stood with the anti-Yerkes forces, and supporters chanted "John J. Coughlin, the next mayor of Chicago" outside of the Workingman's Exchange saloon in response. However, "it will not do to assume that the ordinance is beaten" the *Tribune* warned the next morning. The following Monday night, December 19, 1898, a more solemn council prepared to vote a final time on a watered-down version of the Yerkes proposal, only to have Mayor Harrison bury it in a committee by a vote of 32–31. Alderman William O'Brien leaned toward the two First Ward aldermen and asked, "John! Mike! What the hell's the matter with you? It's a good thing—there's five hundred in it—get on the bandwagon," to which Coughlin supposedly replied, "Billie, we ain't takin' no toothpicks." The pair voted to table the proposal. Alderman Powers, one of the proposal's chief supporters, told reporters after the final vote, "whether the people of Chicago have chosen wisely or not I am not prepared to say. But one thing strikes me, and that is that the last ordinance was a mighty fair one for the city and I doubt if it ever gets more."

Out-of-town newspapers echoed the Chicago mass news media's twin themes of responsible capitalism and pastoralism in response to the final vote. "It is difficult for Mr. Yerkes to understand that city councilmen are responsible to the public," the *Omaha World Herald* wrote, and the *Tacoma* (Washington) *Daily News* observed, "Mr. Yerkes . . . says there is no argument in a rope. But there is, just as there is argument in a roll of banknotes." "Recently Mr. Yerkes lived through the most exciting chapter of his not uneventful life," the *New York Journal* said. "He tried to buy Chicago for a song and Chicago protested against being sold." Coughlin was uncharacteristically brief in his observation on the outcome. "I've recently joined the church," he said to laugher from reporters. "There is intelligence in the Council from the Mayor down," Yerkes grumbled to reporters. "They are eminently fit to settle such a question."

Yerkes retired from Chicago business thereafter, selling all his mass transit interests to out-of-town investors in 1901, and turned his attention to London's mass transit system. While his downfall did not stop political corruption in Chicago, it did signal an end to the carte blanche buying and selling of aldermanic votes, especially after aldermanic salaries were raised and the newspapers made it clear to politicians that they would no longer overlook such overt behavior. Chicago's last traction cable car was electrified in 1906, and with the advent of automobiles a generation later, the city's mass transit system became publicly owned in 1947, six years before Yerkes' planned fifty-year franchise would have expired. As a responsible capitalist gone bad, Yerkes was soon forgotten in Chicago, almost as quickly as a responsible Chicago capitalist of another generation, Samuel Insull, whose fall from grace in the early 1930s helped bring about the Great Depression.[38]

Chicago as the First City

Chicago's mass news media was lobbying for Chicago to become the nation's largest city simultaneously with its crusade against Charles T. Yerkes and the Grey Wolves, the latter adding to the allure of the former in a sense. Initially, the newspapers welcomed the "Second City" moniker when Chicago surpassed Philadelphia in 1890, with a population of 1,099,850 compared to 1,046,964. "Will Chicago have second place?" the *Tribune* asked and answered enthusiastically. "The history of this country has advanced sufficiently to show that Boston, Philadelphia, Baltimore, New Orleans, and San Francisco cannot hope to rival New York, that none of the interior cities stand a chance of running neck and neck with Chicago." A Chicago Board of Education census came up with a count of 1,438,000 in 1892, an increase of 400,000 in two years. "This seems to show that the Chicago census taker still maintains his proud ascendency over those who confine themselves to cold facts," the *Boston Herald* sniffed. One of the final issues of the *Chicago Globe* estimated that the total city and suburban population was over 2,000,000 in 1893. "Judging from the report of the [Chicago] Controller's department it is the 3,500,000 mark that has been passed, and [that] deficit is growing larger," the *Grand Rapids* (Michigan) *Democrat* replied in kind.

The dream became a possibility during and immediately after the World's Fair. "Unless New York annexes Brooklyn before June 1894—a year from now," the *Chicago Evening Journal* predicted, "Chicago will be the largest city in the United States." "Chicago's affectionate regard for Gotham, as shown on Manhattan Day [at the fair], was almost as touching as the loving demonstrations of France to Russia," wrote the *Madison* (Wisconsin) *Journal.* A sixty-eight-year-old Mayor Carter Harrison Sr. told an audience on the day of his assassination, "I believe I shall see the day when Chicago will be the largest city in America and the third city on the face of the globe."

"Is Chicago's population greater than that of New York?" the *Tribune* asked the following year. "Well, if it isn't now it will be. There is no hurry. Don't crowd the mourners." "Some of the Chicago papers are claiming a population of 2,000,000 for the city in 1900," the *Minneapolis Tribune* said. "As to the probable percentage of unemployed persons at that time they are noncommittal." "A Chicago couple have just reported the birth of their twenty-fifth child," the *Buffalo Express* wrote. "It is public-spirited people like these that make a city truly great." The Chicago newspapers dwelled upon and dismissed various proposals for a greater New York area to "be allowed to set up in business for itself as a State, with a Governor, two Senators, etc." or in some other arrangement. "If Chicago doesn't hang [Mayor Carter's assassin] some carping critic will lay it to the greater New York scheme," the *Detroit Tribune* wrote. A *Chicago Daily News* letter writer asked, "Which has the largest population and how much—Chicago or New York?" to which the paper replied, "There is *not much* difference." The following year, the same newspaper expressed the intention to relegate "New York to the position of the St. Louis of the East."[39]

Lacking official records in a noncensus year, it is possible that Chicago surpassed Manhattan Island (New York) to become the nation's largest city in 1896. New Yorkers claimed a population of 1,801,000 in 1892 and 1,851,060 in 1895, but both were "padded, just as the St. Louis census returns of 1860 were, for the purpose of putting the city ahead of Chicago," possible for a city known for its excesses, as asserted by the *Chicago Tribune.* Instead, the normally conservative *Tribune* used an estimate for 1896 New York of 1,600,000 based on the yearly percentage of its population growth between 1880 and 1890. Meanwhile, the 1896 Chicago school board census put that city at 1,619,000. New York's newspapers were largely silent on the issue. The two cities also sparred over city directory population estimates. Chicago's directory put it at 1,828,000 in mid-1897 while New York's directory maker began a practice of not counting laborers and others who moved frequently that year, creating a total that was 20 percent of the previous directory and eliminating any possibility of comparison. "Now, we are the second city of the whole world," the *New York Tribune* rejoiced, putting it ahead of Paris, Berlin, and Chicago and lagging only London. "The compliments of the season to smaller New York," the *Chicago Tribune* replied.

Regardless, clouds began to darken on Chicago's horizon in 1896. Only too aware of the Garden City's gains, New York City and State politicians came to a rare agreement and passed legislation creating a Greater New York City in 1897, set to take place on the following New Year's Day. At the time of the enabling legislation, the *Tribune* scoffed that a new New York City would remain forever "the Second City to the world," ensuring that the entire United States would never be anything better than second best. It also suggested mock names for the new conglomerate including "Yorklyn, Brookyork, Yorkbrook, Yorkland," and "Little New York."

The *Daily News* published an editorial cartoon with the cut line "Pleasant anticipations" showing the New York Democratic Party and Tammany Hall political machine smacking their lips over the boodling prospects of annexation. "[New York] is the first city in the world in the energy, intelligence, and capacity of its habitants for accomplishing results," the *Chicago Tribune* quoted the *New York World*, "yet with all the greatness and grandeur about three-fourths of the inhabitants are discontented and unhappy. Why? Is it because they find that after supporting the owners of the 11,961 dramshops in comfort and idleness, they find themselves pinched with want and destitute of the necessities and comforts of life?" The *Chicago Tribune* quoted the *New York Sun* that the census of 1820 had shown the country that New York was ahead of all other American cities, "and it has kept that lead since." "The concluding statement is erroneous," the *Tribune* replied. "Chicago is the first city in the country now and will remain so for some months to come. This is unpleasant for New Yorkers, but there is no help for it."[40]

Therefore, Chicagoans watched helplessly as New York grew forever out of their grasp on January 1, 1898, and the cities of Brooklyn and Long Island disappeared forever. A few weeks before the annexation, the *Chicago Tribune* published an article titled "Chicago As It Will Be One Hundred Years From Today, A City of Wonders Unbelievable" which asserted that the 1997 Windy City would be "the undisputed sovereign of the States of America, the center of wealth, culture, and political power." Along with predictions of a pneumatic-powered rapid transit system, electric cars, heat, and light, sewage piped to distant farm fields as fertilizer, and sixty-story office buildings, the unnamed writer of the article asserted that Chicago would have a 1997 population of 10 million created by the annexation of surrounding suburbs and prairie land. "At the end of the next century I believe that the city will take in all of Cook County, all of Du Page County, and the northern nine townships of Will County," the author wrote. "Then the South Chicago colony would have extended into Indiana as far as Valparaiso, perhaps. If the state of Indiana will cede that valuable parcel of territory then indeed will Chicago be the Queen of the World."

On the day of the New York annexation, the *Tribune* editorialized, "Chicago has no jealousy in this matter. It wishes Greater New York all kinds of prosperity and sends both bride and groom its congratulations and wishes them a Happy New Year." In response, one of the New York papers welcomed an official Chicago delegation to the celebration with the observation that there was "neither a Hinky or a Dink among them."[41]

While most Chicagoans accepted their second-city fate quietly, the first-city fantasy lingered well into the twentieth century. *Munsey's Magazine* reported in 1907 that "Chicago is the first city in the world in many things—in enterprise, in growth, in energy and in her indomitable optimism and self-confidence. Nowhere else is there such human voltage." "There never existed on the planet Earth such a city as Chicago will be in 1960," the *Chicago Tribune* wrote in 1910, and the Chicago Association of Commerce mounted a $4 million advertising campaign in 1920 to make Chicago "the world's greatest city," a project that promptly crashed over accusations of corruption. "All other cities have heard during several years past is the dark side of Chicago," Mayor William H. Thompson complained to reporters at a press conference the same year, in reference to growing criminal violence. He continued somewhat cryptically, "Now the hammer has been interred."

Cook County District Court Judge Charles Cutting informed commerce association members two years later that "possibly the persons who inhabited the Garden of Eden did not know that some of their descendants would settle along the shores of Lake Michigan, but they did and Chicago is the result." Elaborating upon Cutting's divine intervention theory, University of Chicago Geography Professor J. Paul Goode told a Field Museum audience the following year that the forces of nature "got together and, placing a collective finger on a certain spot on the universe, said: 'We'll fix things up for the world's greatest city to grow here. It will be the city of destiny, for we'll combine our forces to bring every advantage to it. We'll doctor the ground and the air and the people so that some day the world will look to this city and say: "You are king."'"[42]

* * *

The final gasp in Chicago's first-city crusade came at the bequest of idiosyncratic twentieth-century *Chicago Tribune* publisher Col. Robert R. McCormick. Following Joseph Medill's death in 1899, the *Tribune* went through a period of managerial instability until grandson McCormick, a decorated World War I veteran, took control of the paper in 1919. Promising to use all of the *Tribune*'s resources to his end, McCormick initiated a campaign in December 1924 to "make Chicago the first city in the world." Published as part of a larger "Platform for Chicago," McCormick's editorial-page pledge continued through the 1930s, even as residents departed Chicago during the most serious years of the Great Depression, reducing its population.

"Chicago is the biggest hick burg in America," a New York-based letter writer told the *Chicago Tribune* at about the same time. "Chicago will be a great city after New York burns up." In 1931, the son of utilities magnate Samuel Insull predicted that Chicago would have a population of 7.5 million in 1950. When Mayor Edward J. Kelley initiated a "Let's Go, Chicago!" campaign during the World's Fair year of 1933, a *New York Times* letter writer asserted that "New York is America's greatest city and Chicago its greatest American city."

Col. McCormick's first-city platform was repeated nearly daily in the *Tribune* for sixteen years, but his pipe dream died quietly on March 11, 1941, when it was replaced by a new pledge, to "save our republic" from "those who fancy themselves better than other American citizens." A few days later, McCormick told a live audience on WGN, the *Tribune*'s clear channel AM radio station, in perhaps a eulogy to the first-city dream, that "to a Chicagoan, America is incomparably the greatest nation on earth and its heart is Chicago." Employing the imagery of Henry Wadsworth Longfellow's "Hiawatha," a *Chicago Tribune* reporter had written of the 1893 World's Columbian Exposition that the world had laid a slain deer, "the tribute of universal love and admiration," at the feet of Chicago. "At the world's feet," *New Yorker* writer A. J. Liebling (who forever hung the "Second City" moniker on Chicago in 1952) retorted, "Chicago, in return, laid a butchered hog." In the 1953 film noir classic *City That Never Sleeps,* set in a cynical, gritty Chicago, the character Sally "Angel Face" Connors says, "When I first came to this town I was gonna be—oh, there were a lot of things I was gonna do. Become famous. But Chicago's the big melting pot, and I got melted, but good." In the end, like Sally, Chicago's fantasy of being the First City was swallowed up by everyday life.[43]

Notes

Abbreviations

AAN	Accessible Archives
AZ	*Chicagoer Arbeiter Zeitung*
CD	*Chicago Democrat*
CDDP	(Chicago) *Daily Democratic Press*
CDN	*Chicago Daily News*
CFLPS	Chicago Public Library
CG	*Chicago Globe*
CH	*Chicago Herald*
CHS	Chicago Historical Society
CIO	*Chicago Inter Ocean*
CJ	*Chicago Evening Journal*
CP	*Chicago Evening Post*
CR	*Chicago Republican*
CT	*Chicago Tribune*
CTM	*Chicago Times*
FC	(Amherst, NH) *Farmers' Cabinet*
GP	(Chicago) *Gem of the Prairie*
HNMM	*Harper's New Monthly Magazine*
HW	*Harper's Weekly*
ISZ	(Chicago) *Illinois Staats Zeitung*
LT	(London, England) *Times*
MS	*Milwaukee Sentinel*
NYH	*New York Herald*
NYS	*New York Sun*
NYT	*New York Times*
NYTB	*New York Tribune*
PS	*Pittsfield* (MA) *Sun*
WC	(Chicago) *Western Citizen*
WP	*Washington Post*

MANUSCRIPT COLLECTIONS

Douglas Papers	Stephen A. Douglas Papers, Chicago Historical Museum, Chicago.
Handy Family Papers	(Moses P.) Handy Family Papers, University of Michigan William L. Clements Library, Ann Arbor, MI.

Lawson Papers	Victor Lawson Papers, Newberry Library, Chicago.
Lloyd Papers	Henry Demarest Lloyd Papers, State Historical Society of Wisconsin, Madison.
McCormick Papers	Col. Robert R. McCormick Papers, Robert R. McCormick Museum, Wheaton, IL.
Medill Papers	Joseph Meharry Medill Papers, *Chicago Tribune* Archives, Robert R. McCormick Museum, Wheaton, IL.
Sherman Papers	William T. Sherman Papers, Library of Congress, Washington, DC.

Introduction

1. *PS,* 23 Jan. 1840, 3 May 1855; *CD,* quoted in *PS,* 1 Feb. 1849; *CD,* quoted in *PS,* 25 Sept. 1845; *CD,* quoted in *National Era,* 27 Dec. 1855, in *African American Newspapers: The 19th Century,* Accessible Archives (hereafter cited as AAN), item #54442; *WP,* quoted in *CT,* 2 Dec. 1888; *Chicago American,* quoted in *New Hampshire Sentinel,* 22 May 1839; Newman Hall, *From Liverpool to St. Louis* (London, New York, G. Routledge, 1870), 141; *Buffalo Express,* quoted in *CT,* 8 Aug. 1889; *Puck,* quoted in *CT,* 9 July 1893; *Indianapolis Sentinel,* quoted in *CT,* 8 Jan. 1893.

2. *Minneapolis Journal,* quoted in *CT,* 9 Sept. 1893; *Brooklyn Eagle,* quoted in *CT,* 23 June 1889; *Cincinnati Tribune,* quoted in *CT,* 2 April 1895; *London Sketch,* quoted in *CT,* 13 April 1899; *CT,* 26 March 1922, 4 Dec. 1923.

3. The *Chicago Tribune* was one of seven newspapers to introduce the Peanuts comic strip on October 2, 1950. As such, the *Tribune* was influential in decisions about the strip's syndication and managed to keep it out of what it considered to be the competing market of nearby Milwaukee for years.

4. Ruth McManus and Philip J. Ethington, "Suburbs in Transition: New Approaches to Suburban History," *Urban History* 34 (March 2007): 317–37; Clay McSane, Carl Abbott, and Timothy J. Gilfoyle, "The State of the Art in North American Urban History," *Urban History* 32 (Nov. 2006): 582–97; Timothy J. Gilfoyle, "White Cities, Linguistic Turns, and Disneylands: The New Paradigms of Urban History," *Reviews in American History* 26 (Jan. 1998): 175–204; Bessie Louis Pierce, *A History of Chicago* (New York: A.A. Knopf, 1937–1957); Harold M. Mayer and Richard C. Wade, *Chicago: Growth of a Metropolis* (Chicago: University of Chicago Press, 1969).

5. P. L. Berger and T. Luckmann, *The Social Construction of Reality: A Treatise in the Sociology of Knowledge* (Garden City, NY: Anchor Books, 1966); Colin Cherry, *World Communication, Threat or Promise? A Socio-technical Approach* (Chichester, UK: John Wiley, 1978), 26–36; Donald L. Shaw and Maxwell E. McCombs, *The Emergence of American Political Issues: The Agenda-Setting Function of the Press* (St. Paul, MN: West Publishing, 1977); Mary B. Cassata and Molefi Kete Asante, *Mass Communication* (Macmillan Publishing, 1979); W. Phillips Davison, "The Third-Person Effect in Communication," *Public Opinion Quarterly* 47 (Spring 1983): 1–15; Melvin L.

DeFleur and S. J. Ball-Rokeach, *Theories of Mass Communication* (White Plains, NY: Longman, 1989); Denis McQuail, *Mass Communication Theory*, 4th ed. (Thousand Oaks, CA: Sage, 2000); Herbert Gans, *Deciding What's News: A Study of CBS Evening News, NBC Nightly News, Newsweek and Time* (New York: Pantheon, 1979), 42–48; S. A. Lowery and Melvin L. DeFleur, *Milestones in Mass Communication Research* (White Plains, NY: Longman, 1995); B. Paul and M. B. Dupagne, "The Third-Person Effect: A Meta-Analysis of the Perceptual Hypothesis," *Mass Communication and Society* 3 (Spring 2000): 57–85; James Shanahan and Michael Morgan, *Television and its Viewers: Cultivation Theory and Research* (Cambridge, UK: Cambridge University Press, 1999), 1–19.

6. David Croteau and William Hoynes, *Media/Society: Industries, Images, and Audiences*, 3rd ed. (Thousand Oaks, CA: Pine Forge Press, 2003), 3–30.

7. Gunther Barth, *City People: The Rise of Modern City Culture in Nineteenth-Century America* (New York: Oxford University Press, 1980), 58–59.

8. Louis Gottschalk, *Understanding History: A Primer of Historical Method*, 2d ed. (New York: Alfred A. Knopf, 1969), 56; Jacques Barzun and Henry F. Graff, *The Modern Researcher*, 5th ed. (Fort Worth, TX: Harcourt Brace Jovanovich, 1992), 96; Michael G. Kammen, *Selvages and Biases: The Fabric of History in American Culture* (Ithaca, NY: Cornell University Press, 1987), 154–73; Martha Howell and Walter Prevenier, *From Reliable Sources: An Introduction to Historical Methods* (Ithaca, NY: Cornell University Press, 2001), 32; Stephane Levesque, *Thinking Historically: Educating Students for the Twenty-first Century* (Toronto: University of Toronto Press, 2008), 121–22; J. H. Hexter, *The History Primer* (New York: Basic Books, 1971), 86; Arthur Schlesinger Jr., "Worse than Useless," *Newsweek* 61 (Jan. 14, 1963).

9. Finley Peter Dunne, *Observations by Mr. Dooley* (New York: R. H. Russell, 1906), 239–44; Walter Lippmann, *Public Opinion* (New York: Harcourt, Brace, 1922), 331; *Indianapolis Journal*, quoted in *CT*, 1 Sept. 1889; *Allan Nevins on History*, compiled by Ray Allen Billington (New York: Charles Scribner's Sons, 1975), 267–68; *CT*, 9 Dec. 1921; Michael Gartner, "The First Rough Draft of History: An Interview with Benjamin C. Bradlee," *A Sense of History: The Best Writing from the Pages of American Heritage* (New York: American Heritage, 1985), 807–8.

10. Allan J. Lichtman and Valerie French, *Historians and the Living Past: The Theory and Practice of Historical Study* (Arlington Heights, IL: AHM Publishing, 1978), 176; James A. Jones, "Constructing History with Computers," in *Writing, Teaching, and Researching History in the Electronic Age: Historians and Computers*, ed. Dennis A. Trinkle (Armonk, NY: M. E. Sharpe, 1998), 83–88; *Nevins on History*, 264; "Bessie Louise Pierce and Chicago History," in *The Encyclopedia of Chicago*, ed. James R. Grossman (Chicago: University of Chicago Press, 2004), 150.

The use of historical newspaper databases has become more prevalent in dissertations and theses, especially those involving content analysis and related methodologies, but remains less so in journals and books. Since style guides such as the *Chicago Manual of Style, MLA Style Manual*, and *Publication Manual of the American Psycho-*

logical Association (APA) require newspaper titles but not their retrieval method, it is likely that databases are being used but not referenced. For examples, see Richard Junger, "'God and man helped those who helped themselves': John and Mary Jones and the Culture of African American Self-Sufficiency in Mid-Nineteenth-Century Chicago," *Journal of Illinois History* 11 (Summer 2008): 111–32; David Niven, "Objective Evidence on Media Bias: Newspaper Coverage of Congressional Party Switches," *Journalism and Mass Communication Quarterly* 80 (Summer 2003): 311–26; and Sharon Block, "Rape and Race in Colonial Newspapers, 1728–1776," *Journalism History* 27 (Winter 2001–2): 146–55.

Chapter 1. From Zero to 29,963 in Just Fifty-five Years

1. John Clayton, *The Illinois Fact Book and Historical Almanac, 1673–1968* (Carbondale: Southern Illinois University Press, 1970), 15–17; Alfred T. Andreas, *History of Chicago from the Earliest Period to the Present Time,* I (Chicago: A. T. Andreas, 1884), 171; John Moses, *Illinois* (Chicago: Fergus Printing Co., 1892), 278–82; Milo M. Quaife, *Chicago's Highways Old and New: From Indian Trail to Motor Road* (Chicago: D. F. Keller, 1923), 11–28; "Illinois in Spring-Time," *Atlantic Monthly* 2 (Sept. 1858): 483; *CT,* 8 Dec. 1916.

2. *CT,* 8 Oct. 1857, 20 May 1979; Don E. Fehrenbacher, *Chicago Giant: A Biography of "Long John" Wentworth* (Madison, WI.: American Historical Research Center, 1957), 36–38; Bessie Louise Pierce, *A History of Chicago* I (New York: Alfred A. Knopf, 1937), 381; Irving Cutler, *The Chicago-Milwaukee Corridor: A Geographic Study of Intermetropolitan Coalescence* (Evanston, IL: Department of Geography, Northwestern University, 1965), 17; Michael H. Ebner, *Creating Chicago's North Shore: A Suburban History* (Chicago: University of Chicago Press, 1988), 1–2.

3. *GP,* quoted in *CT,* 10 July 1887; *CD,* 22 May 1844, 21 March 1848, 7 April 1848; James W. Carey, "Technology and Ideology: The Case of the Telegraph," in Carey, *Communication as Culture: Essays on Media and Society* (Boston: Unwin Hyman, 1988), 206; Timothy R. Mahoney, "'A Common Band of Brotherhood': Male Subcultures, the Booster Ethos, and the Origins of Urban Social Order in the Midwest of the 1840s," *Journal of Urban History* 25 (July 1999): 619–46; William J. Cronon, "To Be the Central City: Chicago, 1848–1857," *Chicago History* 7 (Spring 1978): 12–21; Carl Abbott, *Popular Economic Thought and Urban Growth in the Antebellum Middle West* (Westport, CT: Greenwood Press, 1981); Carl Abbott, "Civic Pride in Chicago, 1844–1860," *Journal of the Illinois State Historical Society* 53 (Winter 1970): 399–421.

4. *CT,* 21 Jan. 1919, 16 March 1941; *Massachusetts Spy,* 16 March 1786; *Philadelphia Gazette,* 2 Oct. 1894.

5. *CT,* 23 April 1936, 13 April 1958, 4 March 1962, 22 Jan. 1978; John F. Swenson, "Jean Baptiste Point De Sable: The Founder of Modern Chicago," *A Compendium of the Early History of Chicago to the Year 1835, When the Indians Left* (Chicago: self-published, 2000), available at www.earlychicago.com; Helen Horney and William E.

Keller, "The Negro's Two Hundred Forty Years in Illinois—A Chronology," *Journal of the Illinois State Historical Society* 56 (Fall 1963): 433–38; Thomas A. Meehan, "Jean Baptiste Point Du Sable, The First Chicagoan," *Journal of the Illinois State Historical* Society 56 (Fall 1963): 439–53; *Chicago Defender,* 12 Feb. 2000.

6. (NY) *Morning Chronicle,* 21 Nov. 1805; *New York Commercial Advertiser,* 14 Aug. 1807; *New York Evening Post,* 28 Nov. 1807; *Rutland* (VT) *Herald,* 30 Jan. 1808; *CT,* 5 March 1899.

7. *Plattsburgh Republican,* 21 May 1814; *CT,* 8 March 1890; *Richmond Enquirer,* 30 June 1812; *Alexandria Daily Gazette,* 4 Sept. 1812; *Buffalo Gazette,* 1 Sept. 1812, quoted in the (Charleston) *City Gazette and Daily Advertiser,* 25 Sept. 1812; *Western Star,* 19 Sept. 1812; *National Imtelligencer,* 3 Oct. 1812; *Columbian Phoenix,* 3 Oct. 1812; *Constitutionalist,* 20 Oct. 1812; *Federal Republican,* 2 Nov. 1812; *Aurora,* quoted in the *Baltimore Patriot,* 22 Feb. 1813.

8. Paul Chrisler Phillips, *The Fur Trade* (Norman: University of Oklahoma Press, 1961), 274; Hiram Martin Chittenden, *The American Fur Trade of the Far West* (New York: Press of the Pioneers, [1902] 1935); "Chicago in 1856," *Putnam's* 7 (June 1856): 610; Samuel Appleton Storrow, *Narrative of a Tour in the Northwest in 1817,* quoted in Milo Quaife, *The Development of Chicago 1674 to 1914, Shown in a Series of Contemporary Original Narratives* (Chicago: Canton Club, 1916); John H. Fonda, "A Series of Reminiscences," *Wisconsin Historical Collections* 5 (Madison: The Society, 1858); Charles Fenno Hoffman, *A Winter in the West* (New York: Harper & Bros., 1835); *CT,* 9 Oct. 1902, 29 June 1947; Colbee C. Benton, *A Visitor to Chicago in Indian Days: "Journal of the 'Far-off West'"* (Chicago: Caxton Club, 1957); *New York American,* quoted in (Concord) *New Hampshire Patriot,* 21 April 1834; Harold H. Mayer and Richard C. Wade, *Chicago: Growth of a Metropolis* (Chicago: University of Chicago Press, 1969), 3; *New Hampshire Sentinel,* 16 Aug. 1835; *CD,* 7 Oct. 1835; *Connecticut Courant,* 6 July 1835; *Litchfield Enquirer,* quoted in the *Connecticut Courant,* 28 Jan. 1837.

9. *Saratoga Sentinel* (Saratoga Springs, NY), 6 May 1823; *Rhode Island American,* 7 Aug. 1832; Roland Tinkham, quoted in Henry Raymond Hamilton, *The Epic of Chicago* (Chicago: Willett, Clark, 1932); *Salem* (MA) *Gazette,* 24 July 1832; *CD,* quoted in the (Amherst, NH) *FC,* 12 Oct. 1838; *Portsmouth* (ME) *Journal of Literature and Politics,* 20 Oct. 1838; *PS,* 14 July 1859; *New Hampshire Patriot,* 22 Aug. 1850; *CD,* quoted in *FC,* 14 Feb. 1850; *CT,* 5 Dec. 1897; *WC,* 6 July 1843; Newman Hall, *From Liverpool to St. Louis* (London: G. Routledge, 1870), 157; Charles Rosenberg, *The Cholera Years* (Chicago: University of Chicago Press, 1987).

10. *Constitutional Diary,* 18 Jan. 1800; *LT,* 26 Dec. 1807, 7 Oct. 1846, 12 May 1847; Walter E. Houghton, *The Victorian Frame of Mind* (New Haven, CT: Yale University Press, 1957), 183; Thomas Carlyle, *Past and Present* (New York: New York University Press, 1977, 1843), 146.

11. *Rural Visitor,* 1 Oct. 1818; *CT,* 14 April 1905; *Portsmouth* (NH) *Oracle,* 11 April 1818; *Rhode Island American,* 9 May 1823; *Providence* (RI) *Patriot,* 3 June 1829; *Barre* (MA) *Gazette,* 6 Sept. 1839, 9 June 1848, 26 Aug. 1853; *London Quarterly,* quoted

in *New-Bedford Mercury,* 28 Aug. 1837; Francis Wayland, *The Elements of Political Economy* (New York: Leavitt, Lord & Co., 1837), 162; *Pennsylvanian,* as quoted in *Chicago American,* 31 Jan. 1837; *Practical Preacher,* 21 Dec. 1849, McCormick Papers; *Connecticut Mirror,* 22 May 1830.

12. John Dean Caton, "'T'is Sixty Years Since' in Chicago," *Atlantic Monthly* 71 (May 1893): 590; *CD,* 18 Nov. 1835, 22 May 1839, 31 March 1843, 15 May 1844; *Chicago American,* 22 Oct. 1836, 21 Feb. 1837; *Chicago Express,* 28 Oct. 1842; *CD,* quoted in *New Hampshire Patriot,* 24 Aug. 1835; *FC,* 22 Jan. 1846; Henry Blake Fuller, *With the Procession, a Novel* (New York: Harper & Bros., 1895).

13. *New York American,* quoted in *New Hampshire Patriot,* 21 April 1834; *New Hampshire Sentinel,* 14 May 1835; *Utica Whig,* quoted in the (St. Albans) *Vermont State Paper,* 21 July 1835; *New York American,* quoted in *Connecticut Courant,* 6 July 1835; *CD,* quoted in *New Hampshire Patriot,* 24 Aug. 1835; *PS,* 1 Oct. 1835; *Cincinnati Mirror, and Western Gazette of Literature and Science,* circa 1834–35, quoted in (Galveston, TX) *Flake's Bulletin,* 4 May 1867; *CD,* 9 Dec. 1835; *New Hampshire Patriot and Statesman,* 17 Aug. 1837; *Detroit Journal,* quoted in *Connecticut Courant,* 29 June 1835; *FC,* 26 Aug. 1839.

14. Harold M. Mayer, "The Launching of Chicago: The Situation and Site," *Chicago History,* 9 (Feb. 1980): 68–79; *New York Commercial Advertiser,* 5 Feb. 1812; *CT,* 19 April 1891.

15. *LT,* 8 Jan. 1841; *Chicago American,* 21 Jan., 28 Jan. 1837; Rufus Blanchard, *Discovery and Conquests of the Northwest with the History of Chicago* (Chicago: R. Blanchard, 1900), 10; (Portland, ME) *Eastern Argus,* 19 Oct. 1830, *New York Mirror,* quoted in *New Hampshire Sentinel,* 4 Aug. 1836; (Sing-Sing, NY) *Hudson River Chronicle,* 25 Dec. 1838; *New Hampshire Sentinel,* 19 May 1841; Abbott, "Civic Pride," 399–421.

16. *CT,* 21 July 1895.

17. Calhoun to wife, 17 Oct. 1833, quoted in *CT,* 26 Nov. 1883; *CT,* 22 Feb. 1859; *CD,* 26 Nov. 1833, 9 May 1834; *CD,* quoted in *New Hampshire Patriot,* 24 Aug. 1835; Andreas, *History of Chicago* I, 360–71.

18. *CD,* quoted in *PS,* 29 May 1834, 4 Feb. 1836, 16 March 1837; *CD,* quoted in *New Hampshire Sentinel,* 17 Dec. 1835; *CD,* 28 Jan. 1834; Don Harrison Doyle, *The Social Order of a Frontier Community: Jacksonville, Illinois, 1825–70* (Urbana: University of Illinois Press, 1983).

19. *CD,* 26 Nov. 1834, 3 Dec. 1833, 25 Nov. 1835, 3 March 1836, 13 April 1836, 29 June 1836; Franklin William Scott, *Newspapers and Periodicals of Illinois, 1814–1879* (Springfield: Illinois State Historical Library, 1910), 52–53; Pierce, *Chicago* I, 153–57; George Hage, *Newspapers on the Minnesota Frontier, 1849–1860* (St. Paul: Minnesota Historical Society, 1967), 11; *Chicago Democrat* Subscription Books, Chicago Historical Society (hereafter CHS); William Cronon, *Nature's Metropolis: Chicago and the Great West* (New York: Norton, 1991), 61–63.

20. *CD,* 13 April 1836, 11 May, 16 Nov. 1836, 24 Sept. 1860; *CT,* 22 Feb. 1859, 28 Aug., 12 Sept., 22 Sept., 24 Sept. 1860, 5 Jan. 1919, 6 Sept. 1924, 12 April 1959; *NYT,* 24 Sept.,

25 Sept. 1860; *LT,* 9 Oct., 10 Oct., 13 Oct. 1860; Nicholas A. Woods, *The Prince of Wales in Canada and the United States* (London: Bradbury & Evans, 1861), 285–92; Andreas, *History of Chicago* I, 366–71; A. J. Liebling, "Profile," *New Yorker* 28 (12 Jan. 1952): 30.

21. *CD,* 24 April 1839, 1 Jan. 1841, 18 Jan., 8 June 1842, 31 Jan. 1844; *Barre Gazette,* 15 Dec. 1843; *CD,* quoted in *Berkshire Whig,* 14 Sept. 1843; *CT,* 17 Oct. 1888; Andreas, *History of Chicago* III, 838; Fehrenbacher, *Wentworth,* 23, 34–49, 239n10; Donald L. Miller, *City of the Century: The Epic of Chicago and the Making of America* (New York: Simon and Schuster, 1996), 78.

22. *CT,* 23 Feb. 1879; *PS,* 1 July 1847; *Democratic Daily Press,* 10 May 1853.

23. *PS,* 10 Nov. 1853, 1 Oct. 1857, 12 Aug. 1858; 13 Oct. 1859; *CD,* quoted in *FC,* 14 Feb. 1850; *CD* business books, 1833, CHS; Herbert Asbury, *Sucker's Progress: An Informal History of Gambling in America From the Colonies to Canfield* (Montclair, NJ: Patterson Smith, [1938] 1969), 286; *CD,* 30 Dec. 1833; Clifton R. Wooldridge, *Gambling Exposed: True Experiences of Clifton R. Wooldridge* (Chicago: M. Stein, 1918); *Salem Gazette,* 14 Aug. 1835; *New Hampshire Patriot,* 7 Aug. 1837; (New London, CT) *Morning News,* 21 May 1846; *CT,* 30 Jan. 1854, 16 Sept. 1862; *FC,* 20 Dec. 1855.

24. *CT,* 20 Dec. 1853, 9 April 1856, 6 Oct. 1857, 23 Nov. 1857; 14 Jan. 1859, 4 Sept. 1898; John F. Flinn and John E. Wilkie, *History of the Chicago Police Department the Settlement of the Community to the Present Time* (Chicago: Policeman's Benevolent Association, 1887); Walter Cade Reckless, *The Natural History of the Vice Areas in Chicago,* PhD dissertation, University of Chicago, 1925; Herbert Asbury, *Gem of the Prairie: An Informal History of the Chicago Underworld* (New York: Alfred Knopf, 1940); Frederick Francis Cook, *Bygone Days in Chicago* (Chicago: A. C. McClurg, 1910), 157.

25. *CT,* 19 June, 20 June 1857, 8 Feb. 1981; Isabella L. Bird, *The Englishwoman in America* (London: John Murray, 1856), 155.

26. *Cleveland Herald,* quoted in *The North Star,* 7 April 1849, AAN, item #14367; Scott, *Illinois Newspapers,* 54–56; *CT,* 24 Sept. 1859, 21 Aug. 1864, 11 Sept. 1871, 16 April 1877, 23 Feb. 1879, 12 June 1892, 10 June, 12 Dec. 1897, 22 Dec. 1899, 15 Aug. 1941; Kenny J. Williams, *Prairie Voices: A Literary History of Chicago from the Frontier to 1893* (Nashville: Townsend Press, 1980), 371–479.

27. "Story of Great Fire as Told By Joseph Medill," Medill Papers; *CT,* 21 Aug. 1864, 23 Feb. 1879, 9 Oct. 1893, 7 June 1937, 10 Oct. 1942; Williams, *Prairie Voices,* 80; Herbert E. Fleming, "Magazines of a Market-Metropolis: Being a History of the Literary Periodicals and Literary Interests of Chicago," *The American Journal of Sociology* 11–12 (1906): 387–88.

28. *CD,* 31 Aug. 1849; *CT,* 21 Aug. 1864; Lloyd Wendt, *Chicago Tribune: The Rise of a Great American Newspaper* (Chicago: Rand McNally and Co., 1979), 26–27.

29. Andreas, *History of Chicago* I, 401; Wendt, *Chicago Tribune,* 23–25; Susan Thompson, *The Penny Press* (Northport, AL: Vision Press, 2004).

30. McCormick to Miss Clarke, 6 March 1947, McCormick Papers; Richard Norton Smith, *The Colonel: The Life and Legend of Robert R. McCormick, 1880–1955* (Boston:

Houghton Mifflin, 1997), 66–67; *CT,* 10 June 1897, 10 June 1947; Kenneth E. Olson, "The Role of Liberal Arts in Our Journalism Program," *Northwestern University Alumni News* 34 (April 1955), 3–5, in Medill Papers; David L. Protess, "Joseph Medill: Chicago's First Modern Mayor," in *The Mayors: The Chicago Political Tradition,* ed. Paul M. Green and Melvin G. Holli (Carbondale, IL: Southern Illinois University Press, 1995), 1–15; Alice Snyder, *Inventing Medill: A History of the Medill School of Journalism, Northwestern University, 1921–1996* (Evanston, IL: Northwestern University, 1996).

31. *Chicago Chronicle* clipping, n.d., circa 1880s, "Dungannon Address of Joseph Medill," 16 Feb. 1882, "Sons of Temperance certificate for Joseph Medill," 9 Oct. 1847, F. X. Jennings to McCormick, 4 Sept. 1940, (Coshocton, OH) *Practical Preacher* clipping, 21 Dec. 1849, and Medill, "How to Lay the Atlantic Telegraph Cable, 25 March 1866," all in McCormick Papers; *CT,* 23 Jan. 1887, 21 May 1896, 12 June 1955; Wendt, *Chicago Tribune,* 39–41; Abbott, "Civic Pride," 411; Elise D. Nordquist and Edward Caudill, "'. . . to leave this beggarly profession': A Study of Lawyers in Journalism," paper delivered to the American Journalism Historians Association, Coeur d'Alene, ID, Oct. 1990; Frank Gilbert, "The Coming Man is the Coming Editor," *Lakeside Monthly,* 8 (Aug. 1872): 113–15; H. I. Cleveland, "Booming the First Republican President," *Saturday Evening Post* 172 (5 Aug. 1899): 84–85.

32. *National Era,* 19 July 1855, AAN #53056; *NYT,* 21 Feb. 1861; William Herndon to Medill, 22 Feb. 1861, Medill Papers; Barbara C. Schaaf, *Mr. Dooley's Chicago* (Garden City, NJ: Anchor Press, 1977), 18–19; Ernest Poole, *Giant's Gone: Men Who Made Chicago* (New York: Whittlesey House, 1943), 57; McCormick to Katherine Maddock, 11 April [1941?], McCormick Papers; *CT,* 29 May 1893, 23 June 1899, 7 Feb. 1909; Robert R. McCormick to F. T. Moriarty, 3 April 1933, McCormick Papers; "Memo for the Record," 24 Oct. 1974, McCormick Papers; Jay Robert Nash, *People to See: An Anecdotal History of Chicago's Makers & Breakers* (Piscataway, NJ: New Century Publishers, 1981), 6–7; J. H. Montandon to Robert R. McCormick, 31 Dec. 1933, McCormick Papers; Frederick Hartzell, "Reminiscent and Prophetic Words by Joseph Medill," n.d., unidentified newspaper clipping, circa 1900, McCormick Papers; Stephen Longstreet, *Chicago, 1860–1919* (New York: David McKay, 1973), 232–33; Wayne Andrews, *The Battle for Chicago* (New York: Harcourt Brace Jovanovitch, 1946), 49.

33. Hartzell, "Reminiscent and Prophetic Words" and "Joseph Medill" in *Biographical Dictionary and Portrait Gallery of the Representative Men of the United States, Illinois Edition,* ed. John Moses (Chicago: Lewis Publishing Co., 1896), 13–18; Andreas, *History of Chicago* I, 384–402; John Tebbel, *An American Dynasty: The Story of the McCormicks, Medills and Pattersons* (Garden City, NY: Doubleday, 1947), 5–6; Jay Monaghan, *The Man Who Elected Lincoln* (Indianapolis: Bobbs-Merrill Co., 1956), 45–49; Tracy E. Strevey, "Joseph Medill and the *Chicago Tribune* During the Civil War Period," unpublished dissertation, University of Chicago, 1930, 91, 182.

34. Wendt, *Chicago Tribune,* 65–72; *CT,* 28 May 1853, 23 June 1853, 26 Feb. 1855, 21 March 1860; *CT,* 7 Aug. 1865; Thomas M. Keefe, "Chicago's Flirtation with Political Nativism, 1854–1856," *Records of the American Catholic Historical Society of Philadelphia* 82 (Sept. 1971): 131–58; Roger Streitmatter, "Demonizing the American Immigrant," *Journalism Quarterly* 76 (Winter 1999): 673–83; Bird, *Englishwoman in America,* 147–48.

35. Joseph Medill, "First Draft of Know Something Address," Cincinnati, Ohio, Feb. 1853, *CT* archives, McCormick Museum.

36. Harold L. Platt, *Shock Cities* (Chicago: University of Chicago Press, 2005), 237–39; Carl Wittke, "Ohio's Germans, 1840–1875," *Ohio Historical Quarterly* 62 (Oct. 1957): 339–54; *CT,* 15 March 1854, 27 Sept. 1854, 3 Feb. 1855; *CDDP,* 14 March 1855; *ISZ,* quoted in *CT,* 7 Feb. 1855.

37. *CT,* 8 March 1854, 23 April, 24 April 1855, 27 Oct. 1872, 31 Dec. 1872; *PS,* 26 April 1855; *NYT,* 23 April, 24 April, 30 April 1855; *FC,* 3 May 1855; *CJ,* quoted in the *NYT,* 26 April 1855; *The National Era,* 26 April 1855, AAN item #52187; *CH,* 22 Nov. 1885; *CT,* quoted in (Chatham, ON) *Provincial Freeman,* 16 May 1857, AAN, item #39931; "The First Invasion," *Chamberlin Magazine,* mismarked April 1927, more likely 1917, in Chicago Foreign Language Press Survey microfilm collection, reel #13, Chicago Public Library (hereafter CFLPS); *The National Era,* 12 July 1855, AAN, item #52935; David Grimsted, *American Mobbing, 1828–1861* (New York: Oxford University Press, 1998); *CTM,* quoted in *CT,* 21 Aug. 1864; Mahoney, "'Common Band of Brotherhood'"; undated circa 1855 (perhaps not surviving) issue of *CT* quoted in Tebbel, *American Dynasty,* 17; Miller, *City of the Century,* 136–37; Robert G. Spinney, *City of Big Shoulders: A History of Chicago* (DeKalb: Northern Illinois University Press, 2000), 72–73; Finis Farr, *A Personal History of America's Most American City* (New Rochelle, NY: Arlington House, 1973), 50–51; *CDDP,* 17 Jan. 1856.

38. Thomas M. Keefe, "The Catholic Issue in the *Chicago Tribune* Before the Civil War," *Mid-America* 57 (Oct. 1975): 227–45; Alfred T. Andreas, *History of Cook County* (Chicago: A. T. Andreas, 1884), 395; Strevey, "Joseph Medill," 23; Franc B. Wilkie, *Personal Reminiscences of Thirty-five Years of Journalism* (Chicago: F.J. Schulte & Co., 1891), 184;*CT,* 6 June, 17 June, 13 Sept. 1854, 15 Feb., 24 Sept. 1855, 8 Feb., 15 Feb., 29 Feb., 5 March 1856; 3 March 1857, 27 July 1857, 18 April 1859, 9 July 1877, 1 Oct. 1960.

39. *Lakeside Monthly Magazine* 10 (Oct. 1873): 255; *CTM* undated, quoted in John S. Wright, *Chicago: Past, Present, Future* (Chicago: Western News Co., 1868), vii–viii; *Toledo Blade,* quoted in *CJ,* 11 April 1853; John Kirk to the *Youngstown* (Ohio) *Free Press,* 5 May 1854, John Kirk Letterbook, CHS, quoted in Carl Abbott, *Boosters and Businessmen: Popular Economic Thought and Urban Growth in the Antebellum Middle West* (Westport, CT: Greenwood Press, 1981), 126; *HW,* 5 (19 Jan. 1861): 34, 8 (3 Dec. 1864): 771; *Democratic Daily Press,* 10 May 1853; *CIO,* 28 Aug. 1880; *CT,* 19 May 1856; *Putnam's Magazine* 12 (Oct. 1868): 415.

Chapter 2. "Chicago is the Head-Centre, the Mecca, of All Creation"

1. *GP,* quoted in *CT,* 10 July 1887; *CD,* 7 April 1848; *CT,* 21 Aug. 1864, 10 July 1887, 9 Oct. 1893, 23 Aug. 1896; *CIO,* 17 April 1872; *PS,* 20 Jan., 17 Feb. 1848; Kenneth Silverman, *Lightning Man: The Accursed Life of Samuel F. B. Morse* (New York: Knopf, 2003); Maggie Dennis, "The Once and Future Web: Worlds Woven by the Telegraph and Internet," *Journal of American History* 89 (Jan. 2002): 185–87; Tom Standage, *The Victorian Internet* (New York: Walker and Company, 1998).

2. *CTM,* undated, quoted in Wright, *Chicago: Past, Present, Future,* viii.

3. *CD,* 20 Sept. 1842; *Chicago American,* 22 Sept. 1842; *CD,* quoted in *Ohio Statesman,* 25 July 1845; *WC,* 19 Aug. 1842; *Prairie Farmer,* quoted in *PS,* 5 Oct. 1843; Willa Cather, *O Pioneers!* (Boston: Houghton Mifflin, [1913] 1941), 23; Colin Cherry, *World Communication,* 26–27; *CD,* 23 July, 11 Oct., 22 Nov., 23 Dec. 1843, 21 Feb. 1844; *Union Agriculturist and Western Prairie Farmer* 1 (Jan. 1841): 1; *Prairie Farmer,* quoted in *Ohio Statesman,* 7 April 1848; Perry R. Duis, *Challenging Chicago: Coping with Everyday Life, 1837–1920* (Urbana: University of Illinois Press, 1998), 114–15; Cronon, *Nature's Metropolis,* 47; James Parton, "Chicago," *Atlantic Monthly,* 19 (March 1867): 329.

4. *CD,* 21 Aug. 1844; *CT,* 7 March 1954;John G. Clark, *The Grain Trade in the Old Northwest* (Urbana: University of Illinois Press, 1966), 87; Miller, *City of the Century,* 94; *CD,* 25 Feb. 1834, 25 Nov. 1835; *CD,* quoted in *Barre Gazette,* 6 Sept. 1839; "English and American Railways," *Littell's Living Age,* 6 Oct. 1860, 60; *Prairie Farmer,* quoted in *CT,* 25 Nov. 1857; William M. Wood, "A Cruise on the Lakes," *PS,* 6 Sept. 1849; Hall, *Liverpool to St. Louis,* 146; *CJ,* 11 April 1848, quoted in *PS,* 27 April 1848.

5. *Annual Review of the Business of Chicago For the Year 1852* (Chicago: CDDP, 1853): 1–3; Guy A. Lee, "The Historical Significance of the Chicago Grain Elevator System," *Agricultural History* 11 (Jan. 1937): 16–32; *CD,* 11 Oct. 1843, 21 Aug. 1844; *PS,* 25 Nov. 1858; *The Canadian Settler's Guide,* 10th ed. (London: Edward Stanford, 1860), 146.

6. *Frederick Douglass' Paper,* 5 Oct. 1866, AAN, item #77286; *The Christian Recorder,* 15 Nov. 1862, AAN, item #56591; *PS,* 6 Dec. 1855; *FC,* 7 June 1866; Miller, *Chicago,* 108; Blanchard, *Northwest,* 225; *CDDP,* 13 Sept. 1854; *CT,* 7 Feb. 1909.

7. *HW* 3 (10 Sept. 1859): 580.

8. *Prairie Farmer,* 12 (June 1852): 282; *Chicago Commercial Express,* quoted in *NYT,* 26 May 1858; *CT,* 19 July 1858; Chicago Board of Trade, *Annual Report for 1858* (Chicago: Chicago Board of Trade, 1859), 11; *CDDP,* quoted in *Lake Superior Miner,* 17 Nov. 1855; Lee, "Chicago Grain Elevator System," 22; H. C. Emery, *Speculation on the Stock and Produce Exchanges of the United States* (New York: Columbia University, 1896), 35–38; Thomas S. Ulen, "The Regulation of Grain Warehousing and Its Economic Effects: The Competitive Position of Chicago in the 1870s and 1880s," *Agricultural History* 56 (Jan. 1982): 194–211.

9. *CT,* 13 April 1853, 24 Jan., 7 Feb. 1854, 4 May 1855, 21 Jan. 1857, 12 July 1858, 1 Sept. 1862, 10 Oct. 1872, 2 May 1885, 10 June 1947; *NYTB,* quoted in *Weekly Wisconsin Patriot,* 26 June 1858; "The System of Grain Inspection: Its Establishment and Growth,"

American Elevator and Grain Trade 12 (Jan. to April 1894): 226–27, 260–61, 299, 333; *MS*, 17 May, 29 Sept. 1849; James E. Boyle, *Speculation and the Chicago Board of Trade* (New York: Macmillan, 1920), 1045; Jonathan Laurie, *The Chicago Board of Trade, 1859–1905: The Dynamics of Self-Regulation* (Urbana: University of Illinois Press, 1979), 23–29; Pierce, *Chicago History* II, 82–83; (Baltimore) *Sun*, 14 Oct. 1859.

10. *CDDP*, 17 Dec. 1852, 5 Feb., 2 March 1853; *CT*, 16 May 1853, 4 March 1856, 20 April 1857; William Bross, *History of Chicago* (Chicago: Jansen, McClurg, 1876), 81; William Cronon, Nature's Metropolis: Chicago and the Great West (New York: W.W. Norton, 1991).

11. (Chicago) *Daily Commercial Letter*, vol. 4 (Chicago: Wells & Adams, 1859); *CT*, 22 Jan. 1859, 22 Sept. 1862, 18 Jan. 1889; Scott, *Illinois Newspapers*, 69, 72, 86; *NYT*, 18 Jan. 1889.

12. *CD*, 23 April, 19 Sept. 1848; *CT*, 28 Dec. 1850, 31 May 1858; *CDDP*, 17 Dec. 1852, 5 Feb., 2 March 1853; *CDDP*, *First Annual Review of the Business of Chicago for the Year 1852* (Chicago: *Daily Democratic Press*, 1853): 1, 6, back cover; 1854 Annual Review, 8; 1856 Annual Review, all in CHS.

13. *New York Whig*, quoted in *Chicago American*, 23 July 1839; *CD*, 15 April, 4 May 1848; Specimen of "Board of Trade Daily Report," dated 18 Oct. 1859 at 3:00 p.m., in CHS. Others were likely destroyed in the 1871 fire; Miller, *City of the Century*, 108–11; Jeffrey C. Williams, "The Origin of Futures Markets," *Agricultural History* 56 (Jan. 1982): 306–16; "Forty Days in a Western Hotel," *Putnam's* 4 (Dec. 1854): 629; Parton, "Chicago," 339; *New Hampshire Patriot*, 17 June 1857.

14. F. O. Bennett, *History of the Press Club of Chicago* (Chicago: H.O. Shepard & Co., 1888), 73–74; *Flake's Bulletin*, 30 Jan. 1867; Cook, *Bygone Days*, 251.

15. Fehrenbacher, *Wentworth*, 124–37; *CD*, 16 Aug. 1837; Scott, *Illinois*, 65; *CD*, quoted in *FC*, 14 Nov. 1850, 2 Nov. 1859; "Cyrus Hall McCormick," *Biographical Dictionary and Portrait Gallery of the Representative Men of the United States; Illinois Volume* (Chicago: American Biographical Publishing Co., 1876), 185–88; *CTM*, 3 June 1861; Justin E. Walsh, *To Print the News and Raise Hell!: A Biography of Wilbur F. Storey* (Chapel Hill: University of North Carolina Press, 1963), 150; Andreas, *History of Chicago* I, 411, and II, 494–95; Willis J. Abbot, "Chicago Newspapers and Their Makers," *Review of Reviews* 11 (June 1895): 650; L. E. Ellis, "The *Chicago Tribune* During the Civil War," *Illinois State Historical Society Transactions for the Year 1932*, 39 (Springfield: Illinois State Historical Library, 1933): 136–81; Andreas, *History of Chicago* II, 495; William T. Hutchinson, *Cyrus Hall McCormick*, II (New York: Appleton, Century, 1935), 46–47; "Reissues," *Scientific American* 2 (16 June 1860): 398; Charles H. Lanphier to Stephen A. Douglas, 8 Dec. 1860, Douglas Papers.

16. Scott, *Newspapers*, 65–66; John Moses and Joseph Kirkland, *Aboriginal to Metropolitan, History of Chicago, Illinois*, III (Chicago and New York: Munsell & Co., 1895), 54; James L. Crouthamel, "James Gordon Bennett, the *New York Herald*, and the Development of Newspaper Sensationalism," *New York History* 54 (July 1973): 294–316; Jean Folkerts and Dwight L. Teeter Jr., *Voices of a Nation* (New York: Mac-

millan Publishing Co., 1989), 140–42; Patricia Cline Cohen, *The Murder of Helen Jewett* (New York: Knopf, 1998); Karen Halttunen, *Murder Most Foul: The Killer and the American Gothic Imagination* (Cambridge, MA: Harvard University Press, 1998); Timothy J. Gilfoyle, *City of Eros, Prostitution, and the Commercialization of Sex, 1790–1920* (New York: W.W. Norton, 1992), 92–102.

17. *CT*, 4 May 1886; Walsh, *Storey*, 12–38; Andreas, *Chicago* II, 495; Bennett, *Press Club*, 73–74; Wilkie, *Thirty-five Years*, 141–43; J. S. Currey, *Chicago: Its History and Its Builders*, II (Chicago: S.J. Clarke, 1912), 126; Deborah Hayden, *Pox: Genius, Madness, and the Mysteries of Syphilis* (New York: Basic Books, 2003); Suzanne Poirier, *Chicago's War on Syphilis, 1937–1940* (Urbana: University of Illinois Press, 1995); Terra Ziporyn, *Disease in the Popular American Press: The Case of Diphtheria, Typhoid Fever, and Syphilis, 1870–1920* (Westport, CT: Greenwood Press, 1988); John Gassner, ed., *Twenty-Five Best Plays of the Modern American Theatre: Early Series* (New York: Crown Publishers, 1949); Billy Wilder and A. J. Diamond, *Ben Hecht's and Charles MacArthur's* The Front Page, *Revised Final Screenplay* (Hollywood, CA: Universal Studios [1931] 1997).

18. *CTM*, 8, 9 June 1861; *CT*, 29 Nov. 1865; *MS*, 4 June 1861; Walsh, *Storey*, 145–81; Abbot, "Chicago Newspapers," 651; Wilkie, *Thirty-five Years*, 189.

19. Richard Junger, "Praying for God's Help: Upper-Class Courtship in Gilded Age Chicago," *Chicago History* 22 (March 1993): 4–19; Karen Halttunen, *Confidence Men and Painted Women: A Study of Middle-Class Culture in America, 1830–1870* (New Haven, CT: Yale University Press, 1982), xiii; Gilfoyle, *Eros*, 19; Helen Lefkowtiz Horowitz, *Rereading Sex: Battles Over Sexual Knowledge and Suppression in Nineteenth-Century America* (New York: Knopf, 2002), 14; Stephen Longstreet, *Chicago, 1860–1919* (New York: David McKay, 1973), 149; Walter E. Houghton, *The Victorian Frame of Mind, 1830–1870* (New Haven, CT: Yale University Press, 1957), 353–72; Cook, *Bygone Days*, 140; Nell Kimball, *Nell Kimball, Her Life as an American Madam* (New York: Macmillan, 1970), 115.

20. *CTM*, 20 June 1861, 12, 26 Feb. 1864, 10, 17 March 1864, 24 Jan. 1866, 5, 12 Feb. 1866, 12 March 1866; *CTM*, quoted in *Weekly Wisconsin Patriot*, 3 Aug. 1861; *CTM*, quoted in *Daily Ohio Statesman*, 13 Jan. 1865; *CTM*, quoted in *Pomeroy's Democrat*, 3 Feb. 1869; *CTM*, quoted in *Indianapolis Sentinel*, 9 July 1875; *CTM*, quoted in *Baltimore Sun*, 2 June 1862; *CTM*, quoted in the *Owyhee Avalanche*, 20 Aug. 1875; *Baker v. Young*, 44 Ill. 42 (1867); *Holliday v. People*, 9 Ill. 110 (1847); Cook, *Bygone Days*, 358; Henry M. Hugunin, "The Late Wilbur Fisk Storey and his *Chicago Times*," unpublished manuscript, *Autograph Letter Book, LXVI*, 181–84, CHS; Wilkie, *Thirty-five Years*, 151; *CT*, 6 Sept. 1860.

21. *Morrison* (IL) *Sentinel*, quoted in *CT*, 5 Nov. 1863; *CT*, 4 March 1866, 27 May 1875; *Springfield Register*, quoted in *CT*, 11 June 1874; *CT* as quoted in *Wisconsin Daily Patriot*, 12 Aug. 1863; *CT*, quoted in *Indianapolis Sentinel*, 18 Dec. 1875; Horowitz, *Rereading Sex*, 177.

22. *CT*, 14 Feb., 22 Dec. 1862, 12 Sept., 1 Nov. 1863, 18 June 1864, 9, 15 March, 24 Nov. 1867, 15 Oct. 1869, 1 Sept. 1872., 17 April 1875, 3 Nov. 1878; *Freeport* (IL) *Journal*,

quoted in *CT,* 4 July 1862; *ISZ,* 15 Aug. 1874, in CFLPS, reel #13; *Memphis Daily Avalanche,* 4 Jan. 1867; *Springfield Register,* quoted in *CIO,* 31 Aug. 1878; *Little Rock Daily Republican,* 9 Oct. 1873; *CIO,* 10 Aug. 1874.

23. *CTM,* 8 July 1865, 4 May 1867.

24. *CTM,* 13 Feb. 1875; *CIO,* 14 Feb. 1875; *CIO,* 14 Feb. 1875; *CT,* 14, 15, 17, 23 Feb. 1875; *NYH,* 9 Nov. 1874.

25. *CD,* 5 Oct. 1842; "Medill to 'Friend Lincoln,'" n.d., circa July 1858, McCormick Papers; Carl Sandburg, "Papers Amplify Gettysburg Talk," *CTM,* 30 July 1947; *CT,* 12 June 1955; Cleveland, "First Republican President," 84–85.

26. S. S. McClure to Robert R. McCormick, 25 Aug. 1941, McCormick Papers; *CT,* 15 July 1856, 29 Aug. 1896, 7 Feb. 1909, 11 Feb. 1929; *CT,* quoted in *Frederick Douglass' Paper,* 2 March 1855, AAN item #64180; Wendt, *Chicago Tribune,* 37–78; *CJ,* 6 July 1847, quoted in Joseph L. Eisendrath, "Lincoln's First Appearance on the National Scene, July, 1847," *Lincoln Herald* 76 (Summer 1974): 59–62; Cleveland, "First Republican President," 85; Tracy E. Strevey, "Joseph Medill and the *Chicago Tribune* in the Nomination and Election of Lincoln," *Papers in Illinois History and Transactions for the Year 1938* (Springfield: Illinois State Historical Society, 1939): 40–45; Strevey, "Civil War Period," 23; Philip Kinsley, *The Chicago Tribune, its First Hundred Years,* vol. 1 (New York: A.A. Knopf, 1943), 47.

27. *FC,* 16 May 1860; *CT,* 14, 15, 16, 17 May 1860, 7 Feb. 1909; *NYT,* 16, 17, 18 May 1860, *CTM,* 19, 21 May 1860, 2 June 1888, 6 March 1955; *CT,* 14, 15, 16, 17 May 1860; Carl Sandburg, *Abraham Lincoln: The Prairie Years and the War Years* (New York: Dell, 1954), 286; Sandburg, "Strategy to Pick Lincoln Bared," *CTM,* 31 July 1947; *Pomeroy's Democrat,* 21 June 1873.

28. *NYT,* 19, 21 May 1860; *CT,* 19 May 1860; Ray, Scripps, and Medill to Lincoln, 18 May 1860, Herndon to Medill, 25 May 1860, McCormick Papers; Sandburg, *Lincoln,* 288–95; Kinsley, *Tribune* I, 115–20; Alfred L. Lorenz Jr., "Lincoln, Medill and the Republican Nomination of 1860," *Lincoln Herald* 68 (Winter 1966): 203–4; William J. Cronon, "To Be the Central City: Chicago, 1848–1857," *Chicago History* 7 (Spring 1978): 12–21.

29. *Detroit Free Press,* 6 Feb. 1861; *CTM,* 12, 22 June, 11 July 1861, 25 June 1862; Walsh, *Storey,* 145–81.

30. *CTM,* 8, 13 Sept. 1862; O. P. Morton to Edwin M. Stanton, 25 June 1862, and Richard Yates to Stanton, 7 Aug. 1862, both in *The War of the Rebellion: A Compilation of the Official Records of the Union and Confederate Armies,* Series 3, Vol. 2 (Washington, DC: Government Printing Office, 1899), 176, 316; *CT,* 24 April 1861; L. E. Ellis, "The *Chicago Times* During the Civil War," *Illinois State Historical Society Transactions* (Springfield: Illinois State Historical Society, 1932), 167–68; A. C. Cole, *The Era of the Civil War* (Freeport, NY: Books for Libraries Press, 1971, 1922), 303; Walsh, *Storey,* 160–61.

31. *CTM,* 26 Aug. 1861, 21 May, 17, 23, 25 Sept., 1, 3, 9, 10, 22, 27 Oct. 1862, 15 Nov. 1862, 3, 7, 9 Jan., 31 March, 1, 13 April 1863.

32. *CT,* 22 May, 24 May 1862; Wilkie, *Thirty-five Years,* 115–17; Sylvanus Cadwallader, *Three Years with Grant,* ed. Benjamin A. Thomas (New York: Alfred A. Knopf, 1956), 4, 56–57; William Jones to Col. J. P. Sanderson, 17 May 1864, in *The War of the Rebellion,* Series 2, Vol. 7: 276–77; U. S. Grant to Maj. Gen. Stephen A. Hurlbut, 13 Feb. 1863, in *The War of the Rebellion,* Series 1, Vol. 24, part III: 49–50; Robert Harper, *Lincoln and the Press* (New York: McGraw Hill, 1951), 262; Charles Wright Wills, "Diary of Charles Wright Wills" in *Army Life of an Illinois Soldier,* comp. Mary E. Kellogg (Washington, DC: Globe Printing Co., 1906), 146.

33. *CTM,* 7 May 1863; Ellis, "*Chicago Times,*" 148–57; Walsh, *Storey,* 171–73; Craig D. Tenney, "To Suppress or Not to Suppress: Abraham Lincoln and the *Chicago Times,*" *Civil War History* 27 (Sept. 1981): 248–59; Tenney, "Major General A. E. Burnside and the First Amendment: A Case Study of Civil War Freedom of Expression," unpublished PhD dissertation, Indiana University, 1977.

34. *Houston Telegraph,* 3 April, 29 April 1863; *CT,* 4 June 1863.

35. *CJ,* 4 June 1863; *CT,* 6 Aug. 1916; "Gen'l Orders No. 84, 1 June 1863," in *The War of the Rebellion,* Series 1, Vol. 23, part II, 381; A. E. Burnside to Gen. Ammen, 1 June 1863, in *The War of the Rebellion,* Series 2, Vol. 5, 726; John T. Morse, ed., *Diary of Gideon Welles,* I (Salem, MA: Higginson Book Co., [1911] 1990), 321; Wilkie, *Thirty-five Years,* 100; *Chicago Times, The Suppression of the Times* (Chicago: *Chicago Times,* 1863), 19.

36. *CT,* 4 June 1863, 2; Ernest Poole, *Giants Gone: Men Who Made Chicago* (New York: Whittlesey House, 1943), 52–53.

37. Harper, *Lincoln,* 259–60; Wilkie, *Thirty-five Years,* 100–101; Walsh, *Storey,* 174–75; Cook, *Bygone Days,* 51; J. S. Black, "Mr. Black to Mr. Adams," *Galaxy* 17 (Jan. 1874): 116; Pierce, *Chicago* II, 416; *NYT,* 3, 6 June 1863; Bvt. Brig. Gen. James Oakes to Brig. Gen. James B. Fry, 9 Aug. 1865, in *The War of the Rebellion,* Series 3, Vol. 5, 837–38; *Chicago Times,* "Suppression of the *Chicago Times,*" 25–32.

38. *CT,* 5 June, 2 July 1863; *NYT,* 19 July 1864; E. D. Townsend to Major-General Burnside, 4 June 1863, in *The War of the Rebellion,* Series 3, Vol. 3, 252; Stanton to Maj. Gen. A. E. Burnside, 1 June 1863 and Gen'l Order No. 91, 4 June 1863, both in *The War of the Rebellion,* Series 2, Vol. 5, 723–24, 741; Harper, *Lincoln,* 261–62; Tenney, "Lincoln and the *Chicago Times,*" 257–59; Wilkie, *Thirty-five Years,* 101; Maj. Frank S. Bond to Messrs. Storey and Wooden, 18 Feb. 1864, in *The War of the Rebellion,* Series 1, Vol. 34, part II, 363; Gen'l Order No. 17 in *The War of the Rebellion,* Series 1, Vol. 49, Part II, 139; Abraham Lincoln, *Complete Works,* ed. John G. Nicolay and John Hay, 8 (New York: F. D. Tandy, 1905), 292–93; Finis Farr, *Chicago* (New Rochelle, NY: Arlington House, 1973), 83.

39. *Baltimore Sun,* 5 June 1863; *San Francisco Bulletin,* 5 June 1863; *Macon Weekly Telegraph,* 11 June 1863; *NYT,* 9 June 1863.

40. Andreas, *History of Chicago* II, 495; Abbot, "Chicago Newspapers," 651; Wilkie, *Thirty-five Years,* 101–2; Harper, *Lincoln,* 262–63; *CTM,* 5 June 1863; *CT,* 11 July 1922.

41. *New York Times v. United States,* 403 U.S. 713 (1971) at 728, 729.

Chapter 3. The Victory over St. Louis

1. Undated circa 1848 *GP*, quoted in *CT*, 10 July 1887; *CT*, 23 April, 9 May 1856, 12 May 1858, 18 May 1864, 10 Jan. 1865, 10 Aug. 1865; *CTM*, 30 June 1865.

2. *Chicago After Dark, an Insider's Guide for Tourists of the Vices of Chicago* (Chicago: Western News Co., 1868); *Tricks and Traps of Chicago* (New York: Dinsmore, 1859); *CT*, 13 Dec. 1858, 12, 27 Sept. 1871, 8 June 1980; *CTM*, quoted in Wright, *Chicago*, viii; Longstreet, *Chicago*, 61; "Chicago and the West: The Foundations of Many Generations," *New Englander and Yale Review* 12 (Nov. 1854): 511–12; "Illinois in Spring-Time," *Atlantic Monthly* 2 (Sept. 1858): 488; *Weekly Wisconsin Patriot*, 22 Jan. 1869; *Punchinello* 1 (23 July 1870): 267; *Richmond Examiner*, 6 Feb. 1866; *CJ*, 15 Sept. 1871.

3. *CT*, 7 Jan., 18 July, 2 May 1867, 30 May 1869, 11 April 1868, 4 Jan. 1874, 24 Oct. 1911, 8 Nov. 1931; *CTM*, 20 July 1865.

4. Cook, *Bygone Days*, ix–xi.

5. Cook, *Bygone Days*, 164, 205; *CT*, 4 April 1880, 10 June 1896; Juliette Magill Kinzie, *Wau-Bun, or Early Days of the Northwest* (New York: Derby & Jackson, 1856).

6. Cook, *Bygone Days*, 11, 128–60; *CT*, 26 Aug. 1856.

7. *CT*, 23 Dec. 1866, 20 May 1919; F. B. Wilkie, *Walks About Chicago, 1871–1881 and Army and Miscellaneous Sketches* (Chicago: Belford, Clarke & Co., 1880): 12–21, 38–113, 84–89, 128, 144–46; *CIO*, 15 Oct. 1875.

8. *CTM*, 27 May 1874, *CT*, 23 Nov. 1873, 13 April 1892; Wilkie, *Thirty-five Years*, 125–30, 159–60, 231, 237–41; Cook, *Bygone Days*, 331–38; *CIO*, 23 Nov. 1876.

9. *CTM*, 15 June 1865; *The Chicago Diaries of John M. Wing, 1865–1866*, ed. Robert Williams (Carbondale: Southern Illinois University Press, 2002), 7–8, 23.

10. Peter Gay, *The Bourgeois Experience, Victoria to Freud* II (New York: Oxford University Press, 1986), 202; Caro Lloyd, *Henry Demarest Lloyd, 1847–1903* (New York: G. P. Putnam's, 1912), 46.

11. Gilfoyle, *Eros*, 136; George Chauncey, *Gay New York* (New York: Basic Books, 1994), 131; *CT*, 28 Sept. 1858, 14 Nov. 1861, 14 July 1862, 20 Dec. 1873, 26 Sept. 1875, 3 Jan. 1875, 18 May 1879, 24 June 1879, 13 Sept., 21 Dec. 1884, 12 Aug. 1888, 20 Aug. 1900, 13 Nov. 1956; *CTM* as reprinted in *NYT*, 6 Aug. 1874.

12. Wilkie, *Thirty-five Years*, 131; Wing, *Diaries*, 17, 33; 45, 64; Cook, *Bygone Days*, 251; Chauncey, *Gay New York*, 30–45.

13. *CT*, 2 July, 8 Dec. 1858, 20 Jan. 1859, 10 May 1944, 1 Feb. 1951; Wing, *Diaries*, 22; *CTM*, 27 July, 7 Aug. 1865.

14. Pierce, *Chicago* II, 15–16; *CT*, 7, 8, 9 Aug. 1865, 27 Oct. 1878; *CJ*, 7, 9 Aug. 1865; Wing, *Diaries*, 28.

15. *CT*, 24 Aug. 1871; (Little Rock, AR) *Morning Republican*, 4 Oct. 1871.

16. *CD*, 30 Dec. 1835; *CT*, 5, 21, 23 Sept. 1871, 26 Sept., 1, 5, 6 Oct. 1871; *CJ*, 19, 22, 27 Sept., 5 Oct. 1871; *Minnesotan-Herald*, 16, 23 Sept. 1871; *Columbus Enquirer*, 1 Oct. 1871; *Philadelphia Inquirer*, 2 Oct. 1871; *Dakota Republican*, 28 Sept. 1871; *Trenton*

Gazette, 2 Oct. 1871; *Pomeroy's Democrat,* 30 Sept. 1871; Elias Colbert, quoted in Andreas, *History of Chicago* II, 703.

17. Carl Smith, *Urban Disorder and the Shape of Belief* (Chicago: University of Chicago Press, 1995), 21; *CT,* 3, 26 June, 13 Oct. 1870, 10 Sept. 1871; *CTM,* 4 May 1867, 4 Oct. 1871; Andreas, *History of Chicago* II, 704–7; *Punchinello* 1 (21 May 1870): 123; Wing, *Diaries,* 15, 65; Elias Colbert and Everett Chamberlin, *Chicago and the Great Conflagration* (Chicago: J. S. Goodman, 1871), 468–74; Joseph M. Moran and Edward J. Hopkins, *Wisconsin's Weather and Climate* (Madison: University of Wisconsin Press, 2003), 231–34.

18. Perry R. Duis and Glen E. Holt, "Kate O'Leary's Sad Burden," *Chicago* 27 (Oct. 10, 1978): 220–22; *CJ,* 11 Sept. 1871, 9 Oct. 1871; *CTM,* 3 Dec. 1871; *CDN,* 15 June 1894; Richard F. Bales, *The Great Chicago Fire and the Myth of Mrs. O'Leary's Cow* (Jefferson, NC: McFarland & Co., 2002), 54–57; *CT,* 12 Dec. 1871; *Fort Worth Star-Telegraph,* 30 Nov. 1909; *CJ,* quoted in *Critic-Record,* 27 Oct. 1871; *CDN,* quoted in *Kansas City Star,* 15 Oct. 1880; Miller, *City of the Century,* 150; Michael L. Ahren, *The Great Revolution: A History of the Rise and Progress of the People's Party in the City of Chicago* (Chicago: Lakeside Publishing, 1874).

19. Carl Smith, *Urban Disorder,* 287–88; Karen Sawislak, *Smoldering City* (Chicago: University of Chicago Press, 1995), 17–18; *NYT,* 10 Oct. 1871; *CT,* 17 Dec. 1871, 9 Oct. 1893; Andreas, *History of Chicago* III, 702; Colbert and Chamberlin, *Great Conflagration,* 227–35; David Lowe, ed., *The Great Chicago Fire* (New York: Dover Publications, [1915] 1979), 3–9, 43; Denise Gess and William Lutz, *Firestorm at Peshtigo: A Town, Its People and the Deadliest Fire in American History* (New York: Henry Holt and Co., 2002), 5; T. B. Maury, "The Telegraph and the Storm," *HNMM* 43 (Aug. 1871): 398–418; Joseph Logsdon, *Horace White, Nineteenth Century Liberal* (Westport, CT: Greenwood Publishing Co., 1971).

20. James W. Sheahan and George P. Upton, *The Great Conflagration: Chicago, Its Past, Present, and Future* (Chicago: Union Publishing Co., 1871), 91; *CT,* 7 Oct. 1934.

21. *CT,* 12, 20 Oct. 1871, 1 Feb. 1891, 9 Oct. 1893; Lowe, *Great Chicago Fire,* 41–52; Wendt, *Chicago Tribune,* 233–35; Colbert and Chamberlin, *Great Conflagration,* 207; Cook, *Bygone Days,* 172; Kinsley, *CT* II, 129–33.

22. *NYT,* 10 Oct. 1871; Lowe, *Great Chicago Fire,* 45, 52; Andreas, *History of Chicago* III, 744; *ISZ,* 14 Oct. 1871; Miller, *City of the Century,* 147–57; Smith, *Urban Disorder,* 51–55; Sawislak, *Smoldering City,* 77–81; *Manufacturer and Builder* 4 (Nov. 1872): 245.

23. Colbert and Chamberlin, *Great Conflagration,* 356–57; *CT,* 11, 19 Oct. 1871, 25 Nov. 1871; Lowe, *Great Chicago Fire,* 53–60; Miller, *City of the Century,* 157–67; Sawislak, *Smoldering City,* 49–67; *CJ,* 10 Oct. 1871; Clarence A. Andrews, *Chicago in Story: A Literary History* (Iowa City, IA: Midwest Heritage Publishing, 1982), 30–34; *Philadelphia Inquirer,* 14 Oct. 1871; *Baltimore Sun,* 11 Oct. 1871; *New Hampshire Patriot,* 18 Oct. 1871; *San Francisco Bulletin,* 16 Oct. 1871; *Eastern Argus,* 12 Oct. 1871; *Dallas Morning News,* 17 Sept. 1900.

24. Sheahan and Upton, *Chicago, Its Past, Present and Future,* 142; Andreas, *History of Chicago* III, 721; *Pomeroy's Democrat,* 15 Oct. 1871; Wilkie, *Thirty-five Years,* 143–44; *CJ,* 9 Oct. 1871; *CT,* 11, 16 Oct. 1871; Wilkie, *Walks About Chicago,* 78–79; Logsdon, *Horace White,* 199–200; (Chicago) *Daily Commercial Bulletin,* 9–18 Oct. 1871.

25. *Galena Enterprise,* quoted in the (Cooperstown, NY) *Watch-Tower,* 19 Oct. 1829; *CD,* quoted in *Newport* (RI) *Mercury,* 15 Sept. 1838; *PS,* 30 Aug. 1840; Patrick Reynolds, "A River Town that Thrives on Its History," *Americana* 14 (June 2000): 56–60; Carl Abbott, "The Divergent Development of Cincinnati, Indianapolis, Chicago, and Galena, 1840–1860; Economic Thought and Economic Growth," unpublished PhD dissertation, University of Chicago, 1971; Paul M. Angle, "Galena in its Prime," *Chicago History* 5 (Summer 1959): 229–37.

26. Wilkie, *Thirty-five Years,* 191–98; *CT,* 18 Oct., 3, 8 Dec. 1871; *CT,* 31 Dec. 1852, 6 Jan., 16, 28 May 1853, 3 June 1857, 24 Aug. 1858, 19 Oct., 20 Oct., 27 Oct. 1871; *CD,* 30 Jan. 1849; *CDDP,* 6 Jan. 1853; *MS,* 30, 31 Aug. 1850; 10 April 1856, 28 May 1858; *CJ,* quoted in *MS,* 4 Sept. 1846; *Boston Chronotype,* quoted in *MS,* 17 Aug. 1846; *CT,* quoted in *MS,* 8 Nov. 1849; *CJ,* quoted in *MS,* 16 Nov. 1844; *Ohio Statesman,* 17 Aug. 1853; *Missouri Republican,* quoted in *Leavenworth* (KS) *Bulletin,* 22 May 1869; *Wisconsin Patriot,* 14 Feb. 1863.

27. William T. Sherman to John Sherman, undated July and 2 Sept. 1851, in William T. Sherman Papers; *Missouri Republican,* 12 April 1841; Jeffrey S. Adler, *Yankee Merchants and the Making of the Urban West: The Rise and Fall of Antebellum St. Louis* (New York: Cambridge University Press, 1991), 1–60, 115; Susan E. Gray, *The Yankee West: Community Life on the Michigan Frontier* (Chapel Hill: University of North Carolina Press, 1996), 1–4; Lois K. Mathews, *The Expansion of New England: The Spread of New England Settlement and Institutions to the Mississippi River* (Boston: Houghton Mifflin, [1909] 1969).

28. *CD,* 30 Jan. 1849; *NYTB,* quoted in *CT,* 25 Jan. 1856; *NYTB,* quoted in *Weekly St. Louis Pilot,* 26 Jan. 1856; *CT,* 12 Feb. 1857, 7 March 1862; *St. Louis Globe-Democrat,* quoted in *CT,* 5 Oct. 1884, 21 June 1896.

29. *CT,* 28 Dec. 1850, 6 Jan. 1853, 11 Oct. 1859, 12 Oct. 1871; (Brattleboro, VT) *Weekly Eagle,* 19 Dec. 1850; McClure's news service, quoted in *CT,* 21 June 1896; *CD,* 30 Nov. 1848, 19 Feb. 1850, 28 May, 3 Dec. 1853, 27 Jan. 1855, 18, 27 June 1857; *CDDP,* 1, 19 Jan., 14 Feb., 2, 30 March, 18 Nov. 1853, 3 Feb. 1855; *CJ,* 21 June 1854; *Chicago Magazine* 1 (March 1857): 389; *Daily Missouri Republican,* 10 Nov. 1852; *St. Louis Intelligencer,* quoted in *CDDP,* 21 Sept. 1855; *CTM,* 11 Oct. 1859.

30. *Davenport* (IA) *Daily State Democrat,* quoted in *CT,* 27 April 1857; *Hunt's Merchants' Magazine* 28 (May 1853), 557, and 36 (March 1857), 374; Adler, *Yankee Merchants,* 99; *CJ,* 21 June 1854; *CDDP,* 18 Nov. 1853; *CD,* 27 June 1857; *Missouri Democrat,* 8 July 1857.

31. *Iowa State Register,* 23 April 1868; *St. Louis Democrat,* quoted in *San Francisco Bulletin,* 29 May 1869; *Missouri Republican,* quoted in *Minnesotan-Herald,* 10 July 1869; *St. Louis Democrat,* quoted in *Daily State Register,* 16 June 1869; *Brooklyn Eagle,*

quoted in *PS,* 6 Oct. 1870; *Idaho Tri-Weekly Statesman,* 1 July 1869; *CT,* 16 June, 3 July, 7 Aug. 1860.

32. *St. Louis Times,* quoted in *Dallas Herald,* 28 Oct. 1871; *St. Louis Republican,* quoted in *Duluth Minnesotan,* 25 Nov. 1871; *St. Louis Republican,* quoted in *Galveston News,* 11 Dec. 1872; *Sioux City Journal,* 21 Nov. 1872.

33. Mayer and Wade, *Chicago,* 117; *Columbus Ledger-Enquirer,* 11 Oct. 1870; *Detroit Free Press,* quoted in *CT,* 4 April, 18 April 1872; *St. Louis Republican,* quoted in Colbert and Chamberlin, *Great Conflagration,* 512–13; *HNMM* 68 (March 1884): 501; *CJ,* 14 Oct. 1870; *CT,* 8 Oct. 1870; *Houston Daily Union,* 20 Oct. 1870; *San Francisco Bulletin,* 3 Oct. 1870; *Baltimore Sun,* 4 Oct. 1870; (Little Rock, AR) *Morning Republican,* 11 Aug. 1873.

34. *CT,* 25 April 1875, 15 April, 1 July 1878, 1 April 1878; *NYT,* 25 July 1879, 29 April 1889; *Scribner's Monthly* 10 (Sept. 1875): 533, 540–41; *St. Louis Democrat,* quoted in *Sioux City Journal,* 15 Oct. 1873; *St. Louis Democrat,* quoted in *New Hampshire Sentinel,* 29 Jan. 1874; *St. Louis Democrat,* quoted in *CIO,* 19 March 1875; W. H. Bishop, "St. Louis," *HNMM* 68 (March 1884): 501; L. U. Reavis, *The Future Great City of the World* (1871) as quoted in Ann Cook, Marilyn Gittell, and Herb Mack, *City Life, 1865–1900: Views of Urban Life* (New York: Praeger, 1973), 43; (Middletown, CT) *Daily Constitution,* 26 Dec. 1873; *Troy Weekly Times,* 17 July 1869; *CIO,* 23 Jan., 15 July 1878, 21 Aug. 1879; *New Orleans Times,* 21 May 1878; *St. Louis Post-Dispatch,* quoted in *CIO,* 20 Dec. 1879, 13 April 1880.

35. Cronon, *Nature's Metropolis,* 308; *CT,* 11 Feb. 1990.

36. *CT,* 2 July 1870, 3, 11 July 1880; *Philadelphia Inquirer,* 26 June, 7 July 1880; *CJ,* 2 July 1880; *San Francisco Bulletin,* 1 July 1880, *Wheeling Register,* 26 June 1880; *Wisconsin State Journal,* 13 July 1880; *Idaho Stateman,* 3 July 1880; *Idaho Avalanche,* 17 July 1880.

37. *Lake Superior News,* 22 July 1880; John S. Wright, *Chicago: Past, Present, Future Relations to the Great Interior and the Continent* (Chicago: Horton & Leonard, 1870), 115; William Bross, *Chicago and Her Growth* (Chicago: Jansen, McClurg, 1876), 18; Mayer and Wade, *Chicago,* 117; *CT,* 22 Dec. 1871; Wilkie, *Walks About Chicago,* 77; Cronon, *Nature's Metropolis,* 399n82.

Chapter 4. Chicago Radicalism, Nineteenth-Century Style

1. Charles Edward Russell, *These Shifting Scenes* (New York: Hodder & Stoughton, 1914), 100; *Daily News,* 22 Aug. 1936.

2. *ISZ,* 2 Feb. 1887, CFLPS, reel 14; *CIO,* 15 Aug. 1886; *CT,* 15, 18, 19 Jan., 6, 3 Feb. 1897, 10, 24 April 1936; *CDN,* 25, 26, 27 Aug. 1936.

3. *CDN,* 14 Jan., 8 May 1886; Carl S. Smith, "Cataclysm and Cultural Consciousness: Chicago and the Haymarket Trial," *Chicago History* 15 (Summer 1986): 36–53; Bruce C. Nelson, "Anarchism: The Movement Behind the Martyrs," *Chicago History* 15 (Summer 1986): 4–19; Gerald J. Baldasty, *Commercialization of News in the Nineteenth Century* (Madison: University of Wisconsin Press, 1992), 3–9.

4. Jon Bekken, "Working Class Newspapers, Community and Consciousness in Chicago, 1880–1930," unpublished PhD dissertation, University of Illinois–Urbana, 1992, 116–18; Wendt, *Chicago Tribune*, 316; Cook, *Bygone Days*, 185–86; *Stranger's Guide to the Garden City: Chicago Illustrated and Descriptive.... The City As It Appears in 1883* (Chicago: C.D. Relyea & Co., 1883), 68–69; *CIO*, 25 May 1893, 22 Sept. 1895; *CH*, 22 Nov. 1891; (Little Rock, AR) *Morning Republican*, 24 June 1871.

5. *CT*, 18 March 1877, 10 Oct. 1880, 12 Dec. 1880, 28 Feb. 1882, 9 April 1882, 3 Feb. 1889, 25 Jan. 1902, 24 Jan. 1906; Stone, *Fifty Years*, 109–10; Moses Koenigsberg, *King News: An Autobiography* (New York: F. A. Stokes, 1941), 159; Colin Cherry, "The Telephone System: Creator of Mobility and Social Change" in *The Social Impact of the Telephone*, ed. Ithiel de Sola Pool (Cambridge, MA: MIT Press, 1977), 112–26.

6. *CT*, 6, 10 June 1854, 1 March 1868, 12 March 1872, 8 Nov. 1873, 15 Sept. 1890, 23 Nov. 1911; *CTM*, 4 Sept. 1875, quoted in Emmett Dedmon, *Fabulous Chicago* (New York: Random House, 1953), 14; Cherry, *World Communication*, 40–41; Edd Applegate, *Personalities and Products: A Historical Perspective on Advertising in America* (Westport, CT: Greenwood Press, 1998); Jackson Lears, *Fables of Abundance: A Cultural History of Advertising in America* (New York: Basic Books, 1994); Stephen Fox, *The Mirror Makers: A History of American Advertising and Its Creators* (New York: William Morrow, 1984); Daniel Pope, *The Making of Modern Advertising* (New York: Basic Books, 1983); Susan Strasser, *Satisfaction Guaranteed: The Making of the American Mass Market* (New York: Pantheon Books, 1989).

7. Pierce, *Chicago* II, 158–67, Andreas, *History of Chicago* I, 415; Emily Clark Brown, "The Book and Job Printers of Chicago," unpublished PhD dissertation, University of Chicago, 1929; *CT*, 5 April 1856, 25 Dec. 1873; Edward L. Sheppard, *The Radical and Labor Periodical Press in Chicago: Its Origin and Development to 1890* (Urbana: University of Illinois Institute of Labor and Industrial Relations, 1949), 5–10; *Baltimore Sun*, 17 March 1864; *MS*, 25 Jan. 1859; Hartmut Keil and John Jentz, ed., *German Workers in Chicago: A Documentary History from 1850 to World War I* (Urbana: University of Illinois, 1988); Elliott Shore, *The German-American Radical Press: The Shaping of a Left Political Culture, 1850–1940* (Urbana: University of Illinois Press, 1992).

8. Gersh Martin, "Early Journalism and Printing in Northern Illinois," *Rounds Printers Cabinet*, April 1879 as cited in Emily C. Brown, *Book and Job Printing in Chicago: A Study of Organizations of Employers and Their Relations With Labor* (Chicago: University of Chicago Press, 1931); James C. Sylvis, *The Life, Speeches, Labors and Essays of William H. Sylvis, Late President of the Iron-Moulders' International Union and also the National Labor Union* (Philadelphia: Claxton, Remsen & Haffelfiner, 1872), 129–30; *CH*, 26 Oct. 1890.

9. *CTM*, 12 Sept. 1864; Walker Rumble, "The Race is to the Swift: The 1886 National Typesetting Championship," *Chicago History* 28 (Summer 1999): 44–53.

10. Thomas Robinson, "Chicago Typographical Union No. 16, Fifty Years of Development With Emphasis on Its Relations With the Daily Newspaper Publishers,

1852–1902," unpublished MA thesis, University of Chicago, 1925; Milton Cantor, *American Working Class Culture: Explorations in American Labor and Social History* (Westport, CT: Greenwood Press, 1979); Andreas, *History of Chicago* I, 415; *CT,* 19 April, 6 Aug., 7 Sept., 7 Nov. 1864; Arthur Scott White, "Letter to the Editor," *Michigan History* 11 (Jan. 1927): 145; *Workingman's Advocate,* 17 Sept. 1864, quoted in Pierce, *Chicago* II, 162–64 and 500–503; *CTM,* 12 Sept. 1864; Brown, "Book and Job," 41–43; *Macon Weekly Telegraph,* 28 Sept. 1864.

11. Brown, "Book and Job," 475; *CT,* 9 Oct. 1865, 20 May 1866, 4, 5 April, 2 May 1867; *Daily Iowa State Register,* 1 May 1867; Pierce, *Chicago* II, 177–79.

12. *CR,* 1 May 1867; Pierce, *Chicago* II, 177–79; *CT,* 14 Aug. 1860, 3 May 1867; Richard C. Lindberg, *To Serve and Collect: Chicago Politics and Police Corruption from the Lager Beer Riot to the Summerdale Scandal, 1855–1960* (Carbondale: Southern Illinois University Press, 1991), 59–60; *CT,* 3, 4, 8 May 1867; *New Hampshire Sentinel,* 9 May 1867; *Baltimore Sun,* 6 May 1867; *Memphis Daily Avalanche,* 9 May 1867; *NYS,* quoted in *Trenton State Gazette,* 6 May 1867; *Des Moines Register,* 5 May 1867; "The Undersigned in Behalf," 11 April 1867, Medill Papers; Alan Trachtenberg, *The Incorporation of America: Culture and Society in the Gilded Age* (New York: Hill and Wang, 1982).

13. *CT,* 29 May 1892; *Workingman's Advocate,* 23 June, 1 Sept., 10 Nov. 1866, 24 April 1869, 8 April, 4 Nov. 1871, 3, 17 Feb., 11 May 1872, 20 Dec. 1873, 6 March 1875, 5 May, 10 July 1877; Sheppard, *Radical and Labor Press,* 11–18.

14. *CTM,* 6 Jan. 1867; Colbert and Chamberlin, *Great Conflagration,* 251; *CT,* 14 Oct. 1871.

15. William J. Adelman, *Haymarket Revisited,* 2nd ed. (Chicago: Illinois Labor History Society, 1986), 4; *CT,* 14, 26 Oct. 1871; Sawislak, *Smoldering City,* 69–119.

16. Harris L. Dante, "The *Chicago Tribune*'s 'Lost' Years, 1865–1874," *Journal of the Illinois State Historical Society* 58 (Summer 1965): 139–64; *CTM,* 3 Feb. 1869; *CT,* 17 Sept. 1916; Logsdon, *Horace White,* 173–86.

17. Wayne Andrews, *The Battle for Chicago* (New York: Harcourt Brace Jovanovitch, 1946): 49; Sawislak, *Smouldering City,* 127–33; Miller, *City of the Century,* 437–41; *CT,* 15, 21 Oct. 1871; *ISZ,* 31 Oct. 1871, 7 Nov. 1871, CFLPS, reel #13; Walsh, *Storey,* 278–80; *CTM,* 6, 8 Nov. 1871; *CR,* 31 Oct. 1871.

18. Medill to Colfax, 5 Feb. 1872, as copied in *CT,* 7 Oct. 1928; David L. Protess, "Joseph Medill," in *The Mayors: The Chicago Political Tradition* (Carbondale: Southern Illinois University Press, 1995), 1–6; *CT,* 8 Nov. 1871, 16 Jan. 1872; signed Chicago city checks in the Medill Papers, Herndon to Medill, 26 Jan. 1861, both in Medill Papers.

19. *CT,* 2, 21 April 1872; *NYT,* 22 April 1872; Medill to F. S. Phoenix, 21 Nov. 1874, Medill Papers; *Chicagoer Freie-Presse,* quoted in *CT,* 6 Nov. 1873.

20. *CT,* 17 Jan. 1872, 9 Nov., 22, 23 Dec. 1873; *NYT,* 21 Jan. 1872, 27 Dec. 1873; *CT,* 17 Jan. 1872; *Indianapolis Sentinel,* 23, 24 Dec. 1873; *San Francisco Bulletin,* 23 Dec. 1873; *Trenton State Gazette,* 24 Dec. 1873; (Middletown, CT) *Daily Constitution,* 26 Dec. 1873; Protess, "Medill," 8–12; Andreas, *History of Chicago* III, 854–56; *CTM,* 18

Oct. 1871, quoted in *ISZ*, 19 Dec. 1871, 15, 16, 17 Jan. 1872, 8 Aug. 1873, CFLPS reel #13; Adelman, *Haymarket Revisited*, 4, 54; Dedmon, *Fabulous*, 149.

21. Melvin G. Holli, "Ranking Chicago Mayors: Mirror, Mirror, on the Wall, Who is the Greatest of Them All," *The Mayors: The Chicago Political Tradition*, ed. Paul M. Green and Melvin G. Holli (Carbondale: Southern Illinois University Press, 1995), 287; *CT*, 9 Oct. 1893; Wendt, *Chicago Tribune*, 239–40; Protess, "Medill," 5–7.

22. *CT*, 2 Jan. 1874, 23 Feb. 1875, 23 March 1879; Bekken, "Working Class Newspapers, 178–79; *CTM*, 20 Feb. 1875; *CJ*, 9 May 1876.

23. Robert R. McCormick to A. M. Ruge, 6 Oct. 1944, Medill Papers; George Seldes, *Lords of the Press* (New York: Blue Ribbon Press, 1941), 47; *CT*, 12, 29 July 1877, 5 Feb. 1896, 8 March 1897; *CIO*, 3 Aug. 1877; *Philadelphia Inquirer*, 28 July 1877; *Pomeroy's Democrat*, 3 Nov. 1877; Carolyn Ashbaugh, *Lucy Parsons: American Revolutionary* (Chicago: Charles H. Kerr for the Illinois Labor History Society, 1976), 24–25; Henry David, *The History of the Haymarket Affair: A Study in the American Social-Revolutionary and Labor Movements* (New York: Russell & Russell, 1958), 123; Lucy Parsons, ed., *Famous Speeches of the Eight Chicago Anarchists* (New York: Arno Press, 1969, 1910), 7.

24. Shanahan and Morgan, *Cultivation Theory*, 17–18; *CDN*, 18, 20, 23, 24 July 1877; Pierce, *Chicago III*, 245; *NYT*, 23 July 1877; *CT*, 20 July 1877; Paul Slovic, "Perception of Risk: Reflections on the Psychometric Paradigm," in Sheldon Krimsky and Dominic Golding, ed., *Social Theories of Risk* (New York: Praeger, 1992), 117–52.

25. *CT*, 23, 24 July 1877; *CTM*, 24 July 1877.

26. *CDN*, 24, 25 July 1877; Paul Avrich, *The Haymarket Tragedy* (Princeton, NJ: Princeton University Press, 1984), xxx, 29–31; *CT*, 24 July 1877, Stone, *Fifty Years*, 77–78, Charles Dennis, *Victor Lawson: His Time and His* Work (Chicago: University of Chicago Press, 1935), 41–44.

27. *CTM*, 26 July 1877; *NYT*, 28 July 1877; *CDN*, 26 June 1877; Z. L. White, "Western Journalism," *HNMM* 77 (Oct. 1888): 690; Adelman, *Haymarket*, 6–7.

28. *CDN*, 27 July 1877; Pierce, *Chicago* III, 249–50; Lindberg, *Serve and Collect*, 62; *CT*, 28 July 1877, 4 May 1879, 20 March 1898; Avrich, *Haymarket*, 34–35; Currey, *Chicago* II, 372–73.

29. Hanno Hardt, *Social Theories of the Press: Constituents of Communication Research, 1840s to 1920s* (Lanham, MD: Rowman & Littlefield, 2001), 19–34.

30. *CIO*, 29 April, 10 June 1878; Renate Kieswetter, "German-American Labor Press: The *Vorbote* and the *Chicagoer Arbeiter-Zeitung*," in Hartmut Keil, ed. *German Workers' Culture* (Washington, DC: Smithsonian Institute Press, 1988), 137; Avrich, *Haymarket*, 120–25; Michael J. Schaack, *Anarchy and Anarchists* (Chicago: F. J. Schulte, 1889); *AZ*, 3 Aug. 1880, CFLPS, reel 19; Bruce Nelson, *Beyond the Martyrs: A Social History of Chicago's Anarchists*, 1870–1900 (New Brunswick, NJ: Rutgers University Press, 1988), 122.

31. Lindberg, *Serve and Collect*, 61; Howard Barton Myers, *The Policing of Labor Disputes in Chicago: A Case Study*, unpublished PhD dissertation, University of Chi-

cago, 1925, 150; Sheppard, *Radical and Labor Press,* 23–30; *AZ,* 4 Dec. 1884, CFLPS, reel # 19; *The* (Chicago) *Alarm,* 4 Oct. 1884, 24 Jan. 1885, 27 June 1885.

32. *The Alarm,* 30 May 1885.

33. *AZ,* 8 Dec. 1886, CFLPS, reel #14; *CDN,* 14 Jan. 1886; *CIO,* 20 Jan. 1886; Dedmon, *Fabulous,* 155.

34. *CT,* 5 March, 26 April 1886; *CJ,* 19 April 1886; *Chicago Evening Mail,* 1 May 1886; *AZ,* quoted in Sheppard, *Radical and Labor Press,* 29.

35. *CT,* 3 May 1886; Nelson, "Martyrs," 10–14; *AZ,* 3 May 1886; Shepard, *Radical and Labor Press,* 30–31; *Bismarck Tribune,* 1 May 1886; *Dallas Morning News,* 3 May 1886; Carl Smith, "Cataclysm and Cultural Consciousness: Chicago and the Haymarket Trial," *Chicago History* 15 (Summer 1986): 46.

36. *CDN,* 5 May 1895; *CT,* 22 Nov. 1936; Avrich, *Haymarket,* 14–16.

37. *CT,* 6, 8, 9 Nov. 1864, 3 Dec. 1864, 10 June 1947; *CTM,* 9 Nov. 1864; Cook, *Bygone Days,* 49; George Levy, *To Die in Chicago: Confederate Prisoners at Camp Douglas* (Evanston, IL.: Evanston Pub., 1994), 217–33; Wendt, *Chicago Tribune,* 197–200.

38. Shanahan, *Television and its Viewers,* ix; Nelson, "Martyrs," 193; Avrich, *Haymarket,* 243, 338; Smith, *Urban Disorder,* 333; James Green, *Death in the Haymarket* (New York: Pantheon, 2006), 215; P. Muris, et al., "'Danger is Lurking Everywhere': The Relation Between Anxiety and Threat Perception Abnormalities in Normal Children," *Journal of Behavior Therapy and Experimental Psychiatry* 31 (June 2000): 123–36; K. L. Higbee, "Fifteen Years of Fear Arousal: Research on Threat Appeals," *Psychological Bulletin* 72 (Dec. 1969): 426–44; Lowery and DeFleur, *Milestones in Mass Communication,* 137–61; Albert R. Parsons and Lucy E. Parsons, *Life of Albert R. Parsons* (Chicago: Lucy E. Parsons, 1903), 230; Melville E. Stone, *Fifty Years a Journalist* (Garden City, NJ: Doubleday, Page and Company, 1921) 79; Ann Masa, "Chicago Martyrs: A Parable for the People," *Chicago History* 25 (Summer 1986): 59.

39. Stone, *Fifty Years,* 125; *CH,* 5 May 1886; *CIO,* 3, 5, 6 May 1886; Nelson, "Anarchism," 17; *CJ,* 5, 6, 7 May 1886; *CDN,* 2, 5, 6, 12 May 1886; *Knights of Labor,* 8 May 1886; *CT,* 2, 5, 11, 16 May, 27 June 1886; *Critic-Record,* 3 May 1886; *Macon Weekly Telegraph,* 1 May 1886.

40. *CDN,* 20, 21 May, 20 June, 6, 7, 13, 15 July 1886; Dave Roedinger and Franklin Rosemont, *Haymarket Scrapbook* (Chicago: Charles A. Kerr Publishing Co., 1986), 144; Lindberg, *Serve and Collect,* 70–71.

41. *CT,* 21 June, 17 July, 11, 16 Aug. 1886; *CDN,* 29 July, 7 Aug. 1886; *CIO,* 20 Aug. 1886; Harry Barnard, *Eagle Forgotten: The Life of John Peter Altgeld* (Indianapolis: Bobbs-Merrill, 1938).

42. *CTM,* 21, 24 Aug. 1886; *CIO,* 20 Aug. 1886; *CT,* 21 Aug. 1886; *CDN,* 21 Aug. 1886; *The Current* 6 (4 Sept. 1886): 145.

43. Avrich, *Haymarket,* 391–95; *CDN,* 12 Nov. 1886; *CJ,* 11 Nov. 1887; *CIO,* 12 Nov. 1887; *CT,* 12 Nov. 1887; *ISZ,* 12 Nov. 1887, CFLPS, reel #14; *AZ,* 1 Oct. 1888, CFLPS, reel #15.

44. *CT,* 27 June 1893, 4, 7 June 1895, 20 Oct. 1896, 14 March 1915, 14 Nov. 1985, 27 April 1986; Avrich, *Haymarket,* 422–25; *CDN,* 27 June 1893; Stone, *Fifty Years,* 166–77; Jack Tager, *The Intellectual as Urban Reformer: Brand Whitlock and the Progressive Movement* (Cleveland: Press of Case Western Reserve University, 1968): 13–34; "John P. Altgeld," in *Biographical Dictionary and Portrait Gallery of the Representative Men of the United States; Illinois Volume* (Chicago: Lewis Publishing Co., 1896), 76–77; *CG,* 27 June 1893; *CH,* 27 June 1893; *CTM,* 27 June 1893; *Belleville News-Democrat,* 25 May 1908; David, *Haymarket,* 499; *CIO,* 27 June 1893, 12 Dec. 1897.

45. Dedmon, *Fabulous,* 240–41; *CT,* 5 July 1894; *CDN,* 11 May, 26, 29 June, 2, 3, 5 July 1894.

46. *CT,* 1, 2, 3 July 1894, 7 July 1894; *CDN,* 6, 7, 8, 9 July 1894.

47. W. A. Swanberg, *Pulitzer* (New York: Charles Scribner's Sons, 1967), 135; Willis J. Abbot, *Watching the World Go By* (Boston: Little, Brown and Co., 1933), 84–86, 110–11; Abbot, "Chicago Newspapers and Their Makers," 650–52; Walsh, *Storey,* 277–81; *CTM,* 2, 3, 4, 8 July 1894; Ernest Poole, *Giants Gone: Men Who Made Chicago* (New York: Whittlesey House, 1943), 203; *Report of the General Superintendent to the City Council* (1894), quoted in Lindberg, *Serve and Collect,* 73; Norma Green, Stephen Lacy, and Jean Folkerts, "Chicago Journalists at the Turn of the Century: Bohemians All?" *Journalism Quarterly* 66 (Winter 1989): 813–21.

48. Abbot, *World,* 104–6; Walsh, *Storey,* 279–80; *CT,* 26 July, 9 Aug. 1964.

49. "Historic gallows to be sold on auction," Illinois Associated Press, 23 Oct. 2006; *CT,* 8 Dec. 2006.

Chapter 5. The Beauty

1. *CP,* 9 June 1894.

2. Finley Peter Dunne, *Mr. Dooley in the Hearts of His Countrymen* (Boston: Small, Maynard & Co., 1899); Dunne, *Mr. Dooley's Philosophy* (New York: R. H. Russell, 1900).

3. *CTM,* 16 Feb. 1882; *CT,* 16 Nov. 1978; *World's Fair Puck* 15 (19 June 1893).

4. *CT,* 12 Nov. 1899, 6 June 1902, 7 March 1909; *CIO,* 16 May 1883.

5. *CT,* 19 March 1890.

6. Hubert H. Bancroft, *The Book of the Fair* (Chicago: Bancroft, 1893), 37; Pierce, *Chicago* III, 501; *CT,* 15, 23 Nov. 1885.; *CDN,* 2, 16, 17 Nov. 1885; *CH,* 22, 24 Nov. 1885.

7. *CT,* 3, 4 Dec. 1885, 9 Feb., 28 Nov. 1886, 10 Aug. 1889; *CDN,* 8 Dec. 1885.

8. *CT,* 3 May, 7, 14 July 1888; *Boston Journal,* quoted in *CT,* 2 Dec. 1888; *Spectator,* 1 June 1889, quoted in *HW* 33 (10 Aug. 1889): 652; *NYT,* 18 July 1889; *HW* 33 (31 Aug. 1889): 707, 33 (10 Aug. 1889): 652, 33 (21 Sept. 1889): 766.

9. *Puck* 15 (16 Aug. 1893); H. C. Brunner, "The Making of the White City," *Scribner's Monthly* 12 (October 1892): 403; Kipling, quoted in Robert Shackleton, *The Book of Chicago* (Philadelphia: Pennsylvania Publishing Co., 1920), 230.

10. *WP,* 28 Aug. 1877, 1 Aug. 1889, 10 Jan. 1890; *CT,* 26 Feb., 29 April, 7, 18 Nov. 1886, 4, 10, 28, 30 July, 6, 23 Aug., 22 Nov. 1889.

11. Reid Badger, *The Great American Fair* (Chicago: Nelson Hall, 1979), 50; Dedmon, *Fabulous,* 221; *CT,* 30 July 1889, 10, 16, 26 Jan., 1 Oct. 1890; *St. Louis Globe Democrat,* quoted in *CT,* 24 April 1938; *New Orleans Picayune,* quoted in *CT,* 13 Nov. 1889.

12. Robert Rydell, *All the World's a Fair: Visions of Empire at American International Expositions, 1876–1916* (Chicago: University of Chicago Press, 1984); *Puck* 15 (15 May 1893); *WP,* 9 Jan. 1890.

13. *CT,* 18 Sept., 20 Oct. 1871, 18 Nov. 1886; Lloyd Lewis and Henry Justin Smith, *Chicago: The History of Its Reputation* (New York: Harcourt, Brace, 1929), 141–42; *CH,* 22 Nov. 1885; *CDN,* 10 Nov. 1887; *Norristown* (PA) *Herald,* cited in *CT,* 2 May 1886; *New York Ledger,* quoted in *CT,* 13 April 1886.

14. *CT,* 28 June, 10, 14, 17, 20 July, 2 Aug. 1889; *CH,* 11 July 1889; *New York World,* quoted in *WP,* 1 Aug. 1889; *New York Weekly,* quoted in *CT,* 15 Sept. 1889; *Chicago Economist,* quoted in *CT,* 28 July 1889.

15. *CT,* 21, 24, 26, 27 July, 3, 8 Aug., 1 Oct., 1 Dec. 1889; *CDN,* quoted in *WP,* 1 Aug. 1889; *CH,* 27 Nov. 1889; *New York World,* quoted in *CT,* 13 Nov. 1889; *New York Weekly,* quoted in *CT,* 8 Dec. 1889.

16. *CT,* 14 Aug., 23 Oct. 1889, 23, 25 Feb. 1890; *CJ,* quoted in *WP,* 9 Aug. 1889; *WP,* 10, 28 Aug., 22 Nov. 1889, 23 Feb. 1890; *NYT,* 23 Sept. 1889; *NYS,* 12, 13 Nov., 28 Dec. 1889; *NYS,* quoted in *CT,* 10 Nov. 1889; P. T. Barnum, "What the Fair Should Be," *North American Republic* 150 (March 1890): 400; George Berger, "Suggestions for the Next World's Fair," *Century* 17 (April 1890): 895; "The Columbian Exposition and American Civilization," *Atlantic Monthly* 71 (May 1893): 581; *NYS,* quoted in *CT,* 13 Nov. 1889; *Lincoln Journal,* quoted in *CT,* 22 May 1892.

17. *NYS,* 17, 25 Dec. 1889, 2, 8, 16 Jan, 1890; *CDN,* 11 Jan. 1890; *CT,*14 Dec. 1889, 4 Jan. 1890; *CIO,* 5 Jan. 1890.

18. *CT,* 12, 25, 30 Jan. 1890, 20, 21, 22, 23, 25, 26 Feb. 1890; *NYS,* quoted in *CT,* 16 Feb. 1890; *Truth,* quoted in *CT,* 26 April 1896; *Cincinnati Porcupine,* quoted in *CT,* 10 Nov. 1889; *NYTB,* quoted in *CT,* 10 Feb. 1890; *NYT,* 18 Feb. 1890; *CTM,* 1 May 1893; *CIO,* 8 Oct. 1893; *Knoxville Journal,* 20 Feb. 1890; *CH,* 21 Feb. 1890.

19. *CDN,* 23, 24 Feb. 1890; *NYS,* 25 Feb. 1890; *NYT,* 25 Feb. 1890; *CT,* 25, 27 Feb., 1 March 1890, 1 May 1897; *Bismarck Tribune,* 25 Feb. 1890; *Albuquerque Morning Democrat,* 25 Feb. 1890; Lewis and Smith, *Reputation.*

20. Badger, *Great American Fair,* 58; *NYT,* 26 Feb. 1890; *CT,* 23 Nov. 1889, 4, 11, 26 Jan., 23 Nov. 1890; *NYT,* 3 March, 13 July 1890; *New York World,* quoted in *CT,* 22 May 1892.

21. *CIO,* 1 Jan., 19 March 1891, 29 June, 31 Aug. 1893; *CH,* 5 April 1891; *CT,* quoted in *Columbus* (GA) *Enquirer Sun,* 18 Aug. 1892.

22. *CIO,* 28 Feb. 1892; *Macon* (GA) *Telegraph,* 22 Aug. 1890; *Philadelphia Inquirer,* quoted in *CIO,* 25 Sept. 1892.

23. Moses P. Handy, "Promoting the World's Fair," *World Columbian Exposition Illustrated* 2 (October 1892): 169.

24. "Chicago; The Best Location for the World's Exposition of 1892," *HW* 33 (19 Oct. 1889), advertising supplement 1–4; *CT*, 23 May 1976; John Findling, *Chicago's Great World's Fairs* (Manchester: Manchester University Press, 1994), 4; Neil Harris, "Dream Making," *Chicago History* 23 (Fall 1994): 44–57; Phil Patton, "Sell the Cookstove if Necessary, but Come to the Fair," *Smithsonian* 24 (June 1993): 38–50; Strasser, *Satisfaction Guaranteed*, 6–101; Michael Schudson, *Advertising, The Uneasy Persuasion* (New York: Basic Books, 1984), 28–32; Pope, *Modern Advertising*, 45–61; *The Advertising Age Encyclopedia of Advertising*, ed. John McDonough and Karen Egolf (New York: Fitzroy Dearborn, 2003), 755–60, 1319–21.

25. *CT*, 7, 9, 16, 29 Aug. 1889, 13, 21 Dec. 1890, 12 Dec. 1897, 8, 9 Jan. 1898; *World Columbian Exposition Illustrated* 1 (March 1891): 12, 1 (April 1891): 25; "Department of Publicity and Promotion" proposal, circa 1890, Handy Family Papers; Background Notes, Handy Family Papers; Will Irwin, "The Press Agent, His Rise and Decline," *Collier's* 48 (2 Dec. 1911): 24–25.

26. *World Columbian Exposition Illustrated* 1 (March 1891): 2, 1 (Aug. 1892): 128–29; *CT*, 21 Oct. 1892, 14 May 1893; George Everett, "The Age of New Journalism, 1883–1900," *The Media in America*, 5th ed., ed. Wm. David Sloan and James D. Startt (Northport, AL: Vision Press, 2002), 243; Eugene C. Harter, *Boilerplating America* (Lanham, MD: University Press of America, 1991), 17–36; Gerald J. Baldasty, *E. W. Scripps and the Business of Newspapers* (Urbana: University of Illinois Press, 1999); *CG*, 17 June 1893: *CJ*, 22 June 1893; *CIO*, 14 Aug. 1892; *Scientific American* 13 (11 Nov. 1871); E. W. Howe, "Country Newspapers," *Century* 42 (Sept. 1891): 776–83; Mary Balousek, *Famous Wisconsin Inventors & Entrepreneurs* (Oregon, WI: Badger Books, 2003), 107–9.

27. *Chicago Record: History of the World's Fair* (Chicago: Chicago Record, n.d.), 106–8; Miller, *City of the Century*, 492; Peter B. Hales, *Constructing the Fair: Platinum Photographs by C. D. Arnold of the World's Columbian Exposition* (Chicago: Art Institute of Chicago, 1993).

28. Harris, "Dream Making," 44–57; Julian Ralph, *Harper's Chicago and The World's Fair* (New York: Harper & Bros., 1893), 127–33; Badger, *Great American Fair*, 75–76; John E. Findling, *Chicago's Great World's Fairs* (Manchester: Manchester University Press, 1994), 16–17; Donald L. Miller, "The White City," *American Heritage* 44 (July/Aug. 1993): 70–87; Rydell, *All the World's a Fair;* Mayer and Wade, *Chicago*, 193.

29. *LT*, 14, 29 March 1892; miscellaneous departmental correspondence, April, May 1892, Handy Family Papers; *CT*, 2 April, 9 Sept. 1893; *Wheeling Register*, 28 July 1891; Oscar Wilde, *The Picture of Dorian Gray* (New York: Ward, Lock, 1891), 20; *Milwaukee Wisconsin*, quoted in *CT*, 22 May 1892; *St. Paul News*, quoted in *CT*, 30 Oct. 1893.

30. "Scrapbook on the World's Columbian Exposition, Chicago 1893," Special Collections, Rare Books, University of Chicago Library; *World Columbian Exposition Il-*

lustrated 1 (April 1891): 20, 2 (Oct. 1892): 169; Badger, *Great American Fair,* 157–58n28; *CIO,* 10 May 1890, 23 April 1892, 14 Sept. 1893; W. K. Ackerman to Handy, 27 Feb. 1892, Handy Family Papers; *CT,* 7 Aug. 1892; *Chicago Blade,* circa late June 1893, W. D. Boyce to George R. Davis, 26 June 1893, G. R. Davis to Handy, 3 July 1893, Handy to William T. Baker, 27 June 1872, J. P. Holland to Handy, 12 Aug. 1893, in Handy Family Papers; R. A. LaTouche, *Chicago and Its Resources Twenty Years After, 1871–1891* (Chicago: Chicago Times Co., 1892), 168.

31. Will Payne, *Mr. Salt* (Boston: Houghton-Mifflin, 1903), 54–55; Teresa Dean, *Chips* (Chicago: Warren Publishing Co., 1895), 3; *CT,* 19 Feb. 1891, 2 July 1893.

32. *CT,* 1, 2, 22 May, 4 June 1893.

33. *CT,* 21 May 1893; Erik Larson, *The Devil in the White City: Murder, Magic, and Madness at the Fair That Changed America* (New York: Crown Publishers, 2003), 416n293.

34. Findling, *Great World's Fairs,* 29; *CJ,* 11 July 1893; *CG,* 19 June 1893; Dean, *Chips,* 170–71; *CP,* 4 June 1893; *CT,* 9 May, 5 June 1893.

35. *Utica Observer* as quoted in *CIO,* 24 June 1893; *Charlotte News,* 11 Oct. 1893; *Idaho Statesman,* 7 Sept. 1873; *Tacoma Daily News,* 6 July 1893; *Worcester Daily Spy,* 30 Oct. 1893.

36. *CT,* 10, 15 May 1893, 6 April 1937; Findling, *Great World's Fairs,* 27; *CG,* 1 May, 19 June 1893; *Illustrated American,* quoted in Longstreet, *Chicago,* 272; Dean, *Chips,* 157; Dedmon, *Fabulous,* 7; *WP,* quoted in *CT,* 30 Oct. 1893.

37. *CT,* 4 Feb., 15 April, 10, 14 May, 11 July 1893; *CDN,* 10 July 1893; *CJ,* 11 July 1893; Trumbull White and William Igleheart, *The World's Columbian Exposition, Chicago, 1893* (Philadelphia: World Publishing Co., 1893), 158–59; Rydell, *All the World's a Fair;* Longstreet, *Chicago,* 273, 290; *Detroit Free Press* as quoted in *CT,* 12 Dec. 1893; *CG,* 15 May, 19 June 1893; Dean, *Chips,* 307; *CIO,* 8 Oct. 1893; Badger, *Great American Fair,* 91; *Detroit Tribune,* quoted in *CT,* 11 June 1893.

38. *CT,* 21 Aug., 11 Sept., 28, 31 Oct. 1893; Ray Stannard Baker, *Native American: The Book of My Youth* (New York: Scribner, 1941), 285; *CDN,* 30 Oct. 1893; *The Inland Printer,* 12 (February 1894): 400–401; Fred C. Kelly, *George Ade* (Indianapolis: Bobbs-Merrill, 1947), 106; *CG,* 2 May 1893; Dean, *Chips,* 408.

39. Dedmon, *Fabulous,* 189; *San Jose Mercury News,* 21 Nov. 1892; White and Igleheart, *World's Columbian Exposition,* 637; *Buffalo Courier,* quoted in *CT,* 12 Dec. 1893; *CT,* 1 Nov. 1892, 27 May, 20 Nov. 1894, 20 July 1895.

40. *NYT,* 31 July 1895; Longstreet, *Chicago,* 172–82. A fictionalized account of Holmes's crimes can be found in Larson, *Devil in the White City; New York World,* quoted in *CT,* 15 April 1894.

Chapter 6. Second City

1. Edna Ferber, *Showboat* (Garden City, NJ: Doubleday, Page & Co., 1924), 272; Jerome Kern and Oscar Hammerstein II, *Showboat: A Musical Play* (New York: T.B. Harms Co., 1928), 172–74.

2. William T. Stead, *If Christ Came to Chicago!* (Chicago: Laird & Lee, 1894), 19, 27–29; Frank Norris, *The Pit: A Story of Chicago* (New York: Modern Library, 1934, 1902), 58; *AZ,* 12 Nov. 1888, CFLPS, reel #14; Herbert Gans, *Deciding What's News: A Study of CBS Evening News, NBC Nightly News, Newsweek and Time* (New York: Pantheon, 1979), 42–48; Cherri Ketchum, "If a Radical Screams in the Forest, Will She be Heard?" *Journalism* 5 (2004): 31–49; Brian McNair, *The Sociology of Journalism* (London: Arnold, 1998), 38–56.

3. Charles J. Latrobe, *The Rambler in North America* (London: R.B. Seeley, 1836), 206, 209; *CD,* 31 Dec. 1833; Asbury, *Sucker's Progress,* 286; *CTM,* 25 Feb. 1866; Herbert Asbury, *Gangs of New York: An Informal History of the Underworld* (New York: Thunder's Mouth Press, 1990), 61; *NYT,* 5 Oct. 1869, 18 July 1871, 3 Oct. 1875; Longstreet, *Chicago,* 33–34; *Scribner's Magazine,* quoted in Dedmon, *Fabulous,* 135.

4. Gilfoyle, *Eros,* 7–20; Halttunen, *Confidence Men,* xiii–xvi; Marilynn Wood Hill, *Their Sisters' Keepers: Prostitution in New York City, 1830–1870* (Berkeley: University of California Press, 1993), 3–4.

5. *CT,* 20 Feb. 1860, 5 Sept. 1861, 28 Jan. 1864, 2 Oct. 1870, 8 Feb. 1886; *CTM,* 23 May 1861, 11 July 1865, 9 Jan. 1866, 11 Jan. 1885; Kimball, *Madam,* 123, 143; *Detroit News,* quoted in *CT,* 8 Jan. 1893.

6. *CT,* 5 Dec. 1857, 2, 16 April, 15 June 1858, 3 Aug. 1858, 22 July 1859, 9, 28 Jan, 24 Aug. 1864, 9 Jan., 14 Nov. 1866, 30 Nov. 1867, 10 Jan., 4 June 1873, 28 May 1891, 26 Jan. 1936, 27 Dec. 1953; Asbury, *Gangs of New York,* 65; Longstreet, *Chicago,* 257–59; *CD,* 6 June, 4 July 1857, 6 Feb., 18 Dec. 1858; *Ohio Statesman,* 31 Jan. 1856; Cook, *Bygone Days,* 159–60; *Wisconsin Daily Patriot,* 25 May 1860; (Washington, DC) *Critic-Record,* 18 July 1870.

7. Patricia Cline Cohen, Timothy J. Gilfoyle, and Helen Lefkowitz Horowitz, *The Flash Press* (Chicago: University of Chicago Press, 2008), 1–13; *Chicago Sporting Life,* various issues, CHS; *CT,* 14 Feb. 1859, 19 May 1872; *Chicago by Day and Night: The Pleasure Seeker's Guide to the Paris of America* (Chicago: Thomson and Zimmerman, 1892), 95, 99; *CIO,* 22 Nov. 1877, 28 June 1878, 1 Dec. 1887, 8, 24 Feb. 1888; Herbert Asbury, *Gangs of New York,* 130–35; Walsh, *Storey,* 212; Shang Andrews, *Wicked Nell: A Gay Girl of the Town* (Chicago: Comet Publishing Co., 1878), 4, 75; Andrews, *Cranky Ann, the Street Walker* (Chicago: R. H. Andrews, 1877), 14; Dedmon, *Fabulous,* 143–44; Miller, *Chicago,* 507–8; *Indianapolis Sentinel,* 22 Aug. 1876; *New Orleans Times,* 6 Nov. 1876; *Omaha Herald,* 26 March 1905.

8. Gilfoyle, *Eros,* 234; *CT,* 3 Feb. 1857, 8 Feb. 1881, 24 Oct. 1888, 16 Feb. 1890; *Chicago by Day and Night,* 114–19.

9. Chicago City Council, *Proceedings of the City Council,* 1892–93 (Chicago: City Council, 1893), 134–35; Lloyd Wendt and Herman Kogan, *Bosses in Lusty Chicago: The Story of Bathhouse John and Hinky Dink* (Bloomington: Indiana University Press, 1967, 1943), 47; *CG,* 30 June 1893; Theodore Dreiser, *Dawn: A History of Myself* (New York: H. Liveright, 1931), 407–8; May Churchill Sharpe, *Chicago May, Her Story* (New York: Macaulay, 1928), 37–44; Homer Hoyt, *One Hundred Years of Land Values in*

Chicago (New York: Arno Press, 1970, 1933), 103; *CTM,* 15, 26 Feb., 12, 22, 23, 25, 26 March 1874, 17 July, 19 Dec. 1880; *CT,* 17 July, 6 Aug. 1878, 19 Dec. 1880, 15 Jan. 1882, 26 Jan. 1936; *CDN,* 7 May, 1 June 1887; *San Jose Mercury News,* 16 June 1909; Clifton R. Wooldridge, *Hands Up! In the World of Crime or 12 Years a Detective* (Chicago: Thompson & Thomas, 1901), 66–69; *Bismarck Tribune,* quoted in *CT,* 30 Oct. 1893; *Truth,* quoted in *CT,* 7 Jan. 1894; Theodore Dreiser, *The Titan* (Cleveland: World Publishing Co., [1925] 1946), 13–14.

10. *CT,* 19 June 1890, 21 July 1892, 3 Sept. 1896, 19 Dec. 1903, 6 April 1913; *CIO,* 5 May 1876, 4 July 1890; Herbert Asbury, *The Gangs of Chicago: An Informal History of the Chicago Underworld* (New York: Thunder's Mouth Press; distributed by Publishers Group West [1940] 2002), 138–40; *Chicago Street Gazette,* quoted in Dedmon, *Fabulous,* 147; Stead, *Christ,* 248; *Sioux City Journal,* 14 Nov. 1873.

11. *CIO,* 11 Feb., 26 March, 24 Aug. 1875, 3 Nov. 1876, 28 Sept. 1878; *CDN,* quoted in *Columbus Daily Enquirer,* 2 July 1893; *CT,* 23 Sept. 1859; *Pomeroy's Democrat,* 31 Aug. 1878; Theodore Dreiser, *Newspaper Days* (New York: H. Liveright, 1931), 78–79; *Sporting and Club House Directory,* quoted in Dedmon, *Fabulous,* 145; Dedmon, *Fabulous,* 144; Longstreet, *Chicago,* 115–19, 357; Wendt and Kogan, *Bosses,* 80–81; Miller, *Chicago,* 509–10; Lewis and Smith, *Reputation,* 98–99; George Wharton James, *Chicago's Dark Places: Investigations by a Corps of Specially Appointed Commissioners* (Chicago: Craig Press, 1891); Stead, *Christ,* 250; Kimball, *Madam,* 229.

12. *LT,* 13 Nov. 1885, 19 Jan. 1886, 18 April 1912; *CT,* 25, 27 July 1913; Stead, *Christ,* 184; *Washington Critic,* 25 Jan. 1886; *New Haven Register,* 5 March 1894; *Peoria Mirror,* quoted in *CT,* 25 March 1894; *St. Paul Globe,* quoted in *CT,* 1 April 1894; *Kansas City Journal,* quoted in *CT,* 25 March 1894.

13. *Chicago Chronicle,* quoted in *Charlotte Observer,* 6 March 1894; *Macon Weekly Telegraph,* 12 March 1894; *Duluth News Tribune,* 10 April 1894; *CDN,* 6 Feb. 1894; *CIO,* 25 Feb. 1894, 4 March 1895; *CT,* 7, 9 April 1894, 13 Dec. 1894; 21, 22 Nov. 1897, 3 Feb, 21 April 1912; *NYT,* 4 March 1894, 21 Nov. 1897; Stone, *Fifty Years,* 201–2; Richard Digby-Junger, *The Journalist as Reformer: Henry Demarest Lloyd and Wealth Against Commonwealth* (Westport, CT: Greenwood Press, 1996), 164–65; *LT,* 18 April 1912; *Omaha World Herald,* 21 Nov. 1894; *Washington Star* and *Kansas City Journal,* quoted in *CT,* 15 April 1894.

14. *CT,* 19 Feb., 19 Sept. 1894, 2 March 1895, 22 April 1896; *CDN,* 6 Feb., 26 June 1894.

15. *CT,* 17 Feb., 8 Aug. 1907; *CIO,* 18 Feb. 1882, 28, 29 March 1893; *Chicago Chronicle,* quoted in *Fort Worth Star-Telegram,* 15 May 1904; Norman E. Isaacs, "The Crime of Present Day Crime Reporting," *The Journal of Criminal Law, Criminology, and Police Science* 52 (Nov.–Dec. 1961): 405–10; Dreiser, *Titan,* 83; Wendt and Kogan, *Bosses,* 27; *CT,* 8 Aug. 1907; Asbury, *Gangs of Chicago,* 142–44; David W. Maurer, *The Big Con: The Story of the Confidence Man* (New York Anchor Books, 1999, 1940); Wooldridge, *Hands Up!* 93; *NYT,* 5 June 1915.

16. *CT,* 20, 21 Sept. 1894.

17. *CT,* 10 Oct. 1946, 12 Nov. 1938; *Chicago American,* 11 Nov. 1938; *CTM,* 27 July 1865; *CDN,* 12 Nov. 1938; Wendt and Kogan, *Bosses,* 116; C. Johnson and C. Sautter, *Wicked City Chicago: From Kenna to Capone* (Highland Park, IL: December Press, 1994).

18. *CDN,* 11 Nov. 1938.

19. *CT,* 12 July 1868; *CDN,* 11 Nov. 1938; Wendt and Kogan, *Bosses,* v, 11–16.

20. *CT,* 28 Jan. 1877, 22 June 1879, 23 Sept. 1883, 7 July 1891, 12 Nov. 1938; *CDN,* 11 Nov.1938; Wendt and Kogan, *Bosses,* 17–18.

21. Wendt and Kogan, *Bosses,* 20–21; *CT,* 20 May 1888; Longstreet, *Chicago,* 345–51; *CT,* 24 March 1890, 4 Feb, 30 July 1891; *CDN,* 11 Nov. 1938; Dick Simpson, *Rogues, Rebels, and Rubber Stamps: The Politics of the Chicago City Council from 1863 to the Present* (Boulder, CO: Westview Press, 2001), 50–52; Wendt and Kogan, *Bosses,* 26–27; Steven P. Erie, *Rainbow's End: Irish-Americans and the Dilemmas of Urban Machine Politics, 1840–1985* (Berkeley: University of California Press, 1988); *St. Paul Dispatch,* quoted in *CT,* 1 April 1894.

22. *CDN,* 9 Oct. 1946; Wendt and Kogan, *Bosses,* 74–76, 170; *CT,* 7 Jan. 1885.

23. *CT,* 28 Aug. 1891, 11 Oct. 1946; *NYT,* 1 Jan. 1898; Wendt and Kogan, *Bosses,* v, 339; *CIO,* 1 Oct. 1893.

24. *CT,* 18 Jan., 4 Oct. 1893, 22 March 1895, 23 Oct. 1935, 10 Oct. 1946; *CIO,* 4 Oct. 1893, 18 Feb. 1894, 8 March 1895; *NYT,* 9 March 1898; *CT,* quoted in *NYT,* 24 April 1895; *Memphis Avalanche,* quoted in *CT,* 8 Jan. 1893; *Kansas City Journal,* quoted in *CT,* 11 June 1893.

25. *NYH,* quoted in *CT,* 7 Jan. 1894; *CT,* 20 May 1894, 6 March 1895, 10 Oct. 1946; *CDN,* 20 March 1895; Wendt and Kogan, *Bosses,* 170; Irle Waller, *Chicago Uncensored: Firsthand Stories About the Al Capone Era* (New York: Exposition Press, 1965), 13; James Weber Linn, *James Keeley Newspaperman* (Indianapolis: Bobbs-Merrill, 1937), 87.

26. *CT,* 19 March 1894; *CDN,* 17 April 1894; *CP,* 11 Feb. 1896; *NYT,* 4 April 1894; *Columbus* (GA) *Enquirer-Sun,* 31 Oct. 1897; *New York Journal,* 18 May 1898; *Tacoma Daily Journal,* 5 Aug. 1898.

27. *CT,* 30 Sept. 1872, 22 April 1894, 14 Oct. 1895, 30 Sept. 1896, 5 Jan., 9 March 1897; *CDN,* 14 April 1886, 18 June 1894, 25 Feb. 1896, 9 Oct. 1946; Wendt and Kogan, *Bosses,* 59–77, 81, 158–59; *CP,* quoted in Wendt and Kogan, *Bosses,* 114; *NYT,* 30 May 1895, 1 Jan. 1898; *Macon Weekly Telegraph,* 6 April 1899; *Washington Star,* quoted in *CT,* 10 June 1894.

28. Richard L. Kaplan, *Politics and the American Press: The Rise of Objectivity, 1865–1920* (Cambridge, UK: Cambridge University Press, 2001), 162–63; M. Craig Brown and Charles N. Halaby, "Machine Politics in America, 1870–1945," *Journal of Interdisciplinary History* 17 (Winter 1987): 587–612; Terrence McDonald, *The Parameters of Urban Fiscal Policy: Socioeconomic Change and Political Culture in San Francisco, 1860–1906* (Berkeley: University of California Press, 1986); John Teaford, *The Unheralded Triumph: City Government in America, 1870–1900* (Baltimore: Johns Hopkins University Press, 1984), 139; Mary Ryan, *Civic Wars* (Berkeley: University of

California Press, 1997), 6; Philip Ethington, *Public City: The Political Construction of Urban Life in San Francisco, 1850–1900* (Cambridge, UK: Cambridge University Press, 1994), 407–8; Ann Durkin Keating, *Building Chicago: Suburban Developers and the Creation of a Divided Metropolis* (Columbus: Ohio State University Press, 1988).

29. *CT,* 18 March 1877, 10 Oct. 1880, 12 Dec. 1880, 28 Feb. 1882, 9 April 1882, 3 Feb. 1889, 10 June 1897, 25 Jan. 1902, 24 Jan. 1906; *CIO,* 25 May 1893, 22 Sept. 1895; *CH,* 22 Nov. 1891; (Little Rock, AR) *Morning Republican,* 24 June 1871; Melville E. Stone, *M. E. S.: His Book* (New York: Harper, 1918), 293–96; Koenigsberg, *King News,* 159.

30. *CT,* 27 Sept. 1882, 16 March 1890, 23 Oct. 1935; Stead, *Christ,* 182–83; Lincoln Steffens, *The Shame of the Cities* (New York: McClure, Phillips & Co., 1904), 236–37; Dreiser, *Titan,* 11–12; Victor Lawson to Charles T. Yerkes, 25 Nov. 1889, Lawson Papers, Newberry Library.

31. *CT,* 22, 31 Aug. 1890, 6 May 1891, 7 Dec. 1898; *CDN,* 20 Jan., 22 Aug., 25 Oct. 1890, 14 Jan. 1891, 10 Jan., 5 Feb., 10 Oct. 1894; *Bedford's Monthly* 9 (Oct. 1892): 961–63; Mayer and Wade, *Chicago,* 138–42.

32. *CT,* 3 April 1901, 20 May 1935; *Chicago Times-Herald,* quoted in Wendt and Kogan, *Bosses,* 38–40; Sidney I. Roberts, "Portrait of a Robber Baron: Charles T. Yerkes," *Business History Review* 35 (Autumn 1961): 344–71.

33. *CT,* 19 March 1894, 6, 26 Feb., 10 March 1895, 9, 10, 11 Jan., 7 July 1896, 22 March 1898; Wendt and Kogan, *Bosses,* 120, 138–42, 187–99; Finley Peter Dunne, *Mr. Dooley On Inrything and Ivrybody,* ed. Robert Hutchinson (New York: Dover Publications, 1963), 60.

34. (Chicago) *Daily Socialist,* 20 Nov. 1912; *CDN,* 22 March 1899; *NYT,* 10 Oct. 1897; *CT,* 14 Jan., 5, 13, 25, 27 May, 6, 10, 12 June 1897; *Street Railway Review* 9 (April 15, 1899): 250.

35. *CT,* 22 Oct., 19 Nov. 1897; Walter E. Ewert, *The History of the Chicago Inter Ocean,* unpublished M.A. thesis, Northwestern University, 1940, 116–18; *CIO,* 21, 26 Nov. 1897.

36. *CT,* 5, 6, 8, 10 Dec. 1898; *CIO,* quoted in Wendt and Kogan, *Bosses,* 189–90; *New York World,* 12 Dec. 1898, quoted in *CT,* 14 Dec. 1898; Wendt and Kogan, *Bosses,* 186.

37. *CT,* 7, 9, 11 Dec. 1898; Wendt and Kogan, *Bosses,* 190–91; *CT,* 12 Dec. 1898.

38. *CT,* 13, 20 Dec. 1898, 31 Dec. 1905, 23 Oct. 1935, 1 Oct. 1947; *CDN,* 9 Dec. 1895, 24 March 1896, 20 March 1899, 17 Dec. 1908; *Omaha World Herald,* 17 Dec. 1898; *Tacoma Daily News,* 20 Dec. 1898; *New York World,* quoted in *Kansas City Star,* 25 Dec. 1898; *Chicago American,* 26, 30 Aug. 1900, 5 April 1905; *CIO,* 4 March 1895 and *CT,* 1 June 1903, clippings in Lloyd Papers.

39. *CT,* 24 June, 21 July 1890, 6 July, 26 Oct. 1894, 28 Nov. 1895, 11 Jan. 1897; *CG,* 30 June 1893; *CJ,* 12 July 1893; *CDN,* 4 June 1895, 10 Jan. 1896; *CTM,* 3 July 1894; Willis John Abbot, *Carter Henry Harrison: A Memoir* (New York: Dodd, Mead, 1895), 228; *Buffalo Express,* quoted in *CT,* 22 May 1892; *Boston Herald,* quoted in *CT,* 28 Aug. 1892; *Grand Rapids Democrat* and *Minneapolis Tribune,* quoted in *CT,* 7 Jan. 1894.

40. *CT,* 8, 12, 23 May, 30 June, 1, 14, 28 July 1897, 6 May 1898; *CDN,* 10 May 1897; *NYT,* 6 May 1897; *NYH,* quoted in *CT,* 8 May 1897; Hoyt, *Land Values,* 483.

41. *CT,* 2 April 1893, 6, 7, 8 May, 12 Dec. 1897, 1 Jan. 1898.

42. *CT,* 30 Aug. 1898, 13 Feb. 1910, 8 Nov. 1918, 25 June, 31 Dec. 1919, 4 March 1920, 6 Dec. 1922, 15 April 1923.

43. *CT,* 10 Oct. 1921, 22 July 1922, 9 July 1930, 25 March 1931, 18 May 1933, 11, 16 March 1941, 10 July 1955, 14 November 1956; *NYT,* 25 February 1935; *Munsey's Magazine,* quoted in *Chicago Sun-Times,* 26 Jan. 1992.

Index

A former news reporter, **RICHARD JUNGER** is an associate professor of communication and English at Western Michigan University and the author of *The Journalist as Reformer: Henry Demarest Lloyd and Wealth Against Commonwealth.*

The University of Illinois Press
is a founding member of the
Association of American University Presses.

Composed in 10.5/13 Adobe Minion Pro
with Meta display
by Jim Proefrock
at the University of Illinois Press
Manufactured by Cushing-Malloy, Inc.

University of Illinois Press
1325 South Oak Street
Champaign, IL 61820-6903
www.press.uillinois.edu